Playing Fields

Playing Fields

Power, Practice, and Passion in Sport

edited by
Mariann Vaczi

Center for Basque Studies
University of Nevada, Reno

Generous financial support for the publication of this book has been provided by the Basque Government.

Conference Papers Series, no. 8
Series editor: Joseba Zulaika

Center for Basque Studies
University of Nevada, Reno
Reno, NV 89557
basque.unr.edu

Cover and book design: Daniel Montero and Kimberly Daggett
Cover illustration: *Idilios en los campos de sport* (1920) by Aurelio Arteta

Library of Congress Cataloging-in-Publication Data

Playing fields : power, practice, and passion in sport / edited by Mariann Vaczi.
     pages cm
  Includes bibliographical references and index.
  Summary: "Collection of articles treating the subject of play, game, and sports from a variety of academic methodological perspectives"-- Provided by publisher.
   ISBN 978-1-935709-49-7 (pbk. : alk. paper) 1. Sports--Sociological aspects. 2. Sports--Cross-cultural studies. I. Vaczi, Mariann.

GV706.5.P53 2014
306.4'83--dc23

                                2013046399

Contents

Introduction
"THE PLAZA IS ALWAYS JUDGE":
POWER, PRACTICE, AND PASSION IN SPORT
Mariann Vaczi

During the South Africa World Cup soccer competition in 2010, an Adidas commercial promoting the Spanish national team jersey became a highlight of Spanish nation-building. The commercial was titled *"Nace de dentro,"* (Born Within). It features two Basque players and an Asturian as they stand naked from the waist up—handsome, muscular, and sweaty. Digitally, the players start stripping off their own skin, from under which emerges the symbol of the Spanish state and the colors red and yellow—the colors of the Spanish national team jersey. Against a backdrop of slow-motion soccer-field images and dramatic music, a male voice says, "This jersey is history. It is everything that we suffer for, that we fight for, that we feel and live for. That which unites us is born within."

Rarely is the embodiment of a nation rendered so literally; the athletes' bodies are used as a primordial metonymy for a Spain where all are Spanish "under their skin," although they may be Basque, Asturian, or Catalan on the surface. Soccer in Spain functions as a form of cultural and political capital, a powerful ideological apparatus. Historically, the underperformance of the national team, also known as *la Furia Española* or the "Spanish Fury," was often attributed to a lack of patriotism on the part of players from the Spanish periphery (mostly Basques and Catalans). Winning the 2008 and 2012 European Championships and the 2010 World Cup, however, allowed Spain to assume a new image of unity in diversity: a modern country that is politically and socially united at last, and that has overcome its regional divisions.

Or has it? While the national team's successes are hailed by Madrid as uniting the nation, they generate unease in the Basque and Catalan peripheries. Whose desires are really written on the athletes' bodies? Whose state is embodied? The peripheries have been instrumental in the history of Spanish soccer, even while they are at odds with the idea of a centralized "Spain." The sport has become a site of integration and disintegration, simultaneously affecting and inhibiting what Gregory Bateson[1] would call the schismogenic tendencies of Spanish center-periphery relationships, turning the athlete's body into a "contested ideological terrain."[2]

Stripping one's own skin connotes a Spanish expression commonly used in sports: *dejarse la piel*, literally "leaving the skin" or "giving it all." It means hard work and sacrifice for the colors, for the community and the nation. Spain is also called *piel de toro*, "bull's skin," because the shape of the skin cut off the animal after a bullfight resembles the shape of the country. But the lofty ideals of nation, community, dedication, and sacrifice fall flat in the Adidas logo on the national team's jersey. Just as Benetton's socially progressive messages served to cajole customers into buying its products, sport ideals are often appropriated to do the same. They become "Benettonized" as the commercial reveals its real objective: to sell jerseys.

The Spanish team was hailed as the embodiment of a new nation. It "really represented us," Coach Vicente del Bosque said after the World Cup, and proved that the nation "had healthy, good youth." In Spain, "things happened. . . . We have become a modern country, and that is also reflected by our sport."[3]

By men's sports, that is. In Spain, where men's soccer constitutes a "hegemonic sports culture,"[4] women's soccer is thwarted by institutional inequalities, social stigmatization, and financial deprivation. "Twenty-first-century Spain. You are born a woman, and you can become whatever you want: you can be a hunter, a pilot, a ship's captain, a minister—but can you be a soccer player?"[5] This question, asked in a 2010 documentary on women's soccer titled *Cuestión de Pelotas* ("A Matter of Balls") is rhetorical. By 2010, the film argues, women were still not granted professional status by the Spanish Football Federation. They were unable by decree to make a living as soccer players even if their clubs were willing to pay them. As of 2012, the *best* female players earned only semi legal minimum wage-like benefits of about 10,000 Euros a year—sixty times less than the average male footballer.

Playing fields are replete with social significances, which this book approaches from three angles: power, practice, and passion. "Not for

1. Bateson, *Steps to an Ecology of Mind.*
2. Messner, "Sports and Male Domination, 197–211.
3. See www.as.com/futbol/articulo/bosque-supimos-perder-ganamos-estilo/20110121dasdasftb_57/Tes.
4. Markovits and Hellerman, "Women's Soccer in the United States," 14.

nothing did Nelson say," Nabokov writes in a newly discovered short story on boxing, "that the Battle of Trafalgar was won on the tennis and football fields of Eton."[5] Playing fields, sports halls, and stadiums continue to agglutinate power: they have been used to construct and spread the national-imperial ethos and character;[6] to subvert the imposition of the national-imperial ethos and character;[7] to propagandize authoritarian regimes and ideologies;[8] to exert political pressure on authoritarian regimes and ideologies;[9] to mobilize grassroots resistance against hegemonic or dictatorial powers;[10] and to opiate grassroots resistance against hegemonic or dictatorial powers.[11] Sports create a most visible opportunity to deploy the symbols and language of nationalism, and to communicate abstractions like autonomy, identity, national genius, and unity in palpable terms that provoke immediate emotional reaction.[12] They are immersed in global flows, state-of-the-art technology, and science,[13] and yet remain grounded in local bodies, practices, and passions. Playing fields become a theater of hegemonic tendencies, including the proliferation of organized sports at the expense of local motor practices and indigenous games.

As communities insert themselves, as subjects, into history through sports, female bodies remain marginalized in the process.[14] Sports are a favorite source of political metaphor because, if only arguably, in the ludic field an initial "equality of chances is artificially created."[15] "May the best man win" is the credo of all playing fields that aspire to be level, and it is taken with portentous literalness. Vertical inequalities are already coded in what is believed to be a level playfield, forcing us to reconsider concepts of justice, equality, victory, and defeat in sports.

"How do you remember your great jump into the town square?" Maialen Lujanbio, a *bertsolari* (improvising oral poet) and the first-ever female champion of the Basque national improvisational poetry com-

---

5. Nabokov, "Breitensträter – Paolino."

6. Pope, *Patriotic Games*; Mangan, *Athleticism in the Victorian and Edwardian Public School*; McDevitt, *May the Best Man Win*; MacAloon, *Muscular Christianity in Colonial and Post-Colonial Worlds*.

7. Bairner, *Sport, Nationalism, and Globalization*; James, *Beyond a Boundary*.

8. Brownell, *Training the Body for China: Sports in the Moral Order of the People's Republic*; Katzer, Budy, and Köhring, *Euphoria and Exhaustion*; Shaw, *Fútbol y Franquismo*; Large, *Nazi Games*.

9. Booth, *The Race Game*; Hulme, *The Political Olympics*.

10. Guelke, "Sport and the End of Apartheid"; Mangan and Ha, "Confucianism, Imperialism, Nationalism."

11. Shaw, *Fútbol y Franquismo*.

12. Hargreaves, *Freedom for Catalonia?*

13. Giulianotti, *Football*.

14. Hargreaves, *Heroines of Sport*.

15. Caillois, *Man, Play, and Games*.

petition, was asked in an interview in 2009. That most emblematic Basque cultural practice, previously limited to male competitors, is traditionally held at the fronton, the village plaza court of the Basque pelota game. "I started to be known by everyone," she answered. "Because they put us . . . where *we didn't belong*."[16] Bodies at the plaza fronton turn into subjects of public recognition, while cultural performances, including pelota competitions, have been limited to men. Women's "great jump into the town square"—into frontons, sports halls, and stadiums, is a powerful metaphor for access—a qualitative leap toward a subjectivity that has been, and often still is, a male preserve. Discrepancies between male and female visibility in the media are made to appear the norm and are attributed to spectator preferences, although their roots lie in traditional conceptualizations of gendered agency and space, tacitly nurtured by the deep structures of patriarchal power perpetuated in frontons, plazas, and playing fields.

On the pelota fronton in the Basque village of Aldude (Aldudes in French), there is a sign that says: "Play honestly, the plaza is always judge."[17] In traditional Basque society, the plaza was the public stage of the inculcation of values, the performance of identities, the practice of social control, and the negotiation of power. Just as plaza-frontons occupy the central areas of Basque villages, stadiums have come to occupy a central position in modern urban societies. Their playing fields turn into liminal spaces where the *communitas*[18] suspends its everyday life and structures. They condense social processes into ritual events: into "deep play"[19] whose stakes appear irrationally high, into "social dramas"[20] where agonic interactions cause and cope with collective experience, and into "fateful actions"[21] that exhibit virtues normally hidden in safe and momentless living. Sports events continue to resonate with the village plaza; by convening power, practice, and passion, they remain central in public life.

The aim of this volume is to reflect on how games, sports, and motor practices interact with the themes listed above: global-local processes, inequality, gender relations, identity, representation, performance, and emotion. The chapters are characterized by varied modes of analysis, approaches, and style, as well as by disciplinary eclecticism

16. Estitxu Eizagirre, "Interview With Maialen Lujanbio Zugasti," *Oral Tradition*, February 22, 2002. See journal.oraltradition.org/files/articles/22ii/13_eizagirre.pdf (last accessed November 22, 2013).

17. González Abrisketa, *Basque Pelota*, 211.

18. Turner, *The Ritual Process*.

19. Geertz, *The Interpretation of Cultures*.

20. Turner, *From Ritual to Theatre*.

21. Goffman, *Interaction Ritual*.

featuring sociology, anthropology, history, philosophy, and motor praxeology. A special mission of this volume is to fill, at least partially, a lacuna in the academic literature on Basque society. In spite of the fact that Basques are great fans and practitioners of global games, and their traditional indigenous games have always structured their free time and cultural imaginary,[22] the ludic aspects of Basque society remain under-researched. A call for critical feminist approaches to sports in the Basque Country is especially urgent, considering that the male hegemony of public space and cultural performances is widely recognized.

This volume is divided into three parts reflecting three main themes: power, practice, and passion. The chapters in part 1, "Power," consider playing fields as an arena of power and address that Joan Acker would call "inequality regimes"[23] in sports: gender, class, economic, and geographical inequalities. The chapters in this initial section variously discuss gender discrimination; "hard" and "soft" essentialism; the concept of justice in sports; gendered collective embodiment and public agency; countercultural grassroots sports practices; and local-global dynamisms, Americanization, and hegemony. Part 2, "Practice," focuses on the practice of games as, in the words of Pierre Parlebas, "a type of academy in which social connections are experienced by the body." The chapters here use the perspectives and methodologies of motor praxeology, which relate motor practices to the cultural and social context of the bodies that practice them. A thematic focus includes the basic concepts and approaches of motor praxeology; the intellectual history of motor action; conceptualizations of the body; the internal logic of games, and how this logic influences risk-taking attitudes and the experience of emotions. Part 3, "Passion," looks at the affective dimensions of sports and explores how collective desires are communicated through the emotions that playing fields generate. This concluding section features chapters on European soccer rivalries along ethnic, political, and geographical lines; the social and collective functions of sports participation; and the role of sports for the construction of identities. Finally, the concluding chapter gives closure to the aforementioned themes by reflecting on a life-long research career spent on playing fields.

Part 1: Power

In chapter 1, Michael A. Messner explores how, under the guise of

---

22. Originally developed in psychoanalysis, by the term "imaginary" I mean here processes of identification, and collective formations of a cultural self.

23. Acker, "Inequality Regimes," 441–64.

feminist progress, gender binaries prevail in local, national, and international gender orders. For sports, the great achievement of liberal feminism has been doing away with what Messner calls "hard essentialism"—a natural and categorical differentiation between men and women. There remains, however, what Messner terms "soft essentialism"—a more subtle construction and naturalization of binary gender differences at local, national, and international levels. Messner shows how gender in sports is a dynamic "inequality regime" that intersects with other institutionalized inequality regimes, requiring differentiated analysis.

"What do we mean by fairness in sport?" ask Patricia Vertinsky, Cassandra Wells, and Stephanie Van Veen in chapter 2. In line with Messner's argument of "soft essentialism," the authors argue that behind the façade of fairness we see a perpetuation of gender binaries and discrimination. Vertinsky, Wells, and Van Veen examine fairness "as a floating signifier" in three areas: sex-testing through the case of Caster Semenya; judging in aesthetic sports through the 2002 "bloc judging" scandal in ice-skating; and women's access to ski-jumping. Arguing that women's bodies are essentialized and discriminated against in the name of fairness, the authors call for a differentiated approach that considers the complexities around individual judgment, the sport's historical structures, and the social values around male and female sports participation.

"Strong as a lion, and cunning as a fox"; this is the ideal Basque pelota player. What does this ideal mean for Basque masculinities and for women? The ethnographic approach of Olatz González Abrisketa in chapter 3 reveals how deeply the game is embedded in the Basque cultural imaginary, and how it creates a gendered space and agency. The Basque imagined community, González argues, is personified by male bodies at the fronton: the proto-agonic *plaza gizon*, or "plaza-man." The bodies that gather in the plaza to "contemplate" the pelota game turn it into a sacred place of communion from which women are excluded. Through the story of Maite Ruiz de Larramendi, a talented female player who had to stop playing at the age of thirteen, González explores the construction of Basque masculinities and femininities in the public space of the plaza-fronton.

"To play football, tennis, or basketball, one ball is necessary," Jeremy MacClancy quotes an informant in chapter 4, "but to go downhill on a *goitibera*, two are needed." MacClancy situates the Basque pastime of racing downhill in a homemade go-kart-like contraption within the intersection of various power regimes. The spread of this practice coincided with the 1970's movement *La calle es mía* (the street is mine), a grassroots vindication of public space from the state. Goitibera aims to be a purportedly democratic, anti-elitist, popular event that prides itself on local products, namely homemade vehicles, and in which all are meant to participate as equals. Goitibera has become a symbol of counterculture, a metaphor for marginal others, for those living on the edge—as long as they are male. MacClancy shows how goitibera challenges power at some levels and reproduces it at others; it genders public space and action as male and naturalizes toughness, daring, and ingenuity as male attributes.

In chapter 5, Richard Giulianotti explores the power relations, hegemonies, and inequalities that are created by globalized sports. The author considers three aspects of the sports-globalization interface: the "take-off" period, or the twentieth-century acceleration of the globalization process; the "convergence-divergence" debate on whether globalization homogenizes or heterogenizes cultural systems; and the political-economic consequences of globalization. Giulianotti relates the processes of heterogenization, globalization, and creolization to sports, in which emerging and post-transition nations can insert themselves into the international area. While the "hard Americanization" thesis is less relevant in sports than in other global processes, the world economic system of centers and peripheries is detectable in the hegemony of northern- and Western-based sports associations.

Part 2: Practice

In chapter 6, Pierre Parlebas outlines the perspectives and methodology of praxeology, a sports science in which his work is a fundamental reference. Motor praxeology, he argues, studies the body as part of the whole personality of the player, interacting with the emotional, social, cognitive, and expressive dimensions of a person. A basic premise of motor praxeology highlights the body's involvement with its social and environmental context; bodies in action are deciding, taking part, taking risks, reacting, and communicating. Parlebas outlines the theoretical premises and relevance of motor praxeology through concepts like the internal logic of motor situations, participants' relationships, risk-taking, the uncertainty of the environment, and subjective decisions. The author argues with Marcel Mauss that, although motor action has universal elements, it is also culturally specific; the sociocultural nature of motor action is the subject of ethnomotricity.

In chapter 7, Bertrand During offers a reflection on action and technique in sports based on physical education and sports-science practitioners, as well as philosophers and social theorists. The intellectual history of sports discourse, Durand argues, has been character-

ized by a dualistic conceptualization of body and soul that goes back
to Plato. Subsequent notable figures of sports theory such as Pierre
Coubertin or Georges Hébert failed to consider the role of technique.
Coubertin looked at physical exercise for its social and cultural impact,
and Hébert considered it a natural, instinctual process. In a Cartesian
spirit, the educational theory of "structured gymnastics" considered
the body as a mechanism, a material reality juxtaposed on the mind
and the will. Marxist approaches to motor practice were inspired by
human progress, scientific and technical achievements, and placed
the overachieving individual in the center of "red sports." In the 1960s,
motor praxeology challenged dualistic and mechanistic approaches by
introducing a new perspective in which physical action is an intercon-
nected system of psychomotor (solitary), sociomotor (interactive), and
ethnomotor (cultural) dimensions.

"High-risk sportspeople are often portrayed as suicidal, behavioral
deviants who are revolting against the norm." Is this really so? In chapter 8, Luc Collard questions the assumption that the inclusion of dangerous sports in the school curriculum turns students into dangerous
risk-takers in real life. Through designing a P.E. classroom version of
the famous "chickie-run" car scene in the movie *Rebel Without a Cause*,
the author seeks to establish whether extreme sports specialists take
more risks than specialists in other sports. Detailed results show that
high-risk specialists tended to play the chickie-run game more cautiously, and that they minimized their losses. Collard explores how different factors, such as weight, gender, sports specialty, and risk-taking
reputation might influence motor decisions that involve risk. In the
light of the results, Collard proposes that the integration of high-risk
sports in school curriculum is desirable as an "education of composure"—the ability to confront danger with confidence.

In chapter 9, Joseba Etxebeste Otegi explores the relationship
between motor time and emotions in Basque traditional games, and
whether emotions are influenced by the presence or absence of purpose. Conceptions of time, Etxebeste argues, are culturally conditioned
and may be divided into two categories: linear, purposeful time (typical of Western cultures) and nonlinear time of no purpose (in certain traditional cultures). Games, like time, can be categorized along
the lines of the same dualistic theme: linear, purpose-oriented games
with recorded results, and nonlinear, experience-oriented, "anecdotal"
games without recorded results. In the Basque context, these two categories dovetail with cultural conceptualizations of play: competitive,
result-oriented *joko* and noncompetitive *jolas*. Based on the analysis of
376 Basque children's games, Etxebeste explores Basque attitudes to-

ward time and competitiveness.

In chapter 10, Pere Lavega investigates the intensity and nature of the emotions that players experience depending on the internal logic of games: on the relationship between players, the spatial and temporal constraints of the game, the material tools involved, and competitiveness. Players were trained to observe and record the intensity of their positive, negative, and ambiguous emotions while playing. Lavega considers whether men and women reported different emotions of different intensity. The chapter identifies the factors that led to more or less emotional intensity in terms of roles, strategic pacts among the players, the relevance of the final score, and the tools involved.

Part 3: Passion

In chapter 11, Gary Armstrong and Emily Vest explore the ethno-political contention projected onto soccer between Bosnian Croats and Bosniaks in the city of Mostar, Bosnia and Herzegovina. The story of Mostar's football rivalries is a metaphor for the struggles and divisions that characterize ethno-nationalist tensions accumulating in the former Yugoslavia since the death of Tito. Against the complicated background of the Yugoslav war of the 1990s, the Bosnian Croats and Bosniaks of Mostar have used soccer as a major channel for ethno-political negotiations of space, identity, and desires. Armstrong and Vest show how Mostar became a city of dualism, a "ruptured" city structured around a collapsed bridge, and the rivalry between the Croat, west-bank HŠK Zrinjski and the Bosniak, east-bank FK Velež.

In chapter 12, Mariann Vaczi explores the Basque rivalry complex in general and the soccer derby between the Athletic Club of Bilbao and the Real Sociedad of Donostia-San Sebastián in particular. Based on participant observation, Vaczi considers the derby as a cultural performance structured by specifically Basque conceptualizations of play, competition, and cooperation (*joko, jolas*, and *burruka*), and she uses the prisoner's dilemma as an analytical framework—the derby becomes an arena in which each party, each club, will necessarily pursue its self-interest and even "betray" the other, leading to an institutionalized hostility relationship. At the same time, the external meta-consideration that the two clubs belong to the same "gang," the same moral community (Basques in Spain), imposes a mandate of cooperation. The result is a history of derbies as an iterated "war-peace game" in which interaction oscillates between hostile and cooperative.

Loïc J. D. Wacquant discusses the social and moral functions of a Chicago South Side boxing gym in chapter 13. Based on a three-year-long ethnographic field study during which Wacquant became integrated as a boxer, he identified three functions of a gym in the African-American ghetto. First, the gym is a "sanctuary" that protects the individual from the streets. It offers an escape from the "dull misery of a dull existence," and the often violent realities of American ghetto street life. Second, the gym becomes a "school of morality" that inculcates a spirit of discipline, a sense of belonging, and respect for other people and oneself. And third, the gym serves to "make life less banal" by offering engagement with risk, adventure, masculine honor, prestige, and a virile brotherhood.

Historian Richard O. Davies describes in chapter 14 how a match between an American and a Basque boxer in 1931 shaped the identity of the state of Nevada in general, and that of the Basque diasporas in particular. Under a hot July sun, the handsome local favorite Max Baer entered a prizefight against the reigning European champion Paulino Uzcudun, the "Basque Woodchopper." The chapter offers insight into the interfaces of prizefighting, libertarian morals, and conservative economic and political postures in the aftermath of the Great Depression and the Prohibition era. Nevada embraced prizefighting when it was still prohibited elsewhere, which "contributed significantly to an unsavory reputation of Nevada as the 'Sin State.'" Boxing also had an impact on emerging ideals of frontier masculinity and opened sports to women spectators. Davies describes how for the local Basque-American community, the match provided an axis of identification in their new home.

Games and motor practices, especially dance and pelota, have been important manifestations of Basque identity in the American West. In chapter 15, Clara Urdangarin Liebaert visits the annual youth meeting Udaleku (Summer Camp) organized by the North American Basque Organization in the San Francisco *Euskal Etxea*, or Basque Center. The purpose of the camp is to promote Basque culture and heritage, and to reinforce relations between members of the Basque community. "Being Basque," the author stresses, "is acting like a Basque." The narration of Basqueness, the construction of Basque-American identity, happens through motor exercise: ethnomotricity becomes an important function of identity and cultural heritage. Urdangarin also points out the potential impasses of folklorized identity performance and of an anachronistic, traditional model of Basqueness.

"Twenty-seven up/twenty-seven down, no base runners, no errors, walks. Very rare—only twenty in over 120 years—distinction hall of fame. Armando Galarraga from Venezuela pitched a perfect game for the Detroit Tigers on June 2, 2010. Or did he?" In chapter 16, T. David Brent explores the notion of perfection in an actual "perfect game" in baseball, which the umpire stole from Galarraga through upholding an incorrect decision. Technically, this was a perfect game, despite the umpire's call that made it not perfect. However, the overall outcome was perfect; after the game, the behavior of the player, the umpire, the fans, and the media elevated it into perfection. After revisiting definitions and philosophical ideals of perfection, Brent argues that the process of constructing perfection "is a collaborative one, dependent on many complex factors coming together in the right combination over a period of time."

It is fitting to close this volume with Jennifer Hargreaves' personal narrative of her long career in sports education and research. In the concluding chapter, Hargreaves explores the role of memory for research and examines the relationship between the personal and the political by tracing her interest in sports. She identifies the life and world events that influenced her intellectual and theoretical approaches to agency, power, structure, hegemony, Eurocentrism, freedom, and integrity. Hargreaves demonstrates the impact of personal experience on the choice of research orientation, which led her to examine sports through the perspectives of neglected, marginalized, and discriminated groups, "unsung heroines," and "voices of Others."

Bibliography

Acker, Joan. "Inequality Regimes: Gender, Class and Race in Organizations." *Gender & Society* 20 (2006): 441–64.

Bairner, Alain. *Sport, Nationalism, and Globalization: European and North American Perspectives.* Albany: State University of New York Press, 2001.

Bateson, Gregory. *Steps to an Ecology of Mind.* New York: Ballantine Books, 1972.

Booth, Douglas. *The Race Game: Sport and Politics in South Africa.* London: F. Cass, 1998.

Brownell, Susan. *Training the Body for China: Sports in the Moral Order of the People`s Republic.* Chicago: University of Chicago Press, 1995.

Caillois, Roger. *Man, Play, and Games.* New York: Free Press of Glencoe, 1961.

Cuestión de Pelotas (2010). www.rtve.es/noticias/20101014/documentos-tv-cuestion-pelotas/361944.shtml.

Geertz, Clifford. *The Interpretation of Cultures: Selected Essays.* New York: Basic Books, 1973.

Giulianotti, Richard. *Football: A Sociology of the Global Game.* Cambridge:

Polity Press, 1999.

Goffman, Erving. *Interaction Ritual: Essays on Face-to-Face Behavior*. Garden City: Doubleday, 1967.

González Abrisketa, Olatz. *The Basque Pelota: A Ritual, An Aesthetic*. Reno: Center for Basque Studies, 2013.

Guelke, Adrian. "Sport and the End of Apartheid." In *The Changing Politics of Sport*, edited by Lincoln Allison. Manchester: Manchester University Press, 1993.

Hargreaves, Jennifer. *Heroines of Sport: The Politics of Difference and Identity*. London: Routledge, 2000.

Hargreaves, John. *Freedom for Catalonia? Catalan Nationalism, Spanish Identity, and the Barcelona Olympic Games*. Cambridge: Cambridge University Press, 2000. www.as.com/futbol/articulo/bosque-supimos-perder-ganamos-estilo/20110121dasdasftb_57.Tes

Hulme, Derick L. *The Political Olympics: Moscow, Afghanistan and the 1980 U.S. Boycott*. New York: Praeger, 1990.

James, C. L. R. *Beyond a Boundary*. New York: Pantheon Books, 1963.

Katzer, Nikolaus, Sandra Budy, and Alexandra Köhring. *Euphoria and Exhaustion: Modern Sport in Soviet Culture and Society*. New York: Campus Verlag, 2010.

Large, David Clay. *Nazi Games: The Olympics of 1936*. New York: W. W. Norton, 2007.

MacAloon, John J. *Muscular Christianity in Colonial and Post-Colonial Worlds*. London and New York: Routledge: 2007.

Mangan, J. A. *Athleticism in the Victorian and Edwardian Public School: The Emergence and Consolidation of an Educational Ideology*. Cambridge: Cambridge University Press, 1981.

Mangan, J. A., and Ha Nam-Gil. "Confucianism, Imperialism, Nationalism: Modern Sport, Ideology and Korean Culture." In *Europe, Sport, World: Shaping Global Societies*, edited by J. A. Mangan. London and Portland, Ore.: Frank Cass, 2001.

Markovits, Andrei S., and Steven L. Hellerman. "Women`s Soccer in the United States: Yet Another American 'Exceptionalism.'" In *Soccer, Women, Sexual Liberation: Kicking Off a New Era*, edited by Fan Hong and J. A. Mangan. London: Frank Cass Publishers, 2004.

McDevitt, Patrick F. *May the Best Man Win: Sport, Masculinity, and Nationalism in Great Britain and the Empire, 1880–1935*. New York: Palgrave Macmillan, 2004.

Messner, Michael M. "Sports and Male Domination: The Female Athlete as Contested Ideological Terrain." *Sociology of Sport Journal* 5, no. 3 (1988): 197–211.

Nabokov, Vladimir. "Breitensträter – Paolino." In "Vladimir Nabokov`s

Ringside Vision of Art and Life." In *Times Literary Supplement*, by Thomas Karshan. August 1, 2012. www.the-tls.co.uk/tls/public/article1093895.ece. Accessed February 10, 2013.

Pope, S. W. *Patriotic Games: Sporting Traditions in the American Imagination, 1876–1926.* New York: Oxford University Press, 1997.

Shaw, Duncan. *Fútbol y Franquismo.* Madrid: Alianza, 1987.

Turner, Victor. *From Ritual to Theatre: The Human Seriousness of Play.* New York: Performing Arts Journal Publications, 1982.

———. *The Ritual Process: Structure and Anti-Structure.* Chicago: Aldine Publishing Company, 1969.

Part 1

POWER

1

GENDER RELATIONS AND SPORT: LOCAL, NATIONAL, TRANSNATIONAL

Michael A. Messner

In this chapter, I explore how organized sport works as a constitutive element of current gender relations. To state the project this way requires a move away from a common "sociology of sport" perspective that focuses on relations *within* sport, toward a "sport and society" perspective that explores the ways that sport articulates with strains, tensions, and shifting formations of gender in communities, the nation, and the world. Two conceptual frames are important here. First, when I write of *gender relations* I am assuming a multidimensional analytic framework: gender as an important part of the symbolic realm of cultural meanings; gender as actively created through day-to-day interactional processes; and gender divisions of labor and power as a dynamic part of the structure of social institutions.[1] Second, drawing from Australian sociologist Raewyn Connell,[2] I explore the institutional structure of gender in three geographic registers: a local institutional gender regime; a national gender order (of the United States); and a location within the international gender order.

Whether at the level of local gender regimes or at that of national or international gender orders, these concepts never imply a fixity of gender relations. Rather, they are tools we can use to grasp the "state of play" of gender and power, oscillating between moments of crisis and change, and hegemonic moments of relative stability and consensus. Moments of hegemonic stability in turn always create new strains and tensions that foster new possibilities for change, less often radical disruptions, more often contestations over what Connell[3] calls the "steering" of gender relations—within a gender regime, between gen-

---

1. I develop this three-tiered conceptual framework in Messner, *Taking the Field.*
2. Connell, *Gender & Power.*
3. Connell, "Steering toward Equality?"

der regimes, and within larger gender orders. It is my aim in this chapter to move from local to national to international registers of gender relations by looking first at a local study of youth sports, next at the national politics of Title IX in the United States, and finally at the recent case of South African runner Caster Semenya's "gender-verification test" controversy, with the aim of illuminating some strains and tensions in the international gender order. I will argue that my local study suggests an emergent hegemonic moment of postfeminist "soft essentialism," while the national and international foci reveal some strains and tensions that inhere in this moment of gender formation, as well as the limitations of both a local ethnographic study and of an analysis that focuses primarily on gender.

Sport, Gender, and Society

Before moving to the body of this chapter, I will briefly reiterate an argument about how sport figures in U.S. historical gender relations. Following an early twentieth-century burst of athleticism among girls and women that accompanied a powerful wave of feminism, a backlash against vigorous physical activity for women eliminated many women's sports and vastly marginalized those that remained. The resulting binary opposition of athletic males and nonathletic females helped to construct and naturalize a gendered public-domestic split in the mid-twentieth-century U.S.—a divide especially evident in the middle class—and a hierarchical ordering of gender that was premised on ideologies of male superiority. I have called this mid-century ideology "hard essentialism—the shared belief that women and men are *naturally and categorically different* and should thus be sorted into different and unequal spheres that reflect their natures.[4]

The resurgence of a feminist movement in the 1970s led to a new burst of female athleticism, corresponding with (especially middle-class) women's more general move into public life. On one level, this dramatic growth of female athleticism served as a challenge to the ideology of hard essentialism. However, the particular institutional organization of sport differed from that of most other institutions that were undergoing sex-desegregation in the late twentieth century. Unlike higher education, medicine, law, or politics, the integration of girls and women into sport was taking place within an almost entirely sex-segregated structure. Put simply, "equal opportunity" for girls and women in sport has been sought mostly within a "separate but equal"

---

4. I introduce the concepts of hard and soft essentialism in Messner, *It's All For the Kids*, and further develop the concepts in Messner, "Gender Ideologies, Youth Sports, and the Production of Soft Essentialism."

strategy, where male and female bodies, assumed to be naturally different, are sorted into separate binary categories. As equal opportunity is sought, difference is affirmed. Thus, sport becomes a dynamic site for the simultaneous contestation and reproduction of gender equality and inequality, a "contested terrain" of gender relations.[5]

A Local Terrain of Contested Gender Relations

Between 1999 and 2007, I conducted a study of my local community's soccer, baseball, and softball youth sports programs. I was particularly interested in gender divisions of labor and power among adult volunteers (mostly parents), and in the course of the study, I became increasingly focused on how the division of labor and power in youth sport's gender regime (nearly all of the coaches were men and nearly all of the "team moms" were women) tended to articulate neatly with the gendered work and family relations in this professional-class and white-dominated[6] Los Angeles suburb. Much of the book that resulted from this study analyzes the adults' gender formation processes that result in sex segregation.[7] Here, I briefly outline two interrelated parts of this process: first, the ways in which professional-class adults, through talk and actions, "gender" the boys and girls whom they are coaching; and second, the ways in which adults' gendering of kids reflects and naturalizes the gendered work-family divisions of labor and power in their own families, thus helping to construct the ascendant hegemony of "soft essentialism."

Youth sports coaches, including most of the small number of women coaches, tend to view and treat girls and boys in very different ways. Adults applaud their daughters' participation in sports, seeing it as healthy and empowering. When asked to talk about girls, adults often drop into a language of individual choice: they talk of their daughters' futures as realms of choice for which, they believe, sports participation is helping to prepare them. This new articulation of girls as flexible choosers is a remarkable sign of social change, vastly different from earlier generations who tended to view their daughters as destined for domesticity. In particular, it is a dramatic indicator of the success of liberal feminism. However, the limits of this language of choice for

---

5. Hargreaves, "Where's the Virtue? Where's the Grace?"; Willis, "Women in Sport in Ideology"; Messner, "Sports and Male Domination."

6. I emphasize "professional-class and white-*dominated*" here because in fact the community I studied evidenced considerable class and racial/ethnic diversity (for example, only 44 percent of the community is white). However, I argue that youth sports and other community activities are dominated in form, values, and visible leadership by an ascendant (predominantly white) professional class.

7. Messner, *It's All for the Kids.*

girls are revealed in the asymmetrical ways that adults talk about boys. Adults, simply put, are far less articulate when asked to talk about boys and gender. Ultimately, most adults meander to clichés about boys' supposed natural (testosterone-driven) aggression and emotional linearity (as opposed to the supposed emotional complexity of girls), and about boys' natural inclinations for sport in particular and public life in general. I call this shared view of girls as flexible choosers and boys as inflexible biologically driven creatures "soft essentialism." Similar to hard essentialism, soft essentialism is still premised on a belief in natural differences between boys and girls, but soft essentialism no longer posits this difference to be categorical—especially when it comes to girls, who are now viewed as flexible choosers who as adults will be expected to navigate across and between the challenges and demands of public and domestic life. This changed view of girls stands in stark contrast to a largely unreconstructed view of boys.

Soft essentialist ideology, projected onto children, takes on clearer meaning when we consider common patterns of gender relations in professional-class families. Mothers in these families are college educated, often holding graduate degrees, and have spent years building careers in medicine, law, finance, and other professions. On arrival of children in a family—especially second or third children—many of these mothers face a common dilemma—not so much a "biological pull to motherhood," as conservative pundits would have it, but the constraining experience of being stretched to the limits by the combination of inflexible workplaces, career-committed husbands who do minimal family labor, and expanding public expectations for mothers to involve themselves in the "third shift" of community and school-based work necessary for the concerted cultivation of their own children.[8] Thus challenged, some of these women decide to opt entirely out of their high-powered careers, while others change to less demanding (but lower pay and lower status) jobs. These women narrate their resulting shift in attention away from career and toward care of kids in the language of individual choice, inflected with a feminist sensibility.

In short, the gender regime of youth sports has undergone a huge transformation in the past forty years. And there is evidence to support the contention that girls' dramatic movement into sports is correlated with health benefits and has fostered embodiments of a competitive professional-class habitus.[9]

---

8. Blair-Loy, *Competing Devotions*; Lareau, *Unequal Childhoods*; Stone, *Opting Out*.

9. Miller, Sabo, Farrell, Barnes, and Melnick, "Sports, Sexual Activity, Contraceptive Use, and Pregnancy Among Female and Male High School Students"; Miller, Melnick, Barnes, Farrell, and Sabo, "Untangling the Links Among Athletic Involvement, Gender,

However, the youth sports-based construction of girls as flexible choosers and boys as naturally destined for competition in public life plays a largely conservative and stabilizing role in the context of professional-class work-family gender regimes, where highly educated mothers exercise "choice" to opt out or scale back careers, while men continue largely to focus on their public careers. Gender inequalities that persist at the nexus of professional-class work and family gender regimes, rather than being viewed as sites of collective struggle for change, are narrated through soft essentialism as resulting from women's individual, even feminist-inspired choices. The ideology of soft essentialism, constructed in part within youth sports, helps to naturalize the inequalities that inhere in this moment of hegemonic, class-based gender relations.

An obvious limit of my local study of youth sports is my analytic foregrounding of gender. How might the intersecting gender regimes of youth sports, families, and work look through an intersectional analysis that extends beyond the gender/social class matrix at the center of my analysis? This question could be explored by attending more centrally to the experiences of marginalized people within the white, professional-class-dominated community that I studied, or by comparing youth sports in my community to, for instance, youth sports within adjacent working-class and predominantly Latina/o communities. Such a shift in empirical focus would likely reveal the ways in which concepts like "gender regimes" can obscure as much as they reveal. An intersectional analysis that attends as much to class and race relations might better view youth sports not simply as a "gender regime," but as a dynamic "inequality regime" that intersects with other institutional inequality regimes.[10]

And though I do connect my analysis from the local youth sports gender regimes to local family and work gender regimes, such a study can be limited by its very locality, unless it is connected to an analysis of the historical and macro-institutional context in which it is embedded. In the next section of this chapter, I draw out the scope to think more about sport and the national gender order of the U.S. And while there are many potential points of entry into an exploration of gender and sport on a national scale, I will limit my comments here to what the politics of Title IX can tell us about current strains and tensions in the national gender order.

Race, and Adolescent Academic Outcomes."
10. Acker, "Inequality Regimes."

Title IX, Sport, and the National Gender Order

Initiated in the United States in 1972 to ensure equal opportunities for boys and girls in educational institutions, Title IX has had a huge impact on sports, helping to usher in a dramatic and continuing surge of sports participation by girls and women in high schools and colleges.[11] In the terms discussed in the introduction of this chapter, Title IX can be seen as a largely successful legal and political effort at "steering" the gender regimes of schools and universities toward gender equity. This equity steering did not go unopposed; from the start, the patriarchal center of institutionalized U.S. sport, led by the football lobby, opposed Title IX, and over the years many legal challenges to Title IX have been fought.[12] For my purposes here, these conflicts illustrate the unevenness of gender reform within and between gender regimes. With gender regimes more deeply contested by feminism in the 1970s, education, politics, and the law clashed with the more stubbornly conservative and less vigorously contested gender regime of organized sports. Title IX can be seen as a political and legal means of steering the internal gender regime of sport toward consensus and continuity with the gender regime of education, and with that of the larger gender order.

Title IX politics came to a head at the national level in 2002 when the Bush Administration called for a series of public hearings to assess the effects of Title IX. The subsequent regional meetings (I attended and testified at the one held in San Diego) revealed Title IX to be a lightning rod for backlash discourse, but also—and even more so, as it turned out—as a powerful rallying point for supporters of girls' and women's sport. Legal activist Nancy Solomon and I observed that the anti-Title IX discourse at the hearings tended to invoke a language of male victimization by the state, which was viewed as unfairly representing women's interests.[13] We argued that the language of bureaucratic victimization of individual men—especially as symbolized by the threatened male "walk-on"—was a strategy that seemed to find fertile ground among young white males who face a world destabilized by feminism, gay and lesbian liberation, the Civil Rights movement, and major shifts in the economy.

It is striking how anti–Title IX talk is one of the few places in national discourse about sport where men become at least potentially visible as gendered beings ("gender and sport" nearly always implies "women and sport"). But critics' stories veer decidedly away from any possible analysis of boys and men as a socially formed group with shared in-

---

11. Acosta and Carpenter, "Women in Intercollegiate Sport."
12. See Brake, *Getting in the Game*; Suggs, *A Place on the Team*.
13. Messner and Solomon, "Social Justice and Men's Interests."

terests (much less shared privileges) in sport. Instead, the discourse of critics of Title IX consistently invoked the values of individualism, by telling stories of individual men victimized by liberal state policies that promote the group interests of women. And this discourse rested its case on an essentialist foundation—individual men, the critics argued, are just naturally more interested in sports than are women. The critics agreed that it's a good thing for girls and women to have the right to choose to play sports, but they implied that due to their different natures, boys and men will naturally be drawn to sports, whereas fewer girls and women will be.

The critics thus used the values of individualism to smuggle in an articulation of "men's interests" as collectively opposed to Title IX, but this strategy was limited by the actual complexity of men's interests. To be sure, there is a powerful centripetal pull, even for many marginalized boys and men, to the privilege and erotic power that lie at the center of male-dominated institutions like sport. However, under some conditions, some men disidentify with *and* even oppose institutionalized male privilege. It has become common to hear stories, for instance, of fathers who become overnight equity activists when they find suddenly that their daughters have been denied access to sport or have been offered substandard playing fields or unqualified coaches. In these cases, individual men clearly see their own interests as intertwined with the interests of their female family members.

Indeed, collective opposition to Title IX appears to have faded in recent years, and many would say that this is because of the popularity of Title IX and the widespread support for girls and women's sport participation, including substantial support from men. A 2007 national poll conducted by the National Women's Law Center found that of those who recognize what Title IX is, 82 percent support it.[14] Two Women's Sports Foundation studies in 2008 and 2009 in Boston and San Antonio revealed that only half of those polled knew about Title IX, but the vast majority agreed with its goals.[15] And a 2008 national survey found adults widely supportive of girls' athletic opportunities.[16]

In addition to growing pro–Title IX public opinion, it is also likely that the very legal structure of Title IX has allowed for a smoothing of current tensions and for a movement toward a national consensus that stabilizes a hegemonic moment of gender formation. In a cogent analysis of the legal politics of Title IX, Deborah Brake demonstrates how

---

14. National Women's Law Center, *Barriers to Fair Play.*

15. Women's Sports Foundation, *GoGirlGo!*; Women's Sports Foundation, *GoGirlGo! Boston Post-test 2009.*

16. Sabo and Veliz, *Youth Sport in America.*

Title IX strategically melds different (and in some ways, fundamentally contradictory) strands of feminist legal theory. On the one hand, Brake argues, Title IX is premised on the liberal feminist ideal of equal treatment for individuals, based on merit. Under the law, individuals have the right to equal opportunities to participate in sport. However, this individualist focus in the law is continually in tension with the sex-segregated (and still unequal) collective structure of sport. The liberal feminist strand of Title IX, Brake explains, "strives for equal treatment of men and women without questioning the male-dominated structure of sports and . . . the reasons men and women are differently situated in sport."[17]

Counterbalancing the limits of liberal individualism is the strand of "difference feminism" also undergirding the legal theory of Title IX. Difference feminism, according to Brake, "embrace[s] and value[s] women's distinctive interests, needs, and experiences equally with those of men . . . [and] accommodates gender difference in sport by its allowance of sex-separate teams."[18] While helping to protect and extend the collective interests of girls and women, this aspect of Title IX also echoes the essentialism of nineteenth-century "social feminists."[19] Premised on a presumed biologically based need to create and maintain a gendered boundary around girls' and women's sports, the law creates and protects a separate sphere within which female sport participation can grow and thrive, while simultaneously risking—perhaps even ensuring—a marginalization of women's sports that stigmatizes female athletes as inferior and often in need of protection. The tension between these two strains of feminist theory is clear: can individual girls and women ever have truly equal opportunities, resources, and treatment in an institution that is divided in binary terms according to an assumed-to-be-natural hierarchy of male-female bodily difference?[20]

Title IX, then, is an organically evolving law, its contradictory elements giving it a built-in flexibility that allows advocates to use the law as a tool to push for individual equal opportunity while simultaneously arguing that categorical sex difference creates a distinct group-based interest that must be protected and defended. The effectiveness of this melding of "equal treatment" with "difference accommodation"

---

17. Brake, *Getting in the Game,* 9.
18. Ibid., 10.
19. Vertinsky, *The Eternally Wounded Woman.*
20. Most advocates of women's and girls' sports argue that such a separation is needed, while a few feminist critics argue that separate sports for girls and boys will always reproduce gender inequality. See, for instance, McDonagh and Pappano, *Playing with the Boys.*

is evident, according to Brake, in recent legal cases that have dealt with pregnancy among athletes.[21] National advocacy organizations like the Women's Sports Foundation tend to mirror this dual strategy of advocating for individual equal opportunity alongside a defense of women's group-based interests in maintaining different and separate sports.[22]

For my purposes here, I want to emphasize how Title IX's very strengths, and likely too its popularity, are grounded not so much in a revolutionary potential to disrupt gender relations but to the contrary, in the ways that its melding of equal opportunity and essential difference articulates neatly with the emergence of the professional-class ideology of soft essentialism. In particular, Title IX's emphasis on the individual rights of girls and women as flexible choosers tends to affirm professional-class beliefs in individual meritocracy, while deflecting critical focus away from the ways that gendered institutions constrain those very choices. Simultaneously, the law's essentialist underpinnings then naturalize the unequally gendered outcomes of women's (apparently individual) choices. The inherent strains and tensions built into soft essentialism, I argued above, are (1) its tendency to smuggle in a white, professional-class-based ethic, and either to render invisible and/or to impose that ethic on class- and race-marginalized and subordinated others, and (2) to render boys and men as an undifferentiated, unexamined, and thus unreconstructed category. In the U.S., much pro–Title IX advocacy discourse for girls and women in sport does just that. The liberal feminist individualism helps to construct an individual professional-class white subject, while difference feminism's essentialism helps to maintain boys and men as a naturalized and largely unmarked category. As scholars of masculinities and of whiteness have shown, the invisibility of superordinate categories is often central to the reproduction of the privilege that adheres to these categories.

If politics involve the steering of the gender order, then what strategic steering directions might be implied by the current strains and tensions discussed above? I have argued elsewhere that to push the sport gender regime toward greater democratic egalitarianism would involve two strategies. First, while most advocates of girls' and women's sports are committed to the current institutional segregation of girls' and women's sports as necessary to ensure participation opportunities, many community activists are moving toward a more intersectional understanding of the interests of girls and women, creating sports programs targeted to the needs, for instance, of inner-city girls,

---

21. Brake, *Getting in the Game*, 171–77.
22. Heywood, "Producing Girls."

girls of color, Muslim girls, or differently abled girls. Working creatively with this dynamic tension between the collective interests of girls, as protected under Title IX, and the interests of particular groups of girls who are not privileged by professional class, white, or able-bodied status is one of the keys to pushing beyond the class-based individualist limits of Title IX as a strategy for social justice.[23]

Second, a national social-justice strategy would move toward *a* strategic degendering of boys' and men's sports. This would mean three things. First, this degendering would build a broad social recognition that boys, as much as girls, are socially gendered beings and not simply products of a sexed biological nature. Second, youth sports would be constructed as sites where adults could prepare boys to become flexible choosers who, like girls, need to develop the skill sets and emotional flexibilities that allow them to negotiate across and between the challenges of public and domestic realms of life.[24] This would involve, in part, seeing youth sports as a place in which boys can expand (rather than contract) their emotional repertoires. Third, the homosocial boundaries of boys' and men's sports should be challenged, including, especially, by opening up coaching opportunities for women coaches and continuing the integration of girls into previously all-boys' sporting activities. Together, these strategies would push sport away from its current role as a professional-class gender comfort zone.

Using Title IX as a lens through which to view the current state of play of the U.S. national gender order extends our understanding beyond that of the local ethnographic study discussed in the first part of this chapter by connecting the national legal and political "steering" of gender relations to our understanding of local work-family-youth sports gender regimes. I argue that we can see the ascendant class-based gender ideology of soft essentialism at both the local and the national level. At both levels, we can see the expansion of individual equal opportunity for girls as a major accomplishment of feminism (albeit one that disproportionately benefits girls from privileged backgrounds), while also seeing how persistent essentialist beliefs—however "soft" they may be—continue to construct and naturalize gender hierarchy, smuggle in class and race privilege under the guise of feminist progress, and leave boys and men as an unexamined and unreconstructed category.

A Transnational Moment of Gender Trouble

Gender and sport scholars in the United States have recently begun to

---

23. Cooky, "Girls Just Aren't Interested."
24. See Atkinson and Kehler, "Boys, Gyms, Locker Rooms and Heterotopia."

develop a global focus in their theoretical frameworks and empirical analyses. Connell observes that imperialism and globalization have generated institutions—transnational corporations and markets, global media, the United Nations, NGOs—that are part of a world gender order.[25] Such globalization processes are evident in sport[26] to the extent that scholars can now begin to analyze sport as one site for the collision of national gender orders, within a larger world gender order. The case of South African runner Caster Semenya is one such transnational moment of collision for gender meanings and politics.

In 2009, eighteen-year-old South African runner Caster Semenya won the gold medal at the International Athletics Association Federation (IAAF) World Championships in the eight-hundred-meter run. Although the IAFF had previously joined other international sports governing bodies by doing away with mandatory "gender-verification tests," it was still the case that if and when competitors raised questions about an athlete's "true sex," a gender-verification test could be ordered. This occurred in the case of Semenya, setting off an international debate about human rights, "true womanhood," race, and the use of gender-verification testing.

I do not intend here to discuss the incipient scholarly literature on the politics of transgender or transsexual athletes.[27] Nor do I intend to tackle the very complicated task of understanding the full meanings of the Caster Semenya story, either within or outside of South Africa (to do so would risk oversimplification at best, and a re-inscription of an oppressive colonial gaze at worst). Instead, my goal is more modest: I simply want to use this case as an example of a transnational sporting event that makes questions of sex and gender salient and visible, thus revealing some strains and tensions within the international gender order. From this, I hope to gain insight into the limits of my analysis of local and national gender orders. Fortunately, other scholars have developed a sophisticated analysis of the meanings and nuances of the Semenya incident, and I draw here from two such current works.[28]

An understanding of the transnational meanings of the Semenya incident begins with a sketch of the role of sport in the developing gender order of post-apartheid South Africa. Jennifer Hargreaves

---

25. Connell, *Gender.*

26. Campbell, "Staging Globalization for National Projects"; Miller, Lawrence, McKay, and Rowe, *Globalization and Sport.*

27. For foundational works on this topic, see Birrell and Cole, "Double Fault"; Sykes, "Transsexual and Transgender Politics in Sport"; and Travers, "The Sport Nexus and Gender Injustice."

28. Cooky, Dycus, and Dworkin, "'What Makes a Woman a Woman?' vs. 'Our First Lady of Sport'"; Dworkin, Swar, and Cooky, "Sex and Gender (In)Justice in Sport."

conducted perhaps the first such overview. Gathered in 1995, shortly after the formal end of apartheid, Hargreaves's research in South Africa offers a glimpse into the development of sport within an emergent post-colonializing gender order. Hargreaves observes that sport in pre-apartheid South Africa was "a symbol and celebration of racial . . . superiority and White masculinity," and the immediate years following the end of apartheid were characterized by "piece-meal sport reforms . . . [that] systematically prioritized boys' and men's sports."[29] But by 1995, South African sport had also become a site of struggle for race- and gender-justice: "Black women see sport as a channel for self-definition—simultaneously Afrocentric and feminist. Following years of subjugation under apartheid, their struggles in sport today are part of a wider quest for recognition and dignity; their successes reflect a radical independence and autonomy often absent in other areas of life. Sport is an important politico-cultural space for Black people."[30]

A result of these struggles by the South African women's sports lobby was the development of national efforts to promote gender equity in sports, including the 1997–2000 establishment of a "Women in Sport South Africa" initiative within each province. Hargreaves observed that women's sports participation was becoming a visible pillar in the building of a post-apartheid South African national identity. And—of central importance for my purposes here—unlike the white and professional-class values embedded in the promotion of women's sports in the U.S., the development of women's sports in South Africa is intertwined with a state-sponsored movement to resist and transform white supremacy and colonial domination. The Caster Semenya event, a decade later, reveals the strains and tensions at the nexus between this national South African gender order and that of a transnational gender order dominated by the Global North.

Following Semenya's victorious run, the subsequent IAAF imposition of a gender-verification test on Semenya, along with the hand-wringing in the Euro-American sports media, can be seen as the Global North flexing its imperial muscle to impose Euro-American, binary conceptions of gender on a less powerful nation of the Global South. After all, the very organizational structure within which Semenya was competing was created by, and in the image of, the powers of the Global North. But such a simplistic one-way analysis risks re-inscribing a colonial gaze, and—especially important for my purposes here—misses seeing the dialectical nature of such transnational events. As Connell argues, "The interaction of gender orders is not all one-way .

---

29. Hargreaves, *Heroines of Sport*, 18, 28, 30.
30. Ibid., 36.

. . There is no question that the pressure of the metropole on the gender orders of the global periphery is much stronger than pressure the other ways. [However] we should not think of that as simple 'modernization' of gender. [Rather], the wider historical literature on gender and imperialism show turbulence in the process, and sometimes acute tension."[31]

The Semenya incident reveals such turbulence and tensions at the intersection of North-South gender orders, which may provide opportunities for disruption and change not only transnationally but also possibly within the national gender orders of the Euro-American metropole.

First, this focus on a moment of transnational sporting "collision" reveals, even more than my local or national foci, the limits of a simple focus on gender relations. In particular, the Semenya case brings into stark relief the need for an intersectional analysis of gender with that of race and nation. Sociologists Cheryl Cooky, Ranissa Dycus, and Shari L. Dworkin conducted a systematic analysis of media coverage of the Semenya event, comparing South African print coverage of the story with coverage in the United States. In the U.S. coverage, the dominant media frame "centered on the 'medicalized' aspect of sex/gender . . . among scientists and academics on whether or not 'sex tests' could identify and verify 'real' female athletes."[32] In the South African press, the imposition of gender-verification testing on Semenya was not framed simply (or even primarily) as a violation of an individual human right, or even simply as a violation of "women's rights," but as a white, Euro-American insult to the integrity of South African identity. Semenya, for her South African advocates, was not so much seen as a champion of the rights of women or of transgender or intersexed people, but as "our girl," thus revealing the particular way that race and gender configure to construct the emergent post-apartheid South African national identity.

I do not want to imply a romanticized view of South Africa (or anywhere else in the Global South) as a place where sex/gender binaries are less than meaningful, or where gender fluidity is embraced. To the contrary, feminists in South Africa continue to organize around the strategic interests of women as a social category, fighting against stubborn legacies of institutionalized patriarchy in politics, the labor force, health care, and families, as well as struggling against various forms of violence against women.[33] And as Dworkin, Amanda Swarr,

---

31. Connell, *Gender*, 128–29.
32. Cooky et al., "'What Makes a Woman a Woman?'"
33. Dworkin, Colvin, Hatcher, and Peacock, "Men's Perceptions of Women's Rights

and Cooky point out, South African leaders have been no champions of human rights for transgender or gender-nonconforming people. But when South Africans witnessed scientific gender-verification tests being imposed on Caster Semenya by an institution representing the interests of the Global North, this conjured up recent historic parallels with oppressive medico-scientific practices during apartheid that subjected people to "race-verification tests." In response, it appears that the interests of asserting antiracist and anticolonial South African identity were best served not by engaging in debates about gender fluidity, but instead by embracing Semenya as "our girl" and denouncing as racist any questions about her gender. As such, the South African defense of Semenya affirms an antiracist, anticolonial construction of national identity, with women's sports as one pillar of this identity. Simultaneously, this defense reinforces, rather than challenges, an institutionalized gender binary in sport, thus erasing an opportunity to champion gender diversity and fluidity as part of an expanding human rights discourse.[34]

Second, the Semenya case reveals the limited scope of the concept of soft essentialism for thinking about contemporary gender relations in a global context. On the surface, we see in the Semenya case similarities with central aspects of soft essentialism—reaffirmations of binary sex categories; women's sports treated as a realm that requires "protection" (in this case, through gender-verification testing that aims to affirm a protective boundary around women athletes); and a silence surrounding boys and men as an unmarked, never sex-tested, and thus naturalized superior sex category. But the North-South asymmetries in what the category of "women's sports" means, and in how these categories were strategically deployed, reveals some differences. While the sport agencies and mass media of the Global North attempted to impose their own institutionalized (and "science-based") essentialist and categorical male-female sport binaries, when we examine the meanings and strategies that emerge from South African groups, we see that these sex/gender binary categories were deployed not as a way of creating an individual professional-class "choosing" female subject (as in soft essentialist discourse), but rather as a collective form of resistance against white supremacy and control by the Global North.

In the Semenya case, gender categoricalism is reaffirmed in sport by the dominant discourse of both the Global North and the Global South, but it seems to be a very forced categoricalism, strained at both ends by Northern attempts to use science to force Semenya into

and Changing Gender Relations in South Africa."
    34. Cooky et al., "What Makes a Woman a Woman?"

one or the other sex category, and by Southern discourse that insists on Semenya's femaleness by denying the veracity of gender-verification tests, thus erasing potential questions about gender fluidity and even muting the emergence of Semenya's own voice in the matter.[35] Superimposing the concept of soft essentialism onto this transnational moment, then, risks adopting the standpoint of the Global North, thus doing violence to the intersecting interests at stake, and the different ways these interests are played out in sport.

Conclusion

This chapter has been an exercise in examining sport and contemporary gender relations via three registers: a local gender regime, a national gender order, and a site that reveals some dynamics of a global gender order. This exercise is useful in two broad ways. First, it offers a means of expanding my own scholarly standpoint beyond the local or the national levels, thus potentially shifting or disrupting my domain assumptions. For those like myself who mostly conduct scholarly research on gender and sport within the Global North, attempting to look through a standpoint from the Global South hints at broader strategies for change within the metropole. When we observe sporting institutions dominated by the Global North in direct contact with those of the Global South, our assumptions about the momentary hegemonies within the U.S. national gender order and within local gender regimes can face some radical challenges. It is the very insularity of the U.S. scholars' work on gender and sport, my own included, that can lead us to falsely universalize concepts like "soft essentialism," and to assume, for instance (as I have seen in international discussions of gender and sport), that Title IX has some relevance and meaning to those outside the U.S. A transnational focus illuminates the limits (without necessarily denying the local relevance) of local or national concepts and policies.

Second, a shift in geographic registers can help us to understand more deeply how the strains and tensions in local and national hegemonies are already intertwined with larger, transnational structures. I have argued that at the local level of a gender regime of youth sports in a professional-class, white-dominated U.S. community, we can see the emergence of an ideology of soft essentialism that reveals both the success and the limits of a professional-class-based, individualist feminism. At the level of the national gender order of the U.S., I argue, we can see this same soft essentialism at work in the legal and political

---

35. Ibid.

"steering" of the gender regime of school sports. I have acknowledged that the successes of this steering at the local and national levels are impressive, but also limited by the class-based liberal feminist focus on individual equal opportunity, and by the ways that categorical gender discourse and sport policies render the gendering of boys and men as invisible.

Drawing our scope out from national to transnational further complicates the analysis of sport and contemporary gender relations. The controversy surrounding Caster Semenya raises many potential questions, fundamentally among them the question of "what is at stake in questions of gender equality in sport?" (with a tentative reply being, "not always the same things in all situations and all places"). When and how are assertions of categorical sex difference oppressive? When and how can the categorical interests of girls and women be strategically invoked to press for greater equality and distributive justice? When and how might *other* categories (for example intersexed, race, or place) acutely reveal to us the extent to which "gender" itself is a limiting frame through which institutional sex segregation and naturalization of two supposedly dichotomous sexes is accomplished? And how does an intersectional analysis—especially one that goes beyond the trinity of local race/class/gender—help us to understand the complexities and contradictions in pressing for categorical justice? For example, in asserting the rights of girls and women, when does Title IX in the U.S. erase the particular interests of girls and women marginalized by social class, race, or ethnicity, or of people with differently gendered bodies? In South Africa or elsewhere, how might the deployment of women's sports as resistance against white supremacy and colonial domination also simultaneously render invisible the particular needs of differently gendered people who don't (or won't) fit into binary sex categories, however strategically they may be deployed? In other words, by shifting through these different regional registers, we can more clearly see the ways in which gender relations in sport express the complexities of intersectional inequalities, and how "gender politics" can be a means of steering toward one aspect of social justice, while steering away from another.

Bibliography

Acker, Joan. "Inequality Regimes: Gender, Class, and Race in Organizations." *Gender & Society* 20, no.4 (2006): 441–64.

Acosta, R. Vivien, and Linda Jean Carpenter. "Women in Intercollegiate

Sport: A Longitudinal Thirty-Five-Year Update." Brooklyn College (2012): www.acostacarpenter.org/

Atkinson, Michael, and Michael Kehler. "Boys, Gyms, Locker Rooms and Heterotopia." In *Boys' Bodies: Speaking the Unspoken.* Edited by Michael Atkinson and Michael Kehler. New York: Peter Lang, 2010.

Birrell, Susan, and Cheryl L. Cole. "Double Fault: Renee Richards and the Construction and Naturalization of Difference." In *Women, Sport, and Culture.* Edited by Susan Birrell and Cheryl L. Cole. Champaign, Ill.: Human Kinetics, 1994.

Blair-Loy, Mary. *Competing Devotions: Career and Family Among Women Executives.* Cambridge: Harvard University Press, 2003.

Brake, Deborah L. *Getting in the Game: Title IX and the Women's Sports Revolution.* New York: New York University Press, 2010.

Campbell, Rook. "Staging Globalization for National Projects: Global Sport Markets and Elite Athletic Transnational Labour in Qatar." *International Review for the Sociology of Sport* 46, no. 1 (2011): 45–60.

Connell, Raewyn. *Gender & Power.* Stanford: Stanford University Press, 1987.

———. *Gender.* Cambridge: Polity Press, 2009.

———. "Steering toward Equality? How Gender Regimes Change Inside the State." In *Confronting Equality: Gender, Knowledge and Global Change.* Cambridge: Polity Press, 2011.

Cooky, Cheryl. "Girls Just Aren't Interested: The Social Construction of Interest in Girls' Sport." *Sociological Perspectives* 52, no. 2 (2009): 259–83.

Cooky, Cheryl, Ranissa Dycus, and Shari L. Dworkin. "'What Makes a Woman a Woman?' vs. 'Our First Lady of Sport': A Comparative Analysis of United States and South African Media Coverage of Caster Semenya." *Journal of Sport and Social Issues* 37 (2013), 31–56

Dworkin, Shari L., Amanda L. Swarr and Cheryl Cooky. "(In)Justice in Sport: The Treatment of South African Track Star Caster Semenya." *Feminist Studies.* 39, no. 1 (2013), 40–69.

Dworkin, Shari L., Christopher Colvin, Abbey Hatcher, and Dean Peacock. "Men's Perceptions of Women's Rights and Changing Gender Relations in South Africa: Lessons for Working with Men and Boys in HIV and Antiviolence Programs." *Gender & Society* 26, no. 1 (2012): 97–120.

Hargreaves, Jennifer. *Heroines of Sport: The Politics of Difference and Identity.* London and New York: Routledge, 2000.

———. "Where's the Virtue? Where's the Grace? A Discussion of the Social Production of Gender Through Sport." *Theory Culture and Society* 3, no. 1 (1986): 109–22.

Heywood, Leslie. "Producing Girls: Empire, Sport and the Neoliberal Body." In *Physical Culture, Power, and the Body*, edited by Jennifer Hargreaves and Patricia Vertinsky. London and New York: Routledge, 2007.

Lareau, Annette. *Unequal Childhoods: Class, Race, and Family Life*. Berkeley: University of California Press, 2003.

McDonagh, Eileen, and Laura Pappano. *Playing with the Boys: Why Separate Is Not Equal in Sports*. New York: Oxford University Press, 2008.

Messner, Michael A. "Sports and Male Domination: The Female Athlete as Contested Ideological Terrain." *Sociology of Sport Journal* 5, no. 3 (1988): 197–211.

———. *Taking the Field: Women, Men, and Sports*. Minneapolis: University of Minnesota Press, 2002.

———. *It's All for the Kids: Gender, Families, and Youth Sports*. Berkeley: University of California Press, 2009.

———. "Gender Ideologies, Youth Sports, and the Production of Soft Essentialism." *Sociology of Sport Journal* 28, no. 2 (2011): 151–70.

Messner, Michael A., and Nancy M. Solomon. "Social Justice and Men's Interests: The Case of Title IX." *Journal of Sport and Social Issues* 31, no. 2 (2007): 162–78.

Miller, Kathleen, Don Sabo, Michael Farrell, Grace Barnes, and Merrill Melnick. "Sports, Sexual Activity, Contraceptive Use, and Pregnancy Among Female and Male High School Students: Testing Cultural Resource Theory." *Sociology of Sport Journal* 16, no. 4 (1999): 366–87.

Miller, Kathleen, Merrill Melnick, Grace Barnes, Michael Farrell, and Don Sabo. "Untangling the Links Among Athletic Involvement, Gender, Race, and Adolescent Academic Outcomes." *Sociology of Sport Journal* 22, no. 2 (2005): 178–93.

Miller, Toby, Geoffrey A. Lawrence, Jim McKay, and David Rowe. *Globalization and Sport: Playing the World*. Newbury Park: Sage Publications, 2001.

National Women's Law Center. *Barriers to Fair Play*. Washington, D.C.: National Women's Law Center and the Mellman Group, 2007.

Sabo, Donald F., and Phil Veliz. *Youth Sport in America*. East Meadow, N.Y.: Women's Sports Foundation, 2008.

Stone, Pamela. *Opting Out: Why Women Really Quit Careers and Head Home*. Berkeley: University of California Press, 2007.

Suggs, Welch. *A Place on the Team: The Triumph and Tragedy of Title IX*. Princeton: Princeton University Press, 2005.

Sykes, Heather. "Transsexual and Transgender Politics in Sport." *Women in Sport and Physical Activity Journal* 15, no. 1 (2006): 3–13.

Travers, Ann. "The Sport Nexus and Gender Injustice." *Studies in Social*

Justice 2, no. 1 (2008): 79–101.

Vertinsky, Patricia A. *The Eternally Wounded Woman: Women, Doctors, and Exercise in the Late Nineteenth Century*. Urbana: University of Illinois Press, 1994.

Willis, Paul. "Women in Sport in Ideology." In *Sport, Culture, and Ideology*, edited by Jennifer Hargreaves. London: Routledge & Kegan Paul, 1982.

Women's Sports Foundation. *GoGirlGo! San Antonio 2008*. East Meadow, N.Y.: Women's Sports Foundation, 2008.

Women's Sports Foundation. *GoGirlGo! Boston Post-test 2009*. East Meadow, N.Y.: Women's Sports Foundation, 2009.

2

FAIRNESS AS A FLOATING SIGNIFIER: SEEKING GENDER JUSTICE IN ELITE SPORT

Patricia Vertinsky, Cassandra Wells,
and Stephanie Van Veen

> *"The most unaesthetic sight the human eyes could*
> *contemplate was the female athlete."*
> —Pierre de Coubertin

Fairness is an intuitive concept that articulates perceptions informed by a stunning variety of considerations. It is a house with many rooms, and while not all concepts of fairness are equally demanding on those who may adopt them, or generous to those who become their beneficiaries, most people who are interested in sports agree that fairness matters a lot. So what does it take to keep sports fair? What does fairness require? What do we mean by fairness in sports? As Thomas Murray suggests in a recent study by the Hastings Center for Ethics, "It may not be easy to say exactly what fairness means, but the ease with which we can call out unfairness suggests that the task is worthwhile and far from hopeless."[1] Framing his analysis around the media's steady focus on cheating, banned substances, gene doping, technology, and sex-testing in sports, he notes that "from the steroid scandals of major league baseball to analyses of Oscar Pistorius's cheetahs to the sex-verification test of Caster Semenya, questions today about what constitutes fairness in sports are wide-ranging and varied."[2]

The first thing to note, continues Murray, is that a fair sports competition does not require that athletes be equal in every imaginable respect. Some athletes are taller, stronger, quicker, or more agile than others. Almost no one regards such differences in natural talents as unjust or unfair. But the point at which such differences cross the line from inevitable and acceptable to iniquitous and deplorable, he insists, is something that needs to be debated and settled by the people who participate in, understand, and love sports, not by distant and disinterested philosophers.[3]

---

1. Murray, "Making Sense of Fairness in Sports," 13–15.
2. Ibid.
3. Indeed, the International Olympic Committee (IOC) has been a leading voice in

Blatantly missing, however, from the "compelling realities" that Murray addresses above is a commentary on the very nature of modern sport itself and its exclusionary properties that remain among the most discussed and least understood phenomena of our time. Modern sport, writes Alan Guttmann in *From Ritual to Record*, is not play—that most human of spontaneous activities.[4] Rather, in its pure form, it has seven distinguishing characteristics: secularism, equality of opportunity to compete and in the conditions of competition, specialization of roles, rationalization, bureaucratization, and the quest for records. Guttmann's profile shows how modern sport has developed to fill a special competitive and record-driven role in industrial and postindustrial society, but he is less concerned to analyze just how closely sport has mirrored (and indeed enhanced) inequalities of opportunity in today's world (including those around gender, race, class, sexuality, disability, and age). Modern competitive sport in Western society was conceived as an imperialist phenomenon, a male preserve for those who had the means to enjoy it, and it developed with very particular conceptions around fairness, inclusion, masculinity, status, and the rules of the game. Put more plainly, says Jean-Marie Brohm in *Sport: A Prison of Measured Time*, "the watchwords of the sporting canon for the gentlemen playing amateur sport such as fair play, team spirit, all pull together, etc., were manifestations of the essence of bourgeois ideology infused into every nook and crevice of social existence under capitalism." Brohm shows how social inequalities have been reproduced in exaggerated form within sport but have been masked by the pretence of equality between competitors (that everyone starts off under the same conditions). He concludes that it is illusory to think that sport can be reformed or prettified by a purge or by removing certain abuses and deformities.[5] George Orwell held the same view half a century ago. Serious sport, he said, has nothing to do with fair play; it is bound up with hatred, jealousy, boastfulness, disregard of all rules, and sadistic pleasure in witnessing violence. In other words, it is war minus the shooting.[6]

Is educative sport, then, just a myth, and does the reality of sport

---

promoting this view and has worked assiduously over the last decades to reinforce its influence in the sporting world by insisting that fair play is an Olympic goal. In making sports ethics a formal component of Olympic ideology and education, the IOC has been able to take center stage in sport governance and assert its global influence with sport organizations, reinforcing its particular view of fairness at the same time. Grosset and Attali, "Sport Ethics." See also Butcher and Schneider, "Fair Play as Respect for the Game."

4. Guttmann, *From Ritual to Record*.
5. Brohm, *Sport*, ix, 178.
6. Orwell, "The Sporting Spirit."

constitute a blind spot for social consciousness and a dead end for the pursuit of fairness? Is it possible for women to find fairness in sport in which so many male-controlled bureaucracies impose standards and enact policies that rationalize gender segregation or allow women to be kept out of sport altogether? With these questions in mind, we look at three current examples in sport in which issues around fairness may be viewed as being in urgent need of examination, reflection, and resolution: fairness issues in sex-testing stemming from demands to articulate "who is a woman" in competitive sport; fairness issues around judging in aesthetic sports (i.e., the case of ice-skating/dancing and the new code of points in Olympic competition); and fairness issues related to equity and female inclusion in elite sporting competition (i.e., the case of female ski-jumping). Each of them deals with issues of fairness and gender justice in different but interesting ways, and it is upon this area we will focus our discussion.[7]

Issues of Fairness and Gender Justice in Elite Sport

After the requirement of competition itself, gender has always been the main structuring principle of high-performance elite sport. Sport has long been considered a fine way to turn boys into men, and there are few stronger public measures of masculinity than athletic ability.[8] When he ushered in the modern Olympic Games in 1896, Pierre de Coubertin articulated deeply held traditional views about the role of women in sport. Women were to have no part in competitive sport: "The Games were the solemn and periodic exaltation of male athleticism . . . with the applause of women as a reward."[9] More than a century later, women are still playing catch-up in elite sports, as typified by the modern Olympic Games that were nurtured by and for male athletes in sports in which males excelled and that have remained an arena where fairness and gender justice continue to be muted, despite many advances in female opportunities for sport. How fair for women can it be that the Olympics are still, to borrow a term from cultural anthropology, big men societies manipulating others with gifts. We see the typical story of women in sport as a story of continued efforts to break through the barriers that have kept women from the playing fields and constituted women's physicality as different and lesser than men's. Nor have seg-

---

7. We draw here upon Rawls's notion of justice as fairness. He suggests that justice arises from the reciprocal relations of persons engaging in common practices and that fundamental to justice is the concept of fairness that relates to right dealing between persons who are cooperating with or competing against one another, as when one speaks of fair games, fair competition, and fair bargains. Rawls, "Justice as Fairness."

8. Whitson, "Sport in the Social Construction of Masculinity," 21.

9. Coubertin, "The Women at the Olympic Games," 711–13.

regation and exclusion been the only themes; shifting gender norms have encouraged male-controlled sporting bureaucracies to impose national and international standards upon certain sports and to enact policies (in some instances on the advice of medical experts) that made gender segregation, and even prohibitions of women, seem normal and natural.[10]

Speaking about gender justice in sport, Allen Guttmann has made much of the revolutionary changes brought about in the 1970s by second-wave feminism and Title IX in the United States (and similarly in Canada) and their impact upon opening multiple doors to sport for women and girls. To be sure, once it had become a seriously contested terrain of gender relations and meanings, sport could no longer remain a "masculinist" site where "hard essentialism" could be produced unambiguously. But there has remained a stubborn tendency in the sporting world across the twentieth century and into the twenty-first to recreate and naturalize gender asymmetries by clinging to the idea of natural difference: "women are more flexible, men are stronger, women have a wider pelvis, men have more testosterone, women have more fat, women are more susceptible to knee injuries," and so on. This has contributed to an ascendant gender ideology that Michael Messner calls "soft essentialism," a belief system that negotiates the current tensions between beliefs in equal opportunity with stubbornly persistent commitments to the idea of natural difference. Indeed, Messner has clearly demonstrated through extensive fieldwork on children and sport how common narratives that deploy "soft essentialism" appropriate the liberal feminist language of "choice" in ways that continue to recreate and naturalize gender asymmetries at the nexus of workplaces, families, and the sports arena. In the past, he agrees, sport tended to construct a categorical "hard essentialism" in which boys and men were seen to be naturally suited to the aggressive competitive world of sport, while girls and women were not. Today, with girls' and women's massive influx into sport, these kinds of categorical assumptions of natural differences can no longer stand up to scrutiny. Soft essentialism frames sport as a realm in which girls are empowered to exercise individual (albeit continuing gender appropriate) choices while boys continue to be viewed as naturally wired to perform in the arena of sports. "There's no overt discrimination against women," Messner adds. "There's no bad guy in this story."[11] However, individuals' often

---

10. Adams, "From Mixed Sex Sport to Sport for Girls." Once bobsledding, for example, became an elite sport in the 1920s it was, all of a sudden, deemed too dangerous for women. Cronin, "Bobsledding," 144.

11. Messner, "Gender Ideologies, Youth Sports, and the Production of Soft Essential-

unexamined beliefs about gender function to create a skewed gender division in youth sports. And these continued divisions in youth sports reinforce an unfinished feminist revolution in families and workplaces, and of course at all levels of competitive sport.[12] Indeed, despite the dramatic surge in participation and achievements among women athletes in the years since Title IX, feminists themselves have generally not seen sport as a major theater for gender politics and cultural transformation.[13]

It is not hard to see the role of soft essentialism in the ways in which women and girls select and gain access to sports that structure women's bodies by systematizing specifically feminine myths into acceptable sports such as synchronized swimming (the woman as siren or water nymph); gymnastics, sprinting, and high jump (feline suppleness); and skating and ice-dancing (grace and visual beauty).[14] Despite changes in the gender organization of many sports in the last few decades, research and practice confirm the persistence of gender-typed sports accompanied by a litany of regulatory discourses and practices in both competitive and participatory sporting domains.

Sex-Testing and Gender Verification in Sport

The femininity of women in sport, especially in competitive, international sport, has been a concern of sport governing bodies since their inception, and sex-testing practices (in a variety of forms) have been imposed upon women athletes since at least the 1930s.[15] What began with "letters of femininity" signed by athletes' physicians later evolved into visual inspections of female athletes by a panel of doctors (the infamous "nude parades" of the 1960s) and then into laboratory-based inspections of women's genetic and biomolecular material.[16] Although the governing bodies for both international track-and-field (IAAF) and the Olympic Games (IOC) formally abandoned the policy of mandatory sex-testing prior to the 2000 Sydney Summer Olympic Games, the practice has found refuge in new regulations addressing doping and hyperandrogenism (HA).[17] The variety and increasing complexity

---

ism." Though in fact, in the neoliberal climate of the 1980s and 1990s, men effectively gained official control over all aspects of women's intercollegiate sport.

12. See Messner, *Taking the Field.*

13. Heywood, "Immanence, Transcendence and Immersive Practices."

14. Brohm, *Sport*, 181.

15. Heggie, "Testing Sex and Gender in Sports," 157–63.

16. Ritchie, "Sex Tested, Gender Verified," 80–98.

17. HA regulations place an upper limit on the amount of androgens, commonly called "male hormones" because of their androgenic (masculinizing) and anabolic (muscle-promoting) effects.

of sex-testing, as well as recent re-categorizations and re-definitions, points to the difficulty of pinning down a stable and reliable "source" of sex in female athletic bodies. As sex-testing in sports has demonstrated, physical inspections of female bodies could seem to contradict the subsequent chromosome screens. Conclusions about sex presumed by genetic information could be complicated by unexpected hormone levels. And the relationship between any of these measures and athletic performance is not always straightforward. Indeed, the most consistent lesson to be learned from the history of sex-testing in sport may be that searching for the biological conditions that indicate a level playing field for women is like searching for an oasis in the desert—just when it seems within reach, it is revealed as an illusion.

This does not mean that the will to separate men from women in sport has weakened, nor does it mean that the administrative problem of defining what constitutes fairness or cheating has diminished. The value of sexed eligibility rules in sport is rarely questioned, and in fact, these rules have been rightly credited with providing opportunities for girls and women to enter, develop, and succeed in the male-dominated context of high-performance sport. The stated intent of sex-testing policies is to protect women's opportunities to participate in elite sport by ensuring that men, or women with "unfair" masculine physical qualities, do not introduce performance standards into women's sport that female athletes could not realistically meet. Women who perform beyond the presumed limits of female athleticism are therefore seen as threats to the integrity of women's sport, and to the right of less "masculine" women to compete to win. At the same time, measures to limit extraordinary performances by men (when achieved without the aid of performance-enhancing substances or methods) in order to protect the right of less "extraordinary" men to compete to win have never been considered, never mind enacted. Furthermore, sex-testing policies have unfairly excluded many women from competitive sport. Both the gender specificity and the unfair exclusion of women from sport are hallmarks of sex discrimination that have dogged sex-testing in its many historical guises.[18] Female athletes who have "failed" sex tests have also been subjected to serious personal harm; they have faced intense public scrutiny and ridicule, had their sporting accomplishments and records expunged, their sponsorships and scholarships removed, and their relationships and social support networks damaged.[19] While purporting to protect women, create equal opportunity, and assure dignity, integrity, and purity in women's sports, sex tests have actually

    18. Crincoli, "Eligibility," 1–6.
    19. Sullivan, "Gender Verification and Gender Policies in Elite Sport," 400–19.

victimized and disadvantaged women who have no control over their genetic, biological, or social compositions.[20]

As sport philosopher Angela Schneider has argued, underpinning all discussions of women's eligibility for sport is the notion that "sport" and "woman" are incompatible ideals, which makes exceptional acts of female athleticism (achieved without doping) a contradiction in terms.[21] Sex-testing therefore presents at least two paradoxes for the pursuit of fairness in women's sport. First, it attempts to protect women's sport by excluding certain women. And second, it relies on the idea of sex as a natural, universal, and stable binary while demonstrating, with each new method and technology, the very complexity, mutability, and fluidity of human sexuality.

The social categories of "man" and "woman" are codified in sport. Men compete against men and women against women. Yet neither category is formally defined in the rules or regulations of any sport; instead, sport relies on the "I'll know it when I see it" method of gendered eligibility. For the most part, this system works, but not because sex differences are always apparent on the surface of male and female bodies. Sports themselves are defined overwhelmingly in accordance with those physiological characteristics we call "masculine," which sets up a natural-seeming equivalence between sports performance, "masculine" physiology, and maleness itself. The characteristics of maleness are the same as the characteristics required for excellent sport performance, such as height, high muscle-to-fat ratio, and large heart and lungs. It is therefore inevitable "that any woman who is good at sport will tend to demonstrate a more 'masculine' physique than women who are not good at sport."[22] This is the famous double-bind of female athleticism: the better a woman develops as an athlete, the harder it becomes to see her as a woman. While men's sports may be open to a whole host of participants with wide-ranging variations, the woman in women's sport is narrowly defined.

One has only to look at the enormous variation in physique in both sexes to appreciate that unfairness is more often attributable to autosomal genetic variation irrespective of the sex chromosome complement. There are numerous chromosomal variations (not to mention the use of steroids, or access to high-level training, coaches, facilities, and so on that could give women advantages in high-level athletic competi-

---

20. Schultz, "Caster Semenya and the 'Question of Too,'" 228–43; Vines, "Last Olympics for the Sex Test," 39–41.
21. Schneider, "The Ideal Olympic Athlete."
22. Heggie, "Testing Sex and Gender in Sports," 158.

tions that gene-based sex-testing cannot detect).[23] Furthermore, male bodies are not similarly investigated for signs of biological advantage, though genetic variations of all kinds (including sex-linked hormonal variations) provide different men with sports-related benefits that are not considered unhealthy, immoral, or unfair. What the legacy of sex-testing in sport seems to have made clear is that far from being a stable, consistent, dichotomous biological category into which all people can be classified as *either* and *only* one type or the other, sex is actually a fluid and dynamic concept that fails at nearly every level (genetic, hormonal, social, or cultural) to conform to a predicted or desired binary. This is a particular problem in sport, which requires that men and women be clearly distinguishable and mutually exclusive, and has led sport federations to continue the search for an essential, biological clarity to blurred sex boundaries.

The search was nudged further following a particularly egregious example of sex-testing discrimination at the 2009 IAAF World Championships of athletics. New "hyperandrogenism regulations" (HA) were designed to replace the previous "policy on gender verification" in response to the controversy surrounding South African runner Caster Semenya, whose victory in the women's 800-meter event resulted in accusations that her masculine body had afforded her an unfair advantage over her apparently appropriately feminine competitors. Other racers described her as "at least half-man," and therefore athletically enhanced compared to their own presumably "natural" female physiology. As a result, she was required to undergo tests to confirm whether she is fully female. The test results were leaked to media in Australia, and the case made headlines globally. Reports suggested that Semenya possessed both male and female reproductive structures, as well as testosterone levels three times higher than those of an average woman. As the IAAF consulted with medical scientists in a range of clinical specialties to determine her eligibility to compete as a woman, Semenya's sex status became a topic of open speculation, and evaluations of her body, voice, and mannerisms were scrutinized for signs of masculinity. Terms such as *intersex, hermaphroditism, disorders of sex differentiation,* and *transsexual* circulated in media reports as possible diagnoses for the pathology deemed apparent in Semenya's appearance. In the court of public opinion, Semenya's muscular build, dominant athleticism, deep voice, and masculine facial features—all considered effects of elevated testosterone levels—rendered her inadequately female. Her biological "advantage" carried the force of biological "enhancement"—language

---

23. Schultz, "Caster Semenya," 183.

used to describe illegal doping. Though the IAAF has never confirmed these reports, the new policy governing female eligibility in athletics further blurs the line between doping and biological advantage in women athletes. Not only are the rules developed by the same committee (the medical and anti-doping committee), both are also concerned predominantly with androgenic hormones like testosterone.

The IAAF places testosterone in women, and its "masculinizing" effects, at the core of the new eligibility policy. The policy puts an upper limit on how much testosterone a female athlete can possess before she is not female enough to compete as a woman. They argue that androgenic hormones like testosterone are responsible for men's superior athletic performances, as well as the "masculine traits" and "uncommon athletic capacity" of certain women.[24] According to this logic, some women's physiology essentially mimics the effects of performance-enhancing drugs, and although the effects are not the result of external, artificial, or illegal methods or substances, the incursion into masculine territory is nonetheless considered unauthorized, unfair, and illegal. The conflation of sex-testing with discourses of doping seems to be at the heart of the problem of female eligibility in sport. Like doping, sex-testing invokes "the level playing field" to justify its policies and procedures. But unlike doping, sex-testing is designed to detect atypical sex characteristics in women, not to detect illegal substances or procedures (which constitute cheating).

While the decision concerning whether or not to cheat is generally understood by sport governing bodies as an individual moral problem that all athletes (male or female) must face for themselves, sex-testing has been constructed in a way that removes this agency from certain female competitors. Women do not have to intend to cheat to be disqualified from competition. Some women's bodies are simply defined as "unfair."

Fairness Issues Around Judging in Aesthetic Sports: The Case of Ice-Dance Competition at the Elite Level

Performance judging is an inherent part of competitive sport, and one-third of all IOC sports have a judge involved. There are obvious difficulties with ensuring fairness in judging or refereeing in elite sport, and as Graham McFee explains, these difficulties are compounded in aesthetic sports such as gymnastics, diving, or figure-skating in which

---

24. International Association of Athletics Federation (IAAF), "IAAF Regulations Governing Eligibility of Females with Hyperandrogenism to Compete in Women's Competition," 2011. See www.iaag.org/about-iaaf/documents/medical#hyperandrogenism-and-sex-reassignment (last accessed November 25, 2013).

issues of "soft essentialism," as well as high-level politics, abound. He underscores how "for aesthetic-type sports, there is necessarily a judgment of the manner in which the activity is conducted, going beyond the simple judgment of whether or not it is conducted within the rules. Rather, scoring in these sports involves determining the *quality* of the manner of conducting the activity."[25] Judging for quality thus keeps the door wide open for subjective and biased opinions,[26] which have been no stranger to the world of figure-skating and its systematic structure that has allowed vote-trading, favoritism, and corruption for years. In the past, the term *bloc judging* was used by observers to refer to the biased scores made by judges for skaters from particular national federations, including their own.[27] It was precisely the tradition of bloc judging that led to the international judging scandal at the 2002 Salt Lake City Olympics.

In Salt Lake City, Canadian pair skaters Jamie Sale and David Pelletier were at the center of the scandal vying for the gold medal against their Russian rivals, Elena Berezhnaya and Anton Sikharulidze. The Russians represented a strong tradition of dominant pair skaters from the Soviet Union, as the Soviets and Russians had taken Olympic gold in the pairs event at every Olympics between 1964 and 2002.[28] Some considered the Soviet/Russian domination one of the longest winning streaks in modern sports history (demonstrating an aesthetic style that seemed to find particular favor among the judges), and the Canadians were looking to make their mark on the world stage. On the final evening of the competition, after both teams had performed, many skating fans felt sure that the Canadians had produced a program superior to that of the Russians. Hence the skating world was shocked when the Canadians were placed second, leading to media questions about the integrity of the sport and the fairness of its judging. Following an appeal by the Canadian skating federation and uproar from the North American media, a formal investigation into the judging of the event was initiated. Within a few days, the French judge disclosed that she had been pressured by her federation to place the Russians ahead of the Canadians (regardless of how each team skated on the night of the competition). The French federation was thus implicated in a vote-trading deal that ensured a French victory in the ice-dance event if the French

25. McFee, *Sports, Rules and Values*.

26. Even though judges try to be fair, they have natural biases (patriotic, reputation, halo, memory-influenced, social comparisons, order of performance, and conformity) as well as being expected to analyze performances that some experts point out exceed human information-processing capacity.

27. Riley-Senft, *Triumph on Ice*.

28. Hines, *Figure Skating*.

judge placed the Russians ahead of the Canadians in the pairs event. The two pairs teams were eventually both awarded gold medals (a first in Olympic ice-skating history), though not before strong pressure had been brought upon the International Skating Union (ISU) by the International Olympic Committee (IOC) to do so. The ISU was instructed to address the scandal and "clean up" the sport of figure-skating or risk its future inclusion in the Olympic program.[29]

With a certain amount of resistance, the ISU undertook a formal investigation into the scandal and proposed an initiative to increase the objectivity and transparency in the judging process for all figure-skating events. A new International Judging System (IJS) was developed and implemented in 2004, eliminating the majority ruling that had existed in the old 6.0 judging system. To the traditional team of seven judges, two more were added, constituting a panel of nine judges from whom seven sets of scores would be randomly selected. The highest and lowest scores for each event would be eliminated and the remaining five scores averaged.[30] The addition of three officials on a new technical specialist panel was accompanied by extensive documentation regarding scores that could be awarded for varying levels of difficulty for each element a skater might perform. This has resulted in an increased focus on technical difficulty in an effort to objectify skaters' movements and to reduce subjective aesthetic judgments around quality. As with the old judging system, the panel of judges is still responsible for judging the quality of skaters' performances. However, they are now expected to focus on specific ratings based on five components (skills, transitions and movements, performance execution, choreography, and timing) rather than providing "impressionistic" ratings of the skaters' overall programs (compared to their competitors) as they did in the past.

The ISU remains in control of selecting judges for international competitions and for credentialing their education and training. It relies upon member federations to submit a list of eligible judges for international competition who are "competent, reliable, trusted and impartial" individuals accountable to its Official Assessment Commission (OAC). For Olympic competition, thirteen judges are selected for each skating discipline, from whom nine are selected just forty-five minutes before the event. Discussion among judges during competition is forbidden, and individual scores are revealed only to the OAC following an event.

There is also the issue that figure-skating, especially ice-dance, is

---

29. Pound, *Inside the Olympics*.
30. International Skating Union, *ISU Special Regulations and Technical Rules*.

seen more as an art and spectacle than as a sport, hence issues of class, gender, and fairness in judging take on rather more subtle nuances. Though the new judging system ostensibly improves the "fairness" of judging figure-skating by providing more transparency at the political level, the inherent subjectivities in evaluating an "aesthetic" sport remain. Ensuring fairness of judging where the whole nature of scoring depends on recognition and agreement by judges of the manner in which the actions are performed is extremely difficult. Here, despite the extensive work of the ISU in bringing about a new judging code, the element of judgment seems especially problematic since the judgment or recognition of quality in skaters' elements remains deeply influenced by individual backgrounds, experiences, preferences, and knowledge.

Moreover, since figure-skating continues to rank among the most "girlish" of sports, particular built-in subjectivities around gender still prevail. As Mary Louise Adams has pointed out, figure-skating, once an exclusively upper-class male pursuit, became dominated in the twentieth century by female skaters who were expected to display conservative ideals around femininity in their performances.[31] Figure-skating heroines of the past, such as Olympic gold-medal winner Sonja Henie and Canada's 1947 World Champion, Barbara Ann Scott, epitomized traditional feminine stereotypes by focusing more upon flexibility and gracefulness than on performing athletic feats.[32] Despite changes in the judging system and its technical requirements (including more scrutiny of the footwork than in the old system), the movement styles, postures, choreography, and music selections preferred for female skaters continue to reflect and reward "ice-princess" and "Cinderella"-type roles, including hyperfeminine characteristics such as flexibility, spinning, gracefulness, and submission to a male partner in pairs and ice-dancing. Showing how choreography can become an "apparatus of capture," dizzying twizzles and positions where the female demonstrates exceptional flexibility with her blade to her head in a "donut"-like position are awarded top points. Similarly, high scores are awarded to ice-dancing pairs in which the male dancer shows his strength by lifting his "ethereal" female partner with one hand or on one foot. "It's too bad that the 'ice princess' ideal is still so strong," says top U.S. female ice-dancer Meryl Davis.[33] Male skaters (in part fending

31. Adams, *Artistic Impressions*.

32. This is not to say that they lacked athleticism, for these female champions demonstrated considerable athletic talent for women of the time. Rather, it was the media that continued to focus on those feminine practices that fit the "ice princess"-type role.

33. Jennifer Conlin, "Oh to Bring Gold Home and Perhaps the Bacon," *New York Times*, 11 March 2012.

off presumptions of their effeminacy) criticize the new system for encouraging both aesthetic and technical accomplishments, because they wish to demonstrate "more cirque than soleil" and have the sport recognized more for technique (its quadruple jumps) than for its artistry.[34] Female skaters are still required to skate shorter programs than their male counterparts, thus limiting their opportunity to accumulate the same number of points as male skaters.

One has to question, then, the claim of sports' leaders that fair play is about respect for the rules of the game. For whom are the new rules fairer? The ISU's power over its national federations and the direction of figure-skating in general continues to prevail, as seen in the demand that ice-dancers cease theatrical and gender-bending performances and return to a ballroom style and costuming that reemphasizes traditional gender roles and fairy stories.[35] More recently the ISU's rule that insists ice-dancers use "uplifting" and popular music confirms the governing body's control over the sport for commercial purposes that include attracting more young people to a diminishing fan base.[36] Thus any discussion around the fairness of rules (especially in aesthetic sports such as figure-skating and ice-dance) is problematic without considering the complexities around individual judgments, a consensus for "reading the rules," the sport's historical structures, and the societal values around sport participation for male and female athletes alike.

Fairness Issues in Access and Female Inclusion in Elite Sporting Competition: The Case of Female Ski-Jumping at the Winter Olympics

In 2009, fifteen young female ski-jumpers took the Vancouver Organizing Committee for the 2010 Winter Olympic Games (VANOC) to court over the exclusion of a women's ski-jumping event. The plaintiffs, who came from Canada, Norway, Germany, Slovenia, and the United States, declared that "if VANOC plans, organizes, finances and stages ski jumping events for men in the 2010 Winter Olympic Games, then a failure to plan, organize, finance and stage a ski jumping event for women violates their equality rights, as guaranteed in section 15(1) of the Canadian Charter of Rights and Freedoms."[37] VANOC asserted

---

34. Adams, "From Mixed Sex Sport to Sport for Girls."

35. Kestnbaum, *Ice Figure Skating and Cultural Meaning*.

36. International Skating Union, *ISU Special Regulations and Technical Rules: Single and Pair Skating and Ice Dance*, 2010.

37. See www.wsjusa.com/storage/press-releases-pdf/7.10.09_Fenlon_decision.pdf. *Canadian Charter of Rights and Freedoms*, Part 1 of the Constitution Act, 1982, being Schedule B to the Canada Act, 1982 (U.K.), 1982, c 11.

sympathy for the plaintiffs' situation, but claimed that only the International Olympic Committee (IOC) has the right to decide which events qualify as Olympic events.[38] Justice Laurie Ann Fenton of the British Columbia Supreme Court agreed, albeit reluctantly: "In my view, the exclusion of women's ski jumping from the 2010 Games is discriminatory. Many of the men the plaintiffs have trained with and competed against as peers will be Olympians; the plaintiffs will be denied this opportunity for no reason other than their sex. But not every act of discrimination is a breach of the *Charter*. For the reasons that follow, I find that VANOC is not in breach of the *Charter*. I am, therefore, unable to grant the declaration the plaintiffs seek."[39] It was a tricky case for the challengers, less because of the discrimination issue than for the novelty of the state action problem that formally defeated their case.

Thus women did not ski-jump at the 2010 Winter Olympic Games, and American Lindsay Van, who had already set a hill record and recorded the most points for men and women on the ninety-meter hill at the 2007 Canadian ski-jumping championships at Whistler Olympic Park, had to watch as the men ski-jumpers attempted to surpass her record. Only two male jumpers did, and both of them won a medal. Despite the protests, ski-jumping and Nordic-combined (ski-jumping and cross-country skiing) remain the only disciplines in the Winter Olympics still restricted to men, as they have been since 1924. "So much for Canadian values and promises that the 2010 Winter Olympics will showcase the best of Canada," commented journalist Daphne Bramham. "We get law not justice in the exclusion of women's ski jumping."[40] When it comes to the IOC's motto, *Citius, Altius, Fortius* (Faster, Higher, Stronger), *Altius* remains the exclusive quadrennial property of men.[41]

From the perspective of fairness or gender justice, it is difficult to ignore or excuse the continuing lack of parity between men's and women's opportunities to compete in sporting competitions such as the Olympic Games and the persistence of ridiculous stereotypes about appropriate and inappropriate sporting practices for women, such as ski-jumping. Well into the twenty-first century, male officials in the International Ski Federation (FIS), National Ski Federations, and the IOC were publically re-articulating old-fashioned notions about wom-

---

38. Walter Sieber, board member of VANOC and member of IOC committee provided a 200 page affidavit for VANOC to recommend the exclusion of women's ski jumping.

39. Vertinsky, Jette, and Hoffmann, "'Skierinas' in the Olympics."

40. Daphne Bramham, "These Uppity Women Just Won't Go Away," *Vancouver Sun*, 19 November 2008.

41. Harvey Araton. "Soaring into Court, Seeking Inclusion," *New York Times*, 22 April 2009.

en's susceptibility to injuries of the reproductive system, their supposed lack of strength and courage in the face of jumping from heights, and their lack of technical skills and abilities—a parcel of deterministic views that focus on the biological mission of the female and function to poison young athletes' concept of physical self by causing them to perceive their natural processes as a continuing burden.[42] Gian-Franco Kasper, Swiss head of FIS, commented publicly, for example, that the female uterus might burst upon landing. Jumping is not right for women's bodies, he said in 2005. "It's like jumping down from, let's say, about two meters on the ground about a thousand times a year, which seems not to be appropriate for ladies from a medical point of view."[43]

The IOC's ruling that the plaintiffs lacked technical merit was particularly galling, given that this was the very organization that welcomed Eddie (the Eagle) Edwards, the affable, short-sighted, and overweight plasterer from Cheltenham whose poor level of skill in the ski-jumping event earned him a last-place finish for Great Britain at the Calgary Winter Olympics in 1988. Indeed, ski-jumping offers a particularly illuminating discourse in gender stereotypes and expectations since on the one hand women have been prevented from taking part in major international ski-jumping competitions until relatively recently, while at the same time they have long demonstrated that they can participate at equal or better levels than men.[44]

Ann Travers's observations on the ski-jumping "affair" are also pertinent. The Olympic movement's long history of collusion with social injustice and political tampering is so well documented as not to require repetition here, but, she says, why should we really care about this group of young, white, relatively affluent ski-jumping girls and women? Did the legal challenge by the "flying fifteen" accomplish anything at all? After all, the Winter Olympics in their entirety are incredibly elitist, a showcase of northern European and white North American culture in which ski-jumping tends to be available only to those wealthy enough and with access to expensive facilities. The reason to care, Travers suggests, is that it is the collective struggles of excluded groups that have historically driven processes of social transformation, pressing toward a concept of participatory parity as a measure of gender justice. "The

---

42. Of the eighteen members on the FIS executive committee, seventeen were men.

43. Gian-Franco Kasper, quoted in Vertinsky, Jette, and Hoffman, "'Skierinas' in the Olympics," 37.

44. The examples are legion. In Canada, for example, Isabel Courtier from Revelstoke, British Columbia, was the Women's Champion Ski Jumper of the World in 1922. The eleven-year-old Wurtele twins, Rhoda and Rhona, were jumping off the Côte des Neiges senior ski jump in Montreal with daring and skill in the 1930s before being stopped for such unladylike behavior. Rempel, *No Limits*.

ski jumpers challenge to the IOC ruling and to VANOC's role in doing the sexist dirty work of excluding women ski jumpers from the Games was a direct threat to the symbolic cultural power of the Olympic games as a fair and level playing field."[45] As Laurendeau and Adams point out, "the Olympics is a discourse that constructs excellence and fairness as 'within the true' with the IOC protesting that this recent decision is not about gender but about the upholding of Olympic ideals."[46] After all, the Olympic Charter claims to promote ethics and the spirit of fairness and to act against any form of discrimination affecting the Olympic Movement. More specifically, it claims to encourage and support the promotion of women in sport at all levels and in all structures with a view to implementing the principle of equality between men and women.[47]

The silences around race and class privilege in the ski-jumping case reflected a further level of unfairness, "an unthinking complicity in support of far-reaching hierarchical structures by the Plaintiffs, the Defense and the Canadian judicial system."[48] Sanctioned sex discrimination in a publicly funded exercise on the scale of the Olympics needs not to be seen as a small issue. It reinforces and perpetuates a troubling but traditional discriminatory message about women, athletics, and social citizenship. The case may have been just one small moment in the history of women in ski-jumping, but it encapsulated the larger and long-standing gender issues of sport and fairness. The women jump as well, sometimes better than the men, and the evidence is clear that their gender holds them back.

And of course, ski-jumping has always been involved in subjective judging issues in which there is a combination of quantitative appraisal (distance) and qualitative measures of performance. The weighting of style marks has given members of FIS considerable power to influence the development of ski-jumping. Even though new styles did not appeal to their traditional taste, they succumbed when they were accompanied by obvious quantitative improvements. Qualitative changes demanded constant discussions of fairness and the introduction of new regulations around athletes' body-mass index, the length of skis, the position of bindings, and the type of overalls (all issues seen as providing potential competitive advantage to the male gender), as well as countering threats to the heroic masculine image of ski-jumping.[49]

---

45. Travers, "Women's Ski Jumping, the 2010 Olympic Games, and the Deafening Silence of Sex Segregation, Whiteness and Wealth," 129, 137.

46. Laurendeau and Adams, "'Jumping Like a Girl,'" 431.

47. International Olympic Committee, *Olympic Charter*, 15. Retrieved May 6, 2012 from www.olympic.org/Documents/Reports/EN/en_report_122.pdf.

48. Travers, "Women's Ski Jumping," 137.

49. For example, with the introduction of the new V-technique in the 1980s, it be-

People don't look like bones anymore, said Trevor Morrice of Canada, despite the fact that some of the world's best male jumpers continue to struggle with borderline healthy weights and issues related to eating disorders.[50] Morrice is the son of Brent Morrice, chairman of Ski Jumping Canada and part of the Canadian team who were "dead last" in the male ski-jumping team event at the 2010 Winter Olympics.

The ski-jumping case contesting exclusion renewed questions about the dominant historical construction of female athletes as inferior and in need of protection, while also highlighting the irrational fantasies of the IOC as an agent of and for democracy and universality. It was a clear demonstration that the systems of rules by which their exclusion was legitimated were saturated in and reflective of long-standing relations of power around the gender order. At age eighteen, Canadian Zoya Lynch's career in ski-jumping had come to an end. She pointed out that one's peak is actually quite young: "In ski jumping, the younger you are the more pop you have and the lighter you are. I started jumping when I was eight and by the time I was ten I was fighting for women's rights onwards to now . . . even when I stopped ski jumping I couldn't give up the fight. I just want to say I'm devastated that my home country was not able to stick up for women's rights and equalize the Olympics for the first time in the history of the world."[51]

The IOC finally bowed to pressure in April 2011 to allow women to compete as ski-jumpers at the 2014 Winter Olympics in Sochi, Russia. One result of this decision was that Ski Jumping Canada had its budget doubled by Own the Podium (Sport Canada's funding agency to foster Olympic medal winners) primarily because of the belief that the women had a shot at a medal in Sochi. Despite the fact that top female jumpers like Lynch and Nata de Leeuw have left the sport, Brent Morrice now really needs them to sustain the sport and financial health of Ski Jumping Canada. "We're hoping that they see it in their hearts to come back," he said. "If we can get those girls back, Canada will be sitting

---

came evident that the lower the body weight the longer the jump. Since women jumpers tend to be smaller and lighter than males, and because males became anorexic trying to become lighter (and simultaneously becoming more feminine-looking), FIS (using the excuse of rescuing the health of male jumpers) minimized female advantage by making smaller athletes jump with shorter skis. Pfister, "Sportification, Power, and Control," 51–67. One may ask in such circumstances whether the IOC should have begun gender-testing men to make sure that no women competed in their ski-jumping competitions.

50. Jere Longman, "Battle of Weight Versus Gain in Ski Jumping," *New York Times*, 12 February 2010.

51. Aaron Orlando, "Freeskier Zoya Lynch Transitions from Ski Jumping Career After Bitter Equality Struggle Defeat," *Revelstoke Times Review*, 1 February 2010.

quite well on the international circuit."[52] Perhaps he does not fully understand the ambivalence of the expert female ski-jumpers who were told "no" so many times and who could find no avenue to set politics in motion in their quest for fairness, despite their stunning abilities.

Conclusion

In his *Hastings Center Report* on fairness in sport, Thomas Murray suggests that part of the answer to questions of fairness in sport is to recognize that sports are about what can be accomplished under specific limitations. "The limitations each sport chooses for itself reflect a shared understanding of what that sport is meant to display and reward. The rules of sport are arbitrary in the sense that they could be otherwise, and in practice sports modify their rules in response to changes in equipment, tactics and athletes abilities."[53] Yet even he agrees that the rules and the changes wrought in them are far from arbitrary; the new rules must pass muster with the community of those who play and love that sport, keeping alive what the community values and what is meaningful about participating and winning. In other words, power rules, and narrow conceptions of gender equality have proven insufficient to combat its manifestations.

Governments suggest that progress can come from changes in laws that can have a thinking effect and reinforce the moral imperatives of equality and fairness. Fair play can be taught, and it can be learned, goes the official Canadian government statement. "When guided appropriately, athletes begin to realize that the joy of sport is as much in the effort as in the result. Fair play is an attitude, a way of thinking. Once it's learned, it can apply to every aspect of a person's life. That's why fair play is so important and that's why all of us are responsible." [54] As a result of demands for more fairness in access to sport and its benefits (including considerable pressures for gender justice), there have been increased calls for a "fair playing field" for everyone regardless of age, sex, race, or ability. Federal/provincial/territorial sport ministers in Canada clarified their expectations for fairness in sport in the *London Declaration* (2001), agreeing to reinforce the ethical foundations of

---

52. Gary Kingston, "Go Ahead and Jump at Whistler's Olympic Park," *Vancouver Sun*, 21 March 2012. Indeed, Morrice's not-so-subtle pressure to persuade de Leeuw to leave her university studies and come back to the sport is viewed as a move to forestall Own the Podium from removing its funding from Ski Jumping Canada, in which the men are less competitive. Gary Kingston, "Top Skier Jumps Back into the Game," *Vancouver Sun*, 30 March 2012.

53. Murray, "Making Sense of Fairness in Sports," 14.

54. Fair Play Codes, Appendix C. Fair Play Canada, Gloucester, Ont, Canada, 2001. bcla.centraldesktop.com/bcla/media/Forms/Policies/Fair-Play-Codes.pdf

sport in Canada: "Governments are dedicated to providing the opportunity for all Canadians, whatever their location, their sex or gender or their level of ability or interest to experience the joy of sport and to share in its bounty." "Sport requires honesty and fair play," the ministers continued. "Lasting and meaningful athletic performance can only be achieved through fair means."[55] In September 2003, leading sports officials and athletes in Canada held a symposium entitled "The Sport We Want," leading to demands for an organization called The True Sport Movement that now receives government support through a secretariat. Support is also provided to the Canadian Centre for Ethics in Sports, which espouses the notion of fair play as a universally understood concept that underpins all of sport.[56]

Our examples of gender justice in sport, however, show just how far from such notions of fairness elite sport stands. The sporting body is a critical site for the discourses of power, and it has become the focus of fundamental contradictions between the emancipatory and repressive tendencies of the social, cultural, and political order of contemporary capitalism. In today's sport, although athletes are encouraged to construct and use their own skillful bodies, it is clear from our examples that they do not necessarily use them in conditions of their own choosing. Though the constructions they use are overlaid with ideologies, we should remember that these ideologies are not fixed; as they are reproduced in sporting techniques and practices, so they are modified. The government of the sporting body is thus never fixed but always contains oppositional spaces. It is within these oppositional spaces that fairness may be sought.

Leslie Heywood provides an example of such a space. She posits an evolutionary model of sport that she terms *immersive*, which combines elements of both competitive and participatory sport while deemphasizing the negative effects of both. The immersive model, she suggests, accounts for more of our core motivations and the ways in which these inform sport participation. Alongside the competitive desire for transcendence is another experiential modality that focuses on temporality, meaning being in the zone or experiencing the body as connected to, rather than separate from, the world around it. A key determinant is that the activity is performed in the context of safety and cohesion in which there are no direct threats, hence affective balance and fair-

---

55. London, Ontario, August 10, 2001, Conference of the Federal-Provincial/Territorial Ministers Responsible for Sport, Fitness and Recreation. See *Canadian Heritage*, retrieved May 6, 2012 from www.pch.gc.ca/pgm/sc/pubs/london-eng.cfm.

56. CCES, www.cces.ca.

ness can prevail.[57] Immersive sport, suggests Heywood, might weaken gender as one of life's operating principles and provide for women the resources through which they can contest unfair practices and become empowered through a kind of "stealth feminism" in which they become agents of fairness in the scripting of their own embodied and potentially joyous sporting lives.[58]

It is an embodied view that seems to echo Ludwig Wittgenstein's musings that learning to balance one's body by shifting one's posture from one leg to the other contains useful lessons for thinking through difficult philosophical issues such as fairness in ways that might help us escape from our captivity—our rigid adherence to societies' normalizing scripts about the binary nature of gender and its effects. In offering this suggestion, he reminds us that if we want to better understand something that is in plain view we should examine in depth—and from multiple perspectives—the fine-grained complexities of social phenomena and refrain from imposing abstract theory on a recalcitrant reality.[59]

Bibliography

Adams, Mary Louise. "From Mixed Sex Sport to Sport for Girls: The Feminization of Figure Skating." *Sport in History* 30, no.2 (2010): 218–41.

———. *Artistic Impressions: Figure Skating, Masculinity and the Limits of Sport*. Toronto: University of Toronto Press, 2011.

Araton, Harvey. "Soaring into Court, Seeking Inclusion." *New York Times*, 22 April 2009. Retrieved May 2, 2012 from www.nytimes.com/2009/04/22/sports/othersports/22araton.html

Bramham, Daphne. "These Uppity Women Just Won't Go Away." *Vancouver Sun*, 19 November 2008.

Brohm, Jean-Marie. *Sport: A Prison of Measured Time*. Translated by Ian Fraser. London: Ink Links Ltd., 1978.

Butcher, Robert, and Angela Schneider. "Fair Play as Respect for the Game." *Journal of the Philosophy of Sport* 25, no. 1 (1998): 1–22.

Conlin, Jennifer. "Oh to Bring Gold Home and Perhaps the Bacon." *New York Times*, 11 March 2012.

Coubertin, Pierre de. "The Women at the Olympic Games." In *Pierre de*

---

57. Heywood, "Affective Infrastructures," 1–5.
58. Heywood, "Immanence, Transcendence, and Immersive Practices."
59. Wittgenstein, *Culture and Value*.

Coubertin 1863-1937—Olympism: Selected Writings, edited by Norbert Müller. Lausanne: International Olympic Committee, 2000.

Crincoli, Shawn. "Eligibility: The IAAF Hyperandrogenism Regulations and Discrimination." *World Sports Law Report* 9, no.6 (2011): 1–6.

Cronin, Mike. "Bobsledding." In *International Encyclopedia of Women's Sports*. Vol. 1. Edited by Karen Christensen, Allen Guttmann, and Gertrude Pfister. New York: Macmillan Reference USA, 2001.

Fair Play Canada, "The Fair Play Philosophy." Gloucester, Ontario, Canada,2001. Retrieved May 6, 2012 from fscs.rampinteractive.com/parklandpossemla/files/association/CODE%20OF%20CONDUCT.pdf>.

Grosset, Yoan, and Michael Attali. "Sport Ethics: A Powerful Tool for International Sport Leadership, 1963–1988." *Sporting Traditions* 28, no. 2 (2011): 33–52.

Guttmann, Allen. *From Ritual to Record: The Nature of Modern Sport*. New York: Columbia University Press, 1978.

Heggie, Vanessa. "Testing Sex and Gender in Sports: Reinventing, Reimagining and Reconstructing Histories." *Endeavour* 34, no. 4 (2010): 157–63.

Heywood, Leslie L. "Affective Infrastructures: Toward a Cultural Neuropsychology of Sport." *Frontiers in Evolutionary Neuroscience* 3, no.4 (2011): 1–5.

———. "Immanence, Transcendence, and Immersive Practices: Female Athletes in U.S. Neoliberalism." *The Scholar and Feminist Online* 4, no. 3 (2006), published by The Barnard Center for Research on Women.

Hines, James R. *Figure Skating: A History*. Urbana: University of Illinois Press, 2004.

International Olympic Committee, *Olympic Charter*. Lausanne, 2007. Retrieved May 6, 2012 from www.olympic.org/Documents/Reports/EN/en_report_122.pdf.

International Skating Union. *ISU Special Regulations and Technical Rules: Single and Pair Skating and Ice Dance*, (ISU 2010, online ISU www.isu.org.

Kestnbaum, Ellyn. *Ice Figure Skating and Cultural Meaning*. Middleton: Wesleyan University Press, 2003.

Kingston, Gary. "Go Ahead and Jump at Whistler's Olympic Park." *Vancouver Sun*, 21 March 2012.

———. "Top Skier Jumps Back into the Game." *Vancouver Sun*, 30 March 2012.

Laurendeau, Jason, and Carly Adams. "'Jumping Like a Girl': Discursive Silences, Exclusionary Practices and the Controversy over Women's Ski Jumping." *Sport in Society* 13, no. 3 (2010): 431–47.

Longman, Jere. "Battle of Weight Versus Gain in Ski Jumping." *New York Times*, 12 February 2010.

McFee, Graham. *Sports, Rules and Values*. Abingdon: Routledge, 2004.

Messner, Michael. "Gender Ideologies, Youth Sports, and the Production of Soft Essentialism." *Sociology of Sport Journal* 28, no. 2 (2011): 151–70.

———. *Taking the Field: Women, Men, and Sports*. Minneapolis: University of Minnesota Press, 2002.

Murray, Thomas H. "Making Sense of Fairness in Sports." *Hastings Centre Report* 40, no. 2 (2010): 115.

Orlando, Aaron. "Freeskier Zoya Lynch Transitions from Ski Jumping Career After Bitter Equality Struggle Defeat." *Revelstoke Times Review*, 1 February 2010.

Orwell, George. "The Sporting Spirit." *The Tribune* (London), December 1945.

Pfister, Gertrud. "Sportification, Power, and Control: Ski-Jumping as a Case Study." *Junctures* 8 (2007): 51–67.

Pound, Richard W. *Inside the Olympics: A Behind the Scenes Look at the Politics, the Scandals, and the Glory of the Game Inside the Olympics*. Etobicoke, Ont.: Wiley, 2004.

Rawls, John. "Justice as Fairness." *Journal of Philosophy* 54 (1957): 653–62.

Rempel, Byron. *No Limits: The Amazing Life Story of Rhona and Rhoda Wurtele, Canada's Olympian Skiing Pioneers*. Montréal: Twinski Publications; Les Editions Histoire Quebec, 2009.

Riley-Senft, Jean. *Triumph on Ice: The New World of Figure Skating*. Vancouver: Greystone Books, 2010.

Ritchie, Ian. "Sex Tested, Gender Verified: Controlling Female Sexuality in the Age of Containment." *Sport History Review* 34, no. 1 (2003): 80–98.

Schneider, Angela. The Ideal Olympic Athlete: Some Thoughts and Reflections on Gender Differences. Paper presented at the 8th International Symposium for Olympic Research at the International Centre for Olympic Studies, University of Western Ontario, 2006. Retrieved March 31, 2012 from www.la84foundation.org/SportsLibrary/ISOR/ISOR2006ac.pdf.

Schultz, Jaime. "Caster Semenya and the 'Question of Too': Sex Testing in Elite Women's Sport and the Issue of Advantage." *Quest* 63, no. 2 (2011): 228–43.

Sullivan, Claire. "Gender Verification and Gender Policies in Elite Sport: Eligibility and 'Fair Play.'" *Journal of Sport and Social Issues* 35, no.4 (2011): 400–19.

Travers, Ann. "Women's Ski Jumping, the 2010 Olympic Games, and the Deafening Silence of Sex Segregation, Whiteness and Wealth." *Journal of Sport and Social Issues* 35, no. 2 (2011): 126–45.

Vertinsky, Patricia, Shannon Jette, and Annette Hoffmann. "'Skierinas' in the Olympics: Gender Justice and Gender Politics at the Local, National and International Level over the Challenge of Women's Ski Jumping." *Olympika* 18 (2009): 25–56.

Vines, Gail. "Last Olympics for the Sex Test." *New Scientist* 135 (1992): 39–41.

Whitson, David. "Sport in the Social Construction of Masculinity." In *Sport, Men and the Gender Order: Critical Feminist Perspectives*. Edited by Michael Messner and Don Sabo. Champaign: Human Kinetics Books, 1990.

Wittgenstein, Ludwig. *Culture and Value*. [German-English Parallel Text]. Edited by G.H. Wright, in collaboration with H.Nyman. trans. Peter Winch. Oxford: Blackwell, 1980.

3

Bodies out of Place: Gender, Space, and Community in the Basque Sport of Pelota

Olatz González Abrisketa

In her article "Gendering Nationhood,"[1] Joanne Sharp argues that the supreme values of national construction have gender, and that it is primarily male bodies that embody them. Noting both the complicity between theories of nationalism that consider symbol repetition as the main support for the creation of national identity and Judith Butler's performative theory arguing that gender is not made through a founding act but by repeating regulated patterns of behavior,[2] Sharp reveals the gender neutrality with which Benedict Anderson faces his reflection on imagined communities: "The imagined bond between individuals and the nation in narratives of national identification is differentiated by gender. Men are incorporated into the nation metonymically. As the Unknown Soldier could potentially be any man who has laid down his life for his nation, the nation is embodied within each man and each man comes to embody the nation."[3]

This chapter aims to show how the metonymic bond between male bodies and the Basque imagined community is generated and reproduced through the game of pelota, which Humboldt called "the principal festival of the Basques."[4] I will also analyze the consequences that this identification produces with regard to the exclusion of women not only from the sport, but also from the space in which it is played: the fronton, in some cases the town's main plaza.

Research on space and gender is nothing new in Basque anthropology. In 1985, in *Mujer vasca: imagen y realidad* (The Basque Woman:

---

1. Sharp, "Gendering Nationhood."
2. On these two points, see Bennington, "Postal Politics and the Institution of the Nation"; and Butler, *Gender Trouble*.
3. Sharp, "Gendering Nationhood," 99.
4. "Es la fiesta principal de los vascongados," in Miguel de Unamuno's translation. Humboldt, *Los vascos*, 84. See Humboldt, Selected Basque Writings, 55–56.

Image and Reality), Teresa del Valle and her team examined the practices that, having been developed by women, were masculinized by
their incorporation into public life and became sources of recognition
and social status.[5] This work reveals the appropriation of knowledge in
fields as fundamental to Basque society as language and gastronomy,
and shows the traditional lack of compatibility between women and
public life in the Basque imaginary. At the same time, Begoña Aretxaga's work on radical Basque nationalist funerals reveals the different
models of male and female behavior in that context.[6] By focusing on
the analysis of the funerals of members of radical nationalist groups,
which she considers central to the forming of the idea of a separate
Basque community, Aretxaga claims that the symbolic pairing that
makes the liberation of that community possible is the *"Ama Aberria*
(motherland)—hero-martyr son" pairing: "If men must assume the activity of the fight, women have the responsibility of its perpetuation
through sons. The former are oriented outward, the latter contain the
'flame of the fight' and keep it alive."[7] The figure of the son occupies the
space of public action, while the mother waits and keeps his memory
alive in case of his disappearance, death, or exile.

Another notable contribution to studies of the prevailing masculinity in places of social protagonism in Basque society directly related
to sports is that of Carmen Díez Mintegi. This anthropologist, who examines the organization of youth soccer in the province of Gipuzkoa,
states that this sport "acts as reference and legitimization to maintain
a space . . . of specific socialization, which is linked to values related to
social success and social prominence."[8] I myself claim, in a paper dedicated to the first and only professional female pelota players, the *raquetistas*, that "the image of female pelota players occupying the central
space of Basque culture, that which belongs to the *bertsolari* [Basque
improvising oral poet, *bertsolariak* in plural], the politician, or the *plaza-gizon* [plaza-man], the space of the plaza, the fronton, is incompatible with the image that society has created of itself."[9]

The aim of this chapter, then, is to develop the question of gendered space by focusing on the chain of signifiers that constitutes the
symbolic web that denies women's bodies (those that have not become
mothers) the opportunity to embody the community and thus become
protagonists in the public space. To do this, I rely as ethnographic evi-

---

5. del Valle, *Mujer vasca*.
6. Aretxaga, *Los funerales en el nacionalismo radical vasco*.
7. Ibid., 92.
8. Díez, "Deporte, socialización y género," 161.
9. González Abrisketa, "Las raquetistas," 31.

dence on the material drawn from my own fieldwork on sport conducted between 1998 and 2002, and which I analyze in detail in my monograph *Basque Pelota: A Ritual, an Aesthetic.*[10] I also use recent field data
gathered between 2011 and 2012. Furthermore, I will rely on different
ethnographic landscapes within the Basque context,[11] and in other sociocultural environments.[12]

Contemplating Bodies: Sports

As Niko Besnier and Susan Brownell argue in regard to anthropological studies focused on sport, all sports events presuppose an audience.[13]
The size of the audience can be extremely diverse, ranging from a few
friends in a school sport to millions of viewers of the Olympics; nevertheless, "it invariably involves a strong emotional component."[14]

Because of their affective component, sports set collective values
and narratives in motion and become powerful metaphors for the societies that practice them. The *mise-en-scène* of a game is an excellent opportunity to gain access to the imaginary of those who play and watch:
the arena becomes the temple in its etymological sense of being a "place
for observation," in which that imaginary is reproduced.

The emotional bond between the space, the game, and the community is quite remarkable in the Basque Country because there, the
courts of the pelota game are in the main squares of towns and villages. Pelota is played between two individuals or pairs, and consists of
hitting a ball against the walls of a fronton or court in various modalities, either with one's bare hands or using some sort of instrument. At
a worldwide level, its most famous variant is *jai alai* (literally meaning
"lively fiesta" in Basque), which is especially popular in the U.S. state
of Florida. In this modality, players use a long-bellied basket to hit the
ball. This particular game was exported by Basques at the beginning
of the twentieth century. Within the Basque Country itself, the most
renowned modality is that of hand pelota, in which players use their
bare hands. Unlike the other modalities indigenous to specific local
Basque geographical areas, hand pelota is played all over the Basque
Country and also in the neighboring region of La Rioja, Spain. It has
come to represent many of the values associated with Basque male
identity: strength, stamina, nobility, and fair play. The court used for
the game, the fronton, is the town plaza, the space people use to orga-

---

10. González Abrisketa, *Basque Pelota.*
11. Bullen, "Gender and Identity in the Alardes of Two Basque Towns."
12. Vertinsky, Shanon, and Hofmann, "'Skierinas' in the Olympics."
13. Besnier and Brownell, "Sport, Modernity, and the Body," 443–59.
14. Cash and Damousi, quoted in Besnier and Brownell, "Sport, Modernity, and the Body," 450.

nize their main events. The community recognizes both the space and
the cultural narratives reproduced in it as its own. Located next to the
church and the city hall, the fronton is the main square, the venue for
collective events and rituals, from informal knockabouts to the most
formal games, as well as for social meals, dances, political meetings,
music concerts, fiestas, and any other expression of community. People dance, eat, and play in these public places. And there are no gender
or age distinctions, in a clear ethnographic picture of the Edith Turner's *communitas*.[15] Everyone may use the central space.

The communitarian occupation of the public space is complemented, however, with other uses, such as games and formal events.
In this new arrangement, people are located on one side of the fronton
to make room for the main figures, usually male adults. The spectators envelope a central area occupied by the players. During the competition, the bodies of the audience give shape to the arena, an arena
that, as Elias Canneti says, "is a wall of people. The spectators turn their
backs to the city."[16]

The bodies' position for watching a game implies a close relationship as they *con-template*.[17] In other words, the positioning of the audience generates the temple where the main figures perform the play.
It is the spectators' bodies that provide the place. Thus the gathered
audience becomes the physical expression of the social body and the
acceptance of the person who represents it.

Furthermore, sharing the same space for inclusive practices of celebrating the community—neighborhood meals, dances, fiestas, and
so on—with male-specific competitive activities creates an association between them; they are considered events of social belonging and
cultural identity. Thus the plaza, the community space par excellence,
is gendered through the activities emplaced by *contemplative* bodies,
which are primarily masculine. Although anyone can occupy the plaza
informally, events worthy of being *contemplated* are strictly male practices. Only men's games are considered worthy of watching, and the
majority of the spectators are also men. When the plaza takes on this
contemplative shape, when it becomes a temple, the fronton offers the
clearest metaphor for cultural protagonism: singers, politicians, *bertsolariak*, *aizkolariak* (woodchoppers), and pelota players, among others,

---

15. Turner, *Communitas*; Turner, *Dramas, Fields and Metaphors*.
16. Canetti, *Crowds and Power*, 28.
17. The verb *contemplate* is not normally used in English to mean "to watch a game."
I would like to force the verb slightly in order to establish a concept for the collective
positioning of watching an event. According to the *Oxford English Dictionary*, the word's
etymology goes back to the Latin verb *contemplari*, based on *templum* or "place for observation." See Trías, "Prólogo."

embody the hegemonic image of the protagonist.

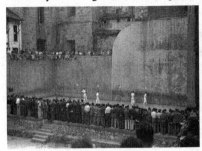 

Hand pelota match at the Trinity   *Hand pelota match at the Beotibar*
fronton, Donostia-San Sebastián, 1943. *fronton, Tolosa, 1934.*
Photograph by Pascual Martin   *Photograph by Jesús Elosegui*

In recent years, some women have become noted performers in the plaza, in the paradigmatic public space. The case of Maialen Lujanbio, the *bertsolari* or improvised poetry champion who won the *txapela*[18] in 2009, is unprecedented. No woman had achieved that kind of leadership in a cultural performance before her. Apart from this notable exception, hegemonic protagonism in the plaza is masculine.

For the last few decades, women have tried to access as protagonists the central places from which they had previously been systematically excluded. There have been great conflicts between women who wanted to take part in the main rituals of their community and those—men *and* women—who did not want to let them participate. One of the most famous conflicts is that of the Alarde, a military-style parade held in the towns of Irun and Hondarribia (Gipuzkoa) in which locals dress as soldiers to commemorate their towns' defense against invading French troops in the sixteenth and seventeenth centuries. In 1996, some women wanted to march alongside men in the most relevant fiesta of their town, but they were excluded. Viewing the implacable opposition to participation by a majority of the population, women who wanted to participate made a legal appeal, which at that time proved them right. Therefore, since 1998, women soldiers participate in parades separately, in mixed processions together with men.[19]

Sports are more complex arenas since they are based on the development of physical skills.[20] Biological and medical arguments are

---

18. The *txapela* is the black Basque beret worn by men. It is the prestigious trophy awarded to winners of various Basque competitive championships (in *bertsolaritza* or improvised oral poetry, cycling, and many other endeavors).

19. The Alarde is still a matter of disagreement in these towns. Since 1998, they have held two separate Alardes—the "mixed march," and the "traditional march" in which only male soldiers participate alongside a few carefully selected women in the traditional role of the *cantinera* or "serving girl." See Bullen, "Gender and Identity in the Alardes of Two Basque Towns."

20. See Messner and Sabo, *Sport, Men, and the Gender Order*; and Birrell and Cole, eds.,

used to maintain gender segregation and male superiority in sports.[21] As Robert W. Connell argues, "men's greatest sporting prowess has become a theme of backlash against feminism. It serves as symbolic proof of men's superiority and right to rule."[22]

Several studies have shown that maintaining the idea of male superiority as an incontestable fact of nature rests in many cases on a corporate intervention that ensures its perpetuation. The sport of ski-jumping is revealing.[23] In the Winter Olympics held in Vancouver in 2010 there was no female category because, as the president of the International Ski Federation, Gian-Franco Kasper, said ski-jumping "does not seem to be appropriate for women from a medical point of view."[24] Although this federation had made the female category official in the World Championship 2009, and at that time it was a woman who held the record in the ninety-meter jumping competition (the American Lindsey Van), women could not participate in ski-jumping in the 2010 Winter Olympics. Instead, Van had to watch from home while her record, which she had set in 2008, was broken by the Swiss skier Simon Ammann, without her being allowed to defend it.

This was not the first time that women who had reached male levels of performance had been prevented from competing in a sport. A similar case was that of Zhang Shan, the Chinese gold and Olympic record winner in the mixed category of skeet-shooting in the 1992 Barcelona Games. Zhang could not defend her title in Atlanta in 1996 because at that time not only were the sexes segregated, but the event was not even open to women. This meant that in Atlanta there were only male sport shooters, and they did not have to endure the seemingly humiliating experience of being beaten by a woman. Today, women are allowed to participate, but the categories differ in the number of shots to be fired (with fewer shots for women), which makes any comparison impossible. The rules have also changed so that Zhang's record has been obscured.

Women, Sport, and Culture.

21. Feminism has debated this issue intensely. Although feminism has been theoretically aligned with the radical critique of sport, considering sport as reinforcing the dominant values, in practice feminism has advocated maintaining sex segregation as a means of promoting the participation of women. For an analysis of this dilemma, see Theberge, "A Critique of Critiques."

22. Connell, *Masculinities*, 54.

23. See Vertinsky, Shanon, and Hofmann's "'Skierinas' in the Olympics"; chapter 2 in this volume; Laurendeau and Adams, "'Jumping Like a Girl'"; and Travers, "Women's Ski Jumping, the 2010 Olympic Games, and the Deafening Silence of Sex Segregation, Whiteness, and Wealth."

24. *Fighting Gravity*, documentary film, directed by Alex Mar (Screen Siren and Empire 8 Production in association with Title IX Productions, 2010).

The physical limitations imposed on female bodies through sex-verification tests can be added to these examples. They have been justified as a way of protecting the allegedly inferior feminine category from superior (i.e., male) intruders, but it can be interpreted as the result of prescribing what a female body should be, besides preserving male hegemony in sport.[25]

What is actually being safeguarded? What is it that, day by day, those *contemplative* bodies protect as live spectators, television viewers, and sports journalists and broadcasters?

Giving Body to the Nation

In the 1990s the link between national identity and gender became one of the most productive conceptual discoveries for political anthropology and feminism. Accompanying postcolonial arguments and on the wave of nationalism studies, feminist thinkers revealed the processes by which narratives on the construction of national identity appear saturated with gender and sexual metaphors. In *Gender and Nation*, Nira Yuval-Davis highlights the crucial role that women play in the production and reproduction of national communities, despite the concealment of women in narratives on the construction of nations.[26] This concealment would be linked, among other things, to the foundation of the modern nation imaginary, which is based on the displacement of the father figure (authoritarian) in favor of the sons (fraternal). Referring to Carole Pateman, although questioning her implicit homogenization of the categories, Yuval-Davis recalls that in the modern liberal state "the system is transformed from patriarchy into fraternity," in which "men have the right to *rule over their women in the* private domestic sphere, but agree on a contract of a social order of equality among themselves within the public, political sphere."[27] This change ideologically supported the passage from the old regime to modernity but did not substantially change gender implications in the construction of nations. Thus, it maintained the agonic dimension as central to the genesis of the community. In this context, we must remember that the *polis*, from which the narrow idea of the public dimension of the political proceeds, is mythically and ritually based on two schemes: the sacrifice of the father,[28] or the struggle between brothers.[29] These

---

25. See Cole, "Resisting the Canon"; Schneider, "On the Definition of 'Woman' in the Sport Context"; and Sullivan, "Gender Verification and Gender Policies in Elite Sport."
26. Yuval-Davis, *Gender and Nation*, 7.
27. Ibid.
28. Freud, *Totem and Taboo*.
29. Girard, *Violence and the Sacred*.

schemes converge in the Western imaginary and are based on terms like *tragos-tragedy*,[30] *duel*,[31] *agon-agora*,[32] and *poleo-polis*.[33] The narratives of national foundation are inseparable from war, and it is in this context that concealing the image of women has been more persistent. The attempts of Yuval-Davis to retrieve images of female soldiers[34] resonates with what Aretxaga finds on gender and Basque radical nationalism: namely, that "to think about female prisoners or refugees requires a conscious effort."[35]

Sharp also highlights the absence of gender in Anderson's outline when she states that there is no more arresting emblem of the modern culture of nationalism than the cenotaphs and tombs of the Unknown Soldier.[36] For Anderson, it is the anonymity of the soldier that holds the myth of the nation and its deep religious roots—anyone can be a member of the fraternity of the imagined community. Sharp points out, however, that "we can all be fairly sure that the soldier is not called Sarah or Lucy or Jane."[37]

Aretxaga shares the astonishment at Anderson's poor vision of gender and emphasizes that, "while Anderson discusses the family metaphor extensively, surprisingly he does not dedicate even a sentence to gender."[38] Aretxaga analyzes sexual metaphors used in political rhetoric on Ireland, highlighting that a gender change was considered necessary to enable the construction of a free and independent Ireland. Irish nationalist intellectuals strove to masculinize the image of the nation, which had been feminized by British colonialism in order to dispossess its capacity for self-determination. To achieve independence, Ireland needed "warrior heroes that might serve as national role models."[39] Despite the active participation of Irish women in the struggle for national liberation, the new nation would imagine and constitute a community of men, and the redemption of the idealized body of the nation was predicated on the progressive control of women's bodies.[40]

---

30. Miralles, "Introducción," xi.
31. Unamuno, *La agonía del cristianismo*, 30–31.
32. Árnason and Murphy, eds. *Agon, Logos, Polis*.
33. Tierno Galván, *Desde el espectáculo a la trivialización*, 6. I develop the idea of the agonic configuration of the modern nation and its place in the sports imaginary in González Abrisketa, *Basque Pelota*.
34. Yuval-Davis. *Gender and Nation*, 93.
35. Aretxaga, *Los funerales*, 73.
36. Anderson, *Imagined Communities*, 9.
37. Sharp, "Gendering Nationhood," 99.
38. Aretxaga, "Does the Nation have a Sex?," 94.
39. Ibid., 98.
40. Ibid.

War narratives, a basic constituent of community foundation, create the body of the nation, which emerges in two complementary body images: that of the mother who gives bodies *to* the nation, and that of the sons who give their bodies *for* the nation. The agonic discourse becomes central to the concealment of women (not mothers) in representations of the community and causes their systematic exclusion from spaces of cultural protagonism. In order to reveal these concealment procedures, Aretxaga recommends examining "the narratives and metaphors that, to put it one way, make up the body of the nation."[41]

Sport, a quintessential sphere of agonic representation in peacetime, offers a wide range of these narratives. It endlessly repeats the imaginary in which the body of the nation can be abstracted only through a male body, a body that is able to attract other bodies and thus embody the community.

Contemplated Bodies: The Protagonists

Proto-agonist is the first *agonist*, the perfect *agonist*, someone who is considered to be gifted at fight, at *agôn*, someone who was born to fight.[42] In Basque pelota, the basic qualities or powers needed to confront and dominate one's opponent are strength and cunning, powers that are hard to find in equal proportions in any single pelota player (*pelotari*). Therefore, every *pelotari* is defined primarily as being either strong or cunning. This difference also marks the position they occupy on the pelota court or in the field—defender or attacker.

Despite the fact that the *pelotari* establishes his ultimate renown at singles, the game *par excellence* in pelota is doubles. Most encounters are doubles games. It is in doubles that the *pelotari* learns and understands his place on the court. Place conditions his character as a pelota player and the way he confronts his opponent in singles. In doubles, each player occupies a determined position on the court, a position that defines the action he needs to execute, and that officially divides players into front-court players and back-court players.

The back-court player occupies the rear squares or areas of the fronton. He is the guardian of the front-court player's back. His responsibility is to take the weight of the rally. His objective is to hit the ball farther than the opposing back-court player, to make it difficult for him to reach the ball, and to impede its interception by the front-court player. The greatest attribute of the back-court player is his strength:

---

41. Ibid., 93.

42. The *Oxford English Dictionary* indicates that *protagonist* comes from Greek *prôtagônistês*, from *prôtos* (first in importance) + *agônistês* (actor). One should also highlight the root of the word *agonist*—*agôn*, which means "fight."

a force of vigor, of a spectacular energy called *indarra* (power) in pelota.[43] The principal task of the front-court player is to intercept the balls that the back-court players exchange. He must be able to finish off the point, cut off the other's intention, and hit the ball out of the opposing player's reach. For the front-court player, whose mission is to finish off the point by deceiving his rival, it is fundamental to be *cunning*. The conjunction of these two qualities is what defines the ideal pelota player—in short, to be "cunning like a fox and strong like a lion."[44] These two attributes are rarely present to an equal degree in any *pelotari*; players usually excel in one or the other. Despite the obvious fact that the combinations embodied in individuals can be innumerable, back-court players are normally *lions* and front-court players are *foxes*. However, there are exceptions like Ogueta (Jose Mari Palacios), Retegi I (Juan Ignacio Retegi), and Goñi II (Mikel Goñi) who, despite strength being their best attribute, possessed an infallible talent for fathoming the game a second before their opponent. For this reason they played in the front squares of the fronton. Such players might be considered *fox-lions* as a means of surpassing the obvious limitations of binarism.[45] I use this binary distinction in general here as something helpful to understand the imaginary of pelota, while at the same time recognizing these limitations.

I term these two ideal types in the competition proto-agonists, that is, deriving from the *agon*. Some of the most memorable pelota games have been played between a lion and a fox. Looking back in history, the greatest rivalries have occurred between two examples of these *pelotari* types. One of them frequently snatches the *txapela*, the symbol of the champion, from the other: strength beating cunning, or cunning beating strength.[46]

The archetypical pattern materialized in the pelotaris' bodies and staged on the court has a powerful effect on spectators, who feel attracted to the fronton by this dialectic conflict between opposing forces. With reference to two *pelotaris* of his youth, Miguel Unamuno puts it this way: "There are *marduristas* [fans of Mardura] and *eliceguistas* [fans of Elizegui], slaves to their blood and temperament; there are those who follow the force of cunning, of calculus and rapidity, and those who adore and believe in blatant and solid strength, open and without

---

43. For a symbolic analysis of the concept of *indarra*, see Ott, *The Circle of Mountains*, 86–89; del Valle, *Mujer vasca*; and González Abrisketa, *Basque Pelota*, 79–126.
44. Salaverría, "El Pelotari," 120.
45. I would like to acknowledge David Brent for helping me clarify this perspective.
46. Vilfredo Pareto's thesis on the alternation of power between conservative, stable persons (whom he terms "lions") and astute, innovative people ("foxes") serves as a curious parallel. See Pareto, *The Mind and Society*.

deceit."[47]

Although the agonic contest of powers is very effective in attracting an audience to the fronton, they do not occupy the same place in the imaginary of the pelota. Cunning and strength are not considered in the same way. The former is less pure than the latter. The foxes, who overcome their opponent by hiding their weapons, are always under suspicion.[48] Strength, however, is considered honest, transparent, and noble. There is nothing dirty about strength. It is straightforward.

Nowadays, TV broadcasting and its emphasis on the spectacular have led to the dominance of the front-court players' game. The foxes receive the greatest applause in the fronton, although the lions continue to embody the prototypical image of the *pelotari*. There is a large discrepancy between the imaginary of the game and what actually happens at the fronton, a discrepancy that, thanks to the moral-aesthetic message, perpetuates the double bind, and thanks to the gym, embodies it. All the current *pelotaris*, despite standing out especially in one of the two powers, are physically robust, something that was not normally the case years ago. Traditionally, a lot of champions, some of them exceptional, did not fit into the image of the strong *pelotari*. In fact, Atano III (Mariano Juaristi), the *pelotari* who has the most frontons and monuments dedicated to him, was just five feet seven inches tall and weighed 145 pounds. Men did not in general have a significantly smaller constitution back then; Atano III's two main antagonists were Azkarate (Hilario Azkarate) and Gallastegi (Miguel Gallastegi), who were both around six feet two inches tall and 220 pounds. The former lost the *txapela* or championship title to Atano III, and the latter snatched it from him.

The symbolic preeminence of strength as the required quality to be a pelota player has less to do with playing than with the type of glorified masculinity related to the sport. Most of the literature that describes the game defines it as virile, manly. Even unmistakably academic articles refer to the manliness of the sport as if it was an absolute signifier. For example, one article published in a medical sports journal describes the care of players' hands in pelota; the authors are concerned about the injuries that hand pelota players suffer because of the inefficient protection they use. What concerns them even more in their conclusions is that boys will give up playing hand pelota and take up other sports—that we will witness "the extinction of one of the most

---

47. Unamuno, "Un partido de pelota," 305.

48. Craftiness is attributed in pelota to women and the left-handed, an association also made in Hertz, *Death and the Right Hand*; Caillois, *Man, Play, and Games*; Needham, *Right and Left*; and González Abrisketa, *Basque Pelota*, 215–21.

beautiful and virile native sports in our country."[49]

Hand pelota as a reinforcement of the physical and moral countenance of men is still one of the most reiterated convictions. Hand pelota shapes the bodies and minds of Basque men; the type of male body people like to contemplate, the quintessential beautiful body is, above all, a strong body. Hand pelota used to feature different types of bodies until gym work was incorporated into the training of *pelotaris* in the late 1980s. Nevertheless, the Basque imaginary of the ideal *pelotari* has above all extolled a strong body type, as we can easily see in the discourse and iconography of the game.

The imaginary is full of strong male bodies that hit the ball openly and therefore honestly. Most of them are *lions* who strike the ball with their arm outstretched or showing their open hand (again, a sign of honesty in their play). These images are relevant since they specify the meaning of strength beyond the mere physical body. These strong bodies that strike the ball openly are not expressing strength, but instead their nobility. And that is where we must seek the patterns of women's exclusion from the spaces in which cultural protagonism is displayed— in the moral-aesthetic connection in which nobility and strength are condensed in the hegemonic male body, which itself becomes an object of contemplation.

Bodies Made Temple: The *Plaza-Gizon*

From childhood on, *pelotaris* learn to admire strength not only in people but also in the objects that they use in their game. Frontons are strong: they are stone walls. Pelotas are strong: they are hard leather balls. Through these objects, *pelotaris* learn what nobility is: they call balls noble if they are perfect for playing. A *pelota* (ball) is noble if it bounces straight and predictably, if it has a path in keeping with the stroke of the *pelotari*. A fronton is noble if it does not cause bad rebounds, if it returns the ball as expected. A person is thus noble if he acts according to the rules, if he behaves as expected, and if everybody feels comfortable with him. In the pervasive reference to the quality "noble," a major cultural message emerges: "Play honestly, the plaza is always the judge," which is engraved on the plaque in the fronton of Aldude (Aldudes), Lower Navarre, a small village in the Northern Basque Country.

This legend urges the *pelotari* to behave nobly because he will be judged by the public, a public that, whether or not people are present, is the plaza itself. The plaza consists of contemplative bodies—the community that is judging the individual's acts. To play honestly is to be-

---

49. García Pérez and Sorozábal, "Cuidado de la mano en el juego de la pelota," 399.

have properly, according to the *common sense*[50] of the community that observes and creates space for the player, bodies that turn the player into a protagonist precisely because they represent common desires. This is the message.

And only the male body, whose proto-agonic qualities can provoke the passion of those who *contemplate* it, can reach the greatest qualifier for a Basque man: to be a *plaza-gizon*, which literally means "plaza-

Pelotaris (1930) by Aurelio Arteta

man." *Plaza-gizon* is the man who excels in the activities that are the greatest sources of collective enjoyment. He ennobles events in which the "common being" is celebrated. There is probably no more precise word to describe it; the plaza-man is the man who embodies the plaza and the plaza is the material expression of the community. Therefore, the plaza-man represents the community.[51]

As Sharp rightly points out, the body that embodies the imagined community is necessarily male. This is also true in the Basque case, in which it even has a specific qualifier. There is no word in Basque for women with the same meaning as that of *plaza-gizon* for men. One could easily enough construct a similar term linguistically: *plaza-andrea* or "plaza-woman." However, this designation did not exist until a group of women from Donostia-San Sebastián established *plaza-andreok*, a feminist political party. This name perfectly expressed the demand that female bodies be present and function as protagonists in public spaces.

For a woman, nevertheless, a formidable obstacle has to be over-

---

50. Geertz, "Common Sense as a Cultural System."

51. For an extended analysis of the meaning of the *plaza-gizon*, see Zulaika, *Basque Violence*; and González Abrisketa, *Basque Pelota*.

come. In order to be a protagonist, it is necessary to have bodies around her to make her one, and those bodies have to achieve some kind of identification with her. They have to share an emotional bond in order to *contemplate* that body; this, however, does not often happen when the female body is placed in the center of the public space.

Pelotari (1970) by Agustín Ibarrola

A Displaced Body: The Case of Maite Ruiz de Larramendi

Besides the centrality of male categories in the sport, which is common to most ball games all over the world, hand pelota does not have a competition for women either at the professional or the amateur level. Women do not compete in hand pelota.

Traditionally, pelota was played in the center of towns and villages, in the square. Almost all young people were involved in this practice in their spare time. Those who stood out and wanted to be *pelotaris* exercised informally and arranged challenges until they made (or not, as the case may be) the jump to professional status by being hired by a manager. Today there is formal training in pelota, and children learn to play in "pelota schools" where they train regularly and under systematic instruction. Some girls train with them, but they can only compete until the age of thirteen. After that, there are no women *pelotaris*.

This absence is not due to poor performance. Girls do not give up pelota because they are not good at it. Usually girls who still play pelota at the age of thirteen are very good, and may even be the best in their group. They give up hand pelota because their environment forces them to do so. It is not a question of not having a future—most boys do not have a future either, because it is extremely difficult to become a professional *pelotari*. For girls, it is a question of not having a place.

It is important to make this distinction because boys and girls go through different processes when they give up pelota. Most boys who play the sport give it up and never become professional. Less than 1 percent of boys who play pelota in childhood will make a living at the game. There are some collective stages in this process, but with so many different factors involved, ultimately leaving the sport is a boy's individual choice. Moreover, this is a personal choice, considering that most parents would not persuade a boy to give up pelota, one of the most popular activities most intimately linked to Basque identity. Besides, being a *pelotari* is also a significant source of status.

In the case of girls, it is neither an individual nor a personal choice. Girls are forced to withdraw from hand pelota even if they are among the best players in their group. When a girl is around twelve or thirteen years old, social and medical arguments start working against her persistence in the activity she likes most and in which she excels. There are many examples of this process in the Basque Country, and here I focus on the case of Maite Ruiz de Larramendi simply because it made the headlines recently. This case shows how in Basque society, as elsewhere, women's bodies do not fit the image of the protagonist, or put another way, there are no bodies willing to allow them to be protagonists.

Born in 1973, Ruiz de Larramendi won the Navarrese government award for the best Navarrese sportswoman of 2011. She is a *pelotari* of the only modality of Basque pelota in which there is a women's championship: *paleta goma* or "rubber paleta." This is a nonprofessional modality that is played in several countries; it is especially popular in Argentina, but attracts little interest in the Basque Country itself. People do not go to watch *paleta goma* just as they do not go to watch the other nonprofessional modalities. That said, there are people involved in these modalities because they are part of the official pelota federations. As such, there are various championships, and most world champions in the Basque Country come from these pelota modalities.[52] Nevertheless, they receive little attention because people prefer to watch professional games. Nonprofessional pelota is neither a job nor a source of status.

Ruiz de Larramendi is an X-ray technician at the main hospital in Pamplona-Iruñea, and she competes as an amateur, despite her five

---

52. This, despite the fact that there is no officially recognized Basque Federation. The Basque Federation team does not play in the world championship, only in the World Cup. Most of the players who play in the Spanish Federation and the French Federation are Basques because it is a sport mainly played in the Basque Country and Navarre.

world champion titles and being named "Best *Pelotari* in the World Championship" in 2010, a title for which both men and women are eligible. Ruiz de Larramendi, however, does not enjoy widespread recognition beyond her small Navarrese village, Eulate, and its environs. Nobody asks her for an autograph when she walks through the streets of Bilbao, Donostia-San Sebastián, or Pamplona-Iruñea, which might have been the case had she been a professional hand pelota player as she dreamed she would be when she was a child.

Ruiz de Larramendi was an excellent hand pelota player when she was a child. If she had been a boy, people would probably have called her an up-and-coming talent. People did not call her that, of course, but she still believed she fit that description. When she was twelve years old, she beat one such emerging talent, Rubén Beloki, who nine years later would become the youngest champion in the history of hand pelota. Beloki retired in 2011 after twenty years as a professional *pelotari*. He is now the sports manager of one of the two professional hand pelota companies[53] and a talent scout searching for promising new players, young boys who will become professional in the near future.

A year after her victory against Beloki, Ruiz de Larramendi began to feel the pressure to give up pelota. She was thirteen years old. Apparently, some of her father's friends started telling him that she was too grown up to go on playing hand pelota. Her father tried to persuade her to give up, but she did not want to listen to him. It was inconceivable to her. "I loved playing hand pelota and it was what I did best," she remembers.[54] Her mother, who had always supported her, also tried to talk her out of it. Ruiz de Larramendi remembers their conversations as being completely absurd. The fact that she was a girl made no particular difference to her, and her mother tried to explain it with arguments that obscured the question even more. "You will damage your hands," she said. "But I haven't even started using protectors yet," she replied.

Hand pelota frequently causes hand injuries. Children start playing with a soft ball that is later exchanged for harder ones when they grow up. Since the 1960s, pelota players have protected their hands with foamed PVC and surgical tape known as *tacos* ("wedges"). They start learning how to use *tacos* when they are around ten years old. Their use of protection depends on how much pain they feel when playing. Ruiz de Larramendi had not yet started using *tacos* because her hands were

---

53. Professional hand pelota is managed by two private companies: Aspe and Asegarce. They have their own pelotaris, trainers, bookmakers, as well as specific contracts with frontons and TV channels. Their pelotaris compete in championships organized by the Professional Hand Pelota Companies League (LEPM).

54. Personal communication, Altsasua (Navarre), May 16, 2012.

strong enough and never gave her problems. The argument about damaging her hands seemed ridiculous to her. "It is because I'm getting boobs," she concluded. "No, no, no," replied her mother, embarrassed. Both of them knew that the only reason she could not continue playing hand pelota was precisely that. She was becoming a woman, and a woman is out of place competing in the plaza. In the end, she gave up playing pelota and took up another pastime, playing the Basque accordion with her uncle as her father had advised her to do.

Six years later, when she was nineteen, the Navarre Federation called her for a trial to play *paleta* on the Spanish team. She was excited because she wanted to play pelota again. She knew that *paleta* was not the same as hand pelota, the modality she liked most, but at least she would be able to compete again. That same year, in 1993, Beloki, her most famous rival when they were children, won the second division hand pelota singles championship, and two years later, at the age of twenty, he became the *manomanista*[55] champion, the youngest *txapeldun* (champion) in the history of the modality. Ruiz de Larramendi had dreamed of doing just that when she was a child. Now she doubts she could have been *manomanista* champion in a combined category with both men and women playing together. She cites the biological argument, the anatomical differences between men and women, but there is not total conviction in her words—after all, she remained unbeaten in the youth categories. She repeats the *common sense* argument (understood in an anthropological and non-logical way), and immediately complains that she was not even allowed to try and compete with men. Nobody from her pelota school became a professional pelota player. Her contemporaries gave up the game at different stages for different reasons, but no one did so when they were among the best, as she had to do.

Bodies Out of Place

Michael A. Messner points out an emergent hegemonic moment of "soft essentialism" whereby sexual binarism is reaffirmed by establishing "natural" differences between the sexes, along with the argument that they are not a deciding factor in the role a person, especially a woman, adopts in society.[56] By examining the discourse of adults concerning children in sport, Messner realizes that the discourse about girls in sport is much more elaborate than that about boys. Apparently, girls can decide to play any sport and their parents will encourage

---

55. Singles hand pelota championship.
56. Messner, "Gender Ideologies, Youth Sports, and the Production of Soft Essentialism."

them; they think it will be helpful for their future, helping them to face adult life as good workers and model citizens. This presentation of girls as "flexible choosers" reveals a societal change that has taken place in recent decades; however, it also reveals an underlying soft essentialism inasmuch as boys are considered constructed as "biologically driven creatures." Discourse about boys, as Messner verifies, is nonexistent; boys are seen as naturally well-disposed to sports and public life. If the female body has been naturalized, Messner tells us that it is the male body that remains nonquestionable, at least in Western societies. It is the way it is—natural and physically superior to the female body.

Messner's concept of "soft essentialism" is very useful in understanding something that anyone from a Western country who has children can corroborate. If I have a little girl, I can dress her as a boy and no one will notice. However, if I take my little boy to kindergarten dressed as a girl, he will most likely be made to change clothes that very day, I will be told not to do that again on the second day, and on the third day I would be in trouble with social services. My little boy would not be dressed—he would be dressed *up*–and to be dressed up as a girl would be seen as damaging to his honor, an honor that society as a whole feels it has to protect. This could also be the reason why, when in doubt, people refer to a non-gendered baby (one without earrings, colored ribbons, or any other gender sign) as a boy. Even if this is a mistake, it is still perceived as better to call a girl a boy than the other way around, which would be considered humiliating. In short, natural male bodies are dishonored through contact with female markers, whether clothing or other designations.[57]

Another relevant point here is the case of Caster Semenya, the South African athlete who won the eight-hundred-meter event at the 2009 World Championships and whose gender was questioned by the IAAF International Committee. Both Messner (chapter 1) and Patricia Vertinsky, Cassandra Wells, and Stephanie Van Veen (chapter 2) analyze the case in this volume. Vertinsky, Wells, and Van Veen consider sex-testing in sport an expression of the intention "to protect women's opportunities to participate in elite sport by ensuring that men, or women with 'unfair' masculine physical qualities, do not introduce performance standards into women's sport that female athletes could not realistically meet." Thus, the purpose of the testing is to protect women's sports from the threat of male superiority that supposedly jeopardizes their equal chances of winning. Vertinsky, Wells, and Van Veen review various developments concerning practices in which the

---

57. Mary Douglas's concept of pollution comes to mind here. See *Purity and Danger*.

mere possibility of women reaching male levels of performance, as in ski-jumping, are aborted by reconsidering the regulations of the sport itself. Messner argues that the Semenya case unveils latent imperialism when it comes to the interpretation of gender. Apart from considering it a clear expression of "soft essentialism," Messner points out that "the Semenya case brings into stark relief the need for an intersectional and transnational analysis of gender with that of race and nation."

References in South Africa to Semenya as "our girl" and the disappointment there over the indictment, in contrast to the Western version of the issue as an obvious forgery, suggest that there is a hegemonic vision of what a woman is and should be. The case illustrates a classic concern of feminist studies—the essentialization of a particular type of woman, stripped of other characteristics of her identity, such as race, nation, or class.

My own point of view on this issue is based on the image of *contemplative* bodies, those bodies that are positioned or placed to make someone a protagonist.

In her ethnography on Basque soccer, Mariann Vaczi reminds us that the female team of Athletic Bilbao won the Spanish championship several times in the period 2002–2012, while the men's team has not won a title since 1984. In spite of this, the women's team is not eager to play in the club's main stadium, where men also play.[58] They are afraid that fans will not come and the stadium will be empty. In other words, they are afraid they will not be able to attract enough *contemplative* bodies to turn them into protagonists.

In order to examine the significance of bodies, we have to consider the choreography in which they are involved. A body's place depends on how it is related to others. The position of a body depends on other bodies' disposition to create a place for it. If this can be metaphorical in social life, it is absolutely physical in sports and other cultural events. Cultural protagonism is granted by contemplative bodies, by particularly *disposed* bodies that create the specific place that is indispensable in order to fight, to participate. In the Basque fiesta of the Alarde (in Hondarribia, Gipuzkoa), as I mention at the beginning of this chapter, people who oppose the participation of women greet the mixed parade of men and women with black umbrellas, behind which they hide their bodies. The wall of black umbrellas substitutes for bodies, which is a symbolic way of saying to the women who march in this traditionally all-male parade: "We are not *con-templating* you, because you do not

---

58. Vaczi, "A Matter of Balls."

represent us." And in more commonplace terms they say: "We didn't come here to see *you!*"

Caster Semenya's sex-verification test was another way of protecting the sight, the *common sense* of contemplative bodies that constitute the imagined global community watching and supporting modern global sports events. Her body was not seen as fitting into the image of the female athletic body that the *contemplative* community wants to watch. A boy dressed as a girl may also constitute a damaging image. And there are not many Western eyes that can contemplate such "transgression" without opening their umbrellas to cover their gaze.

Conclusion

The sociologist Nirmal Puwar argues that there is a somatic norm behind every space: "certain types of bodies . . . are tacitly designated as being the 'natural' occupants of specific positions."[59] The bodies that do not fit into the norm, which she calls "invaders," are almost always expelled or made invisible.

As I have argued, the game of pelota shaped social life in the main squares and plazas all over the Basque Country. Such was the popularity of the game between the nineteenth and twentieth centuries among people, mostly men, that frontons were constructed in the center of towns and villages. These frontons became the central plazas. Bodies watching the game, turning their backs on the city, were replaced by stone and shaped the plaza. The stone survived longer than the bodies, and generations of Basques have conceived of pelota as their main sport, playing the game whenever they have the chance. Only a ball is necessary to play, and wherever the continuing presence of bodies turns the place into the central communal space, the exchange of hits shapes the bodies and minds of Basque men. By playing pelota, they learn their individual skills and position with regard to others. They also reproduce the moral messages implicit in the game. The game in the plaza becomes an eternal circle: the bodies make the place, the place makes the bodies. The bond may become so strong that some bodies become places, "plaza-men," representing other bodies and specifying their connection. They become symbols of the community.

In the Basque imaginary, the protagonists' bodies become the community itself, the embodiment of the idea of "us." The relationship between the Basque community and its *plaza-gizon* is similar to the relationship between God and Jesus Christ. The only female body around is the mother, who becomes a protagonist only through her son.[60]

---

59. Puwar. *Spaces Invaders*, 7.
60. Joseba Zulaika refers to this bond in *Basque Violence*.

Other than in their role as mothers, women's bodies cannot represent the cultural link that is staged in the plaza, which is primarily a fraternal bond between brothers. In global, Western hegemonic contexts, these men—executives, federation representatives, judges, and so on—concede that their sisters compete against each other for the glorification of the nation and decide under what conditions they should do it. These competitions have to avoid confusion and mixture, and may not challenge male superiority by allowing women to reach male levels of performance, or by allowing male bodies to have feminine attributes. Cases like that of Caster Semenya show the confusion that masculine women and feminine men still cause in the international plaza.

In the context of professional pelota, this danger does not exist because there is no female category that can display so "harmful" an image. However, the logic is similar: the public needs to know what it is *contemplating*. There is a great need for transparency in sports, and a female body in the plaza is considered a body out of place. Maite Ruiz de Larramendi first suspected this when, after playing an exhibition match in the fiestas of her village, the organizer of the game gave the other three players a small remuneration, but not her. All of them were the same age, but she was the only girl. Ruiz de Larramendi's body was physically there, but the organizer did not even *contemplate* the notion of her being a protagonist, and therefore deserving of a fee.

Now her niece, Olatz, is also an accomplished hand pelota player. She is nine years old and trains with the boys. Ruiz de Larramendi told me that when Olatz was five years old she spent all summer in the fronton. When the school year started, Olatz's mother offered her a lot of activities to occupy her—except pelota. Olatz did not understand why. After all, her brother, only three years older than her, played hand pelota. She did not dare mention pelota to her mother, probably suspecting some kind of inadequacy in herself; meanwhile, she rejected the other activities. In the end, her mother suggested: "You like pelota a lot. Maybe we should enroll you in pelota?" Olatz's face lit up. "Oh, Mom, I thought you would never ask," she answered. The idea of girls as "flexible choosers" still has its rigid limits, as the case of Basque pelota shows.

The definitive link between male bodies, collective places, national games, and the imagined community itself, which in the Basque context is specified in the figure of the plaza-man, is then especially significant when it comes to understanding the exclusion of women from being protagonists in sports in particular and in public spheres in general.

Bibliography

Anderson, Benedict. *Imagined Communities: Reflections on the Origin and Spread of Nationalism*. Revised edition. London and New York: Verso, 1991.

Aretxaga, Begoña. *Los funerales en el nacionalismo radical vasco*. Donostia: La Primitiva Casa Baroja, 1988.

———. "Does the Nation Have a Sex? Gender and Nation in the Political Rhetoric of Ireland." In *States of Terror: Begoña Aretxaga's Essays*. Edited by Joseba Zulaika. Reno: Center for Basque Studies, University of Nevada, Reno, 2005.

Árnason, Jóhann Páll, and Peter Murphy, eds. *Agon, Logos, Polis: The Greek Achievement and Its Aftermath*. Stuttgart: Steiner, 2001.

Bennington, Geoffrey. "Postal Politics and the Institution of the Nation." In *Nation and Narration*, edited by Homi K.Bhabha. New York: Routledge, 1990.

Besnier, Nico, and Susan Brownell. "Sport, Modernity, and the Body." *Annual Review of Anthropology* 41 (2012): 443–59.

Birrell, Susan, and Cheryl L. Cole, eds. *Women, Sport, and Culture*. Champaign, Ill.: Human Kinetics Books, 1994.

Bullen, Margaret. "Gender and Identity in the Alardes of Two Basque Towns." In *Basque Cultural Studies*, edited by William A. Douglass, Carmelo Urza, Linda White, and Joseba Zulaika. Reno: University of Nevada Press, 1999.

Butler, Judith. *Gender Trouble: Feminism and the Subversion of Identity*. New York: Routledge, 1990.

Caillois, Roger. *Man, Play, and Games*. New York: Free Press of Glencoe, 1961.

Canetti, Elias. *Crowds and Power*. Translated by Carol Stewart. New York: Viking Press, 1962.

Cole, Cheryl L. "Resisting the Canon: Feminist Cultural Studies, Sport, and Technologies of the Body." *Journal of Sport and Social Issues* 17, no. 2 (1993): 77–97.

Connell, Robert W. *Masculinities*. Berkeley: University of California Press, 2005.

del Valle, Teresa. *Mujer vasca: imagen y realidad*. Barcelona: Anthropos, 1985.

Díez, Carmen. "Deporte, socialización y género." In *Culturas en juego: Ensayos de antropología del deporte en España*, edited by F. Xavier Medina and Ricardo Sánchez. Barcelona: Icaria, 2003.

Douglas, Mary. *Purity and Danger: An Analysis of the Concepts of Pollution and Taboo*. London: Routledge, 2002.

Fighting Gravity. Documentary Film. Directed by Alex Mar. Screen Siren and Empire 8 Production in Association with Title IX Productions, 2010.

Freud, Sigmund. *Totem and Taboo: Some Points of Agreement Between the Mental Lives of Savages and Neurotics.* London: Routledge & Kegan Paul, 1960.

García Pérez, G. J., and F. J. Sorozábal. "Cuidado de la mano en el juego de la pelota." *Archivos de Medicina del Deporte* 9, no 36 (1992): 389–99.

Geertz, Clifford. "Common Sense as a Cultural System." *Antioch Review* 33, no. 1 (1975): 5–26.

Girard, René. *Violence and the Sacred.* Translated by Patrick Gregory. London: Continuum, 2005.

González Abrisketa, Olatz. "Las raquetistas: Un caso de olvido." *Ankulegi* 3, (1999): 29–34.

———. *Basque Pelota: A Ritual, an Aesthetic.* Translated by Mariann Vaczi. Foreword by Joseba Zulaika. Reno: Center for Basque Studies, University of Nevada, Reno, 2012.

Hertz, Robert. *Death and the Right Hand.* Aberdeen: Cohen & West, 1960.

Humboldt, Wilhelm von. Selected Basque Writings: The Basques and Announcement of a Publication. Translated by Andreas Corcoran. Reno: Center for Basque Studies, 2013.

———. *Los vascos.* Donostia-San Sebastián: Roger, 1998.

Laurendeau, Jason, and Carly Adams. "'Jumping like a Girl': Discursive Silences, Exclusionary Practices and the Controversy over Women's Ski Jumping." *Sport in Society* 13, no. 3 (2012): 431–47.

Messner, Michael A. "Gender Ideologies, Youth Sports, and the Production of Soft Essentialism." *Sociology of Sport Journal* 28, no. 2 (2011):151–70.

Messner, Michael, and Donald F. Sabo. *Sport, Men, and the Gender Order: Critical Feminist Perspectives.* Champaign, Ill.: Human Kinetics Books, 1990.

Miralles, Carlos. "Introducción." In *Aeschylus, Esquilo: Tragedias Completas.* Madrid: Planeta, 1993.

Needham, Rodney. *Right and Left: Essays on Dual Symbolic Classification.* Chicago: University Press of Chicago, 1973.

Ott, Sandra. *The Circle of Mountains: A Basque Shepherding Community.* New York: Oxford University Press, 1981.

Pareto, Vilfredo. *The Mind and Society.* Translated by Arthur Livingstone. New York: Harcourt, Brace, and Co., 1935.

Puwar, Nirmal. *Space Invaders: Race, Gender and Bodies Out of Place.* Oxford: Berg, 2004.

Salaverría, José María. "El pelotari." In *La gran enciclopedia vasca.* Donostia–San Sebastián: N.P., 1974.

Schneider, Angela J. "On the Definition of 'Woman' in the Sport Context." In *Philosophical Perspectives on Gender in Sport and Physical Activity*, edited by Paul Davis and Charlene Weaving. London and New York: Routledge, 2010.

Sharp, Joanne. "Gendering Nationhood." In *BodySpace: Destabilizing Geographies of Gender and Sexuality*, edited by Nancy Duncan. London and New York: Routledge, 1996.

Sullivan, Claire F. "Gender Verification and Gender Policies in Elite Sport: Eligibility and 'Fair Play'." *Journal of Sport and Social Issues* 35, no. 4 (2011): 400–19.

Theberge, Nancy. "A Critique of Critiques: Radical and Feminist Writing on Sport." *Social Forces* 60, no. 2 (1981): 341–53.

Tierno Galván, Enrique. *Desde el espectáculo a la trivialización*. Madrid: Tecnos, 1987.

Travers, Ann. "Women's Ski Jumping, the 2010 Olympic Games, and the Deafening Silence of Sex Segregation, Whiteness, and Wealth." *Journal of Sport and Social Issues* 35, no. 2 (2012): 126–45.

Trías, Eugenio. "Prólogo." In *La fundación de la ciudad: Mitos y ritos en el mundo antiguo*, edited by Pedro Azara et al. Barcelona: UPC, 2000.

Turner, Edith. *Communitas: The Anthropology of Collective Joy*. New York: Palgrave Macmillan, 2012.

Turner, Victor. *Dramas, Fields, and Metaphors: Symbolic Action in Human Society*. Ithaca: Cornell University Press, 1984.

Unamuno, Miguel. *La agonía del cristianismo*. Madrid: Alianza, 1986. English-language version: *The Agony of Christianity*. New York: F. Ungar, 1960.

———. "Un partido de pelota." *Euskal-Erria* 20 (1889): 301–11.

Vaczi, Mariann. "A Matter of Balls: Women and Soccer in the Spanish Basque Context." Forthcoming in *Soccer and Society* 15, no. 1 (January 2014).

Vertinsky, Patricia, Jette Shanon, and Annette Hofmann. "'Skierinas' in the Olympics: Gender Justice and Gender Politics at the Local, National and International Level over the Challenge of Women's Ski Jumping." *Olympika* 18 (2009): 25–56.

Yuval-Davis, Nira. *Gender and Nation*. London: Sage, 1997.

Zulaika, Joseba. *Basque Violence: Metaphor and Sacrament*. Reno: University of Nevada Press, 1988.

4

WHAT'S UP? WHAT'S GOING DOWN?
GOITIBERAK IN THE BASQUELAND

Jeremy MacClancy

In the early 1990s I convened a seminar series at the Institute of Social Anthropology, Oxford University, on sport and identity, which I then edited as a book.[1] One reason I organized these talks was my fear that sport was not being taken seriously as an object of study by the majority of my colleagues. I worried that the topic was regarded askance by most of my peers, as a form of leisure pursuits capable of giving great pleasure yet unworthy of sustained, serious academic scrutiny. My fears were realized by two incidents.

First, a Cambridge research fellow attended, to my surprise, one of the seminars, which focused on British Pakistanis and cricket. He also wrote for the sports section of *The Times*. His subsequent piece was entitled, "Much Hot Air Expended in the Oxford Cricket Test." In it, he discussed the content of the seminar in a consistently jokey manner and chose to emphasize something the speaker had not even mentioned in her talk—the supposedly deeply phallic symbolism of the game.[2]

Second, I invited a close colleague of mine, who had done extensive, distinguished fieldwork in the Karakorams of north Pakistan, to contribute a paper on polo in that area. His talk was in fact more a detailed research proposal than a finished paper. When he then applied to his university for a small grant to do the extra fieldwork to complete his study, its rector's comments on his application were, "This one has to be NO" (original in capital letters). My colleague ended up funding the trip himself. In my opinion, his chapter proved one of the best in the book.[3]

---

1. MacClancy, ed., *Sport, Identity and Ethnicity*.
2. *The Times*, December 23, 1992.
3. Parkes, "Indigenous Polo and the Politics of Regional Identity in Northern Pakistan."

These days it is difficult to imagine the executive head of a UK university being so brazenly off-hand about promising research into sport. Why? What has changed?

The key response is money, lots of it—indeed, increasing amounts of it. The first factor here has to be the sustained shift in the West from an economic model based on manufacturing to one grounded on the provision of services. In the beginning, the production of physical commodities was outsourced to countries where labor costs were significantly lower, mostly in Asia. Nowadays, the operation of some services (for example, call phone centers) has been shifted continentally as well. This economic revolution dovetails with—in fact, is underpinned by—the ever-increasing degrees of mobility, whether of humans, goods, or information. Today more people move across national boundaries than ever before in the history of humankind. They tend to move above all for the sake of jobs (labor migration) or, for the well-to-do, the promise of self-enhancement (lifestyle migration). Also, the movement of goods has massively increased in recent decades, thanks primarily to the invention of containers, which may be considered the most underrated revolution of the last century. And on top of all that, of course, is the recent rise of information technologies, particularly the Net. Difficult to imagine: the first website was only created in 1991.

The sum consequence of these changes is the contemporary form of globalization, generally regarded as the most extensive, intrusive form yet seen. Its maintained advancement goes hand in hand with the spread of neoliberal political policies, popular since the days of Reagan and Thatcher.

The effects of all these changes on sport are both patent and difficult to overestimate. Football and the Olympics can be our exemplars. Soccer is now indisputably global in dimensions that did not even exist twenty years ago. Today, leading European football teams, the wealthiest on the planet, act in effect as clearing-houses for the most talented players from anywhere in the world. The rise in the number of TV channels and the continuous improvement in televisual technology has made the selling of transmission rights to games a major new and increasingly valuable source of revenue. This went hand in hand with the realization of how much money could be made by commercially astute exploitation of teams' merchandise—shirts, scarves, etc. One result of these developments is the establishment, whether in wealthy Norway, impoverished parts of Africa, or other spots on the globe, of fan clubs for particular British teams.[4] It is not surprising that, in the UK at least, the most skill-

---

4. On Norway see Hognestad, *Norway Between Bergen and Middlesborough*.

ful footballers have become key protagonists in the rise of what is termed celebrity culture, that is, their tweets are worth following.

An indication of just how the hierarchy of these clubs thinks is given in a recent interview with David Gill, the chief executive of Manchester United, the most profitable and successful club in the UK. He stated that "we are acting more like a FTSE 100 company," citing deals with Turkish Airlines, which features players in safety videos, and with DHL, to sponsor training equipment, worth £40,000,000 over four years. "Our revenue is one-third match day, one-third commercial revenue, and one-third from TV. It is a very spread risk. Commercial revenues are very high margin and long term."[5] Similarly, in May 2012 the Business Intelligence Manager of FC Barcelona stated that the club was moving, very successfully, into social media, which they intended to exploit commercially. The aim, he said, was "to monetize the Barça brand."[6] Statements like these would have been unthinkable twenty-five years ago.

If football is the most prominent global game, the Olympics are the most-viewed global sports event, in ways unimagined by Baron Pierre de Coubertin. The Olympic Games have been made so important primarily because of sustained investment by national governments in their teams and by the open, highly competitive rivalry between countries to stage them. In 2012 the British Government agreed, without much apparent debate, to provide out of the deeply constrained national budget an extra £20,000,000 to cover the ballooning costs of the Games in London that year. As a government spokesman stated, the money would be well spent, because the publicity given to the country by the Games was worth at least four times that.

In other words, as I stated above, sports are now taken so seriously because of the cash they bring in. In the process, sports are becoming a central phenomenon in contemporary global life. This is the key logic behind the creation of so many "sports studies" courses in British universities in the last twenty-five years. Indeed, Loughborough University is regarded as so sports-oriented that it is commonly known as "Sports University UK." This would have been unthinkable in the 1980s.

It is therefore disappointing that the emergent anthropology of sports appears to concentrate on canonical sports. Football was the first game to achieve academic respectability in the UK, primarily because what was termed hooliganism was seen as a major social problem and its further understanding worthy of extended, funded study.[7]

---

5. "United's Tactics A Whole New Ball Game," *Financial Times*, 17 April 2012, 21.
6. See www.bbc.co.uk/news/business-18065300.
7. For example, Armstrong and Giulianotti, eds., *Entering the Field*; Archetti, *Masculinities*.

Similarly the Olympics quickly became a focus of academic investigation because of their political prominence and ideological weight.[8] Other forms of organized sports, whether in indigenous or economically developed societies, are also now examined by anthropologists.[9] I take the fact that in early 2012 I was invited to participate in *three* one-day interdisciplinary workshops all more or less on the same topic, the Olympics as a generator of identity, as an indicator of both the recognition of what anthropology can bring to the discussion, and of the over-attention on spasmodic, major events at the expense of other, seemingly lesser activities.

What appear to have been relatively neglected in this recent shift to research topics are street games and juvenile sports or pastimes. The reasons are plain: at first glance, street games are minor pursuits, of no apparent commercial or political importance. They are lightly organized or constituted by a minimal set of regulations. They appear fleeting; they come, they go, after a while they may come back, but little significance is granted to them by many scholars. The case is similar with juvenile activities. They are part of the fun of childhood and, for many, are to be seen as such. Except for the odd child psychologist or folklorist, how many researchers think them an appropriate object of serious contemplation? Whenever I asked Basque colleagues or acquaintances about the subject of this paper, the first reaction was usually a smile, then a few flippant comments about their own involvement in go-karts as juniors. I still cannot judge whether this response was surprise and embarrassment at me taking the topic seriously, a well-humored recollection of almost forgotten pleasures, or some mix of the two.

I have written this paper because I regard go-karts as serious play, in a variety of dimensions. And I have written most of the above, about the different broader contexts within which an anthropology of sports should be placed, because much of the rise in go-kart popularity and competitions may be viewed as direct responses and reactions to the ever more commercialized world of contemporary, organized sports.

This paper is as much about identity as it is about sport, and I need to broach anthropological approaches to it, however briefly. First, a caveat: it is so easy for anthropologists to mis-tread here, to treat "identity" as an entity, bordering on a thing, or worse, as an unproblematic category. Because it is neither. Trying to deploy "identity" as an anthropological term for the sake of cross-cultural comparison and the genera-

---

8. For example, Brownell, *Beijing's Games*.
9. For example, Yelvington, "Cricket, Colonialism, and the Culture of Caribbean Politics"; contributors to Jeremy MacClancy, ed., *Sport, Identity and Ethnicity*.

tion of broad generalizations is a dangerous, fundamentally misguided enterprise.[10] Identity should be treated as an object of analytical study, nothing else. In other words, we anthropologists study other people's conceptions of identity as ethnographic data; we don't come up with our own. In fact, in order to move away from any temptation to regard "identity" as a freestanding, or even semi-detached, entity, it seems best to focus on modes of identification. That holds the promise of making us attend to people as agents and to their strategic deployment of their notions of identity, in what contexts, for what reasons, when, to what effect.

In this sense, there is no Basque identity. Rather, there is a rainbow-like diversity of Basque identities, formulated and exploited by different people at different times for different reasons. As far as I see it, it is our job as anthropologists to follow them as they go, and try to make contextualized sense of what they are up to, what is going on, and how we could assess their activities.

A second caveat: we need to be very careful not to bang "identity" and "sport" together as though they were the academic equivalent of billiard balls. All too often, statements are made that sporting events bring people together, create *communitas*, by some laudable but unexamined mechanism. The Olympics are often given as the greatest example possible. Yet we should expect the encounter of identification and sporting activities to be much more indeterminate and unpredictable. Solidarity does not mean consensus. The Olympics are indeed the best example here, but for the wrong reasons. While many in the West used to regard the Olympics as an open, avowedly nonpolitical event that lauded the values of fair play, the Communists running Russia and its satellite states viewed the Games in politico-ideological terms, as run by capitalists and aristocrats. (Remember de Coubertin's hereditary title). Promoting participation for the sake of political jockeying, they adopted a win-at-all-costs attitude that, in their minds, justified drug abuse and the exploitation of minors. "Vast numbers of ordinary Soviet citizens believed that the Soviet sport system represented all that was bad in the regime's policies: hypocrisy and sham, paramilitary coercion, grossly and immorally distorted priorities, and the abuse of children."[11] I should add that a few years ago I met a Basque member of the Spanish Olympic squad, his way of life as a professional practitioner of a martial art wholly supported by the state. He stated that two years previous he had appeared in an international competition under

---

10. MacClancy, *Expressing Identities in the Basque Arena*, chap. 1, 1–21.

11. Brian Oliver, "Obituary: Jim Riordan," *The Guardian*, 21 February 2012, ii. See also Riordan, "The Rise and Fall of Soviet Olympic Champions," 25–44.

the banner of Spain, but with a small *ikurriña* (Basque national flag) stitched on his jacket. Because of this gesture, his place in the Olympic team, as anything more than a reserve, was placed in permanent doubt. As his overseer told him, "I am suspicious of you." Further examples would only reinforce the point; the history of the Olympics is as much one of division, exploitation, nation-state self-exultation, and the drug industry, as of humans scaling ever-higher levels of physical coordination and attainment.

In sum, we should assume the least possible, and see where the material leads us. If I have to nail my methodological colors to the mast, they would be those of a discriminating electician.

A quick qualifier: In the 1980s anthropologists calling themselves "postmodernists" turned into a theoretical and methodological principle what some anthropologists had been practicing since the murky start of the discipline over a hundred years before—reflexivity. The idea was to undercut pretensions to authority by having anthropologists confess the conditions of their fieldwork: just how much or how little they were able to learn, how they had managed to do so, and how, on reflection, it affected their own conceptions of individual and social life in their quotidian existence once back from the field.

Out of respect to those who still term themselves "postmodernist," I here expose myself in this increasingly conventional manner. I lived in the Casco Viejo of Iruñea-Pamplona for a year in the mid-1980s. Nine months later I returned to live in a village, Cirauqui (Zirauki in Basque), between Iruñea-Pamplona and Estella-Lizarra, for nearly two years. The Camino de Santiago (the pilgrim route to the shrine at Santiago de Compostela) literally passed beneath my first-floor balcony. During the fiestas of my second year in the village, a go-kart competition was staged. Multi-man contraptions rattled and clattered down its cobbled slopes, with haybale piles at the corners to save the crews from damaging themselves too much. I gave a hand placing and shifting the bales as the more dangerous points became more obvious. I found this event easily the most exciting of the nine day-long festivities. Here was something qualitatively different from pottering down the gentle slopes of suburban London, as I had done in the late 1950s, on the four-wheel go-kart made by my eldest brother.

I never saw go-kart competitions in the general area again, though I'd spot occasional photos of them in articles in the local press during my repeated visits to the Basque territories. It struck me as an interesting, in its own way passionate activity, whose study had been ignored. Hence my research. I had wanted to do some face-to-face fieldwork for this article, but, to put my work into its contemporary economic contexts, the present budgetary crisis meant I was not invited to teach in a Basque university this year. So I did not visit the area in 2012, but have had to voyage via surfing the Net or sending my words down a telephone line. Several Basque friends and colleagues, via the phone, email, Facebook, or even face-to-face, attempted to answer my queries, and I am grateful to them.

And reflexivity? None yet, other than the trivial confirmation of how impoverished was my own attempt at making a go-kart for our son five years ago in Spain. Maybe other dimensions are yet to appear.

The Basques have been going downhill for years.

Though most local accounts place indigenous go-karts within a timeless traditionality, as an integral part of an atemporal Basque folklore, it is most probable that they are in fact a by-product of industrialization. Go-karts are made above all of cast-offs, the scraps and detritus of adult activity: planks, nails, screws, nuts, wheels, and maybe bearings as well. While planks and nails were produced in pre-industrial times, screws, nuts, wheels, and bearings only became cheaply available with the establishment of the mass production of cheap metal items in the late nineteenth century. These materials came mostly from broken-down cars or the waste thrown out by the factories, docks, or mines where the fathers of would-be karters worked. It is possible that wooden cylinders tied to the main frame predated the use of metal wheels for go-karts. The only evidence I have of that comes from the north Navarran village of Lezaun, where *carritos* were made with wooden wheels. But few were constructed, and even fewer worked. "Towards the 1960s, thanks to the fact it was getting easier to find material, karts were made which worked well"—that is, with metal wheels.[12]

The general aim of this playful activity is clear: to construct as cheaply as possible a simple vehicle that achieves velocity by overcoming inertia on a downward slope. The durability of the item is less important than its function. So long as it goes, how long it lasts is secondary. The Basque term is equally unpretentious and to the point: *goitibera*, from *goiti* (above) and *bera* (down). In other words, "from above to down."

In April 2012 Joseba Etxebeste most generously conducted, for my sake, a telephone interview with María Josefa Otegi Bakaikoa, born in 1932, who was brought up in Errenteria (Rentería), Gipuzkoa (Guipúzcoa). She remembered go-karting as a child there in the 1930s. It was a summertime activity, she stated, because in winter the rain made the kart very difficult to control. The kart's seat was made of a fish-box, stuffed

---

12. Etniker Euskalherria, *Juegos infantiles en Vasconia*, 714.

with old newspapers and rags to make it more comfortable. There were
no brakes: to slow down, a karter had to take his feet off the front plank
and drag his heels against the ground. Karting was easily possible then
because there were so few cars. The only complication was having to co-
ordinate the runs, bearing in mind the passage of the local tram, about
every ten minutes, across the lower section of the slope. Karters did not
organize races or time runs. Hence there were no winners or losers; the
aim of the amusement was simply to go down the run as quickly as possible without having an accident. María Josefa Otegi emphasized that
karting was almost exclusively practiced by boys. Girls did not dare to
mount a vehicle; they were considered to be less "skillful" or "brave." She
did it because she was a tomboy (*mari-chico*).[13]

The only systematic study I have found on customary go-karts is that
done by the Basque folklore group Etniker which, overseen by the mag-
isterial Basque anthropologist José Miguel de Barandiarán (1889–1991),
carried out a survey of traditional *goitiberak*[14] in the Basque territories in
the 1980s. Deploying a functional definition, they found a mild diversity
of types. In Portugalete, Bizkaia (Vizcaya), the go-karts were made in the
form of an isosceles triangle, with the acute angle forward and truncated,
a small wheel at the front, a pair of larger ones at the back. The bearings
for the wheels needed to be tightly fixed; to secure them well, they might
be nailed in. The two axels were held in place with screws, and then fixed
with nuts. The base of the triangle, a broad plank, acted as the seat.

In Galdames, a Bizkaian town southwest of Bilbao, the front wheel
was larger than the posterior ones, and a transverse plank was nailed
over the truncated edge; its ends acted as footrests. In Artziniega, Araba (Álava), a hole was made in this frontal plank, then filled by a screw
that acted as an axis for the front bearing. This way the go-karter could
try to steer by using his feet on the plank. Some *goitiberak* in the town
were made with four wheels (two by two), rather than three. In the
Ribera Alta region of Araba, a stick was attached to the front bearing,
sufficiently long so that it could be moved from right to left by the feet
and thus act as a form of steering. In the Navarran village of Artajona
(Artaxoa in Basque), only a few kilometers east of Cirauqui, go-karts
might have a central stick attached to a gyratory axis, which served to
steer the kart. According to the Etniker folklorist who studied the locality, village lads either sat or kneeled on their karts as they sped down
riverside paths. In Lekunberri, Navarra, *goitiberak* were made with just

---

13. I am deeply grateful to Joseba Extebeste for conducting this unprompted interview, held April 24, 2012, which he translated for me from Basque to Castilian.

14.In Basque, the plural marker is -k, which has been preserved when desribing the
goitibera in plural in the chapter title and throughout.

one plank and four wheels.[15]

These differences might appear trivial to most, but they serve to underline the range of construction within the basic template of a triangular form supported by wheels. They also serve to belie those modern-day commentators who transmit an essentialist vision of *goitiberak* as of one type only.[16] Folklorists are often criticized by academic anthropologists as unthinking obsessives accumulating data in an outdated manner without sufficient regard for contemporary modes of analysis or the ultimate aims of gathering material.[17] All too often, fieldnotes gather dust in unvisited archives or are collated into rarely consulted reference books. But the force of this denigratory vision of folklorists' labor is strongly undercut in this case, thanks to the corrective that their rich material can supply to the restrictive model of *goitiberak* put out by uninformed contemporary commentators. Just because tenured anthropologists can pride themselves on their years of training, ability to keep up with the literature, depth of perspicacity, and sustained power of analysis is no reason to hastily dismiss the dogged footwork done by folklorists. It is time to celebrate their contribution, not participate in their precipitate sidelining.

The material collected by Etniker serves a further purpose, moreover, because it highlights a central problem of translation. In most areas where Euskera is still spoken or was until relatively recently, the vehicles we are studying are called *goitiberak*. But in Zerain, Gipuzkoa, karts with this name may have as few as two wheels, if used for going down slopes, and none if employed for sliding down pastured areas. In English, the latter would be classed a toboggan, not a go-kart. Similarly, in Bermeo, Bizkaia, triangular karts with three wheels were not called *goitiberak* but *karrikotxiberak*, while in the Araban town of Moreda, vehicles very similar to *goitiberak* but noticeably narrower were known by the Castilian term *patinetas* (scooters). In the Navarran locality of Lezaun, as mentioned, the karts were called by the Castilian word *carritos*. *Carricos* (*-ico* is a suffix taken by Navarrans to mark the Navarran dialect) were made in the Navarran village of San Martín de Unx with wooden boxes but without wheels, which were then hard to find. These vehicles were pushed down slopes or pulled along alleys. As wheels became more available, locals made *carricoches*: triangular, three-wheeled vehicles with a frontal axis to support the feet and tied to a rope used for steering. These were virtually identical in all but name to the *goitiberak* made by their co-evals to the north.

---

15. Etniker Euskalherria, *Juegos infantiles en Vasconia*, 712–14.
16. For example, www.goitibera.com/.
17. Chapman, *The Gaelic Vision in Scottish Culture*; Azcona, *Etnia y nacionalismo vasco*.

The obvious question raised by this material is, what to include in this article? How should I circumscribe the object and the activities I am trying to discuss? For the immediate riposte to my title, given my listing of this data, is that by restricting the subject of study to what locals termed *goitiberak*, I am prescriptively and arbitrarily excluding closely related phenomena from geographically contiguous areas where Euskera was once spoken as an everyday language but has not been practiced within living memory. At this point, I just wish to highlight this conundrum, to make it clear that I am aware of its compounding difficulties, and wish that it will be borne in mind throughout the following section, only to be commented on again in the concluding paragraphs.

By the early 1970s—*los años del hambre* ("years of hunger") long past and the rise of an affluent society now firmly grounded—more and more people were mobilizing politically. Franco might have beaten many of his opponents down in the past, but he could not beat death. Now an old man with a weakening grip on his sclerotic regime, he was failing more and more to control popular protest. In overreaction to mass demonstrations, his paramilitary and armed police forces strove aggressively to retain control of public space. *La calle*, as it was termed, became contested ground, with the more active on both sides energetically seeking to assert their domination of the urban layout. This competition continued into the Transition. In 1976, a year after Franco's death, increasing numbers of people complained about the brutal police repression of demonstrators exercising their democratic rights. The infamous response of Manuel Fraga, then Minister of the Interior (*Ministro de Gobernación*), was to proclaim *"¡La calle es mía!"* ("The streets are mine!") In other words, in his opinion, the streets did not belong to "the people" but to the state.

It is in this context of agitation and disputed territory that we can place the otherwise surprising reinvention of *goitiberak* in the mid-1970s. These modern versions were not crude affairs of wood and rusty screws powered by bored village boys, but properly soldered metal constructions driven by young men, often accompanied by several teammates, who openly competed for prize money in organized races staged by town halls throughout the Basque Country. According to the Basque anthropologist Kepa Fernández de Larrinoa, who go-karted as a child in a Bizkaian village (now part of peripheral Bilbao), these competitions should be viewed as an indirect, supposedly apolitical way of people asserting control of *la calle*.[18] By adapting

---

18. Kepa Fernández de Larrinoa, personal communication.

a formerly unquestioned rural pastime of juveniles, the organizers, participants, and spectators could exploit the ambience of childish innocence surrounding traditional go-karts for very modern-day ends. What policeman, heavily armed or not, could object to what appeared as a novel take on child's play? As far as I am aware, none did. None of these kart races led to mass confrontation with the forces of the state.

This unexpected popularity of go-kart races was built upon by budding *aficionados* who soon began to organize their leisure pursuit into a communal regulatory body. From the beginning, in 1974 and 1975, minimal norms were laid down, dictating the permissible size of the wheels (at that time, only metal wheels were allowed) and the maximum dimensions and weight of the karts. The next year the karters came together in Araba to celebrate the first Championship of Goitiberak of Euskadi, an event staged annually from then on. After several years, in 1992, committed go-karters collectively decided on a list of different race-tracks where races were held that allowed racers to qualify for the Championship. Three years after that, they approved the use of tires, regulating the allowable diameter and number of wheels, the size of a kart, and the number of members within each karting team. By this time, Navarran karters had instituted their own Open Championship, though participation in this or its homologous contest in the Basque Country was not limited to indigenes. By 2001 there were an estimated eight hundred practitioners of go-karting in the Basque Autonomous Community (*Communidad Autónoma Vasca*), and their spokesmen thought their practice sufficiently well-grounded for them to petition the Basque Government for go-karting to be recognized officially as a sport, with all the possibilities for subvention and other forms of support that this would entail. Their Navarran homologue made similar complaints eight years later.[19]

The general form of a karting race has come to take on the following characteristics. It is held in an urban setting, a small town, suburb, or city center with steep slopes, as an integral part of the area's annual patronal fiestas, with the agreement and assistance of the relevant municipal authorities. Each race starts with one or two trial runs by each karting team, followed by two to four timed runs by each. A final run, purely to entertain spectators, may also be held. Participants in any one race can range from 5 karts and 15 karters, to 23 goitiberak and 60 participants (as occurred in Estella-Lizarra, Navarre, October 2009), or 30 vehicles and 45 team members (in Iruñea-Pamplona, June 2009). Num-

---

19. *Noticias de Navarra*, 27 October 2009.

bers can go even beyond that. The highest participation I have found so far was 90 karts and 170 karters (in Sesma, Navarre, September 2009). Size does matter, though; in the 2009 celebration of the annual Sanfermines Txiki, the organizers of the *goitibera* race were pleased that the numbers had gone down because the smaller size of the competition made the run "more agile and thus more fun for the spectators."[20] Vehicular velocity can reach up to an estimated 130 km/h, though even 50 to 60 km/h is still a very impressive speed in the narrow Old Quarter streets of many participating towns. Mayors may boast to visiting journalists how popular their town's track is with both karters and the viewing public, because of its difficulty—particularly steep slopes and very tight turns. This is the case in Sesma, which is only a small hilltop town of less than 1,500 inhabitants.[21] The popularity of *goitiberak* has led to subdivision and diversification. Many race events are now subdivided into *goitiberak* (with separate classifications for metal-wheeled or tired karts, and for the most original or best-designed ones); scooters; skates (of different kinds); luges; skeletons; and so on.

Municipal authorities are usually very keen to provide logistical support and backing for the event, because civic support makes festivities more festive and draws in people from neighboring areas and participating teams from even further afield. If the prize money is sufficiently attractive, and the race event a constituent one for the regional Open or the Championship of Euskadi or Spain, teams may come from Asturias, Galicia, and Castile and León. To encourage those who come from afar, the town hall may dedicate space for visiting teams and spectators to pitch tents and may put up a marquee in the main square where they can cook and eat. As the mayor at one of these grander events stated, "In the marquee we have eaten and dined all of us together. The truth is that it is a lively scene, with all participating. Given that it is a national-level race, people come from different parts of the country and it is interesting to get to know them."[22] The bigger the event, the greater the chance it will pull a large crowd, which is what bar-owners and refreshment stall-holders want. The sum total is that the mayor and his/her councillors keep the populace content, both with the excitement of the day and their ability to make them proud of their locality. Little wonder that elected representatives are so ready to speak to the local press if a journalist can be persuaded to attend. It's just one more way to hang on to their posts.

The festive frame of these events is made patent in some towns

---

20. *Diario de Navarra*, 28 June 2009.

21. *Diario de Navarra*, 13 September 2009.

22. Ibid.

where the race is held on the same stretch of urban roads as the local *encierro*—for example, in Arguedas, Navarre. In the words of one journalist, "The curiosity of this trial was to be present at the passing of the karts for the habitual route of the cow-running. An ideal track for slipping down."[23] In some places the event is made not grander or homologous with traditional practices, but is elaborated in order to heighten the festive ambience. For example, in Mungia, Bizkaia, in 2011, go-karters were allowed to bring only their helmets to the event. Each team was given the materials to make its own kart and to make it as quickly as possible. The three karts completed first were given timed advantages over the rest. To increase the sense of event and excitement, teams had first to gather in one part of the town and then be led through the streets by a brass band, followed by a large number of eager spectators, to the assembly point. Since construction was so rapid that teams did not have time to "tune" their karts, some opted for humor over speed by donning outlandish costumes. "From psychedelic wigs to monkey outfits, participants park their shame at home and throw themselves, down the slope 'to an uncertain destiny', as the jokey organizers of the event put it."[24] Kart races can become so popular or so renowned that they come to be seen as emblematic of their town.[25] Those of Otxaran, Bizkaia, for instance, have been held annually since 1983 and are now lauded as "the most characteristic part of its fiestas," "a classic."[26]

The vaunted popular, indeed *democratic* essence of the sport is emphasized throughout by all concerned—karters, organizers, promoters, and the public. As one Web server put it in a 2006 blog, "And when will we have a *goitibera* team? Fuck elite sports."[27] The bumper sticker "Less football, more go-karting" is seen increasingly in the area. To put these remarks in context, it was the Basque well-to-do who made football popular, and the game is still associated with class in the Basque Country; hence, reacting against football for the sake of promoting go-karts is an openly class-based statement, and is meant to be seen as such. Much the same point was made in an old Basque song, though more indirectly:

> *Dicen que vas a subir,*
> *que vas a subir en aeroplano,*
> *subiras en aeroplano,*
> *bajaras en goitibera.*

---

23. Ibid., 21 September 2010.
24. *Deia*, 30 June 2011.
25. Ibid., 23 August 2010.
26. Ibid.
27. See www.noticiasdenavarra.com/opinion/foros/viewtopic.php?f=3&t=19838&start=0.

> They say you are going to ascend,
> That you will go up in a plane,
> You will go up in a plane,
> You will go down in a go-kart.[28]

I do not think it too fanciful to take that to mean, among other things, that one might go up in the world or have one's head in the clouds, but one will still come down to earth, go downhill at speed, on a go-kart. It is, as it were, a way to have fun yet keep your feet close to the ground.

Karters' boasts about the cheapness of the vehicles are another way of underlining the essentially open, popular nature of the activity. Though a few karters with continental aspirations might boast about their exploitation of modern developments to increase their karts' speed (e.g., aerodynamic considerations, use of disc brakes, and GPS), the great majority of practitioners still underline that their karts are always homemade. One was proud to reveal he had made his with bits from an old bed and a wheelchair: "I enjoyed myself a lot," he told a local journalist.[29] In the words of another pair, "We love (motor-car) speed trials, but we don't have money. Thus *goitiberak* are a good solution so that we can do what we most like." With the help of a friend, they would spend hours soldering pieces together. Their model for the 2010 season combined parts from a motorized scooter and a car.[30] Relevant websites are full of veteran karters giving advice to neophytes on how best to build *goitiberak*.[31] As the financial comment above suggests, some people go-kart because they can't afford anything else. Thus some karters who go on to earn sufficient moneys abandon the pastime and buy stock-cars to race in.[32] To this extent, for some, go-karting is a transitional culture framed by financial considerations.

The potential popularity of the sport is boosted by the lack of any age restriction, high or low. Some events have special sections for children; in others, teams are frequently composed of a father and his sons. Journalists like to emphasize this age-range. One sixty-six-year-old Galician participating in a Navarran race confessed that he used to participate with his children, "But they retired, so only the old guy is left. In 1964 I went to Estella to work, I made very good friends and, since then, I've a special affection for Navarre. I come to these races by invitation, and this has been my form of rendering homage to this

---

28. "Carmen O" in miniaturista-minisypx.blogspot.co.uk/2011/01/goitibera.html.
29. *Diario de Navarra*, 30 August 2008.
30. Ibid., 25 July 2010.
31. For example, www.forocoches.com/foro/showthread.php?t=1459109.
32. Thanks to Olatz González Abrisketa for this point.

land."[33]

In 2011 one Tafallan blogged that her husband had participated in its *goitiberak* race, which included slopes dubbed "heart-attack specials." He had, she wrote, "enjoyed it like a child."[34]

There is no limitation on age, nor of aspiration. Here, go-karts give underdogs the chance to bark. The 1993 film *Cool Runnings* (entitled *Elegidos para el triunfo* in its Spanish version) is a comedic version of the history of the Jamaican bobsleigh team, which trained on local go-karts then participated in the 1988 Winter Olympics. In 2010, in frank emulation of their daring, a seventeen-year-old from Basauri, Bizkaia, who had practised on *goitiberak* since the age of two, was trying to make the shift from asphalt to ice, from go-kart to skeleton (a brakeless frame on which the racer lies chest down), in order to get into the Winter Olympics. He would have been the first Spaniard to do so in that sport, let alone the first Basque.[35] In these varied senses, of homemade manufacture and with no restriction of age or aspiration, *goitiberak* fit smoothly into the common local festive context of determinedly unpretentious pastimes incorporated in mass, public, popular events where all are meant to participate as equals.

Village-size fiestas, whether held in rural settlements or town suburbs, are usually meant to be celebrations, to an important extent not just of community but of moral community, where the ethical code is one of egalitarianism. This sense of moral equality is often in tension with an ever-emergent threat of hierarchy. I well remember reading correspondence in Navarran newspapers by Iruñea-Pamplonans complaining about the publicity given by local periodicals to the self-styled *divinos*, men who ran every day, every year in the *encierro* (running of the bulls) of Sanfermines, as skillfully as possible, and were proud to be known as such. Their corresponding critics acknowledged both their talent and their bravery but damned their self-promoted importance. To them, bull-running was above all about popular participation, without discrimination (other than gender). It was very much *not* a place for a self-chosen few to make their reputations shine, year after year. A similar tension is implicit within *goitiberak* events. Even though races are constituted as competitions, with prizes awarded, and even though champions are crowned, equality is lauded over hierarchy. Winners are praised and granted their laurels, but throughout, the ludic spirit is given prominence. Karters, for instance, may dub their vehicles "Death

---

33. *Diario de Navarra*, 13 September 2009.
34. "Marinela" in miniaturista-minisypx.blogspot.co.uk/2011/01/goitibera.html.
35. *Deia*, 22 October 2010.

to Football" or "Skinny."[36] It is true that kudos go to the fastest (in fact, those with the greatest experience, commitment, and talent), but the important point is to participate, to enjoy oneself, and to either entertain or thrill others in the process. And by bothering to assemble a go-kart and throwing oneself down a slope, one is not just participating but contributing as well, indirectly acknowledging one's recognition of community and one's role in its continuing construction. Basque go-karting is for speed-merchants, not rebels.

Though karting is used to celebrate broad community, there is one limitation on which no one comments. *Goitiberak* might be traditional or modern, but either way it remains a male-only pastime. I have yet to learn of a female member of a karting team, or of a criticism of this gender bias. The solitary counter-example I know is the eighty-year-old woman quoted earlier, who saw herself as a tomboy when young. It is most probable that even today, decades after the rise of feminism in the Basque Country, the self-image of local young women still does not include physical, dangerous behavior.

The masculinist edge to karting is clear in the line that some karters like to quote: "To play at football, tennis, or basketball, one ball is necessary, but to go downhill on a goitibera, two are needed." Along with commentators, karters emphasize the thrill of speed, the emotions that a run engenders, the risks they run.[37] This is integral. Some underline the fact that in the past juvenile go-karters might have given themselves a smack on the body, but no major damage was (usually) done; as one put it, "a very useful apprenticeship for the rest of life."[38] Some extend the point by making video-clips of their activities at races, usually paced to a rock soundtrack. These productions, posted on YouTube and similar sites, act as a record for themselves and others, highlighting their manufacturing skills, their daring, and their masculinist ability to project their own image.

Karters' daring is not just boyish make-believe, to impress themselves and others, because accidents do happen. To my surprise, one newspaper described the two accidents at one race as increasing the sense of event: "The go-kart race was a real spectacle, including the transfer of the wounded by ambulance to hospital."[39] The aim of race-organizers is thus to ensure that there are no unnecessary accidents. In 1995 an accident during the race at Trapagaran, Bizkaia, led

36. *Diario de Navarra*, 28 June 2009, 21 September 2010.

37. Ibid., 21 September 2010; *Noticias de Navarra*, 10 July 2010.

38. See sinquimicanohaybiologia.blogspot.co.uk/2009/12/las-goitiberas.html.

39. See www.diariovasco.com/20090915/bajo-deba/romeria-txakoli-bajada-goitiberas-20090915.html.

to its town hall not staging another for fifteen years. In 2010 the mayor and councillors ceded to pressure from the town's Fiestas Committee to re-stage the event, but this time with fences, truck-loads of hay-bales, and two ambulances at the site.[40] The next year, in the races at Mungia, which has a particularly difficult track, the spokesman for one karting club assessed the outcome so: "Only the most skillful reached the end without harm."[41] Karters want thrills, but not at the price of plaster casts for broken limbs and self-exclusion from upcoming rac-es. It is not surprising, then, that the minutes of the annual assembly of the Basque Inertia Sports Federation (*Euskal Herria Inertzia Kirolen Federazioa*) always begin with a race-by-race assessment of track safety, listing their recommendations for the respective town-halls—usually more haybales in dangerous spots and the provision of ambulances.[42]

The development of go-karts, from wood to metal, from single driver to teams, from child's play to organized public events, enables nostalgia, a backward-looking view made all the longer by advances in *goitibera* technology. This attitude creates a space to laud and linger over memories of pre-affluent days. For example, web-savvy retirees can detail on the Net how much fun could be had in the face of adver-sity: "The worst [go-karts] were those made in a hurry; anything went, boards from boxes of fish—*a slight smell remained, so all the cats of the neighbourhood followed you back to your home. The wheels . . . the worst were of eighth hand, each of a different size.*"[43] In the words of anoth-er, "What memories."[44] The town hall of Abanto, Bizkaia, has tried to exploit this nostalgia, revive traditional go-karting, and integrate local youth and the aged by having local retired men hold a workshop in *goi-tibera* construction.[45]

Although I have argued that go-karts are for lovers of adrenaline, not kickers against the pricks, some stress the rare thrills they offer if you are prepared to make it so risky that few will follow. This is a way to turn karting into a component of counterculture, or what poses as such, or perhaps karting is here being made to act as a metaphor for a certain marginal or extreme style of life. *Al infierno en goitibera* ("To hell on a go-kart") is the name a hardcore punk band formed in Laudio (Llo-

---

40. *Deia*, 26 August 2010.

41. Ibid., 30 June 2011.

42. www.goitibeherak.org/.

43. blogs.deia.com/parecequefueayer/tag/goitibera/.

44. See also blogs.que.es/1585/2005/10/07/la-infancia-me-toco-vivir/; gentedigital.es/comunidad/allendegui/2009/02/24/la-goitibera/.

45. See www.deia.com/2010/04/28/bizkaia/margen-izquierda-encartaciones/com-plices-intergeneracionales. See also "Maribel" in miniaturista-minisypx.blogspot.co.uk/2011/01/goitibera.html.

dio, Araba) in 2002 calls itself. Another group, *Niños suicidas* ("Suicide kids"), starts one of their songs, "La goitibera mi primera arma suicida" ("The go-kart my first suicide weapon"), with the lines:

> *La goitibera mi primer arma suizida*
> *bajar las kuestas los kotxes pa arriba y sube la adrenalina*
> *Aki empezo la kuesta abajo de mi vida*
> *a pie de asfalto se krian los niños suizidas*
> *niños suizidas suizidas suena al ritmo de su vida*
>
> The go-kart my first suicide weapon
> Down the slopes the cars above and the adrenaline rises
> Here started the downward slope of my life
> With a foot on the asphalt the suicide kids bring themselves up.
> Suicide suicide kids sounds like the rhythm of their life.[46]

In stark contrast, the Basque Government tries to take advantage of the positive connotations of go-karting by naming its magazine for those who monitor youth groups *Goitibera Aldizkaria*. They want to exploit the sport's associations with fun-charged youth, not with those who wish to be seen as living on the edge.

In the 1980s, folklorists collected several terms in the Basque territories for karting, a few in Euskera, several in Castilian. Today only *goitibera* is used. In effect it has become the *batua* term for the sport, replacing all other variants. As such, it is a further reflection of the standardization of Euskera across the contemporary Basque-speaking zones of the Peninsula, and a way of incorporating races held in southern Navarre within Euskera terms.

For some participants, local karting races take on clear Basquist and even nationalist dimensions. As one website boasts, in 1995 the first Basque-French karting race was celebrated in Sara.[47] The name for the federation of the sport in the CAV is given in Euskera, and many of the conversations on its website are conducted in the same language. Furthermore, karts, T-shirts, and other associated accessories may all be in the colors of the Basque flag, or *ikurriña*. Some, emphasizing both its Basquist and Basquizing international dimensions, claim that "the goitibera is only made in the Basque Country and Uruguay, established by some Basque worker who had to emigrate."[48] Non-Basques may contest these claims. For example, one Leonese *aficionado* has pointed out that karting races are termed *goite* in his home region. He takes this to

---

46. www.facebook.com/groups/93777207975/.
47. www.euskalnet.net/goitiberagaldames/goiti.htm.
48. Ibid.

mean that they may well be related to Basque *goitiberak*, but that they may have been invented by his compatriots, not by their neighbors to the north.[49] However, as far as I am aware, the nationalist dimensions of the sport and counterclaims by others do not go any further—yet. Goitiberak's nationalist potential thus remains relatively unexploited. At present, the predominant aim seems to be promotion of the sport itself; where participants come from is secondary.

Goitibera races are greatly enjoyed by some Basques, but others remain ignorant of their sustained popularity. Despite the efforts of regional journalists, it appears that support for the sport is relatively localized. When I emailed one friend in Cirauqui (Navarre) about its incidence, her main reaction was one of surprise: she did not even know goitibera races still continued. Her impression was that they had been something out of the ordinary, economical to do, entertaining to watch, which enjoyed a certain level of success in certain years, but that fashions had moved on. The anthropological point to be made here is that just because something is not long-lasting is no reason for not studying it. For too long, social anthropologists have usually focused on enduring phenomena. If our pretensions to represent the people we study are not to be exposed as merely that, we also need to attend to more sporadic phenomena whose popularity may rise and fall, and which tend to be otherwise neglected in the literature.

Karting, in sum, is an activity exploited in different ways by different groups: by boys seeking a cheap thrill, spectators making the most of a break from the mundane, town mayors seeking to maintain their local support, and self-proclaimed marginals who choose to underline karting's potential dangers. Despite some individualist tendencies within the sport, it is primarily a vector of social integration, simultaneously celebrating individual ingenuity and bricoleurs' ability to make a laudable item out of industrial castoffs, as well as strengthening a sense of local community. Perhaps above all, participants extol, by public exhibition, socially valued masculinist traits: individual daring and the unflinching ability to face a certain degree of physical risk. An avowedly popular pursuit, karting is non-elitist, indeed stridently anti-elitist at times.

Finally, karting is a further demonstration of the performative nature of local identity. For karters, the ultimate point of their hobby is just getting on with it, downhill. As a friend in Cirauqui stated in his reply to my queries about *goitiberak*, "Nada de filosofías" ("No philosophies").

---

49. www.diariodeleon.es/noticias/contraportada/el-goite-_640892.html.

Bibliography

Archetti, Eduardo. *Masculinities: Football, Polo and Tango in Argentina.* Oxford: Berg, 1999.

Armstrong, Gary, and Richard Giulianotti, eds. *Entering the Field: New Perspectives on World Football.* Oxford: Berg, 1997.

Azcona, Jesús. *Etnia y nacionalismo vasco: Una aproximación desde la antropología.* Barcelona: Anthropos, 1984.

Brownell, Susan. *Beijing's Games: What the Olympics Mean to China.* Lanham, MD: Rowman and Littlefield, 2008.

Chapman, Malcolm. *The Gaelic Vision in Scottish Culture.* London: Croom Helm, 1978.

Etniker Euskalherria. *Juegos infantiles en Vasconia.* In *Atlas etnográfico de Vasconia.* Vol. 6. Bilbao: Etniker Euskalherria, 1993.

Hognestad, Hans. *Norway Between Bergen and Middlesborough: Football Identities in Motion.* Oslo: Norwegian University of Sport and Physical Education, 2004.

MacClancy, Jeremy, ed. *Sport, Identity and Ethnicity.* Oxford: Berg, 1996.

———. *Expressing Identities in the Basque Arena.* Oxford: James Currey, 2007.

Oliver, Brian. "Obituary: Jim Riordan," *The Guardian*, February 21, 2012.

Parkes, Peter. "Indigenous Polo and the Politics of Regional Identity in Northern Pakistan." In *Sport, Identity and Ethnicity*, edited by Jeremy MacClancy. Oxford: Berg, 1996.

Riordan, Jim. "The Rise and Fall of Soviet Olympic Champions." *Olympika: The International Journal of Olympic Studies* 11 (1993): 25–44.

Yelvington, Kevin. "Cricket, Colonialism, and the Culture of Caribbean Politics." In *The Social Roles of Sport in Caribbean Societies*, edited by Michael A. Malec. Amsterdam: Gordon and Breach, 1995.

YouTube

"Goitibeherak 2009" www.youtube.com/watch?v=N942OCtxoiI

5

GLOBALIZATION AND SPORT: A SOCIOLOGICAL ANALYSIS OF CRITICAL THEMES AND ISSUES

Richard Giulianotti

Sport has been perhaps the most significant cultural force associated with globalization since the late nineteenth century. In many ways, we might regard sport as both a motor and a metric of globalization, in the dual sense that sport both advances and allows us to measure forms of global interconnections and global change.[1] Sport boasts several global mega-events—the Olympics, the World Cup, and so on—that have worldwide TV audiences, notwithstanding the tendency of global sport-governing bodies to exaggerate the estimated figures. Moreover, sport facilitates transnational integration for different societies, as illustrated partly by the fact that the Olympic and the soccer world governing bodies—the International Olympic Committee (IOC) and the Fédération Internationale de Football Association (FIFA), respectively—each has more national members than the United Nations. And, in economic terms, one recent market research report estimated that, at the global level, professional sports generate the not-inconsiderable sum of $120 billion in annual revenues.[2]

While modern sports largely began in the eighteenth and nineteenth centuries, globalization is a rather older process. Indeed, globalization may be seen as going back to at least the fifteenth century, as marked for example through the first wave of European colonization of the Americas. Globalization is therefore a far longer phenomenon than is sometimes assumed to be the case—as, for example, with those social scientists and social movements that equate globalization with the rise of transnational, neoliberal capitalism from the 1970s onward,[3]

1. Giulianotti and Robertson, "Sport and Globalization," 107–12.
2. First Research Inc., *Professional Sports Teams and Organizations*.
3. Bourdieu, *Acts of Resistance*; Wolf, *Why Globalization Works*.

or simply with the rise of (Western) modernization.[4] Globalization is also a multidimensional process that has crucial historical, cultural, economic, political, and social aspects.

In this chapter, I propose to follow the position of Roland Robertson, who defines globalization as a concept that "refers both to the compression of the world and the intensification of consciousness of the world as a whole."[5] Thus, globalization is characterized by intensified transnational connectivity (for example, through migration and satellite communication), and greater social reflexivity about the world in general. A further point to be borne in mind here is that globalization does not simply negate or destroy "the local," as might otherwise be assumed from the way in which "the local" is typically contrasted with "the global." Rather, to move beyond this simple binary opposition, the local and the global should be interpreted as being in an interdependent or mutually implicative relationship. Moreover, globalization may actively promote or sharpen forms of particularism or localism, such as by spreading the expectation across the world that different societies will express themselves or differentiate themselves in distinctive ways.

In the following discussion, I consider three aspects of the sport-globalization interface. I begin by exploring the historical aspects of global sport, particularly the "take-off" period that drove the transnational diffusion of many sports. Second, I examine the sociocultural aspects of global sport with particular reference to the "convergence-divergence" debate. Third, I consider key political-economic issues in global sport, in particular the continuing relevance of the nation-state and national identity, and the impacts of hypercommodification and neoliberalism. In the concluding section, I consider some of the future possibilities and issues that may take center stage to shape the future of global sport. Much of what is argued here is explored at greater length in other publications, notably in collaborative work with Roland Robertson.[6] The principal focus here is largely on elite professional sports that operate mostly at the global level, and which are in the main male-dominated.

Historical Aspects of Global Sport

Turning first to consider the historical aspects of sport, we may say that the record here extends back into ancient civilizations. In ancient

---

4. Giddens, *The Consequences of Modernity*.

5. Robertson, *Globalization*, 8.

6. See the following works by Richard Giulianotti and Roland Robertson: "The Globalization of Football," "Glocalization, Globalization and Migration," "Sport and Globalization," "Forms of Glocalization," "Recovering the Social," *Globalization and Football*, and "Glocalization and Sport in Asia."

Greece, of course, there were the original Olympic Games, while in ancient China some forms of "soccer" (*cuju*) were played.[7] However, the direct modern origins of many sports are located in Britain, notably through the rise of the "games cult" that took hold in schools and universities from the mid-nineteenth century onward.[8] One illustration is provided by association football (the original term for soccer), the formal rules of which were established by the new Football Association in 1863, drawing heavily on the rules for soccer at Cambridge University that had been formulated in 1848. The establishment of the rules of different sports, and their prevalence within the educational systems, provided the institutional bases for the national and international spread and development of these sports over the long term. We should of course underline that this was an intrinsically male process from which women were largely excluded; indeed, much of the ideologies surrounding these sports then and even today is centered on the making of hegemonic masculine identities through physical culture.

According to Robertson,[9] globalization has been through five phases and is now in its sixth (or "millennial") phase. A critical period in the globalization of sport came during the third phase of globalization, known as the "take-off" phase, which ran from 1870s through to the 1920s.[10]

In broad terms, the take-off phase witnessed the intensification of globalization processes. In this period, sport became increasingly central to globalization processes in general. Personal and national identities, the institutional frameworks of nation-states, international relations, and conceptions of global humanity were all given much stronger definition and thematization. For example, principles of national identity and self-determination were more clearly accentuated, while national "traditions" underwent strong processes of invention.[11] Meanwhile, major international associations and events were established and staged. Sport also entered a take-off global phase, as soccer, imperial games like cricket and rugby, and many Olympic disciplines (for example, in track and field, fencing, and equestrianism) underwent international diffusion. Local elites and entrepreneurs were critical catalysts in promoting sports across local populations.[12] Of course,

---

7. Guttmann, *Sports*.

8. Mangan, *The Games Ethic and Imperialism*.

9. See the following works by Roland Robertson: *Globalization*, "Open Societies, Closed Minds?," and "Global Millennialism."

10. Giulianotti and Robertson, *Globalization and Football*.

11. Hobsbawm and Ranger, eds., *The Invention of Tradition*; Robertson, *Globalization*, 146–63.

12. Kaufman and Patterson, "Cross-National Cultural Diffusion."

this was not simply a British story of sporting colonization, because alternative flows and fields of sport globalization were also evident. The *Turnverein* (German gymnastic movement) challenged British sporting hegemony in Europe in the late nineteenth century, the Gaelic Athletics Association served to institutionalize Irish sports in opposition to "colonial" British games, while North American exceptionalism was signified through the popularization of "national" sports like baseball, football, hockey (especially in Canada), and later basketball. Baseball in particular reflected American regional hegemony, as the game was popularized in Central America and parts of the Caribbean, as well as in Japan and its colonies.[13] The Olympic Games, first staged in 1896 and thereon quadrennially, provided early international exhibitions of nation-based sport competition.[14] Soccer's world body, FIFA, was founded in 1904, along national membership lines. The failure of Britain's football associations to participate fully within FIFA provided an early signal of the nation's long-term international and imperial decline. Again, the take-off and diffusion of these different sports were largely underpinned by hegemonic masculine norms and values—typically centered on themes of toughness, virility, and varying levels of violence and pain—though with significant class, ethnic, national, and regional inflections and variations.

At the same time, sports became a focus for the "invention of tradition" at both national and international levels; for example, the modern Olympics were founded to "recreate" ancient Greece's games, while (false) foundation myths were established around the first "playing" of particular sports, such as with the American General Abner Doubleday in baseball, and with William Webb Ellis in rugby union. "National" styles of play began to develop, enabling forms of distinctive masculine national identity to be explored and signified. The successes in sport of non-European nations—for example, by Australians in cricket, New Zealanders in rugby union, and Uruguayans in football—helped to build strong senses of national identity and solidarity across immigrant-based populations. Finally, with regard to humankind, in many different international settings sport became one important sociocultural space in which those marginalized by class, "race," ethnicity, or gender struggled to overcome their social exclusion, to engage and to compete with more powerful social groups. Thus, for example, in Latin America and the Caribbean, nonwhites struggled to participate in soccer and cricket respectively.[15]

---

13. Guttmann, *Games and Empires*.
14. Guttmann, *The Olympics*.
15. Beckles and Stoddart, eds., *Liberation Cricket*.

Given the patriarchal ideologies that were inculcated through sports, some of the strongest forms of marginalization were experienced by women. Yet following their wholesale deployment as a "reserve army of labor" in the early twentieth century and the pursuit of political and social emancipation particularly among upper- and middle-class sections, women undertook significant forms of sporting resistance in regard to participation, such as among wealthier groups within the educational system and among some lower-middle and working-class groups (notably, the Dick Kerr Factory women's soccer team in England until the late 1920s).[16]

Overall, this take-off period was critical in the transnational diffusion of sport. It also served to set in place many of the social themes and conflicts that would remain apparent for the next century in the globalization of sport.

Sociocultural Aspects of Global Sport

One of the most contested debates in social science on globalization centers on the "homogenization-heterogenization" problem. In simple terms, theories of homogenization posit that globalization gives rise to strong processes of cultural sameness, uniformity, and convergence. Alternatively, theories of heterogenization contend that the direction is the other way, as globalization is marked by cultural difference and divergence. Let us look at these opposing standpoints before considering a more integrative approach.

Turning first to the homogenization side, most social scientists who adopt this position are highly critical of its manifestation and are concerned that it is underpinned by structurally unequal and unfair distributions of power. In broad terms, many homogenization approaches identify forms of cultural imperialism as underlying these processes of convergence. For example, in regard to global communications, proponents of the cultural imperialism thesis highlight the ways in which media corporations from the Global North are able to swamp societies in the Global South with images of advanced consumerism and pro-North ideologies.[17] In a variation on the cultural imperialism thesis, the American sociologist George Ritzer[18] has advanced the keyword, "grobalization," to capture how, in his view, cultural homogenization is driven by three "grobal" forces: capitalism, via expansionist major corporations; Americanization, via US corporations and culture products; and "McDonaldization," through transferring the highly ef-

---

16. Hargreaves, *Sporting Females*; Giulianotti, *Football*.
17. Hamelink, *World Communication*; Schiller, *Communication and Cultural Domination*.
18. Ritzer, *The Globalization of Nothing*.

ficient, disenchanting, and tasteless organizational principles of the McDonald's fast food chain into other fields of social life.

These arguments are not without supporting evidence. We might, for example, consider how their key points fit with global sport mega-events: in the Olympic Games, most of the designated sports derive historically from the Global North, while television coverage is saturated with multifarious commercial messages, usually from the Global North's transnational corporations. In addition, applying globalization theory, the Olympics and soccer's World Cup finals have been strongly influenced by American corporations—for example, with respect to event management and television revenues. They are also organized in highly efficient and rational ways.

However, there are weaknesses in the homogenization arguments. It may be that these approaches are too pessimistic in failing to recognize sufficiently the capacity of most sociocultural actors to engage critically and creatively with "global" cultural phenomena. Thus, media imperialism theory exaggerates the extent to which television viewers and newspaper readers simply absorb and internalize media messages, rather than engage selectively and critically with media content. Meanwhile, grobalization theory puts too much emphasis on the commercial production and sale of cultural phenomena, such as in regard to tourism or cuisine, rather than paying sufficient attention to the interpretative and normative aspects of culture—for example, in respect of different cultural aesthetics, styles, meanings, and techniques.

Ritzer's grobalization theory does encourage us to consider one significant strain of the homogenization thesis—Americanization theory. This approach contends that the United States and American corporations—such as Coca-Cola, CNN, Disney, McDonald's, Microsoft, and Nike—are the dominant forces of cultural imperialism, in promoting American values, lifestyles, products, worldviews, and practices across the world.[19] We might say that these Americanization processes have two main levels: "hard Americanization," which features the domination of American products and practices at the expense of local alternatives; and conversely, "soft Americanization," which involves the specific influence of everyday Americanisms within different societies at everyday level.

There are some significant weaknesses in the Americanization thesis in general terms. First, the association of Americanization with free-market global commercialism does not entirely fit with all of the practices of US major league sports, as illustrated by some rev-

---

19. Crothers, *Globalization and American Popular Culture.*

enue-sharing within sport leagues and also by the "draft system" for distributing players across teams.[20] Second, most North American sports—particularly football and baseball—have had regional rather than global impact. Their development has been focused largely at the national level, some might say in a "solipsistic" rather than imperialistic way.[21] Conversely, soccer, as the world's most popular sport, has had limited historical impact in the United States and remains outside the list of the "Big Four" American sports (football, baseball, basketball, and hockey). Finally, the very term *Americanization* is increasingly misrepresentative in geographical and sociological terms. It refers not to the American continent but to one specific nation, the United States. The term also implies that the United States is a culturally uniform nation, yet this has never really been the case, and is particularly inapplicable now, given the long-term impacts of mass migration and multicultural cosmopolitanism.

Given these points, the attractions of the "hard Americanization" thesis start to break down within sports. The "soft Americanization" thesis is perhaps more plausible, in being able to account for how specific American practices have had influence within other sports—for example, in pre-event razzmatazz, in marketing techniques, and in the use of television production techniques in covering non-American sports.

Overall, these points help to capture the broader argument that homogenization theories, while not without their merits, are at their weakest when obliquely applied to sport and do not allow us to probe the cultural complexity and diversity of sport in different settings.

Theories of heterogenization, in contradistinction, point to cultural divergence and differentiation in globalization. Again, there are a variety of theories and keywords that utilize different facets of the heterogenization approach. The theory of creolization explores how peoples in peripheral societies engage critically and selectively with the cultural phenomena of other societies to produce creolized cultural forms.[22] The concepts of hybridity and hybridization perform similar functions in drawing out the cultural mixing and blending that has long occurred across different societies, as illustrated in music, dance, and sports, particularly in postcolonial contexts.[23] Additionally, theories of indigenization register the development and growing significance of

20. Szymanski and Zimbalist, *National Pastime*.

21. Martin and Reeves, "The Whole World Isn't Watching (But We Thought They Were)."

22. Hannerz, *Cultural Complexity*.

23. Burke, *Hybridity*; Pieterse, "Globalization as Hybridization," 45–68; Pieterse, *Ethnicities and Global Multiculture*.

indigenous cultural-political identities in recent years, such as among "First Nation" or native peoples in North America and Australasia.[24]

These different aspects of creative heterogenization are illustrated in different ways in sport. The most radical instances feature fundamental changes to the rules and ethics of particular sports in order to fit with local conditions and contexts. For example, North Americans transformed the games of folk football, or rugby, and rounders to produce the "national" sports of football and baseball. More spectacularly, Trobriand Islanders transformed cricket, the quintessential English pastime, into an elaborate local ritual that helped to build positive relations between different communities.

It is more common for local peoples to indigenize or creolize the content rather than the form of those sports that have undergone at least some level of international diffusion. In this way, different societies come to produce their own aesthetic, technical, and normative versions of the sport. For example, in soccer, Latin American societies place relatively high value on individual artistry compared to soccer cultures in northern Europe, particularly the UK; and in cricket, the Indian subcontinent has historically placed greater emphasis on slow bowling skills and techniques compared to other regions that play the game. Indeed, it might be argued that India has "hijacked" this English colonial sport by developing its own styles of playing and narrating cricket, and more recently by taking the lead in the game's political and economic development, most obviously through the creation of the world's most lucrative club tournament, the Indian Premier League (IPL).[25]

Theories of hybridity and hybridization help to explain how, for example, sporting cultures emerge from a variety of influences and interests. For example, in Latin America different soccer societies have drawn in part upon forms of dance to reimagine the sport, such as with Brazil and samba, Argentina with tango, and Colombia with salsa.[26]

Meanwhile, the influence of indigenism in sport is manifested in several ways. Traditional games and folk sports have maintained and extended their appeal in many societies, such as the Basque pelota, the Scottish Highland Games, the Breton Games (see papers in this volume).[27] First Nations peoples have also staged their own international events, such as the Inuit Games, which feature sporting disciplines

24. Friedman, "Indigenous Struggles and the Discreet Charm of the Bourgeoisie."

25. Appadurai, *Modernity at Large*; Rumford, "More Than a Game: Globalization and the Post-Westernization of World Cricket," 202–14.

26. Burke, *Cultural Hybridity*, 27–28; Bellos, *Futebol*, 35; Archetti, *Masculinities*.

27. Jarvie, *Highland Games*; Eichberg, "Travelling, Comparing, Emigrating."

that are derived from traditional forms of physical culture or labor. Some First Nations populations have also staged prominent protests around major sporting events, with a focus for example on their denial of key civil and human rights (for example, Australian Aboriginals around the Sydney 2000 Olympics).[28] Thus, overall, heterogenization theories hold substantial traction within sport and help to mark out the ways in which diverse social groups engage creatively with different sporting movements.

To find a middle way that allows for the possibility of homogenization and heterogenization in sport, the concept of glocalization has particular benefits. Glocalization has been widely discussed and debated in social science since its introduction to explain the sociocultural aspects of globalization.[29] Thus far, most analysts of glocalization have tended to associate it with processes of heterogenization, partly in order to challenge more deterministic arguments regarding cultural convergence. However, glocalization has a deeper sociological meaning, in referring to the mutual interdependency of the local and the global.[30] Glocalization theory thus allows for the "duality of glocality"—that is, the interplay of convergence/homogenization and divergence/heterogenization tendencies with respect to global culture.[31]

The concept of glocalization has been applied to explain different aspects of sport, such as the broad global aspects of soccer, the identities of transnational soccer fans, and the key aspects of Asian sport.[32] In modern sport, we find that homogenizing impulses may be apparent in the way in which national sports federations and governing bodies are structured. In contrast, heterogenizing tendencies are more evident in the diverse aesthetic codes and historical and social identities of sports clubs and nations.

Overall, the duality of glocality reflects my wider understanding of how, following Robertson,[33] the sociocultural aspects of globalization feature a complex interplay between the local and the global, convergence and divergence, and the universal and the particular. I will now consider some of the major political-economic aspects of globalization

28. Lenskyj, *The Best Olympics Ever?*

29. Robertson, "Mapping the Global Condition: Globalization as the Central Concept," 15–30; Robertson, *Globalization*; Robertson, "Glocalization"; Holton, *Global Networks*; Roudometof, "Transnationalism, Cosmopolitanism and Glocalization"; John Tomlinson, *Globalization and Culture*.

30. Robertson, *Globalization*, 173–74; Robertson, "Globalization Theory 2000+."

31. See Giulianotti and Robertson, "Forms of Glocalization."

32. See the following works by Giulianotti and Robertson: "The Globalization of Football," "Glocalization, Globalization and Migration," "Sport and Globalization," *Globalization and Football*, and "Glocalization and Sport in Asia."

33. Robertson, *Globalization*.

in relation to sport.

Political-Economic Aspects of Global Sport

Here, I examine two critical debates—on the nation-state and on the world economic system—with regard to the political-economic aspects of globalization and their relevance to global sport.

First, there has been significant debate among social scientists on the continuing relevance or otherwise of the nation-state in an age of advanced global connectivity and consciousness. Some analysts have dismissed the nation-state as a "zombie-category,"[34] and others as outmoded by "hyperglobalist" tendencies that promote transnational industries, consumption patterns, and identities.[35] Conversely, it might be argued that nation-states continue to have crucial relevance in political and other senses. They remain the core political units of intergovernmental organizations such as the UN or European Union. They may also be said to have adapted significantly in regard to national identities and ideologies—for example, by prioritizing forms of civic rather than ethnic citizenship across their multicultural populations.[36]

In sport, we might certainly point to ways in which the status of the national has been squeezed or undermined. Club- or "franchise"-level competitions dominate the week-by-week organization and presence of most team sports, for example in baseball, basketball, soccer, football, rugby union, rugby league, and more recently in cricket through the high-profile IPL tournament. Individual sports are focused even more on the production and competitive interplay of transnational stars, such as in tennis, golf, and track-and-field athletics. In line with Ohmae's analysis, in hyperglobalist terms we find that sport shows strong transnational features comparable to industries as sports leagues like the NBA or the English Premier League pursue global markets; to identities, as top clubs like Manchester United, the New York Yankees, and the Chicago Bulls develop supporters worldwide; and to consumption patterns, as individual consumerism is promoted for the transnational sale of sports merchandise.

Yet notwithstanding these points, sport remains one field of social life in which the nation-state and national identity are especially relevant and prominent. Politically, many nations still place particular political store on their competitive status and presence within international sport. The right to stage sport mega-events continues to be prized by many nations, because it affords one way in which emerging

---

34. Beck, "Rooted Cosmopolitanism."
35. Ohmae, *The Borderless World*; Ohmae, *The End of the Nation State*.
36. Nairn, "Breakwaters of 2000," 91–103.

or post-transition nations (such as Brazil, Russia, and Qatar) are able to establish themselves in the international arena. In broader terms, these mega-events also enable different societies to explore and to celebrate exceptional forms of nationalism, for example when flags and other signifiers of national allegiance suddenly adorn public spaces during soccer's World Cup finals.

Sport has also allowed individuals, social groups, and nations to explore new forms of national identity—such as civic or dual identity—for example among second- and third-generation ethnic minorities in Western Europe. This observation points to a further, broader issue regarding the complex and uneven ways in which sport serves to position or reposition marginalized groups within the nation. Historically, ethnic minorities have struggled for the right to participate and to represent (and thus to embody) the nation on equal terms within major international sports events—as illustrated, for example, by the endeavors of black Latin American soccer players or West Indian cricketers to captain their national sides.[37] Sport also provided a critical site of wider struggle in South Africa when much of the international community, led by African nationalist movements, boycotted sporting and other cultural links with the apartheid regime.[38] The position of women within national sport is also highly important here, because women too have struggled for the right to participate and to represent the nation, most obviously in regard to pressing to increase the number of events and female competitors at the Olympic Games over the long term. While some iconic, world-beating women athletes might be presented as "trophy nationals"—notably Cathy Freeman in Australia—far deeper issues continue to be apparent as women athletes struggle for levels of public recognition, financial backing, and competitive opportunities that come near to matching their male peers. Indeed, some nations continue to suppress explicitly women's sport, for example by refusing to send any female athletes to global events such as the Olympic Games.

Thus, overall, the nation-state continues to play a particularly prominent role within global sport and connects in complex and uneven ways to distinctive struggles for participation and inclusion by marginalized social groups. These issues are thrown into sharper relief when we explore the wider contemporary political economy of global sport.

A substantial component of globalization studies within social science has centered on the "world economy" or "world economic sys-

---

37. Carrington, *Race, Sport and Politics*.
38. Booth, *The Race Game*.

tem" over the long term, and more recently on the predominance of neoliberal or free-market policies in shaping this world economy since the 1970s.[39] For "world systems" analysts, the modern world economy is dominated by "core" nations and regions (notably North America, Western Europe, and Japan) at the expense of "peripheral" (for example, African) and "semi-peripheral" (for example, Eastern European) nations and regions. Many analysts also point to the power of transnational corporations (or TNCs), which operate beyond national confines with regard to labor, investment, and general trade, across the "global system."[40] However, while being careful not to underplay their economic scale and transnational range, we must acknowledge that many TNCs still harbor significant affiliations with their nation of origin—for example, in their brand identities, recruitment strategies, and strategic headquarters.[41]

Significant aspects of the world economy or global system are inevitably to be found in global sport, particularly in elite professional, male-dominated sport systems. For example, in soccer, the "core" league systems are found in Western Europe, particularly the "Big Five" soccer markets of England, Germany, Spain, Italy, and France, which indulge in heavy recruitment of players from poorer, semi-peripheral, and peripheral regions, such as Eastern Europe, Latin America, and Africa.

TNCs are increasingly prominent in sport, particularly in regard to merchandise, media, and sponsorship. Thus, Nike and others have developed international divisions of labor that provide further structural underpinnings for the hegemony of "core" nations and regions; the Sky pay-TV network has used premium sport to "batter" its way into global television markets, in close partnership with core sports leagues. TNCs in electronics, fast food, finance, telecommunications, and transport, largely based in core nations, have become heavily involved in the high-visibility sponsorship of elite sports. Additionally, it has been argued elsewhere that the world's most highly valued professional sports clubs are like TNCs in regard to global brand status, international divisions of labor, and their world consumer basis.[42] Moreover, these "TNC sports clubs" are similar to other TNCs in maintaining some of their distinctive kinds of local or national particularity, retaining, for exam-

---

39. Wallerstein, "The Rise and Future Demise of the World Capitalist System"; Wallerstein, *The Decline of American Power*; Arrighi, *The Long Twentieth Century*; Harvey, *A Brief History of Neoliberalism*.

40. Ohmae, *The End of the Nation State*; Sklair, *The Transnational Capitalist Class*.

41. See Doremus, Keller, Pauly, and Reich, *The Myth of the Global Corporation*.

42. Giulianotti and Robertson, "The Globalization of Football"; Giulianotti and Robertson, *Globalization and Football*.

ple, a specific playing style or ethos, distinctive "home" locations (the home stadiums), and featuring iconic "home-grown" players in their teams. To put it another way, these TNC clubs appear as "glocal" entities, sharing some common features while also marking themselves out in distinctive ways, particularly in terms of their identities and cultural contents.

Since the early 1990s, the world's largest clubs and the leading core sports leagues have gained the most financially and in competitive status from the greater influence of neoliberal policies within elite sport. Thus, for example, elite sport leagues are broadcast on pay-TV networks worldwide, while the world's leading sports teams are increasingly committed to recruiting athletes from a worldwide pool of talent, while playing games or going on consumer-building tours into new markets (particularly in East Asia).[43]

The "hypercommodification" of sport gives rise to a variety of social and political conflicts and tensions. First, there is intensification of competitive inequalities, purely on the basis of financial factors, between elite clubs or "core" nations and the rest. Thus, for example, the Champions League—the most prized tournament in European club soccer—has been dominated by a small pool of teams from the "Big Five" nations since the mid-1990s. Similar forms of structural inequality arise in nations where neoliberal principles are allowed to take the strongest hold. Second, the politics of access and distributive justice take on greater importance, for example in the distribution of tickets to elite sports events such as the Olympics or the major soccer cup finals. There have been concerns that such events fail to distribute tickets on a fair basis by overcharging or by prioritizing corporate sponsors rather than the most committed fans or those who have worked the hardest to support the sport. Third, just as a "liberalized" financial sector engendered the world economic crisis from 2007 onward, so a deregulated free market in sport can produce intense financial volatility, as marked for example by the high levels of debt within parts of European club soccer. Fourth, sport may be used to promote the neo-liberalization of other areas of society. For example, CCTV systems were effectively piloted at UK sports stadiums before being deployed in public spaces in order to regulate populations and cities.[44] More recently, preparations for the hosting of mega-events in Vancouver and London (Olympics), South Africa (World Cup), and Brazil (both) have involved forms of social "clearing" and the transformation of urban areas into relatively

---

43. See Walsh and Giulianotti, *Ethics, Money and Sport.*

44. Giulianotti, "Soccer Casuals as Cultural Intermediaries; Giulianotti, "Social Identity and Public Order; Armstrong and Giulianotti, "From Another Angle."

sterile, privatized spaces.

On the other hand, we should note too that the hypercommodification of sport is not an absolute or uncontested process. First, there are significant differences between different clubs, nations, and sports systems in regard to their political economy and governance structures. In soccer, for example, elite English clubs are privately owned, whereas in Germany, Spain, and Latin America many clubs are at least majority-owned by club members (in effect, the fans). In this sense, we might say that "glocalization" is at play in partly differentiating the corporate governance of clubs. Moreover, the European football governing body, UEFA, has introduced "fair play" rules in a bid to ensure that the competitive balance of competition is not upset by club owners who operate beyond their team's annual income by using their private wealth to buy success.

Second, it is also important to recognize that a relatively wide circle of stakeholders is seeking to exert political influence within sports. These forces include sports federations, clubs, athletes, agents, spectators, club members, nation-states, intergovernmental organizations, the mass media, transnational corporations, and nongovernmental organizations and social movements. Moreover, each of these entities harbors substantial differences and schisms—for example, between national sports federations or sports clubs that compete at different levels. At different junctures, opposing voices and alternative models with regard to the neoliberalism of sport may be put forward by at least some of these groups.

Conclusion

In this chapter, I have set out the interface of globalization and sport with a focus on three main dimensions. First, in historical terms, the take-off phase was critical in the diffusion of sport and in setting the context for the future social manifestation of sport within different locations. Second, in sociocultural terms, sport continues to be shaped by processes of homogenization and heterogenization; the latter in particular spotlights the cultural agency and creativity of different social groups in their sports participation. The concept of glocalization is useful in capturing the interpenetration of the local and the global within sport, and also in allowing for the interrelationships of homogenization and heterogenization. Third, in political-economic terms, global sports demonstrate the continuing relevance and changing contents of the nation-state and national identity. At the same time, the world economy or global system, and the predominance of neoliberal economic policies, provide the basis for core or leading athletes, clubs, and sports institutions to dominate global sport. However, as I have also indicated, there are significant forces in world sport that offer alternative visions and models for the institutionalization, organization, and sociocultural manifestation of elite professional sports.

To finish, I will conclude by saying that social conflicts have always been evident within sport, at local, national, and transnational levels. These conflicts have regularly centered on the position of marginalized social groups and their rights and opportunities to participate and to be included in sports. Class, gender, sexuality, "race," ethnicity, and age/generation continue to be the critical fault-lines along which these conflicts are defined and played out. These conflicts tend to take on "glocal" characteristics, of course, in being manifested in different ways in different national and regional settings. Neoliberal economic and social policies tend to sharpen social inequalities and divisions, and thus provide a basis for the further marginalization of these communities within sport and other social fields. On one hand, this raises real issues about social justice, and whether the sports participation and involvement of individuals and social groups—such as in attending sports events, accessing reasonably priced sports facilities, and being part of wider sporting communities—should really be determined by market forces. On the other hand, this raises further problems for the reproduction of sport. So many of the innovative, spectacular, and compelling aspects of sport are derived from the creative agency and critical engagement of individuals and social groups from marginalized social groups. If these communities start to lose their footholds within sport and perhaps turn to other, more meaningful and inviting cultural fields, then sport itself will be much the poorer.

Bibliography

Appadurai, Arjun. *Modernity at Large: Cultural Dimensions of Globalization*. Minneapolis: University of Minnesota Press, 1996.

Archetti, Eduardo P. *Masculinities: Football, Polo, and Tango in Argentina*. Oxford: Berg, 1998.

Armstrong, Gary, and Richard Giulianotti. "From Another Angle: Police Surveillance and Football Supporters." In *Surveillance, Closed Circuit Television and Social Control*, edited by Clive Norris, Jade Moran, and Gary Armstrong. Aldershot: Ashgate, 1998.

Arrighi, Giovanni. *The Long Twentieth Century: Money, Power, and the Origins of Our Times*. London: Verso, 1994.

Beck, Ulrich. "Rooted Cosmopolitanism: Emerging from a Rivalry of

Distinctions." In *Global America? The Cultural Consequences of Globalization*, edited by Ulrich Beck, Natan Sznaider, and Rainer Winter. Liverpool: Liverpool University Press, 2004.

Beckles, Hilary McD., and Brian Stoddart, eds. *Liberation Cricket: West Indies Cricket Culture*. Manchester: Manchester University Press, 1995.

Bellos, Alex. *Futebol: The Brazilian Way of Life*. London: Bloomsbury, 2002.

Booth, Douglas. *The Race Game: Sport and Politics in South Africa*. London: Frank Cass, 1998.

Bourdieu, Pierre. *Acts of Resistance: Against the Tyranny of the Market*. Translated by Richard Nice. New York: New Press, 1999.

Burke, Peter. *Cultural Hybridity*. Cambridge: Polity, 2009.

Calhoun, Craig. *Nations Matter: Culture, History and the Cosmopolitan Dream*. London: Routledge, 2007.

Carrington, Ben. *Race, Sport and Politics: The Sporting Black Diaspora*. London: Sage, 2011.

Crothers, Lane. *Globalization and American Popular Culture*. Lanham, MD: Rowman and Littlefield, 2007.

Doremus, Paul N., William W. Keller, Louis W. Pauly, and Simon Reich. *The Myth of the Global Corporation*. Princeton: Princeton University Press, 1999.

Eichberg, Henning. "Travelling, Comparing, Emigrating: Configurations of Sport Mobility." In *The Global Sports Arena: Athletic Talent Migration in an Interdependent World*, edited by John Bale and Joseph Maguire. London: Frank Cass, 1994.

First Research Inc. *Professional Sports Teams and Organizations*. Austin, Tex.: First Research, 2012.

Friedman, Jonathan. "Indigenous Struggles and the Discreet Charm of the Bourgeoisie." *Journal of World-Systems Research* 5, no. 2 (1999): 391–411.

Giddens, Anthony. *The Consequences of Modernity*. Cambridge: Polity, 1999.

Giulianotti, Richard. "Soccer Casuals as Cultural Intermediaries: The Politics of Scottish Style." In *The Passion and the Fashion: Football Fandom in the New Europe*, edited by Steve Redhead. Aldershot: Ashgate, 1993.

———. "Social Identity and Public Order: Political and Academic Discourses on Football Violence." In *Football Violence and Social Identity*, edited by Richard Giulianotti, Norman Bonney, and Mike Hepworth. London: Routledge, 1994.

———. *Football: A Sociology of the Global Game*. Cambridge: Polity, 1999.

Giulianotti, Richard, and Roland Robertson "The Globalization of Football: A Study in the Glocalization of the 'Serious Life.'" *British Journal of Sociology* 55, no. 4 (2004): 545–68.

———. "Glocalization, Globalization and Migration: The Case of Scottish Football Supporters in North America." *International Sociology* 21, no. 2 (2005): 171–98.

———. "Sport and Globalization: Transnational Dimensions." *Global Networks* 7, no. 2 (2007): 107–12.

———. "Forms of Glocalization: Globalization and the Migration Strategies of Scottish Football Fans in North America." *Sociology* 41, no. 1 (2007): 133–52.

———. "Recovering the Social: Globalization, Football and Transnationalism." *Global Networks* 7, no. 2 (2007): 144–86.

———. *Globalization and Football.* London: Sage, 2009.

———. "Glocalization and Sport in Asia: Diverse Perspectives and Future Possibilities." *Sociology of Sport Journal* 29, no. 4 (2012): 433–54.

Guttmann, Allen. *Women's Sports: A History.* New York: Columbia University Press, 1991.

———. *The Olympics: A History of the Modern Games.* Champaign: University of Illinois Press, 1992.

———. *Games and Empires: Modern Sports and Cultural Imperialism.* New York: Columbia University Press, 1994.

———. *Sports: The First Five Millennia.* Amherst: University of Massachusetts Press, 2004.

Hamelink, Cees J. *World Communication: Disempowerment and Self-Empowerment.* London: Zed Books, 1995.

Hannerz, Ulf. *Cultural Complexity: Studies in the Social Organization of Meaning.* New York: Columbia University Press, 1992.

Hargreaves, Jennifer. *Sporting Females: Critical Issues in the History and Sociology of Women's Sports.* London: Routledge, 1993.

Harvey, David. *A Brief History of Neoliberalism.* Oxford: Oxford University Press, 2006.

Hobsbawm, Eric, and Terence Ranger, eds. *The Invention of Tradition.* Cambridge: Cambridge University Press, 1983.

Holton, Robert J. *Global Networks.* Basingstoke: Palgrave, 2008.

Jarvie, Grant. *Highland Games: The Making of the Myth.* Edinburgh: Edinburgh University Press, 1991.

Kaufman, Jason, and Orlando Patterson. "Cross-National Cultural Diffusion: The Global Spread of Cricket." *American Sociological Review* 70, no. 1 (2005): 82–110.

Lenskyj, Helen. *The Best Olympics Ever? Social Impacts of Sydney 2000.* Albany: SUNY Press, 2001.

Mangan, J. A. *The Games Ethic and Imperialism: Aspects of the Diffusion of an Ideal.* London: Viking, 1986.

Martin, Christopher R., and Jimmie L. Reeves. "The Whole World Isn't Watching (But We Thought They Were): The Super Bowl and *American Solipsism.*" *Culture, Sport, Society* 4, no. 2 (2001): 213–36.

Nairn, Tom. "Breakwaters of 2000: From Ethnic to Civic Nationalism." *New Left Review* 1/214 (1995): 91–103.

Niezen, Ronald. *The Origins of Indigenism: Human Rights and the Politics of Identity.* Berkeley: University of California Press, 2003.

Ohmae, Kenichi. *The Borderless World: Power and Strategy in the Interlinked Economy.* New York: Profile, 1994.

———. *The End of the Nation State: The Rise of Regional Economies.* New York: Free Press, 1995.

Pieterse, Jan Nederveen. "Globalization as Hybridization." In *Global Modernities,* edited by Mike Featherstone, Scott Lash, and Roland Robertson. London: Sage, 1995.

———. *Ethnicities and Global Multiculture: Pants for an Octopus.* Lanham, MD: Rowman & Littlefield, 2007.

Ritzer, George. *The Globalization of Nothing.* Thousand Oaks, Cal.: Pine Forge, 2004.

Robertson, Roland. "Mapping the Global Condition: Globalization as the Central Concept." *Theory, Culture and Society* 7, no. 2 (1990): 15–30.

———. *Globalization: Social Theory and Global Culture.* London: Sage, 1992.

———. "Glocalization: Time-Space and Homogeneity-Heterogeneity." In *Global Modernities,* edited by Mike Featherstone, Scott Lash, and Roland Robertson. London: Sage, 1995.

———. "Globalization Theory 2000+: Major Problematics." In *Handbook of Social Theory,* edited by George Ritzer and Barry Smart. London: Sage, 2001.

———. "Rethinking Americanization." In *Global America? The Cultural Consequences of Globalization,* edited by Ulrich Beck, Natan Sznaider, and Rainer Winter. Liverpool: Liverpool University Press, 2004.

———. "Open Societies, Closed Minds? Exploring the Ubiquity of Suspicion and Voyeurism." *Globalizations* 4, no. 3 (2007): 399–416.

———. "Global Millennialism: A Postmortem on Secularization." In *Religion, Globalization and Society,* edited by Peter Beyer and Lori Gail Beaman. Leiden: Brill, 2007.

Roudometof, Victor. "Transnationalism, Cosmopolitanism and Glocalization." *Current Sociology* 53, no. 1 (2005): 113–35.

Rumford, Chris. "More Than a Game: Globalization and the Post-Westernization of World Cricket." *Global Networks* 7, no. 2 (2007): 202–14.

Schiller, Herbert I. *Communication and Cultural Domination.* Armonk, N.Y.: M. E. Sharpe, 1976.

Sklair, Leslie. *The Transnational Capitalist Class.* Oxford: Blackwell, 2001.

Szymanski, Stephan, and Andrew S. Zimbalist. *National Pastime: How Americans Play Baseball and the Rest of the World Plays Soccer.* Washington, D.C.: Brookings Institute, 2006.

Tomlinson, John. *Globalization and Culture.* Cambridge: Polity, 1999.

Wallerstein, Immanuel. "The Rise and Future Demise of the World Capitalist System." *Comparative Studies in Society and History* 16, no. 4 (1974): 387–415.

———. *The Decline of American Power: The U.S. in a Chaotic World.* New York: New Press, 2002.

Walsh, Adrian, and Richard Giulianotti. *Ethics, Money and Sport: The Sporting Mammon.* London: Routledge, 2007.

Wolf, Martin. *Why Globalization Works.* New Haven: Yale University Press, 2004.

Part 2

PRACTICE

6

Motor Praxeology: A New Scientific Paradigm

Pierre Parlebas

The body has long been neglected in university studies and scientific research. As a result of this, physical activity, games, and sports have generally been seen as infantile pastimes or, at best, accepted as a way of letting off steam or recharging intellectual batteries. However, over recent decades numerous research projects in many different disciplines have challenged these perceptions. Studies carried out in biology, neuroscience, the humanities, and the social sciences have shown that physical activity makes demands on many aspects of the personality—in a physical sense, of course, but also in regard to cognition, emotions, and relationships. Playing ball games like baseball or four square, running a marathon, taking on a tennis player, or steering a yacht deeply affects individuals and offers them infinite possibilities for expressing themselves.

The Science of Motor Action

Playing means deciding, taking part; and taking action is communicating. Every year there are new research findings that confirm beyond any doubt the important role of physical activity in children's development, adults' self-fulfillment, and the collective welfare. Through using different means, motor action makes demands on personality in just as rich and fruitful ways as verbal action. Action is the word.

This statement can hardly be contested. Traditionally, the study of games and sports has been treated as mere applied sciences in the service of established disciplines; in the amphitheater of knowledge, traditional physical games and sports do not get more than standing room at the back. Yet the findings of recent studies have brought about a real turnaround in this perspective. It would be justified to talk about a Copernican revolution in this regard, because physical activity has been moved from the periphery toward the center. We go from movement toward action. We are moving toward a change of paradigm, which has an original object of study: motor action. Not movement, nor the "body"—a concept with far too many meanings that lead to confusion—but "motor action," a more precise and better defined concept that studies corporeality as part of the whole personality of the acting individual.

Whether we like it or not, the idea of movement reduces physical activity to the biological machine's displacement, and this greatly and inappropriately overvalues its technical description. In sharp contrast, the concept of motor conduct and, more generally, the concept of motor action focus on the acting individual in particular, along with the motor methods that express his or her personality.

When a soccer player runs into the opposing team's area and shoots forcefully at the goal, when a 100-meter relay runner passes on the baton at full speed, when a canoeist paddles against fierce rapids, or when a dodge ball player throws the ball at his opponent, it is not enough to explain these physical activities as mere "movements" of a body-machine. These are motor conducts that involve a person's fundamental dimensions: their biomechanical dimension, of course, but also their emotional, social, cognitive, and expressive dimensions.

Our soccer player has to communicate with the other players and decode body signals; the relay runner has to accept being part of a shared action; the canoeist must detect the relevant indicators and make various decisions about the risks involved; and the dodge ball player has to judge distances, calculate paths, and plant the seed of doubt in his adversary by feigning. The acting individual is a person who collects and stores information, who draws up and carries out motor strategies. In this sense, physical education could become a real school for decision-making. As one can see, we have come a long way from the simple notion of movement!

This is the basis of a new discipline—motor action or motor praxeology. This gives an indisputable identity to a field of activity that has been considered until now of lesser importance; it gives unity to a multitude of games and sport practices that seemed highly heterogeneous, such as, for example, swimming, discus-throwing, boxing, red rover game or basketball. Motor praxeology offers a new perspective, an original approach to types of activity that have almost always been discussed from a distance by academia. This is a consequence of motor praxeology's specificity, which distinguishes it from other disciplines and avoids any encroachment from uncontrolled territories. These three characteristics—identity, unity, and specificity—enable us to classify praxeology as a science to an extent that makes it possible to investigate a clearly identified area, using both qualitative and quantitative scientific procedures.

Motor praxeology aims to follow two clearly defined principles: on the one hand, to uncover the specific characteristics of physical activity by investigating its many different manifestations from a new point of view; and on the other, to study real situations in games and sports under the constraints of conceptual analysis and the strict demands of scientific methodology.

The Internal Logic of Motor Situations

One of praxeology's first objectives is to uncover the internal logic of each motor situation. By the "internal logic" of games or sports activity I mean the group of features of motor action that are used when carrying out the activity—in other words, the cluster of relevant features. How is a volleyball match, a judo contest, a game of tag or a skiing time-trial carried out? Do the participants have to collect information and take motor decisions straightaway, or simply carry out automatic actions that they previously learned? Should they start off with cooperative or with aggressive actions?

Basketball requires certain ways of controlling the ball and of communicating among players; rugby and kickball require other ways, which are very different and much more varied. This motor logic leads to the creation of specific strategies for each game. Here, internal logic is not based on an appreciation of individuals' biomechanical or psychological qualities in the same way it was conceived in the past; rather, it is based on the analysis of the whole motor situation in the context of all of the actors. This analysis is carried out in terms of the system; what is taken into account is not an isolated player but rather the relationships that players have with their environment, the equipment they use, and the other participants. What happens among the players is of prime importance.

The most important features of the motor situation are expressed in terms of relationships—relationships with space, equipment, time, and other participants: teammates and/or adversaries. All of these factors can be specifically observed and studied objectively; they match motor behavior that can be identified on the field of play. In some senses, a sporting game's internal logic is its identity card; it is the "kernel" of the most relevant characteristics of its motor action. One could say that it reveals the "grammar" of the "sporting game" in question.

Each sporting game has its own particular alchemy. What takes place among the players? Can the role of body communication be demonstrated? Are the relationships between those taking part established by body-to-body contact or at a distance? Is the game's motor logic a logic of solidarity or of violence?

In order to answer these questions, it is vital that we carry out an X-ray of each sporting game from the point of view of the objective characteristics of motricity that make up its fundamental structure. This does not mean biology or sociology, but rather a completely new approach—that of praxeology, which focuses on motor action in its own right. This area is vast and to date has hardly been touched by scholarly research. However, there are some general *modus operandi* rules, adopted by many international teams, which have considerably altered the research landscape with regard to the domain of physical activities.

Information Uncertainty in Motor Activities

One of the key problems is finding objective indicators in order to facilitate a complete understanding of all sports and physical activities. Such an understanding should enable a classification that identifies each sporting game in terms of its main characteristics of praxis. I have been able to demonstrate three criteria for internal logic that define the main characteristics of motor activities

Participants' Relationship with the Material Environment

The relationship with space is fundamental. If the environment is arranged and standardized, as in athletics, gymnastics, and swimming, motor action is orientated toward an automatism that is carefully repeated and fine-tuned during training. The sequence of movements produces astonishing ability or exceptional audacity, such as in apparatus gymnastics. This is all based on sequences programmed long in advance; participants don't need acquired information, and they do not have to make any decisions during the event itself.

On the other hand, when the environment is "wild" and not standardized, as in windsurfing or adventure canoeing, participants carry on a continuous motor dialogue with space; they collect data, try to evaluate the obstacles in advance, and continually take preemptive action. This internal logic requires the acting individual's competence in dealing with this information. We can therefore identify a "dimension" that can be either "controlled" or "wild," and depending on which of the two is the case, all motor activities can be classified according to the degree of information uncertainty they produce. Motor activities can all be classified by a continuum ranging from "wild" at one extreme and "controlled" at the other. It is clear that this information has a decisive influence on actors' motor behavior and on specific features of the corresponding motor learning.

Participants' Relationships with Others as Cooperative Motor Interaction

Interactions take place among teammates; this is defined as motor communication. This is a relationship of body cooperation and has varying degrees of openness; it can take place through body contact or at a distance, and with or without equipment (climbing ropes, canoes, sails, and so on).

Participants' Relationships with Others as Motor Interaction Among Adversaries

These interactions take place among adversaries, in contact or at a distance, and they include counter-communication interactions (as in boxing, fencing, tennis, and so forth).

Counter-communication, such as tackling in rugby, should not be confused with cooperative communication, such as passing. The motor exchanges between two boxers are not the same as those between two climbers roped up on a rock face. In the former example, the purpose of each participant's motor action is to fool the adversary and to floor him; in the latter, all the motor actions of the participants are designed to help their partners achieve a shared objective.

These three criteria apply to the subjective implication of the acting individuals: the actors all try to reduce uncertainty by decoding the situation. The common factor in these three situations is the influence of information uncertainty, both in regard to the classic, non-intentional determinism of the material environment, and to the intentional reactions, whether helpful or not, stemming from the human environment. In fact, it is the notion of information and meaning that guides the participants' motor conduct and motor praxeology places this at the center of the subject of physical and sports activities.

Domains of Motor Action

Dichotomous Classification Tree

By taking into account the presence or absence of each of these three criteria, we can draw a dichotomous classification tree with eight domains of motor action. Each of these domains has particular characteristics regarding social links and relationships with the environment (see figure 6.1).

The eight domains of this classification can be reorganized into

Figure 6.1 Classifying physical activity in terms of motor actions.

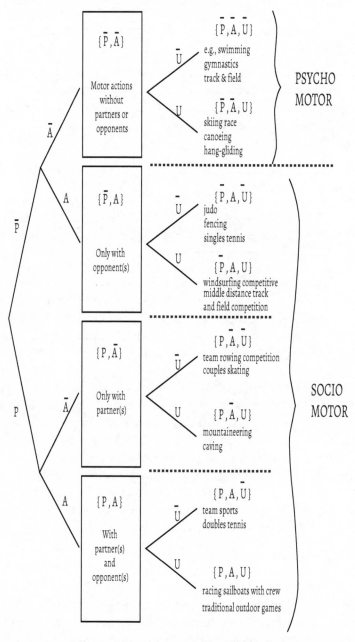

Three criteria are used: interaction with partners (P), interaction with adversaries (A), and uncertain information produced by the environment (U). Symbols that are not relevant are overscored. This creates an eight-branch dichotomous tree that shows the essential categories of motor actions.

subgroups, each one of which has a more global motor action meaning. In this way one can distinguish between two major sectors: the psychomotor area, in which participants work alone without building up instrumental motor interactions with other people (as in canoeing, stilting, pole-vaulting, solo climbing, and so on); and the sociomotor domain in which motor interaction among players is necessary. Moreover, there are three main types of action domains in the sociomotor area: sports and games in which motor interaction is exclusively antagonistic for instance, in duels between individuals (such as wrestling, judo, and fencing), and in games in which the principle "everyone for themselves" applies (for example, duck, duck, goose game, spud, and blind man's buff game); sports and games in which interaction is exclusively cooperative (for example, lead and top rope climbing, acrobatic gymnastics, sailing and rowing in crew, and children's hand clapping games); and sports and games in which there is both opposition and cooperation, particularly in duels between teams (such as volleyball, football, baseball, and dodge ball).

Each domain of motor action is based on dealing with the uncertainty that comes from the material and/or the human environment. It is, in fact, the notion of information that is at the core of the classification scheme and its coherence.

Simplex Classification

The diagram in figure 6.1 may be converted into an S3 class simplex with eight reference points; it reflects exactly the same data, but organized according to the subgroups U, P, and A (U = Uncertainty; P = Partners; A = Adversaries) in the simplex (figure 6.2). This simplex has the advantage of offering a very "expressive" formulation that can be analyzed by using its vertices, edges, and faces. This approach enables us to obtain extremely clear comparisons between domains of motor action, and emphasizes how one might potentially reorganize them according to their social and cultural interpretations.

For example, the simplex in figure 6.2 categorizes the 309 sports at the 1992 Olympic Games in their respective eight domains of motor action, according to the three criteria U, P, and A. A detailed look at the empirical data from this global sporting showcase reveals that the reality of the situation spectacularly contradicts official claims. In other words, the Olympic Games in fact value individual prowess far more than collective success; they pay far more attention to automated actions than to actions involving decision-making; they give more value to situations involving confrontation than to activities involving coop-

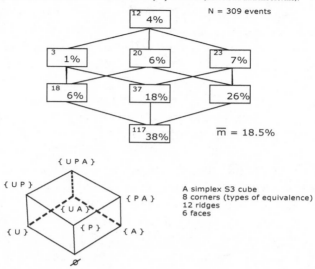

Figure 6.2 Distribution of events at the '92 Olympic Games (Barcelona and Albertville).

eration; and they maintain stereotyped male and female roles.[1] Formalizing data by using rigorous methodology allows us to go beyond the received ideas that are often so prevalent in the world of sports.

The Player and the Game

Researchers inevitably come across two apparently contradictory points of view in the analysis of all social situations, including that of sporting games: the actor and the system in the case of the former, and the player and the game in the case of the latter.

Games take place as a result of the behavior of biologically separate individuals; the players are the basic components of each game. However, players act in accordance with rules that impose the internal logic of the games' system, which brings about very diverse motor action domains. Individual action is necessarily subject to the "social contract" that the participants agree to when they enter the game, and it must conform to all the system's norms and regulations. In other words, individuals' motor participation and the constraints imposed by the structure are continually intermeshed; on the one hand, the players' individual actions flow faithfully through the system's social mold, and, on the other, this collective system only makes sense and becomes real as a result of the players' individual behavior.

I have just emphasized the actors' motor behavior with regard to their environment, their way of dealing with uncertainty, and finally,

---

1. Parlebas, *Jeux, sports et sociétés*.

their subjective experiences with regard to decision-making. I have already noted that the emphasis on players leads to their repositioning in the context of norms. I am now going to look at the characteristics of games as a universal cultural system that involves certain regular features. I will identify certain "universal" features—objective structures that, according to my hypothesis, are present in every game.

A Cultural Construction: Ethnomotricity

Motricity has long been considered to be an individual, biological fact. In fact, motor action is also a social event. All motor conduct bears witness to a culture. Games are the creation of a culture and the result of history. I would even go so far as to say that they form a genuine cultural heritage.

Traditional games reflect the place where they were born. They reflect a way of life and behavior, a way of interacting with the environment and with other people. Linked to ancient beliefs, inspired by religious ceremonies and sacred rites, and derived from folk and seasonal customs, many games figure among the most deeply rooted cultural activities in the societies from which they evolved. In short, cultural heritage includes ways of playing as well as ways of writing and building.

What makes this area unique is that it is corporal heritage based on motor action. Above all, games create a dynamic just like stories, but in this case they are based on a type of action; games carry the memory of past centuries. Participants may breathe new life into this heritage through their own body movements, gestures, kinesthetic sensations, and motor relationships with their fellow players. Traditional sporting games reveal a type of culture that consists of action, a culture that is re-lived through the body's movements.

Marcel Mauss clearly pioneered this approach to play, body, and culture from 1934 onward by uncovering the eminently cultural facet of "body techniques." Ways of running, swimming, dancing, fighting, and playing, he writes, "each society has its own special habits."[2] Mauss states that body techniques depend greatly on ways of life, "habitus," that are also connected with education, social conventions, and prestige. By "habitus" we should understand socially acquired attitudes that underpin and partially predetermine every individual's thinking, feeling, and behaving, and noticeably influence people's relationship with their bodies. This concept has recently gained strength once more as the cornerstone of Pierre Bourdieu's theory of social tastes, particularly

---

2. Mauss, "Body Techniques,"457.

with regard to sports.[3] The use of the body, Mauss argues, depends on "systems of symbolic assemblages" created by social "habitus" whose presence Bourdieu underlines in class conflicts.

By playing, children unknowingly learn about their social universe and all about the culture to which they belong. All games form part of a specific ethnological game culture, "ethnoludicity." The internal logic of sporting games is connected to values from the social context. The armed races that concluded the original Olympic Games twenty centuries ago were as much part of the culture then as windsurfing or Formula 1 racing is today. Social groups and nations are distinguished by their games: Scottish tossing the caber, American baseball, English cricket, Basque pelota, African canoe racing, and Afghan buzkashi are as distinctive cultural forms as subsistence or family structure. I have therefore come to theorize an ethnology of motricity, which I call "ethnomotricity." I take ethnomotricity to be the field and the nature of motor activities from the point of view of their relationship with culture and the social context in which they develop. Rooted in many different cultures, physical activities span an extremely wide spectrum of motor action diversity.

The Universals of Sporting Games

Does this effervescent diversity of sporting games condemn observers to search far and wide, and get lost in a kaleidoscope of actions that are all original and cannot be related?

It is true that everything seems to differentiate sporting games from each other: the ways of playing and communicating, the playing arenas, the type of equipment used, the length of the encounters, the criteria for success, and so on. Some games are played with a ball or with a puck, others with racquets, with baskets, and with bats, while still others use stones, scarves, or flags, and there are even some that use no equipment at all. Sometimes the adversaries confront each other body-to-body, while in other games a net keeps them apart. Twenty-two participants play on a particular field, a dozen on a particular wooden floor, two in a particular ring or dojo; in yet another game there are thirty participants in the open air. Faced with this extravagant multiplicity of situations, the overriding feature of sporting games seems to be their diversity.

But is this infinite variety in fact deceptive? Behind the exuberance of motor conduct and an apparent disorder of phenomena, might there be solid organization deep down? In the same way that an im-

---

3. Bourdieu, *Distinction*.

mense variety of linguistic utterances masks the uniformity of syntactic and phonological mechanisms, does the astonishing multiplicity of games hide an extremely influential underlying unity? By examining the dynamics of generating motor behavior (a fact that establishes the differences between motor activities), we see that a finite number of rules affecting a finite number of players and objective data lead to an infinite possibility of game sequences. Basketball, football, or the "capture the flag" game cannot be reduced to a jumble of actions that are merely improvised and random. Behind the infinite glimmer of encounters that always repeat themselves, is it possible to identify stable and common structures?

In-depth analysis and observation of these situations of play suggest the possibility of advancing the hypothesis that the games of all cultures are based on unvarying systems that lie beneath the apparent variation. In other words, underneath the disorder swarming on the surface there is a deep structural order that determines game actions. Player initiatives have to take place against the backdrop of a pre-established canvas common to all the participants. Whatever their physical and psychological characteristics may be, each participant's actions conform to these underlying imperative structures—the "universals of sporting games."

These universals are not vague, mysterious essences but rather operational models that show the basic structure of all sporting games and contain their internal logic. These systems of precise, relevant characteristics can be objectively identified in each game. We will present them as logical, mathematical models, which makes them subject to critical analysis. These models show the principles of action in games in a schematic way; they illustrate player dynamics and their possibilities of motor action. Seven universals have been identified: the network of motor interactions, the graph of goal interactions, the scoring system, the social motricity role structure, the network of subroles, and the code of motor praxis and motor gestures that are linked to indirect body communication. These internal logic characteristics systems depend on rules, and form the matrix of sporting games. Each culture stamps its original seal on the action, reaction, and preemptive action that make up each game. Standing on a common platform, ethnomotricity leads to multiple creations with hundreds of faces, all of which are active agents of social transformation as well as witnesses to their particular cultural origin.

Illustrations

It is hardly possible to explore the varied content of these different universal features in this chapter. However, a few illustrations may serve as examples in order to give an idea of the potential that this type of modeling has both in terms of formal description and in anthropological interpretation.

The Network of Motor Interactions

Each sporting game has a network of motor interactions. This can be very simple, such as in psychomotor games (hopscotch, pinball, javelin throwing contest and so on), and they are sometimes extremely dense, such as in sociomotor games (for example, dodge ball, red rover, soccer and so on). This type of universal is rigorously defined in each game. All basketball players—whether they are Chinese, Russian, or American—act within the same network of communication, scrupulously following itineraries preestablished by the internal logic that is derived from the rules. All over the world, any given sport is based on a unique interaction network.

However, it is clear that there are differences from game to game.

Figures 6.3. Solidarity and rivalry relations of motor communications.

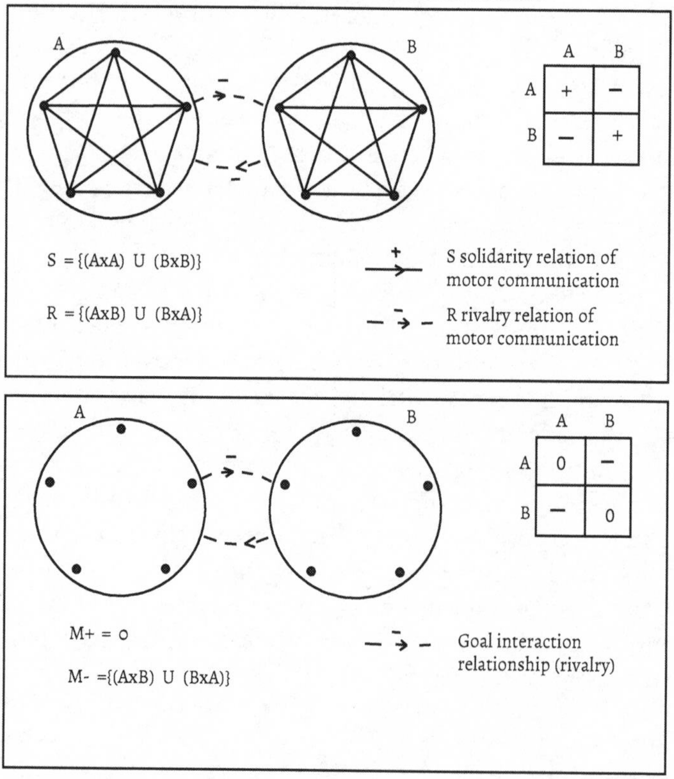

S = {(AxA) U (BxB)} $\xrightarrow{+}$ S solidarity relation of motor communication

R = {(AxB) U (BxA)} $-\ \dashrightarrow\ -$ R rivalry relation of motor communication

M+ = o

M- = {(AxB) U (BxA)} $-\ \dashrightarrow\ -$ Goal interaction relationship (rivalry)

Figure 6.4. Diachronic network of goal interactions in "foxes, chickens and snakes" games.

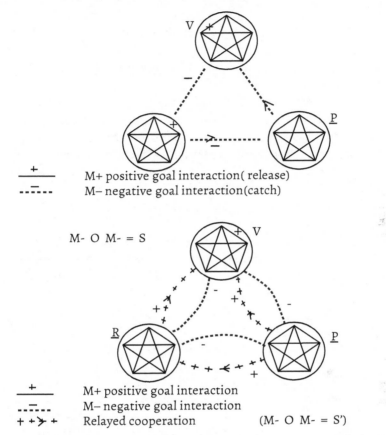

	M+ positive goal interaction(release)
+	M– negative goal interaction(catch)

M- O M- = S

	M+ positive goal interaction
+	M– negative goal interaction
+ +≻ +	Relayed cooperation

(M- O M- = S')

The network of hide-and-seek obviously differs from that of volleyball! Each game has its own network that is different from that of other games. Each "universal" therefore corresponds to a "meta universal" or an abstract model that brings together a large number of different manifestations, each of them forming part of networks strictly defined by each sporting game. This second-degree phenomenon may seem complex, but in fact it is long-established in our understanding of the world around us. To take a simple example, the concept "dog" includes multiple manifestations such as bulldog, dalmatian, spaniel, chihuahua, and so on. The universal concept is generic and includes a whole range of specific differences. I will illustrate my remarks by looking more specifically at basketball and the game *poule renard vipère* or "fox, chicken, snake," in which the respective networks are like species from the same genus.

In figure 6.3, the basketball motor interaction network is indicated on a complete binary graph made up of two subgraph groups showing positive cooperation in which absolute confrontation is indicated on a two-part subgraph in relation to antagonism. This bipolarized structure can be found in all well-known international sports in which two teams (football, hockey, volleyball, and so on) or two individuals (combat sports, fencing, tennis, and so on) confront each other. The interaction matrix is highly expressive; these are "team duels" or "individual duels" in which the interest of two individuals or of two strongly united teams is diametrically opposed. Using the "universal of goal interaction network" in figure 6.4 enables us to complete this basic network; it shows that only successful confrontation interactions, points, are taken into account and recorded in the scoring system. The fact that the final result of matches is thus based exclusively on the confrontation score offered by the official record can be verified in all institutionalized sporting games.

It is easy to reach an overall interpretation of these two universals: sports represent real combat that aims to make the winner's domination clear, considering that the initial equality of conditions makes it possible to evaluate the final inequality of results.

In comparison, as seen in figure 6.4, the motor interaction network in traditional games such as "poule renard vipère" has a completely different structure.[4] Foxes catch chickens, which catch snakes, which catch foxes. In other words, when foxes catch chickens they catch their own protectors, and by doing what they have to do to win, they do what will make them lose! This irrational, intransitive triangular relationship is radically different from the frank, dyadic, and unambiguous relationships of sporting duels. This game is "paradoxical": it puts players in a contradictory situation, close to what the social psychologist Gregory Bateson terms a "double bind."[5] In other words, players have to choose between two contradictory options that are mutually binding.

The game's disturbing ambivalence creates a tension that challenges the concept of non-contradiction, which is a central premise of Western logic. This game is a classic example of the many paradoxical games with varying degrees of "binds" involved, including traditional games like "la Balle assise," "le Gouret," "Accroche-décroche," "l'Ours et son gardien," and "la Galine." Sports cannot tolerate such a transgres-

---

4. A traditional children's game in France whereby participants are organized into three teams: foxes, chickens, and snakes. The goal is for each team to catch another (for the foxes to catch the chickens, the chickens to catch the snakes, and the snakes to catch the foxes). When a team member is caught they become a prisoner in their opponents' camp. Yet because each team is both predator and prey, the more successful it is the weaker it becomes.

5. Bateson, *Steps to an Ecology of Mind*.

sion of relational logic; institutional practices have totally rejected all paradoxical games with "perverse" effects, as the sociologist Raymond Boudon has demonstrated in general terms.[6] At the same time, paradoxical games bring about situations with ambivalent and flexible relationships, questioning the usual order of things; they bring about original forms of social relationships that may prove excellent for open experiences of socialization.

The operational analysis of the interaction network in all of these games uncovers many other unexpected situations: sudden changes of allegiance (red rover game); non-symmetrical duels (cops and robbers); games with convergent network (chain tag game) and with permutation network (What's the time, Mr. Wolf? tag game); games with shared, nonexclusive competition (blind man's buff game). Clearly one of the considerable advantages of universals is that they offer methodological tools that help compare games, leading to well-argued suggestions and interpretations. They also develop observation grids for motor behavior and a host of "indicators" that give us valuable empirical data that enable detailed field analysis.

The Transition Network of Sociomotricity Sub-roles

The universal that places the observer at the center of motor action during a game is without doubt the sociomotricity sub-roles transition network. In order to explore this, it is first necessary to identify sociomotricity roles (in other words, the main action categories defined by the rules), and to complete the graph with their role-to-role authorized shifts figure 6.6 shows the network of sociomotricity roles in the traditional game "Accroche-décroche" (also known as "les Petits fagots"). Nowadays this game is played by young children; during the Renaissance era it was a pastime for aristocrats at the French Court. Second, each role is broken down into sub-roles that show the range of motor action elementary strategic units, which can be updated by the person carrying out each role. The network of roles can be developed into a transition graph of sociomotricity sub-roles associated with their matrix, which shows all the possible motor behavior sequences allowed by the rules (see figure 6.5).

The network of social motricity sub-roles is the clearest proof of the generating power of universals. Every single player, whoever they are, will take one of the preestablished paths in the sub-roles graph. Whether they wish to or not, whether they are tall or short, whether they have blue or brown eyes, all players necessarily take a route that has been

---

6. Boudon, *The Unintended Consequences of Social Action.*

Figure 6.5. Sociomotor role changes network and associate matriz (grid). The blank spaces show possible role changes, the shaded spaces show forbidden combinations.

Hooked and unhooked game

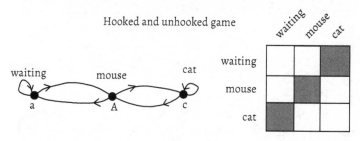

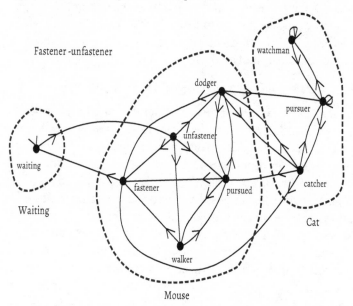

Figure 6.6 Sociomotor subrole changes network. The roles are divided into subroles that represent the minimal strategic action units that are likely to organize themselves in predictable sequences.

previously marked on the sub-roles graph. Obviously, players of each game are "enrolled," and it seems inevitable that this "enrollment" should involve consequences of acculturation that influence participants' behavior and personality both in the near and distant future.

Local or Global?

Games, in a sense, are a type of an academy in which social relationships are experienced by the body. Analysis of communication networks objectively updates the structures that enable social relations to be woven; the characteristics of these networks bear witness to the preferential values that are encouraged by sporting games and, as an extension, by the cultures that include them. Games thus reveal, explicitly or implicitly, certain cultural tendencies.

The standardization of sports allows every community to take part together in the same event. There is undoubtedly a rallying aspect to this. However, sports conform to a unique competitive model that is highly restrictive, invented by western societies with high technology, and in which media power is fundamental. This lessens the importance of regional cultural creations, although such domination and colonization does not necessarily mean that local communities should not develop their own sporting motor activities as much as those of the colonial power.

Local games—in other words, traditional games—are characterized by activities of incredible diversity. They bear witness to physical and ludic characteristics specific to local values and express local identities. Local games have exploited their sporting options, which have yielded extremely varied results. Consequently, traditional games worldwide are like a highly colored kaleidoscope with astonishing variety. Should we be surprised by this? This diversity seems justified inasmuch as it reflects a visible tendency in all cultural constructions: the desire to demonstrate originality, to stand up for a local area, to defend heritage.

The multicolored world of sporting games is unified by the underlying principle of universals, which offer a universal cultural matrix based on the participants' motor action. It would be well worth researching the balance between the global standardization necessary for consensual participation, and the genuineness indispensable for local identities to exist.

Bibliography

Bateson, Gregory. *Steps to an Ecology of Mind*. St. Albans: Paladin Frogmore, 1973.

Bourdieu, Pierre. *Distinction: A Social Critique of the Judgment of Taste*. Translated by Richard Nice. Cambridge: Harvard University Press, 1984.

Boudon, Raymond. *The Unintended Consequences of Social Action*. New York: St. Martin's Press, 1982.

Mauss, Marcel. "Body Techniques." In *Incorporations*, edited by Jonathan Crary and Sanford Kwinter. New York: Zone, 1992.

Parlebas, Pierre. *Jeux, sports et sociétés: Lexique de praxéologie motrice*. Paris: INSEP Publications, 1999.

7

ACTION, TECHNIQUE, AND COMMUNICATION

Bertrand During

"In the reality of technique, culture ignores a human reality."[1] Questions as to the status of *techniques* in games and sports have received multiple, contradictory responses, which can be illustrated by evoking two foundational approaches. In the first essay ever devoted to the place of games in culture, Johan Huizinga regards humanity as the result of *games*, calls humans "Homo Ludens," and worries about games' transformation into work—which signified for him their replacement by *sport*.[2] At the same time, in another foundational text Marcel Mauss proposes studying "body techniques" as determined by the cultures within which they are developed. In his proposed classification, no particular place is given to games, and a relatively minor one to sports.[3] Games without technique on the one hand, techniques without games on the other. It is interesting to look back on those arguments in the light of developments through the twentieth century, and to run through the range of different positions they prompted.

In order to preserve what they consider a space of liberty, certain thinkers celebrate motor practices as a rediscovery of nature—that of the world and that of human nature. They minimize technique and deprecate its being related to scientific advances as an unnecessary complication. Others meanwhile are more sensitive to the way analogies between body and machine can lead to a rationalization of exercise, and they go so far as to make the science of exercise a subheading to the science of machines.

It is possible, then, that approaches to sport constitute a privileged ground for analysis and for a more general reflection on action and

1. Simondon, *Du Mode d'Existence des Objets Techniques*, 9.
2. Huizinga, *Homo Ludens*.
3. Mauss, "Body Techniques," 455–77.

technique. Here I will attempt to demonstrate this both on the basis of current conceptions in physical education and sports science, and on the rich reflections on questions of action, communication, and technique contributed by some authors quite external to the field. In short, creating a dialogue between researchers who rarely meet will illustrate the hypothesis proposed by Norbert Elias, that "knowledge of sport is the key to knowledge of society."[4]

A Matter of Courage: Technique Relegated to the Background

In his *Republic*, Plato defines gymnastics and music as the two branches of an education addressed "to the two temperaments"[5] of our soul—our passionate nature and our philosophical nature. He adds that the first is not aimed at satisfying the requirements of the body "except incidentally."[6] Gymnastics is the education of courage, necessary for the good of the City. Once this principle is established, everything else follows: "For why should one recite the list of the dances of such citizens, their hunts and chases with hounds, their athletic contests and races? It is pretty plain that they must conform to these principles and there is no longer any difficulty in discovering them."[7]

Even if the *Republic* simplifies thinking that will become more complex in *Timaeus*, Plato's reasoning is clear: education properly speaking is only for the soul, and gymnastics cultivates courage, one of the soul's two temperaments. In the twentieth century this principle was translated into the concept of virile culture (in relation to the necessities of warfare) and courageous action in general. The techniques of sports and exercise were secondary, as was any benefit they might have for the body; indeed, the body itself—the prison and tomb of the soul—was also regarded as secondary. Despite the importance he accords to gymnastics, Plato never enters into any description or analysis of what is actually practiced. What counts is the *orientation* of the action and its implications for effort, courage, and risk-taking.

In an apparent paradox, the study of gymnastics, physical education, and sport pays little attention to the activities that compose them, while it accords major importance to the moral and social ends wherein lie their educational value. The dualism that separates body and soul is extended into a separation between what gives action its meaning on the one hand, and what makes it possible on the other. Everything to do

---

4. Elias and Dunning, *The Quest for Excitement.*
5. Plato, *Republic*, Book 3, 412. At www.perseus.tufts.edu/hopper/text?doc=Plat.+Rep.+3.412a&fromdoc=Perseus%3Atext%3A1999.01.0168
6. Ibid., 411e.
7. Ibid., 412b.

with technique is thus devalued.

Three approaches illustrate this long tradition of thought and the different forms it can take. The first, a brief evocation of the work of Pierre de Coubertin, corresponds to a refusal to concentrate on technique; although it is not excluded, it is put to the service of a new institution, a new culture. The second is embodied by Georges Hébert and attempts to justify interest in technique by arguing that it is an extension of nature, a response to needs dictated by instinct. The third approach, which we find expressed in the contemporary sports media, will enable us to underline the dangers of praising the simplicity of action, particularly when it is accompanied by denunciations of reflection and culture. In short, since the nineteenth century the notion of technique in physical activity has been treated as superfluous and secondary (because of its naturalness), or it has been elevated in praise of brutality and the absence of thought.

The first attitude stems from the indifference already shown by Plato, which is shared by Coubertin. Although he was a devoted sportsman open to many different experiences, as well as a perceptive observer, Coubertin nonetheless refers only rarely to the characteristics of physical practice, to questions of learning and training procedures. For him, "the technique of physical exercises . . . is learnt above all by practicing them."[8] Coubertin, who organized competitions and sports for schoolboys and is most renowned for his role in creating the modern Olympic Games and the Committee that oversees them, was both a reformer of the educational system and a politician concerned with social and international peace. He wisely left technique to the technicians; his aim was to go higher and further than that. His approach does not *exclude* technique but underpins a notion that goes far beyond technique alone; in other words, technique is interesting as long as it helps organizational formations, illustrates values, and helps to transmit them.

Schematically, Coubertin proposed and perpetuated a dual system.[9] First, he articulated the relations between the sports themselves, highlighting individual excellence in various measured and/or judged events, dueling aptitude, and collective combat. Then, on a second level, he connected events, ceremonies (opening, closing, and award ceremonies), and structures (the Olympic village, the torch relay), which make it possible to create a relationship between excellence, the extreme manifestation of liberty, equality, and fraternity. This approach

---

8. Coubertin, "Extract from a Report to the Minister of Public Instruction, 1915," 413.

9. One might add that the Games are part of the same system as the Congress, and that the sporting activities can be related to popular education projects.

gives cultural and political issues a central place, which is firmly in the liberal tradition; as a result, the study of sporting action as it actually happens is relegated into the shadows. Whereas the "technician" sees the high jump as the conclusion of an accelerating race that advances from a jumping-off point and overcomes an obstacle, Coubertin for his part was more interested in the human will expressing its liberty and its capacity to take risks and to transcend bodily limits.

Coubertin (1863–1937) was a prolific author (his works are estimated to amount to more than twelve thousand printed pages).[10] Yet the younger Georges Hébert (1875–1957) is no less impressive, particularly if we consider that he devoted nearly ten thousand printed pages almost exclusively to physical activities and the creation, defense, and illustration of his "natural method of physical, virile, and moral education."[11] It is worth mentioning the relationship between Coubertin and Hébert; they have common points, and also certain disagreements. Most important, Hébert was a practitioner; he attended the Physical Education Congress in 1913 accompanied by a large group of naval cadets and marines whose spectacular demonstrations were enthusiastically received by both the public and the press. One might obviously expect him, therefore, to be a technician. But that is not the case; as he wrote himself, the quality of these demonstrations resulted from the fact that, strictly speaking, the performers were not performing techniques. Hébert's pupils did not learn complex movements at their master's dictation, as was the custom at the time. Moving around continuously, they carried out work that led them to spend lots of energy in sequences that Hébert called "the gestures of our species," the activities of the "active primitive," or "natural movements."[12]

Coubertin left technique to others and focused on the organization of sport as well as its cultural and social impact. Although Hébert devoted his life and energy to observing, analyzing, and perfecting motor techniques, he believed that what was essential in sports lay elsewhere. He is an ambiguous figure in terms of his relationship with technique, embodying a paradox we often see. Throughout the twentieth century there were many trainers and teachers who, like Hébert, thought that motor techniques were inscribed in the structure of the human organism made for walking, running, and jumping.[13] Naturism and fi-

---

10. Jean Durry estimates twelve to fifteen thousand pages in his *Le Vrai Pierre de Coubertin*.

11. Hébert, *L'Education Physique Virile et Morale par la Méthode Naturelle*.

12. Ibid.

13. Hébert organizes motivity into ten natural families of movements (walking, running, jumping, crawling, climbing, balancing, throwing, lifting-carrying, attack-defense, and swimming) that, presented in that order, constitute the plan for every les-

nalism go together. The man of nature, whom Hébert terms "the active primitive," guided by instinct and need in his daily struggle to survive, achieves the best possible development; exercise has to be included in the city-dweller's daily routine in order to recuperate those lost qualities. "There is in fact a way of working that is essentially appropriate for the development of the human organism as well as that of the animal: it is at the basis of *movement* in its most diverse forms, and is enhanced by varied utilitarian efforts. We call it natural or *fundamental* work."[14]

At the beginning of the first in a series of five volumes, Hébert postulates that motor techniques are natural. He devotes his attention to their study and cannot avoid illustrating their cultural character. Here we should note a coincidence: 1936 was the year of the publication of both Volume I of the "Natural Method" and of Marcel Mauss's foundational article,[15] which shows that the simplest, most elementary "body techniques" are fashioned by culture. There are no natural techniques, because techniques are learned.

By making his work dependent on a false anthropology and insistently proclaiming the "intangible" character of principles that do not stand up to examination, Hébert condemned the rest of his not inconsiderable work to lie untouched on library shelves. His figure illustrates a common situation in the domain of corporal techniques: those who master them see no point in studying them and consider that there is no way of acquiring them other than through practice. And because it is not made explicit, learning by practice is taken to be natural.

This position is sometimes extreme, accompanied by a total lack of reflection. On occasion, the "man of action" is not satisfied with rallying against those who seek to understand rather than act, and chooses instead to condemn them. This can be illustrated with an example borrowed from the French sports daily *L'Équipe*. According to an article in this publication during the mid-1970s, "The woolly minds that haunt the higher spheres of PT—Pseudo-sporting Twaddle" have the ridiculous ambition (this is in 1976) of creating a university to "cultivate the inimitable gibberish" that they take for thinking.[16] As Roland Barthes writes about the way certain populists aim to discredit "intellectuals," "here we perceive the inevitable basis of all anti-intellectualism: the

---

son, carried out in nature along a course punctuated by obstacles, or more simply on a platform, in the schoolyard, always in a continuous movement of waves.

14. Hébert, *L'Education Physique*, 7.

15. Mauss, "Body Techniques."

16. Marcel Hansenne, "En toute liberté," *L'Équipe* (Paris), 30 October 1976, p. 7. With two million copies sold on Mondays, *L'Équipe* was the largest-circulation daily at the time in France.

suspicion of language, the reduction of all adverse speech to a noise."[17]

After a few variations on the theme of the simple, natural, and spontaneous character of sporting practices and some raillery at the expense of those who strive to complicate matters and put young people off, the article in *L'Équipe* finishes by calling for a purge: "Sport in schools. God knows how many spears we have broken trying to convince skeptics from the outside. But even if we win that victory one day it won't be enough. We also need to get rid of certain costly parasites— male and female—who still flourish inside."[18]

This anti-intellectual discourse resonates with the Pétain dictatorship in France (1940–44), whose ideology juxtaposed rural authenticity with the perversity of cities, honest work with vain speculation, racial purity with cosmopolitan populations, and strength with culture. It is no surprise that we have reached this point. Considering motor practices as natural leads people to think of human beings as the product of their bodies. But as Lévi-Strauss underlines, taking sides with Mauss, arguing for a cultural basis of corporal techniques is "a project eminently well fitted for counteracting racial prejudices, since it would contradict the racialist conceptions which try to make out that man is a product of his body, by demonstrating that it is the other way around: man has, at all times and in all places, been able to turn his body into a product of his techniques and his representations."[19] There are considerable obstacles to the development of a technology of corporal techniques, and they have not been completely overcome—far from it. The apparent innocence of things that seem obvious on the surface hides heavy consequences that generally remain implicit, latent, or repressed.

From Mechanistic Models to Criticisms of Technique

One of the typical components of physical education in schools is gymnastics. It is made up of precise movements executed by pupils who line up facing a master, who in turn demonstrates the progress of the exercise by showing its repetitions and dictating its rhythm. The justifications for this are first of all anatomical; according to the founder of gymnastics, the Swede Per Henrik Ling, execution should be almost surgical in its precision. The avowed aim is to straighten the body and strengthen the musculature of the spinal column. It requires knowledgeable masters and disciplined pupils as part and parcel of the laborious atmosphere of traditional schools.

---

17. Barthes, "Poujade and the Intellectuals," 207.
18. Hansenne, "En toute liberté."
19. Lévi-Strauss, *Introduction to the Work of Marcel Mauss*, 8–9.

This sport, often referred to as "structured gymnastics," defines the body as a mechanism whose structure needs to be reinforced before it can be put to work. As a consequence, Raoul Fournié, president of the French Physical Education League, wrote:

> In our bodies, which are made up of superimposed segments, everything works like a mechanical construction, piling up layers on top of one another. The construction stands—or is stood up—but the joints have not been sufficiently tightened. It only takes a heavy object placed on the edifice for the construction to give way at its weakest points, lean in one direction or another, and collapse. The same goes for human mechanics. The objective should dictate the measures: to ensure the solidity of the human construction, we need to train those human joints, the extensors. But what exercise are we to use? That of localized, correct movements, constructed analytically . . . The Swedes have understood this and quite rightly tightened their screws, and now we can admire one of the finest races in the world.[20]

The body "made up of superimposed segments"—bones as levers, articulations as pulleys, muscles as ropes—is that found in the mechanics of Descartes, who opposed extended, geometrical substance to thinking, immaterial substance. Corrective, structured, maintenance gymnastics is based on a separation between the material reality of the body on the one hand, and on the other hand the mind and the will, which sit inside the machine like the captain on board his ship. It consists of stretching, strengthening, and straightening exercises for the muscles and bone structure, aimed at allowing articulations to function properly and correcting bad posture and unfavorable attitudes. From this point of view it does have a certain efficacy and is still found today at the start of physical education classes and in weight-training rooms.

This mechanistic view of the body is extended by reference to a second generation of machines. Progress in the study of physiology made it possible to draw a parallel between the body and thermodynamic machines that make use of atmospheric oxygen to transform available energy resources into work, heat, and waste. Here, too, the transfer of knowledge about the behavior and production of machines contributed to a more and more precise method of regulating the intensity of preparation and training exercises.

But beyond that contribution (which should not be underestimated), there remains the question as to the limits of these machine-models of the body. The consequence of making those models as precise as

---

20. Raoul Fournié, *L'Homme Sain* 1 (1945).

possible (after all, no model can aspire to be the same thing as the complex reality it tries to account for) was to call the resulting techniques into question, and to make people wonder if it was possible to continue thinking of the human organism on the basis of our knowledge of machines.

Criticism of structured gymnastics was first triggered by a tardy realization of its limited results. Between 1945 and the late 1950s, all physical education students in France had lessons in structured, maintenance gymnastics aimed at straightening curved spines—more in the name of an aesthetic norm, incidentally, than on the basis of any confirmed biomechanical knowledge. But this was far from successful, as shown by the dispersion in measured inter-vertebral angles observed in X-rays of students admitted to the École Normale Supérieure (a special higher-education establishment outside the mainstream framework of the French public universities system), who were arguably the elite of physical education training.[21] Failures encountered in physical education based on mechanics led some professors to question the approach, along with the conceptions on which it was based. Monist references replaced dualism; the body defined as a machine in need of straightening and consolidation was substituted by the idea of people involved in a significant relationship with their material and human environment. Following the phenomenology of F. J. J. Buytendijk and Maurice Merleau-Ponty,[22] Gestalt theory, and genetic psychology, psychomotor practitioners replaced "puppet gymnastics" with individualized work that emphasized awareness, thereby shifting from the imitation of external models to the consideration of proprioceptive references and the construction of a body schema.

At the same time that it was called into question by people who shared its goals but wanted it developed on a more solid foundation, structured gymnastics faced competition from other conceptions of physical education and sports. At first the debate struck a compromise; basic gymnastics structuring the body and applied gymnastics putting it to work were seen as complementary on the basis of a shared dualism. But the need emerged to replace the old references that gave meaning to physical exercise (sport was first and foremost moral, virile education, a training of the will), and the supporters of sports education also turned toward a monist approach. Given their taste for science and technique—and the fact that it was the dominant philosophy in French intellectual life at the time—they were led to base their ideas

---

21. Research carried out by Dr. F. Macorigh and published in *Les Cahiers Scientifiques d'EP* (March 1964).

22. Buytendijk, *Attitudes et Mouvements*; Merleau-Ponty, *Phenomenology of Perception*.

on Marxism.

According to these ideas, humans produce history by putting techniques to work and shaping the history of the material world they live in, which shapes them in return. Scientific progress leads to technical progress, creating a new world and a new Man. From this point of view, just as industry overtook manufacturing, sporting techniques were superior to those of the games and gymnastics that preceded them. Progress and the search for optimum production had the same value in productive work and in sporting competitions. The miner Alexey Stakhanov, the cosmonaut Yuri Gagarin, and the high-jumper Valeriy Brumel were "heroes of the Soviet Union" because they demonstrated (in work, space exploration, and sports, respectively) the superiority of the "new man." By demonstrating how human progress had been made possible by the emergence of a new society through its record-breaking exploits, "Red sport"[23] promoted an ideal that called for the transformation of human beings by science.

Massification corresponds to industrialization, and planning to the scientific organization of work. Technique, art, and action in all their forms, in every domain, freed from the quest for profit, were now at the service of the proletarian revolution. Medicine only ever takes care of people with illnesses; from this point of view, it was opposed by a science of maximal performance, which its main advocate termed "anthropomaximology."[24]

From my perspective, and lacking the space to devote this story to the thorough analysis it deserves, I would simply argue that the univocal relationship that placed technique, art, and action under the direct aegis of the sciences led to a twin failure. First, brilliant results were often driven by propaganda and, in sports, under the cover of "scientific" preparation, the organized, systematic use of performance-enhancing drugs. Also, it is necessary to recognize that art or technique cannot be reduced to science: the artist and the technician cannot be satisfied with *knowing*, with being able to explain the actions they have mastered. They also need to *do*, to *create* a work, object, or performance. As Kant wrote, "Art regarded as human skill differs from *science* (as *can* from *know*) as a practical faculty does from a theoretical, as Technic does from Theory (as mensuration from geometry). . . . Only that which a man, even if he knows it completely, may not therefore have the skill to accomplish, belongs to Art."[25] And, I would add to this, technique.[26]

---

23. Riordan, *Soviet Sport*.
24. Kuznetsov, "The Potentialities of Man and 'Anthropomaximology.'"
25. Kant, *Critique of Judgment*, 110.
26. As Georges Canguilhem points out in *La Connaissance de la Vie*, 122, this text from

The irreducibility of technique to science, of the organism to a machine, goes beyond the criticisms that reproach sport for transposing the logic of alienated work into leisure, and which developed from the 1960s onward at the same time as physical education was striving to become more sport-oriented. Those criticisms considered that "modern sport is the typical activity of an industrial society based on the scientific organization of work."[27] And in this society, "the worker who repeats the same movement all day has no closer brother than the runner who goes round and round a concrete track as mechanically as the arms of his stopwatch."[28] Athletes thus became doubly alienated; their liberty was confiscated by their trainer and by sporting institutions, and their right to play, to take pleasure in their endeavors, was redirected toward the ascetic search for performance. Consequently, athletes became archetypal of the "one-dimensional man" for whom administered liberty and intellectual repression become endlessly renewed sources of productivity.[29] The analogy between sport and industrial work is not without interest or relevance, yet it is nonetheless worth questioning the limits of its validity. The breaking-down of tasks by a division of labor pushed to the extreme, consisting—as the influential proponent of Taylorism, American mechanical engineer Frederick Winslow Taylor, recommended—of thinking of human functioning in terms of machines, turned out to be counterproductive in terms of quality and was inhumane for the workers. It is also important to mention that, since at least the mid-twentieth century, there emerged a critical tradition arguing that beyond a certain level of the division of labor and specialization there are negative effects, to the point of cancelling themselves out.[30] Finally, it appeared that technically superfluous movements that would have been suppressed by the comparison of the organism to a machine are often biologically necessary. This was another way of proving the irreducibility of the organism to a machine, which helps emphasize the limits of the analogy between athlete and robot.

Work and Interaction: Bodily Techniques and

the *Critique of Judgment* is quoted by Paul Krannhals, *Der Weltsinn der Technik* (Munich and Berlin: Oldenbourg, 1932), who sees it as the recognition of the fact that all technique contains, essentially and positively, a vital originality which is irreducible to rationalization.

27. Brohm, "Sociologie Politique du Sport," 19.

28. Laguillaumie, "Pour une Critique Fondamentale des Sports," 44.

29. Marcuse, *One Dimensional Man.*

30. Georges Friedmann, in *The Anatomy of Work*, quotes numerous U.S. authors who question the limits of Taylorism.

Tactics–Beyond an Opposition?

The foundational articles of motor praxeology appeared in 1967. They are linked to the context by two observations. A profound change came to be added to the "splitting-up" of physical education that gradually called the old dualist conceptions into question and placed at the heart of renewed physical education not the articulation of techniques approached in a mechanistic way or ascetic values, but the unity of a person involved in the action.

Reading what he wrote at the time, Pierre Parlebas seems divided between two attitudes. One stressed the importance of technique in the broad sense: "We have to consider that we are involved in a precise era, principally technical and industrial, and we must accept that."[31] From this point of view, he clearly refutes Hébert's discourse on "natural" motivity: "All the means Hébert made use of—words, language, knowledge, gestures, material means—are techniques. And if we *can* speak of human nature, is it not human nature to gain access from birth to culture?"[32] Here he develops the concept to its fullest.

The other attitude points to a much more restricted meaning of "technique" identified with mechanical repetition of formal gestures (calling structured gymnastics into question) and with learning conventional gestures borrowed from certain specialties (this is aimed at the sporting-education current). In short, "today is the era of technicism: the prestige of technique, measurement, and immediate efficacy is considerable. There is a growing tendency at the moment to adopt a few shining specialties and to overvalue them outrageously, to attempt through them a so-called complete development."[33]

One should link these positions to the observation from which Parlebas proposes analyzing the profound transformation of physical education through the 1960s, a sort of silent "Copernican revolution" that seems to reject technical conceptions because it refutes the old dualist conception, putting the unity of the person (not the dualist association of mechanics and morality) at the heart of physical education. "The advent of the psychomotor approach as a fundamental event is not the fruit of a brutal revolution, but of a slow evolution. Exercises tend to become no longer ends in themselves, but means of psychomotor enrichment. It is no longer technique and know-how that are fundamental, but the student who uses them. Our attention is directed away from the movement, and oriented toward the person who moves."[34]

---

31. Parlebas, "L'Education physique en Miettes," 11.
32. Ibid.
33. Ibid., 9.
34. Ibid., 13.

To summarize, it really seems that we are dealing here with a conception that associated technique and industry, affirming that it is a matter of a universe we cannot escape. In the background one can detect (the reference to fragmented work is a hint) that the analogy between the world of production and that of physical activities is seen as a danger for the latter. The mechanization of bodies by structured gymnastics and long repetitions constitutes a training that leads to a strict, closed adaptation. If we add that the advent of the psychomotor approach radically calls the dualist model into question, it appears that we can no longer talk of the body as a separate entity; we must think in terms of the unity of the active person engaged in a significant interaction with the environment and with others.

Parlebas suggests a science of motor action defined as an approach to phenomena of motor communication—a semiology of motivity. The essential concepts of this new discipline are presented in his *Contribution à un Lexique Commenté en Science de l'Action Motrice* (Contribution to a lexicon discussing the science of motor action, 1981), the third edition of which was published in 1999 with the title *Jeux, Sports et Société* (Games, sports, and society).[35] Communication implies the presence of a source of uncertainty, possibly situated in the physical environment where constructed spaces (a stadium, gymnasium, or pool, for example) are juxtaposed with open nature, whose difficulties have to be overcome. Uncertainty can also come from another person, and one has to learn to properly communicate; opposition may also heighten the level of uncertainty. In this regard we may identify three criteria, the combinations of which result in eight classes of physical activity.[36]

The first class contains numerous activities in which the subject acts alone in a stable space: running, jumping, throwing, acrobatics, and so on. There is no uncertainty in the physical environment and no one else is involved in these actions. Alone, and after much practice and repetition, the athlete manages to exhibit highly effective motor actions in which proprioceptive regulations are dominant. Performances are measured or judged, and the athlete strives for the best output. These motor situations express individual excellence and illustrate the ascetic search for the best possible human performance, something Jürgen Habermas terms "the bourgeois ideology of achievement" (*Leistungsideologie*), which "displaces assignment of status according to the standard of individual achievement from the market to the school system."[37]

---

35. Parlebas, "Classification," 7.
36. Ibid., 5–20.
37. Habermas, "Science and Technology as Ideology," 251.

We might consider that Coubertin, an advocate of education reform through sport, contributed to this displacement by replacing moderate, collective gymnastics with deliberately excessive, individualist sports. Moreover, if we return to Habermas's fundamental distinction between work (a "purposive-rational action") and interaction (a "communicative action" mediated by symbols),[38] it does seem that the sporting situations under consideration follow the logic of work and techniques of production.

As to the second class of motor actions that regroups cases in which the subject is alone but confronted with the uncertainty of the natural environment, one can ask to which of Habermas's two categories they belong. On this subject Habermas evokes a different relationship with nature, as proposed by Marcuse—rather than treating nature as an object (*Gegen-stand*) that we can make use of technically, we can go out and meet nature as a partner (*Gegen-spieler*) in a possible interaction. We can seek a fraternal nature instead of an exploited nature, and communicate with nature rather than simply working it without the slightest communication.[39] We must however recognize that even if this is an interesting way of distinguishing activities in nature from those in a constructed environment and from work activities, communicational action cannot be substituted for technical action because these two forms are complementary and cannot be dissociated.

All of the six other classes of motor activity are characterized by the presence of others either as partner and/or as adversary, both in stable and in uncertain environments. What is dominant here in defining the logic of motor situations is the semiological dimension. Action involves coordination with one's partner(s) in order to deceive one's opponent(s). From duels between individuals to duels between teams, the problematic is the same: we are in a world where gestures and acts are signs, and where the rules of games and sports constitute the codes that give them their meaning.

Parlebas's approach has led to a great many developments over the last half-century. Lacking space to mention them all here, I will conclude (following up on the concepts of Habermas[40]) with the question of what place they allow for technique.

In his thinking about knowledge, action, and power, and following Max Weber, Habermas distinguishes between two universes: that of work or "purposive-rational actions" and that of "communicative

---

38. Ibid., 244.
39. Ibid.
40. The following text is based on table in Habermas, "Science and Technology as Ideology," 245.

action" governed by "consensual norms."[41] The first group contains instrumental activities: those based on rational choice or guided by scientific knowledge, or those that combine both characteristics. Examples of these include athletics, swimming, gymnastics, and all other sporting activities that follow an experimental logic that varies the conditions of execution (all other things being equal) in order to control the effects on performance. Activities that proceed analytically, and in which training strategies are largely similar to the methods of life sciences form part of these purposive-rational actions. Incompetent performances result in failure, which is often measurable and always objectifiable. Here we are truly in the world of technique, of work, and we must often turn to the sciences[42] in order to develop the principles whose success is the basis of achievement.

The second universe is made up of *"communicative action,* symbolic interaction. It is governed by binding *consensual norms,* which define reciprocal expectations about behavior, and which must be understood and recognized by at least two acting subjects."[43] If we apply this definition to games and sports based on interaction with others, we see obvious points of convergence as well as differences.

The rules that orient action are indeed norms. They are present in everyday language, which defines for example the nature of possible interactions and the tolerated degree of violence in any given society. Language defines roles: they may be fraught with images as in games in which one is identified with a bear, a wolf, or a cat; or they may be more operation-oriented in sports with keepers, attackers, and defenders. By identifying with these roles, players are able to expect certain behaviors in response to their own. Learning, assimilating, and the interiorization of roles that resemble other roles all show a relationship between games, sports, and improvisational theater, the *commedia dell'arte.* In communicative action, the sharing of roles is the basis for maintaining the institutions that guarantee the rules, whose power serves to ensure the success of the spectacles they organize. Caught up in articulated roles, actions tell a story that an observer can transform into a narrative, and which the public can share. Finally, since rules have a normative origin in communicative activity, maintaining the game requires the presence and intervention of referees and judges who are invested with the power of sanction by the institution, to the extent that what the referee does not see can lead to deceptive successes.

There is a true convergence between the theory of action as pro-

---

41. Ibid., 244.
42. As opposed to the empirical practices of the past.
43. Habermas, "Science and Technology as Ideology," 244.

posed by Habermas (following Weber) and Parlebas's intention to tackle and classify motor situations according to their meaning. Hence situations with a low degree of "semiotricity"[44] resemble "purposive-rational actions," and situations of motor communication in which someone else is present and whose internal logic implies that presence resemble "communicative action." So much so that if we stretch the argument too far—since purposive-rational action is identified with work—one might consider that an important part of modern sport (that is, every situation in athletics, gymnastics, and swimming in which the athlete is acting alone) consists of introducing the logic of work (as characterized in industrial societies) into the sphere of leisure. This would result in dehumanized sports and alienated athletes in the same way that there is fragmented work for subservient workers; other sports are rich in interaction and properly human, and yet they are threatened, like these others, by an impoverishment of tasks, stereotyping, and alienation. Yet as I demonstrated earlier, reducing humans to machines, even from the simple point of view of the organism, is of limited efficacy; it is also difficult to defend theoretically. The opposition between purposive-rational action and communicative action is not the same as the opposition between man and machine, or between the "kingdom of nature" and the "kingdom of ends."[45] Both modes of action are human and form part of culture. This is the organizing principle in Parlebas's approach to motor situations: solitary activities termed "psychomotor" and interactive practices termed "sociomotor" are both part of the ensemble of "ethnomotor" practices, which signifies the range and cultural signification of all forms of motor action.

Conclusion

The purpose of this chapter is to illustrate the usefulness and potential range of reflection on games and sports. In order to do this, I chose the central question of action and technique.

My first objective was to show the dangers of common representations that, in the name of spontaneous play, simplicity, and liberty of sport, consider action in sports to be the result of the liberation of nature. This line of argument is often tainted with anti-intellectualism and aims to discredit intelligent approaches in order to keep a tighter control over people's bodies. Moreover, it has sometimes led to the ex-

---

44. Semiotricity refers to "the nature and field of motor situations seen as putting in play systems of signs directly associated with the motor behavior of participants." Parlebas, *Jeux, Sports et Sociétés*, 324.

45. "Reich der Zwecke" as opposed to "Reich der Natur," in Kant, *Groundwork of the Metaphysics of Morals*, 101.

altation of strength.

Second, I discussed an already long tradition based on the working of machines as a way of understanding and exercising the body—a construction to be straightened and consolidated; a thermodynamic machine; an engine one breaks in by making it run at different speeds; a cybernetic machine whose information-processing capacities can be enhanced. The body and its practices in this tradition of thought are part of the universe of techniques and sciences. Despite their contributions, however, the limits of these models lead me to conclude that the organism is not reducible to a machine, nor is technique reducible to science. If these distinctions are not maintained, we begin to risk viewing sports as merely the mechanization and taming of the body, following the logic of industrial labor.

Third, I aimed to overcome the difficulties encountered in the first two traditions. By making a connection between the analyses of Parlebas and Habermas, I sought to show that, whereas the opposition between purposive-rational action and communicative action covers the distinction between psychomotor and sociomotor practices, the convergence between the two forms of motor practice defined by their internal logic (that is, from the point of view of their meaning in the context of ethnomotricity) leads me to note (1) the presence of meaning where techniques oriented toward a result are present, and (2) the search for a result where phenomena of praxic communication are essential and define the rules of action. There is no separate mechanized motivity "in fragments" on one hand, and meaningful socialized motivity on the other; rather, there are bodily techniques and tactics on both sides, like two faces of the same coin.

Bibliography

Barthes, Roland. "Poujade and the Intellectuals." In *Mythologies*. Translated by Richard Howard and Annette Lavers, 206–14. New York: Hill and Wang, 2012.

Brohm, Jean-Marie. "Sociologie Politique du Sport." In *Sport, Culture et Répression*, edited by Ginette Berthaud, Jean-Marie Brohm, François Gantheret, and Pierre Laguillaumie. Paris: Maspero, 1972.

Buytendijk, F. J. J. *Attitudes et Mouvements*. Brussels: Desclée de Brouwer, 1957.

Canguilhem, Georges. *La Connaissance de la Vie*. Paris: Librarie Hachette, 1952.

Coubertin, Pierre de. "Extract from a Report to the Minister of Public

Instruction, 1915." In *Textes Choisis, T3: Pratique Sportive*. Zurich: CIO Weidmann, 1986.

Durry, Jean. *Le Vrai Pierre de Coubertin*. Paris: CFPC, 1997.

Elias, Norbert and Eric Dunning. *The Quest for Excitement: Sport and Leisure in the Civilizing Process*. Oxford and New York: Blackwell, 1986.

Fournié, Raoul. *L'Homme Sain* 1 (1945).

Friedmann, Georges. *The Anatomy of Work: Labor, Leisure, and the Implications of Automation*. Translated by Wyatt Rawson. Westport, Conn.: Greenwood Press, 1978.

Habermas, Jürgen. "Science and Technology as Ideology." In *Jürgen Habermas on Society and Politics: A Reader*, edited by Steven Seidman. Boston: Beacon Press, 1989.

Hansenne, Marcel. "En toute liberté." *L'Équipe* (Paris), October 30, 1976.

Hébert, Georges. *L'Education Physique Virile et Morale par la Méthode Naturelle*. Paris: Vuibert, 1936.

Huizinga, Johan. *Homo Ludens: A Study of the Play Element in Culture*. New York: Roy Publishers, 1950.

Kant, Immanuel. Critique of Judgment

———. *Groundwork of the Metaphysics of Morals*, edited and translated by Mary Gregore and Jens Timmermann. Cambridge: Cambridge University Press, 2011.

Krannhals, Paul. *Der Weltsinn der Technik*. Munich and Berlin: Oldenbourg, 1932.

Kuznetsov, V. V. "The Potentialities of Man and 'Anthropomaximology.'" "Sporting Life: Its Political, Social and Educational Aspects." Special issue, *International Social Science Journal* 34, no. 2 (1982): 277–89.

Laguillaumie, Pierre. "Pour une Critique Fondamentale des Sports." In *Sport, Culture et Répression*, edited by Ginette Berthaud, Jean-Marie Brohm, François Gantheret, and Pierre Laguillaumie. Paris: Maspero, 1972.

Lévi-Strauss, Claude. *Introduction to the Work of Marcel Mauss*. Translated by Felicity Baker. London: Routledge and Kegan Paul, 1987.

Marcuse, Herbert. *One Dimensional Man: Studies in the Ideology of Advanced Industrial Society*. Boston: Beacon Press, 1964.

Mauss, Marcel. "Body Techniques." In *Incorporations*, edited by Jonathan Crary and Sanford Kwinter. New York: Zone, 1992.

Merleau-Ponty, Maurice. *Phenomenology of Perception*. Translated by Donald A. Landes. London and New York: Routledge and Kegan Paul, 2012.

Parlebas, Pierre. "Classification." In *Contribution à un Lexique Commenté en Science de l'Action Motrice*. Paris: INSEP, 1981.

———. "L'Education physique en Miettes." In *Activités Physiques et Education Motrice*. Dossier EPS 4. Paris: Revue éducation physique et sport, 1990.

———. *Jeux, Sports et Sociétés: Lexique de Praxéologie Motrice*. Paris: INSEP, 1999.

Plato, *Republic*. Book 3. At www.perseus.tufts.edu/hopper/text?doc=Perseus%3Atext%3A1999.01.0168%3Abook%3D3%3Asection%3D411e.

Riordan, James. *Soviet Sport: Background to the Olympics*. Oxford: Basil Blackwell, 1980.

Simondon, Gilbert. *Du Mode d'Existence des Objets Techniques*. Paris: Aubier, 1989.

8

The Taste for Risk in Sportspeople: How Do They Play a "Chickie-Run" Game?

Luc Collard

A Love of Danger?

When I was a young physical education teacher, my colleagues and I used to organize an annual high-risk sports camp for our high school classes. The students were unruly teenagers having problems at school, and the program involved outdoor climbing, rafting, canoeing, and bungee-jumping. Throughout these years and despite many difficulties, we never had a single accident. Nevertheless, one day our principal asked us to stop this program of high-risk activities for these kinds of students—in other words, we were obliged to stop offering potentially dangerous sports to such "hotheads." Instead, according to him, they needed to learn how to control themselves and not to become risk-takers (which they already were in any case). I have never been convinced by this point of view, which is the reason I chose to write my thesis on the educational interest of high-risk sports. Unfortunately, I found that most of the scholarly literature concurred with my principal's arguments.

In the literature, some athletes are often accused of irresponsible behavior and have been compared to risk-taking deviants—drug and sex addicts, delinquents, and so on—who are rebelling against established norms.[1] Thrill-seeking in sport has been linked with the psychological trait of impulsiveness, "fleeing from self-consciousness,"[2] and the quest for a state of euphoria. Given the lack of reference points in society itself, the player in search of meaning in his/her life supposedly poses the ultimate question: life or death? They abandon themselves to sensory exhilaration, unhesitatingly agree to put themselves through a

---

1. Assailly, *Les jeunes et le risque*; Peretti-Watel, *Sociologie du risqué*.
2. Lafollie, "Detection of High-risk Personalities in Risky Sports."

life-threatening ordeal,[3] and adopt an extreme attitude to the task at hand; in short, specialists in dangerous outdoor sports are sometimes described as being blinded by their love of danger.[4] Despite their realistic judgments regarding their higher probability of being seriously injured while participating in their sport (in comparison with the average sportsperson), practitioners of dangerous sports believe in their abilities to cope with risk, inducing lower feelings of vulnerability.[5]

Even though the interviews or questionnaires used in these studies provided information on how high-risk sports specialists say (or think) they behave, these tools did not assess the sportspeople's true behavior. Hence, given the lack of *in vivo* validation, we decided to assess the hypothesis relating to a "thirst for risk" by observing the actions of sixty-six sportspeople during a game that enabled true risk-taking. We sought to establish how these extreme sports specialists behave and whether or not they take more risks than specialists in other sports.

The novelty of this approach relates to the consideration of physical games or sports as a laboratory for human behavior in general.[6] Indeed, depending on the type of game, one can witness drama, inhibition, pleasure, aggressiveness, inventiveness, and humor.[7]

In order to measure risk-taking, one can use a "paradoxical" game in which the protagonists must position themselves with respect to a dual constraint: (1) the need to protect themselves from the worst-case scenario by obtaining little reward, and (2) the prospect of obtaining greater reward by becoming dependent on the other players' benevolence. Players are thus subjected to a dilemma that they resolve according to their risk-averse or risk-taking nature. Game theory provides many models for which one can calculate the ideal behavior if players play perfectly rationally in order to maximize their gains and minimize their losses.[8] Thus, one is able to estimate the ideal behavior and compare it with the players' true behavior in a motor situation. In fact, this approach enables the objective measurement of subjectivity. The combination of rationality and reality within a play activity is the domain of behavioral game theory.[9] The literature on the topic reports deviations between ideal behavior and what is actually observed in practice.

3. Le Breton, *Conduites à risque.*

4. Donnelly, "Sport and Risk Culture," 29–58.

5. Martha, Laurendeau, and Griffet, "Comparative Optimism and Risky Road Traffic Behavior Among High-risk Sports Practitioners," 429–44.

6. Parlebas, "Elementary Mathematical Modelization of Games and Sports."

7. Parlebas, "Jeu sportif, rêve et fantaisie."

8. von Neumann and Morgenstern, *Theory of Games and Economic Behavior*; Shubik, *Game Theory in the Social Sciences.*

9. Kagel and Roth, eds., *Handbook of Experimental Economics.*

These deviations are related to several different factors, ranging from "reasons to believe" (for example, erroneous perception of probabilities related to the player's level of experience of games in which chance has a role);[10] through individual preferences for risk-taking (as in the private value auction game); to compliance with a moral stance (as in the coordination game).[11] However, to the best of my knowledge, none of the experiments to date have involved the physical resolution of this type of game.

How to Play "Chickie-Run" and Survive

"Chickie-run" takes its name from the famous car challenge in the 1955 movie *Rebel Without a Cause*, starring James Dean. It is similar to the famous "prisoner's dilemma" game developed by Albert W. Tucker.[12] Here, the sum of individual interests does not necessarily lead to a collective optimum.[13]

Starting from opposite ends of a gym (20 meters/65 feet apart), two players (Player L, the "line" player, and Player C, the "column" player, by reference to the score matrices presented below) run straight toward each other (figure 8.1a). If the two players collide {*Continue, Continue*}, they each lose two points (figure 8.1b). If both "chicken out" at the last moment {*Defect, Defect*}, each player scores two points (figure 8.1c). If one defects and the other continues {*Defect, Continue*}, the defector scores nothing and the non-defector scores four points (figure 8.1d).

The following additional rules and safety measures were implemented:

- In order to avoid a collision when both players defected, the latter were told to always deviate to their right.
- Any contact whatsoever between the players was counted as {*Continue, Continue*}.
- To ensure that the players ran at roughly the same speed, they had to arrive within a three-meter/ten-foot central zone (marked out with cones) at the same time.

Each participant played only once against each of the other players (in other words, sixty-five matches per player). The personal payoffs in each match (−2, 0, +2, or +4) were noted on a summary table. Before

---

10. Condorcet, *Essai sur l'application de l'analyse à la probabilité des décisions rendues à la pluralité des voix*; Allais, "Le Comportement de l'homme rationnel devant le risque: critique des postulats et axiomes de l'école Américaine."

11. Harsanyi, "A New Theory of Equilibrium Selection for Games with Complete Information."

12. Tucker, "A Two Persons Dilemma."

13. Harsanyi, "Morality and the Theory of Rational Behavior."

each match, players were able to consult information on their opponent's past strategy. This was a full-information game because each player was aware of (1) his/her possible actions, (2) the actions that could be adopted by the other player, (3) the full range of possible outcomes and the corresponding gains and losses, and (4) the other player's motives and reputation, as well as his or her own. To gain time, six matches took place simultaneously within a number of parallel tracks in the gym. Each match lasted an average of one minute (from meeting the opponent until the outcome). The need to organize 2,145 matches during three half-day sessions and the recording of the results in a double-entry table did not allow us to take account of the order of the matches; each player chose an opponent when one was available, without worrying about his or her position in the "league table." Once the table had been completed, it was impossible for the researchers to assess the "reputation" effect, even though the players may have taken account of it in the heat of the action.

Each player had to note his or her name, sport, and body weight on the table so that this information was available to their opponents. Indeed, body weight may be a potential confounding factor by inciting lighter players to defect more readily when faced with heavier players.

Figure 8.1. The chickie-run game.

a. *Starting from opposite ends of the gym, the two players run straight toward each other.*

b. *If both players continue straight on, they collide in the 3-meter/10 foot-long central zone and each loses two points.*

c. *If the player in white "chickens out" before the central zone and the player in black crosses the line without deviating, the player in white scores no points and the player in black scores four points.*

d. *If both players deviate from the line, each scores two points.*

e. *At the end of the match, the players enter their score in a summary table and then go on to play against each of the remaining players. Players are able to consult their future opponents' results on the summary table.*

We studied 66 adult sports students (25 young women and 41 young men). The mean ± standard deviation (SD) age was 20.3 ± 1.2. All players participated voluntarily in the study. Thirteen participants weighed under 55 kilos (approximately 120 pounds), thirty-six weighed between 55 and 70 kilos (120 to 155 pounds), and seventeen weighed over 70 kilos (155 pounds).

We sought to compare the behavior of the high-risk sports specialists (climbing, diving, and so on, coded as *ClimbDive*; n=9) with that of three other categories of sportspeople: specialists in individual sports that take place in highly predictable physical and human environments (gymnastics, swimming, and so on, coded as *GymSwim*; n=14), players in team sports that take place in a partly controlled environment (coded as *SoccerRugby*; n=32), and indoor combat sports specialists (wrestling, boxing, and martial arts, coded as *Combat*; n=11). All students were experts in their respective sports who trained several times per week and played competitively.

From a Rational Point of View

The dilemma in "chickie-run" consists of an absence of dominant tactics. In other words, neither *Continue* nor *Defect* tactics dominate in absolute terms (figure 8.2).

The first figure in parentheses corresponds to the score (payoff) for player L ("Line"), and the second corresponds to the score for player C ("Column"). With this payoff matrix and in an iterated game (65 matches), taking risks ("Continue") is not better than playing cautiously ("Defect").

Figure 8.2. Score matrix for the chickie-run game

Player C

		Defect	Continue
layer L	Defect	(+2, +2)	(0, +4)
	Continue	(+4, 0)	(−2, −2)

The best of a bad situation corresponds to the "best possible worst case" scenario. Playing *Maximin* equates to playing {*Defect, Defect*} all the time. Even if the opponent changes his or her tactics (by playing *Continue* to move from +2 to +4, see figure 8.3), playing *Maximin* guarantees at least 0 (instead of +2 if the opponent also plays *Maximin*), which is always better than -2. This way, the worst case scenario is avoided. If each player plays *Maximin*, the chance of reward is {+2, +2} each time.

On a scale from -2 to +4, this score is satisfactory. However, this is not a balanced situation. If one player maintains his or her chosen tactics, the other will gain by changing tactics.

There is a second solution: the Nash equilibrium. In this type of game, playing the equilibrium consists of "minimizing the opponent's maximum."[14] This way, neither of the players is tempted to change tactics if the other maintains his or hers.[15] This solution was offered by John Nash, whose life is featured in the movie *A Beautiful Mind* (2001).

From a purely strategic standpoint, this game has two Nash equilibriums: {*Continue, Defect*} and {*Defect, Continue*}—{+4, 0} and {0, +4}. However, these are suboptimal for the player scoring 0. Because the game is iterated against all the other players, there is a mixed-strategy Nash equilibrium that can improve the overall outcome for the two players (L and C). This consists of playing safe once every other time (p=0.5).

When considering the results, we used the term "Maximin profile" to refer to players who deviated in more than 75 percent of the matches (because this value corresponds to the average of the probabilities for the Maximin and Nashian strategies). In contrast, a player who deviated less than 50 percent of the time was classified as reckless (the "risk-taker" profile). Finally, a player adopting the intermediate, balanced position (independently of the opponent's reputation) was referred to as "Nashian."

Nice Guys Finish First

None of the subgroups of sportspeople played exactly as expected. For the population as a whole, the 2,145 matches generated 2,166 points—that is, a score per match E_{real} of +1.01 Pt/m, almost exactly what a mixed-strategy Nash equilibrium would yield. The tactical combination {*Defect, Defect*} was observed in 30.2 percent of cases, instead of 25 percent (or half of 50 percent) for a *Nashian* strategy and 100 percent for *Maximin*. The {*Continue, Continue*} combination occurred in 21.3 percent of matches (instead of the 25 percent expected for *Nashian* and 0 percent for *Maximin*).

As with the GymSwim players, the ClimbDive players defected in 75 percent of cases (the Maximin profile). They were more cautious than the Combat players, who continued in more than 50 percent of the matches. The SoccerRugby players were at the equilibrium (the Nashian profile). The "thrill-seekers" obtained the best aggregate score

---

14. Barbut, "Jeux et mathématiques," 857.

15. Nash, "Equilibrium Points in N-person Games," 48–49; Nash, "Non-Cooperative Games," 286–95.

per match (+1.34). (The scores in intra-subgroup matches were not taken into account).

Figure 8.3. Percentage of tactical combinations in each subgroup (lines) versus the other sportspeople (columns).

		Other players	
GymSwim players	N = 728 ↗	Defect	Continue
E* = +0.88	Defect	35% (254)	38% (277)
	Continue	12% (88)	15% (109)

		Other players	
"High-risk sports"	N = 513 ↗	Defect	Continue
ClimbDive players	Defect	46% (236)	27% (139)
E* = +1.34	Continue	16% (82)	11% (56)

		Other players	
Combat players	N = 605 ↗	Defect	Continue
E* = +0.9	Defect	24% (145)	19% (115)
	Continue	26% (157)	31% (118)

		Other players	
SoccerRugby players	N = 1088 ↗	Defect	Continue
E* = +1.01	Defect	23% (250)	26% (282)
	Continue	26% (284)	25% (272)

* E= expected gain per match; ** The three other subgroups of sportspeople (column) confronted with the "line" subgroup.

Because the goal of the present research was to measure the appetite for risk in extreme sports specialists, figure 8.4 compares their strategies with those of other types of sportspeople (with a total of 513 matches = 9 ClimbDive x [14 GymSwim + 11 Combat + 32 SoccerRugby]), and displays the strategies of each subgroup vis-à-vis the three others. Even though all the head-to-head matches took place (2,145), the presentation in figure 8.4 excludes the 678 matches between players from the same sporting subgroup; we wanted to accentuate any differences by opposing the various subgroups. The GymSwim subgroup played 728 matches against the three other subgroups (14 x [9 + 11 + 32]), the Combat group played 605 matches (11 x [9 + 14 + 32]), and the SoccerRugby group (the largest population) played 1,088 matches (32 x [9 + 11 + 14]). The detailed results show that the high-risk sports specialists (ClimbDive) tended to play cautiously (the Maximin profile). This phenomenon was also observed in the GymSwim subgroup, with one difference: they only obtained 0.88 Pt/m, compared with 1.34 Pt/m for the ClimbDive subgroup (with a significant difference in Student's T test, T=2.9, Degrees Of Freedom [DOF] =21, p<0.01). Not only were the dangerous sports specialists the most cautious, they also minimized their losses. The fact that caution can maximize gains is one of the characteristics of this type of n-player, namely no zero-sum game.[16] In practical terms

---

16. Harsanyi, "Morality and the Theory of Rational Behavior."

and when the game is repeated, cooperative (cautious) strategies tend to dominate egocentric (risky) strategies.[17] This was this case for the *ClimbDive* subgroup but not for the *GymSwim* subgroup.

The *Combat* subgroup was the most reckless and played *"Continue"* in over 50 percent of matches (figure 8.3). This appetite for risk did not pay off and yielded only 0.9 Pt/m (that is, a significantly [p<0.05] lower score than *ClimbDive* [$T=2.44$, DOF=18]). The *SoccerRugby* subgroup adopted a mixed equilibrium strategy (*Nashian*), enabling an average score of 1 Pt/m.

An analysis of the 678 intra-subgroup matches showed that the members of each family of sports specialists played against each other in the same way as they did against the members of other subgroups (Chi-squared=1.44, DOF=3, ns).

Given that the four sports subgroups were not matched in terms of sample size, gender, and body weight, it was necessary to refine the results. In order to see whether cautiousness (*Maximin*) is indeed related to the sport practiced and not (through a linkage effect) to other explanatory factors (gender or weight), we performed a logistic regression using the TRI2 software developed by Philippe Cibois.[18] All 2,145 parties (that is, including the 678 intra-subgroup matches) were taken into account.

Let us take a reference situation: MALE MIDDLEWEIGHT SOCCERRUGBY (with MAXIMIN as the dependent variable, figure 8.4), accounting for 14.3 percent of the population. For each of the other modalities, we calculated the marginal effects, all other things being equal. Female gender (Female) increased the likelihood of cautious behavior (MAXIMIN) by 8.1 percent (odds ratio [OR]=1.73). Being heavy (HEAVYWEIGHT) or light (LIGHTWEIGHT) had the same, negative effect (OR=0.43 and 0.64, respectively), and individuals in these subgroups were 4.7 percent and 7.6 percent more likely to take risks, respectively. However, these three aspects were only trends and did not achieve statistical significance. Only belonging to the CLIMBDIVE and GYMSWIM subgroups appears to be significantly explanatory at p<0.01 (OR=7.67, +41.8 percent and OR=6.94, +39.4 percent). Hence, the high-risk sports specialists were more cautious than the other sportspeople because of their sporting background and not because of their gender and body weight characteristics. Indeed, they shared these characteristics with the *GymSwim* subgroup.

---

17. Axelrod, "Effective Choice in the Prisoner's Dilemma"; Axelrod, "More Effective Choice in the Prisoner's Dilemma"; Axelrod and Hamilton, "The Evolution of Cooperation."

18. Cibois, *Les méthodes d'analyse d'enquêtes.*

The dependent variable is MAXIMIN, and the reference situation is MALE MIDDLEWEIGHT SOCCERRUGBY. Some characteristics are more important than others in the explanation of prudent behavior (MAXIMIN). They are evaluated in terms of the odds ratio and the corresponding marginal effects (as a percentage). The most strongly explanatory elements are the CLIMBDIVE and GYMSWIM (***, p<0.01) specialties. The other factors did not have a statistically significant influence (ns).

Figure 8.4. Logistic regression for identifying explanatory factors for cautious behavior (Maximin).

Dependent variable: MAXIMIN					
		Coeff.	Chances	Percent.	
Reference situation:		−1.7916	0.1667	14.3	
			Odds ratio	Marg. effect	Test
Gender	MALE	Ref.			
	FEMALE	0.5467	1.73	8.1	ns
Bodyweight	LIGHTWEIGHT	−0.4477	0.64	−4.7	ns
	MIDDLEWEIGHT	Ref.			
	HEAVYWEIGHT	−0.8395	0.43	−7.6	ns
Sport	COMBAT	−0.0003	1.00	0.0	ns
	SOCCERRUGBY	Ref.			
	CLIMBDIVE	2.0369	7.67	41.8	***
	GYMSWIM	1.9378	6.94	39.4	***

High-Risk Sports Specialists Are Not Risk-Takers

Given the current state of our research, it is impossible to say whether the observed correlations were causal. Why did the high-risk sports specialists play the game more cautiously than the others and end up with a better overall score? Are there psychological factors that predispose certain people to take up extreme sports? Or does the intensive performance of extreme sports tend to modify attitudes when playing "chickie-run"?

One possible explanation may be found in the physical (motor) relevance and novelty of the "chickie-run" dilemma. A mathematical game is an abstract system that is entirely controllable by abstraction; once a player has decided on his or her strategy, he or she can simply note it on a piece of paper and then leave the room, and the game is over before it even begins! In the "chickie-run" game described here, the player's choice of strategy (*Maximin/Nashian/Risk-Taker*) is just the start. Regardless of the underlying, abstract plan, the game consists of a motor act. When two players face off against each other, there is only one imperative: to make the opponent deviate, or at least try to make that happen. To this end, the players must use "motor intelligence"— that is, intimidation (making the opponent comply with my demands) and persuasion (preventing the opponent from believing that he or she has dominated me). How, then, can this motor intelligence be implemented? By waiting until the last moment to take a deviate/continue decision and by counting on the opponent's fear of collision—this is the basic principle behind a game that, regrettably, became even more famous when James Dean died in a head-on car crash.

Depending on their particular sporting experience (in training and competition), participants may vary in their ability to decipher and mask behavioral patterns without panicking. The low score in the *GymSwim* group appears to bear this out. The absence of a direct opponent and the standardization of gymnastics equipment are unlikely to prompt frequent "motor decisions." However, in this strategic game, is it not strange that sportspersons used to dealing with uncertainty generated by other players (namely, the *Combat* and *SoccerRugby* groups) had lower scores (figure 8.3) than sportspersons confronted only with the unpredictability of the natural environment (that is, *ClimbDive*)? Were the team sports and combat sports specialists victims of their familiarity with two-player and zero-sum games? In the world of sporting duels where one player's loss is the other's gain, only antagonistic behavior (holds, punches, and shots) changes the score. In "chickie-run," things are different; strategies are conditional and an overly high frequency of aggressive interactions {*Continue, Continue*} resulted in lower gains for the *Combat* and *SoccerRugby* groups. The transfer of sporting behavior patterns to inappropriate motor situations has already been observed.[19]

A second explanation has to do with the reputation that the sportspersons build up blow-by-blow. Because the game is always played against different players and full information is available, each player can identify his or her future opponent's past behavior and adjust the strategy accordingly: "defect" when faced with an opponent known to "continue" more than 50 percent of the time and "continue" when the opposite is true. Our experimental protocol did not enable us to take this variable into account because the order of the matches was not recorded. It doubtless had some impact, however. With over two thousand matches, would extreme sports specialists have exhibited greater cognitive abilities in odds estimation and anticipation (that is, taking into account how their opponents had played in their previous matches) than the other subgroups?

The results nevertheless suggest that people who are often described as "extreme sports" specialists are far from extreme in terms

---

19. Oboeuf and Collard, "Agressivité motrice"; Collard and Loyer, "'La bataille des nageurs.'"

of their behavior. This conclusion confirms two surveys performed ten years apart.[20] Briefly, the surveys were based on indirect questionnaires and examined the participants' statements about risk. This made the surveys less robust but easier to administer than measurements of motor behavior. In comparison with standard psychometric tests and interviews, the two surveys were novel in as much as the responders did not have total control over their responses. To this end, we used the Condorcet method,[21] in which pairs of items are submitted to a ballot by the responders. In my 1998 survey and in that performed by Mariani in 2011, the ballot items were characteristic traits in high-risk sports: "control" (over a tricky situation), "nature" (synchrony, harmony with the wildness of the natural environment), "novelty" (the use of novel equipment and movements), "risk" (potential danger that could lead to an accident), and "thrill" (a strong emotion that disrupts the usual equilibrium). These items are presented in pairs; for each of the ten distinct pairs, the responders circle the item that motivates them most. The 2011 survey was based on a sample of 61 surfers, 98 windsurfers, 148 kite-surfers, and 48 multiple sports specialists (surf + kite-surf or surf + windsurf), all of whom performed at an international level. The 1998 work surveyed 91 French sports students who were national-level high-risk sports specialists.

With this type of arrangement, the responders' memory cannot totally condition their choice in logical terms. Although the question is not ambiguous and demands an immediate judgment, it can reveal some absurd rankings known as "cursed triplets." For example, it is possible for an answer to highlight an illogical ranking such as thrill > nature > risk > thrill (where ">" means "preferred to"). The presence of an intransitive triplet (a famous "cursed triplet") is symptomatic of the Condorcet effect (CE). In a five-item ballot such as this, a given response can have five intransitive triplets. The greater the CE (that is, the higher the number of intransitive triplets), the more difficult it becomes to differentiate between the items.

The result given most frequently by the 91 sports students was transitive, and the collective choices were apparently homogeneous. Strikingly, "risk" was ranked in last place as a motivating factor in "high-risk" sports. This confirms the "chickie-run" findings and contrasts with the supposed "passion for risk" and "suicidal violence" described in the scholarly literature. Mariani's 2011 results are similar in

---

20. Collard, *Sports, enjeux et accidents*; Mariani, "Le risque en question dans le loisir sportif de nature."
21. Condorcet, *Essai sur l'application de l'analyse à la probabilité des décisions rendues à la pluralité des voix.*

all respects to my 1998 findings.

What motivates our specialists above all are strong emotions and the mastery of imbalance (the "thrill" trait) in synchrony with the natural environment (the "nature" trait) and the "novelty" associated with the use of new techniques. In the wild, these sportspeople are seeking unhindered adventure, which requires significant self-control. The "thrill" trait is the most captivating; it attracted 70 out of 91 votes when paired with the novelty trait, 77 votes when paired with "control," 65 votes when paired with "nature," and 51 votes (namely, 5 more than the majority of 46 votes) when paired with "risk." In other words, the inversion of 6 "thrill vs. risk" votes (6.5 percent of the total) would be enough to change the shape of the majority ballot and increase the CE to the maximum level possible. In fact, the majority of responders preferred the "nature" trait to "risk" (66 votes), "novelty" (84 votes), and "control" (72 votes). The "novelty" trait won twice, against "risk" (68 votes) and "control" (54 votes). The control trait received only 1 majority vote (against "risk," with 75 votes nevertheless). By inversing the 6 votes between thrill and risk, three intransitive triplets would appear in the majority ballot: thrill > novelty> risk > thrill, thrill > nature > risk > thrill, and thrill > control > risk > thrill. Three intransitive triplets (out of a possible maximum of five) correspond to a CE of 60 percent. The group's apparent homogeneity is, then, illusory. It masks latent heterogeneity suggesting that it is difficult to determine the underlying, motivating factors in high-risk sports.

Processing the individual data reveals a 10-percent CE, with only one "cursed triplet." For these responders, the intransitive triplets were always related to the "risk/thrill/nature" triplet (six as "thrill > risk > nature > thrill" and three as "thrill > nature > risk > thrill"). For example, "risk" is preferred to "thrill" and "thrill" preferred to "nature," but then "nature" is preferred to "risk"! This sign of incoherence (found nine times in the survey) is doubtless due to subjective overlap between the judgment criteria—dangerousness is associated with a radical change in the internal equilibrium and is characteristic of the wildness of the natural environment. These three traits (with similar connotations) probably explain the confusion expressed by our young responders.

The presence of a CE in individual data and for 6.5 percent of the votes in the group ballot testifies to the responders' difficulty in expressing their attraction for high-risk activities in a purely cognitive mode (that is, by verbalization). This may explain the disparity between the literature findings on risk-taking sportspeople on the basis of interviews and psychometric tests (namely the attraction of danger and disdain for death) and what is observed here "in the flesh" with game theory applied to the "chickie-run" experiment (that is, securitizing behavior and an aversion to deliberate risk-taking). This mismatch between words and acts appears in an extraordinary narrative by Douglas Robertson in *The Last Voyage of the Lucette* (2005).[22] On board their forty-three-foot schooner *Lucette*, the Robertson family set sail from the south of England in January 1971. Eighteen months seaborne in the middle of the Pacific, *Lucette* was holed by killer whales and sank. Four adults and two children survived the next thirty-eight days adrift in a nine-foot dinghy before being rescued by a Japanese fishing vessel. The author describes the day-by-day hell that he and the other survivors endured, and the self-control they needed to perform acts such as drinking their own urine (or that of others) or injecting sea water via the rectum. However, Dougal Robertson (the father) remembered this odyssey with nostalgia and reported the comments made by two of his children after they had been rescued: "Douglas told me even before we had reached Panama that he would thank me every day of his life for giving him such an adventure, and Neil stated in a moment of shipboard boredom that he preferred it on the raft."[23]

However, the reader knows better; neither of the two children said as much when adrift after the sinking. This is typically termed "making a virtue of necessity," and contemporary television programs exploit this vein. For example, ex-Special Forces soldier Bear Grylls deals slickly with high-risk situations in *Man vs. Wild*. However, the show often forgets to mention that Grylls is surrounded by a whole safety team—yes to risk-taking, as long as there is no danger!

Not So Rebel, and with a Cause

High-risk sports (motocross, sea diving, kite surfing, and so on) have a number of identifiable characteristics that set them apart from other social activities. Indeed, high-risk sports are the only legal, life-threatening social activities that are apparently practiced for their own sake. What do we expect and what do the participants expect from the "roll of the dice" in these situations?

Sportspeople are often stereotyped as suicidal, behavioral deviants who are revolting against the norm. As surprising as it may seem, our observations strongly indicate that high-risk sports participants have a special distaste for risk. If our findings turn out to be correct, one could reasonably include high-risk sports in physical education programs in which the ultimate objective is safety. To this end, it may be valuable

22. Robertson, *The Last Voyage of the Lucette*.
23. Ibid., 348.

to introduce learners to motor situations with high levels of subjective but low levels of objective risk. This situation works as a paradox. To be safe, one must avoid danger. However, by always avoiding danger, one is deprived of the opportunity to confront it with confidence.

"The main utility I see in my erstwhile mountaineering days was the education of my composure, which enabled me to sleep upright on the narrowest ledge while overlooking an abyss," wrote Marcel Mauss in 1934 before adding (with respect to education): "It consists especially of education in composure. And the latter is above all a retarding mechanism, a mechanism inhibiting disordered movements; this retardation subsequently allows a coordinated response of coordinated movements setting off in the direction of the chosen goal. This resistance to emotional seizure is something fundamental in social and mental life."[24] This quality also enabled the players to maximize their gains in the "chickie-run" game.

This fundamental aptitude is an important issue in our educational system. The balance of the skier, the skillfulness of the motorcyclist, and the confidence of the climber are not the sole determinants of sporting success but constitute its main objective. Physical education can help schoolchildren acquire this "resistance to emotional seizure" by offering them the opportunity to perform sporting activities with an aura of risk and adventure.

Bibliography

Allais, Maurice. "Le Comportement de l'homme rationnel devant le risque: critique des postulats et axiomes de l'école Américaine." *Econometrica* 21 (1953): 503–46.

Assailly, Jean-Pascal. *Les jeunes et le risque: Une approche psychologique de l'accident.* Paris: Vigot, 1992.

Axelrod, Robert. "Effective Choice in the Prisoner's Dilemma." *Journal of Conflict Resolution* 24, no. 1 (1980): 3–25.

———. "More Effective Choice in the Prisoner's Dilemma." *Journal of Conflict Resolution* 24, no. 3 (1980): 379–403.

Axelrod, Robert, and William D. Hamilton. "The Evolution of Cooperation." *Science* 211 (1981): 1390–96.

Barbut, Marc. "Jeux et mathématiques: Jeux qui ne sont pas de pur hazard." In *Jeux et sports*, edited by Roger Caillois. Paris: Encyclopédie de la Pléiade, 1967.

Cibois, Philippe. *Les méthodes d'analyse d'enquêtes.* Paris: Presses Univer-

---

24. Mauss, "Body Techniques," 474.

sitaires de France, 2007.

Collard, Luc. *Sports, enjeux et accidents*. Paris: Presses Universitaires de France, 1998.

Collard, Luc, and Frédéric Loyer. "'La bataille des nageurs': Illustration d'un conflit entre préférences individuelles et intérêt collectif." *Mathematics and Social Sciences* 188, no. 4 (2009): 41–53.

Condorcet, Antoine. *Essai sur l'application de l'analyse à la probabilité des décisions rendues à la pluralité des voix*. Paris: De l'Imprimerie Royale, 1785.

Donnelly, Peter. "Sport and Risk Culture." In *Sporting Bodies, Damaged Selves: Sociological Studies of Sports-related Injury*, edited by Kevin Young. Boston: Elsevier, 2004.

Harsanyi, John C. "Morality and the Theory of Rational Behavior." *Social Research* 44, no. 4 (1977): 623–56.

——. "A New Theory of Equilibrium Selection for Games with Complete Information." *Games and Economic Behavior* 8, no. 1 (1995): 91–122.

Kagel, John H., and Alvin E. Roth, eds. *Handbook of Experimental Economics*. Princeton: Princeton University Press, 1995.

Lafollie, Delphine. "Detection of High-risk Personalities in Risky Sports." *L'Encéphale* 32, no. 2 (2007): 135–41.

Le Breton, David. *Conduites à risque: Des jeux de mort au jeu de vivre*. Paris: Presses Universitaires de France, 2002.

Mariani, Guillaume. "Le risque en question dans le loisir sportif de nature: enquête sur les pratiques de surfs." *Ethologie & Praxéologie* 15 (2011): 31–50.

Martha, Cécile, Jason Laurendeau, and Jean Griffet. "Comparative Optimism and Risky Road Traffic Behavior Among High-risk Sports Practitioners." *Journal of Risk Research* 13, no. 4 (2010): 429–44.

Mauss, Marcel. "Body Techniques." In *Incorporations*, edited by Jonathan Crary and Sanford Kwinter. New York: Zone, 1992.

Nash, John. "Equilibrium Points in N-person Games." *Proceedings of the National Academy of Sciences of the USA* 36, no. 1 (1950): 48–49.

——. "Non-cooperative Games." *Annals of Mathematics* 54, no. 2 (1951): 286–95.

Neumann, John von, and Oskar Morgenstern. *Theory of Games and Economic Behavior*. Princeton: Princeton University Press, 1944.

Oboeuf, Alexandre, and Luc Collard. "Agressivité motrice: Habitudes et transferts dans trois sports collectifs." *Sociologos* 3 (2008). At http://socio-logos.revues.org/1233.

Parlebas, Pierre. "Jeu sportif, rêve et fantaisie." *Esprit* 446 (1975): 784–803.

——. "Elementary Mathematical Modelization of Games and Sports."

In *The Explanatory Power of Models*, edited by Robert Franck. Netherlands: Kluwer Academic Publishers, 2002.

Peretti-Watel, Patrick. *Sociologie du risqué*. Paris: Armand Colin, 2000.

Robertson, Douglas. *The Last Voyage of the Lucette (Survive the Savage Sea, 1973)*. New York: Sheridan House Inc., 2005.

Shubik, Martin. *Game Theory in the Social Sciences: Concepts and Solutions*. Cambridge: MIT Press, 1982.

Tucker, Albert W. "A Two Persons Dilemma." Mimeo, Stanford University, 1950.

9

BASQUE GAMES AND EMOTIONS: A QUESTION OF TIME

Joseba Etxebeste Otegi

In *Alice's Adventures in Wonderland*, Lewis Carroll describes the curious game of the Caucus-race and the emotions it provokes:

> First it marked out a race-course, in a sort of circle, ("the exact shape doesn't matter," it said,) and then all the party were placed along the course, here and there. There was no "One, two, three, and away," but they began running when they liked, and left off when they liked, so that it was not easy to know when the race was over. However, when they had been running half an hour or so, and were quite dry again, the Dodo suddenly called out "The race is over!" and they all crowded round it, panting, and asking, "But who has won?"
>
> This question the Dodo could not answer without a great deal of thought, and it sat for a long time with one finger pressed upon its forehead (the position in which you usually see Shakespeare, in the pictures of him), while the rest waited in silence. At last the Dodo said, "everybody has won, and all must have prizes."[1]

A young researcher takes notes while an informant reminisces about the last play in the final of the Basque pelota championship during the festivals honoring the local patron Saint Lucia: how the ball flew against the left wall, how he stretched out his arm cutting the ball short. In the man's wrinkled face and the tension in his eyebrows, the young man could see the impact of the ball in his hand, the furrowing in the air, the poisoned slice hitting just above the line, the useless effort of the adversary, and the rebirth of the pride of victory.

An informant explains how, as a child, she felt a mixture of fear and desire when she went near the forbidden pool where the son of a neigh-

* This study has received funding from Spain's Ministry of Science and Innovation through R+D+i projects: DEP2010-21626-C03-01, DEP2010-21626-C03-02 and DEP2010-21626-C03-03.

1. Carroll, *Alice's Adventures in Wonderland*, ch. 3, 34–35.

bor from her village had drowned. The water was black, or at least that is how she remembers it, and in the blackness, in the darkest spot, that is where the greatest number of trout was to be found. Terrified and seduced, she lowered her fishing rod down from the bridge and waited for it to vibrate in her hand during that vacation with her cousins in the Leitzaran Valley, Gipuzkoa, in the Basque Country at the height of the post-Spanish Civil War period.

A child who was afraid of water never learned to swim; a great swimmer who took part in pool races became anxious, imagining he could see monsters while swimming among the rocks of the mouse-shaped peninsula known as Ratón de Getaria (Gipuzkoa); a young man is full of pride, joy, and happiness when he wins the local cycling race while his closest rival hides in embarrassment among the crowd, avoiding all contact with his neighbors. We feel emotions when we act, and we remember the actions with the feelings that they produced. Narrations of motor experiences are tinged with joy, happiness, humor, anger, friendship, sadness, embarrassment, surprise, compassion, fear, rejection, and love. If, according to Pierre Parlebas, affectivity is the key to physical activities,[2] its recollection—whether immediately afterward or as a distant memory—enables us to understand the relation between motor culture and the subject's emotional experiences. The aim of this chapter is to explore the idea that Basque people have of motor time, and the emotions described by individuals when they participate in traditional games. This is a study, in other words, of the social system and of the experience of those involved in the sentimental education of the Basque people.

Cultural Time: Succession or Cloud of Points?

Time in Western culture is conceived as something external to human nature, like the continuous flow of water in a stream. Cultural time becomes something so evident and natural that in the end we forget that it is socially constructed. This means that we should take some precautions and care when it comes to clarifying the concepts of purpose, intention, result, and linearity.

If we take into account the behavioral study of natural phenomena and their classification, active behavior can be differentiated according to the intentionality it has behind it: "The term purposeful is meant to denote that the act or behavior may be interpreted as directed to the attainment of a goal—i.e., to a final condition in which the behaving object reaches a definite correlation in time or in space with respect to

---

2. Parlebas, *Activités Physiques et Education Motrice*.

another object or event. Purposeless behavior then is that which is not interpreted as directed to a goal."[3]

To clarify the distinction between the presence and absence of purpose, we could think of a clock, a machine that measures time. The device is designed to "tell the time," which enables individuals to co-ordinate their activities in society. Its correct use enables us to arrive on time at a conference, board a plane before it takes off, or arrive at the table before mealtime is over. The use that we make of the clock, something highly useful in the modern world, does not mean that the artifact has any purpose in itself. Even if we get to the conference late, miss the plane, or end up without any food, the clock continues to "tell the time." The machine, whose tick-tock makes the hands move around the face, does not move toward any end, does not produce any other event, but just continues to tell the time while hidden in the belly of Peter Pan's crocodile. The clock has no purpose nor is it aimed at any goal.

If the clock has an alarm, things are different. The turning of the bevel gears that drive the hands causes the lever that supports the tiny hammer to spring into action. A mechanical force strikes the mallet against the metallic dome producing a shrill hammering. This gadget can be used to make a bell ring, to turn on the heating, to open blinds, or to set off a bomb. The watch that has been programmed does not need to "tell the time" like a normal timepiece, but rather to set off an-other event at the end of a fixed period of time. The bomb will explode when the clock that controls it reaches zero unless James Bond or an-other hero manages to stop it. A machine, a behavior, or an event with a purpose inevitably produces another event.

The reference to a clock here is not gratuitous if we consider the words of Norbert Elias: "Especially in urban societies they make and use clocks in a manner reminiscent of the making and using of masks in many pre-urban societies: one knows they are made by people but they are experienced as if they represented an extra-human existence. Masks appear as embodiment of spirits. Clocks appear as embodiment of 'time.'"[4]

It is feasible to think that subjects' emotions can be influenced by the presence or absence of purpose in the event in which they are tak-ing part. One could even argue that, in general terms, while one cul-ture may be mainly oriented toward active behavior with a purpose, for another culture the opposite may be true, with behavior lacking any intention. Through an analysis of language, Dorothy Lee demonstrates this possibility by comparing the nonlinear culture of the Trobrianders

---

3. Rosenblueth, Wiener, and Bigelow, "Behavior, Purpose and Teleology," 18.
4. Elias, *Time*, 118.

of Papua New Guinea and the linearity of American culture. According to the author, the way the experience of reality is formulated will determine the way in which subjects experience hope, motivation, and satisfaction and thus to a large extent determine individuals' emotions.[5]

The Trobrianders structure their accounts without any temporal connection between objects, and when this occurs, temporality has no meaning. Different verb tenses do not exist in their language; there is no distinction between past and present, activities and events are not organized according to ends and means, and there are no causal or teleological relations; instead, all form part of a general model of behavior. Trobriander culture does not employ purpose or intention in its codification of reality.

In Western culture, direction, reason, and purpose are so evident that we take them for granted. They underpin not only our way of thinking but also our aesthetic perception; the emotional climax has a fundamental value for us and, in fact, gives meaning to life itself. We have assumed linearity as an axiom in our way of thinking about personality and character, and it is present both in induction and deduction, in the course of the evolution of the species as well as in historical events. Linearity is axiomatic, omnipresent, and inescapable, and we are incapable of questioning the reality of its presence.

Lee argues that there are two main reasons why linearity is used as a guide in our culture when we consider events or experiences linked to the ego, which is to say to emotions and subjectivity. On the one hand, we feel the need to organize events chronologically in a linear order. For the Trobrianders, what would correspond to our history is in their context a collection of anecdotes—unrelated points that are told without regard for chronological sequencing, development, or causality. On the other hand, we have the need to order events into a climactic sequence, whether by size, intensity, emotional significance, or some other principle. We organize events linearly not because we are interested in historical causality, but rather because the present is the culmination point of our history, the climax of the plot. When the Trobrianders relate events there is no agreement established for their development, no building of emotional tone. Their stories have no plot, linear development, or denouement. In summary, our conception of character formation, our emphasis on the importance of success, and of failure and frustration in general, are based on the underpinning axiom of linearity, of purpose. Such a determination is avoided, however, in cultures such as that of the Trobrianders insofar as their sentimental

---

5. Lee, "Lineal and Nonlineal Codifications of Reality," 151–64.

education is concerned.

We have seen that cultures are guided in terms of the presence or absence of purpose, and that this also conditions the character and feelings of the people. It is not unreasonable to think that games and sports, insofar as they are cultural constructs, can also be organized according to this characteristic. According to Pierre Parlebas, it is worth analyzing how games and sports are concluded. There are two main ways in which sporting games are concluded: on the one hand we have those that end depending on the rules of the game (an internal logic) and, on the other, those that end as a result of an external event beyond the rules of the game (an external logic).[6]

To explain a little further, a sporting event can have an end that is determined by the rules; the game advances inexorably toward its own conclusion, toward its sole purpose, which is the determination of a winner of the contest. These are termed "score memory games," of which there are four different types.

The first type of score memory games are based on a classification system. Victory is determined by a system of "homogenously classifying" the contestants after participation. All the participants are put in order according to a certain scale: time, distance, score based on an aesthetic code, frequency obtained, or something else. These are usually contests and races. In the world of sport, this includes artistic gymnastics, trampolining, the one-hundred meters race, the two-stage Olympic lift of the weightlifter, stock car races, riding wild bulls at the rodeo, throwing the javelin, shooting a bow and arrow. These are just a few examples of the many possibilities of classification system contests. This system is also highly developed in traditional Basque games for adults, the *Herri Kirolak* (literally, "popular sports"): betting on the dragging of huge stones with bulls, *trainera* races (traditional rowing boats), stone lifting, cutting grass with a scythe, and anvil lifting all use this system. In children's games, the one-legged race, skipping stones, and catapult-shooting contests also illustrate the same principle.

Another type of game focuses on an end that has a time limit. The result in a sporting game is verified at the end of a "fixed time," which is to say at the end of an agreed time when a winner is appointed. This is the case with soccer, basketball, and football, which end when two halves of a specific amount of time come to an end. In some games there is no specific time period; baseball, for example, ends after nine innings rather than a set time.

In yet another type of game, the end has a score limit. The end can

---

6. Parlebas, *Juegos, Deporte y Sociedades*, 438.

come about when a specific result is obtained, such as with tennis in which two or three sets have to be won and in which the best of three or five is played, as is the case in volleyball too. Basque pelota also follows this principle. Hand ball modality games in pelota last until one of the competitors achieves twenty-two points, modalities played with a basket or jai-alai until one team achieves thirty-five points, and with a racquet forty-five points. In traditional modalities like *rebote*, *laxoa*, or *bote luzea*,[7] a system is used that varies between nine and thirteen games.

Other games are shaped around both a score and a time limit. The last case of recorded results refers to sporting games that end either after a time limit or with a limit result, as occurs in boxing, judo, and taekwondo matches. Here, the fighter loses or wins "points" at the end of rounds of fixed duration or by knocking out the adversary, thereby obtaining a score that gives the fighter an immediate victory.

Games with a winner or with a scoring memory are games with a purpose and, like a programmed clock, are destined to lead to their own self-destruction, advancing to the end, to an emotional denouement that coincides with the designation of a winner. The sequences are chronological and addictive, the result condenses the action of what has occurred, and the sequences correspond to a linear codification of the reality of the game with temporal causality as its axis.

By contrast, there are sporting games that do not require a winner to be appointed in order to prevail. The rules of such games, their internal logic, do not determine the end. In the same way that a clock tells the time repeatedly without stopping, games without scoring memory start up over and over again in an endless chain. Play is stopped only when something outside the rules makes the game come to an end, such as the weather or because the players want to stop, or because it is time for a break, the end of playtime, or time to go home. Like the pocket watch that never stops telling the time, the sequences of the game are chained together in a continuous cycle until the mallet of external logic breaks the game.

Let us now consider the case of a well-known game without score memory, which is known as tag in English, *pilla-pilla* in Spanish, and *harrapaketan* in Basque. The participants decide on a catcher (an "it") by drawing lots, and they also specify a clear and wide enough space in which to play. The catcher has to try to catch the free players while they do all they can to avoid being caught. Races and chases ensue. The catcher is at the center of the action and all the other players move depending on this player's movements. If the catcher is quick and skill-

---

7. The *rebote*, *laxoa*, and *bote luzea* are different modalities of pelota. Played face to face, each of these modalities has its own court, instruments, and rules.

ful, the players will be careful to keep a distance; if the catcher is a bit clumsy and slow, then the other players will get closer to challenge and dodge him. At any point, a careless move on the part of a player or the talent of the catcher will enable him to catch a free player. At this point, the two players, the catcher and the caught, change roles, much to the indifference of their playmates, who are busy weighing up the new catcher. The old "it" is no longer the center of attention now that he has given up the post to a new pursuer. The role-changes become a sequence of chains in this game without purpose or goal, without the victory or defeat of any of the participants. These kinds of role-changes are known as permutations, but other potential cases also exist.

It may be that the temporal sequences do not result in a role-change. The customs and rules of the hunt do not establish an end to the activity as the different players caught turn into an endless chain in a pursuit without end. Linear time disappears. The idea of nonlinearity appears in the Basque myth of the priest who, because of his extreme fondness for hunting, misses Mass and is condemned to hunt a hare for eternity. It should be noted that even if that which is caught, fished, or picked is useful or of interest, the activity still lacks purpose. In the same way that the game of catch can be enjoyable and practical for the players, or just as the clock is built to tell the time, the event or behavior does not have any purpose, intention, or goal in the sense in which it is meant in this article. Games of hunting, fishing, and catching are activities without recorded results, without purpose.

It seems that behavior, languages, and sporting games can be divided into two main areas: on the basis of the absence or presence of purpose, linearity, or score. Omnipresent American linearity contrasts with the point cloud of the Trobrianders, just as the emotional denouement of the victory of football differs from the cloud of affective anecdotes of tag and the clock that illuminates the time on a stopwatch that makes a supermarket blow up. The different names and the different ways they are applied reveal a profound phenomenon that is linked to the cultural notion of time. The efforts made by some experts in historiography, such as Walter Benjamin, should be noted. These scholars attempted to abandon the linearity of universal history and to advocate the study of what are known as "monads"—points in which the messianic cessation of happening can be recognized.[8]

Time in Basque Culture and Its Sporting Events

Time is a system of orientation, a system of references just like space.

---

8. Benjamin, *Illuminations*, 265.

A compass marks our north and enables us to situate ourselves in relation to space, just as the Year Zero in the Christian era allows us to situate ourselves in relation to time. Both are cultural creations, not objective data but rather social constructs. The terms outside, within, before, and after can be used for both space and time and put us in contact with the references that we use both in terms of time and space. As Norbert Elias argues, "the concepts 'time' and 'space' are among the basic means of orientation of our social traditions."[9] For him, "timing thus is based on people's capacity for connecting with each other two or more different sequences of continuous changes, one of which serves as a timing standard for the other (or others)."[10] This connection of sequences, as we have seen, should be purposeful or purposeless.

A study of the calendar used by the Basques allows us to unravel their idea of time. In traditional Basque culture, the calendar is a system of temporal reference of great importance that organizes the spiritual and earthly life of its subjects. The idea of time being unfolded underpins the liturgical calendar of the Church of Rome, which is applied in the Basque Country as well as across most of Europe. The ecclesiastical calendar is a succession of festivities. Specific days are set aside to honor saints and martyrs, the Virgin Mary, the Holy Trinity, and the birth of Christ. In general terms, the festivals of the liturgical calendar are divided into two main groups: the festivities with fixed dates and those with movable dates.

The main holidays with fixed dates are those of the Calendar of Saints —that is, the days designated for honoring the lives of various saints. They are fixed because they occur on the same day every year, according to the solar calendar; for example, the festival of San Fermín of Pamplona-Iruñea is always on July 7. On the other hand, the calendar of movable feasts celebrates the birth, life, death, resurrection, and ascension of Christ and the descent of the Holy Spirit. These are understood to be movable because they are calculated by the lunar calendar, on the basis of when Easter Sunday or the Resurrection is celebrated, which, following the Jewish tradition, occurs after the first Sunday of the first full moon after the spring equinox. Movable feasts are not fixed in the solar calendar; for example, Easter Sunday in 2010 was on April 4, in 2011 on April 24, in 2012 on April 8, and in 2013 on March 31 (always, of course, on a Sunday). The movable calendar divides the year into phases, and these are calculated so that the dates indicated can be celebrated on the same day of the week, with the day of the year being changed. Easter Sunday, Ash Wednesday, and Ascension Thursday are

---

9. Elias, *Time*, 98.
10. Ibid., 72.

all examples of this calendar.

Considering the purpose of the calendars, there are significant differences between fixed and movable festivals. The Calendar of Saints has traditionally organized the earthly life of the Basque people—when to sow, reap, slaughter animals, fish different species, or when to have trade and market days. This popular wisdom is stored away in the sayings that give advice on agriculture, weather, relations, and even magic. For example, there is a tradition of planting garlic before the Feast of Saint Martin on November 11. As a traditional saying goes, "Garlic, why have you turned bad? Because you didn't sow me before Saint Martin."[11] Festivals with a fixed date are events with a purpose, and lead to other events; they sow today and reap tomorrow, which is necessary for cycles of agriculture, animal-breeding, or life at sea. In contrast, the calendar of movable dates symbolically represents the life of Christ—his birth, death, and resurrection—and guides the spiritual life of the Basque people. Catholics aim to live a life that resembles that of Christ, whom they take as their model. They celebrate his birth, death, resurrection, ascension to heaven, and the descent of the Holy Spirit as a cycle in which festive states occur that are not causal, linear, or chronological, but merely occur one before the other. In the same way as the clock that tells the time, each phase of the year reveals an exemplary image of the life of Christ, whether it is his birth or resurrection. Dorothy Lee shows this same "recreation or realization of a mythic model" in the great ceremonial expedition known as the Kula of the Trobrianders.[12] Basque people in traditional society seem to experience a codification of reality that is both linear and nonlinear, a balance between the presence and absence of purpose that follows the monastic idea of *ora et labora*, prayer and work—two practices needed in the life of a good Catholic. The affective structuring of the Basques seems to be balanced between the need to organize an emotional plot in a dramatically climactic way, and the desire to accept small anecdotes that are not organized into parts of a more general sentimental model. The study of the presence or absence of purpose in Basque ethnomotricity enables us to determine how emotional models that are structured by the calendar lead to motor-skill games. Do Basque children's games end by declaring a winner or, by contrast, does play continue until an external event ends it? The study that I present here is based on the corpus of motor-skill

---

11. Other examples in Spanish: by All Saints Day, wheat should be sown and all fruit stored away at home; kill the chicken for Saint Catherine's Day and the turkey for Saint Nicholas Day; kill your cattle for Saint Andrew's Day whether good or bad, just as the cattle is; for Saint Blas you will see storks, and if you don't there will be a year of snow.

12. Lee, "Lineal and Nonlineal Codifications of Reality," 151–64.

games collected in the ethnographic atlas *Juegos Infantiles en Vasconia* ("Basque children's games") produced by Etniker Euskalherria.[13] I identify and describe 861 different motor skill games; I include a summary sheet that takes into account elements such as internal logic, the presence or absence of recorded results, external logic, and the presence of girls and/or boys.[14] By proceeding this way, we can use simple or more complex statistical analyses ranging from the distribution of occurrences to the analysis of multiple correspondences, and highlight only the necessary results in order not to overload the text.

We saw previously how the absence or presence of purpose in motor skill games resulted in an absence or presence of score memory: a game of tag without a winner that concludes when the players arbitrarily stop playing, or a game of handball that concludes when one side achieves 22 points (or goals), for example. The results are highly significant for understanding the importance of these kinds of games in Basque culture; games with no score memory that are restarted again and again without any particular goal make up 56.3 percent of the total (485), and sports games with a score memory that ends with a winner being declared constitute 43.7 percent of all activities (376).

The data obtained shows how the ludic time of motor culture is divided into two relatively balanced halves, with a certain tendency toward nonlinear codifications of reality. Games, like the liturgical calendar, lead members of the Basque community to codify reality on the basis of both the presence and absence of purpose, balancing the weight of the result with the value of the process and victory with the cyclical repetition of game sequences, guiding the subjective experience of subjects in a fair way toward both an emotional denouement as well as toward the random ordering of sentimental anecdotes.

These models are still very pertinent today, not only in children's lives but also for adults. It can be observed, for example, in the Tour of the Basque Country (Euskal Herriko Itzulia in Basque), the most important cycling race organized in the country. In actual fact, the Tour includes different races in one competition. The time of all the stages is counted, and a general winner is declared depending on who has clocked up the shortest time. A mountain winner and a consistency winner are also declared according to the points they obtain on the sprints and targets throughout the whole course. Different scales of classification are at play simultaneously; this is a race with a purpose, result, and record. Another important race organized in the Basque Country is known as the *Korrika* (Running). Like the cycling route, the

---

13. Etniker Euskalherria, *Juegos Infantiles en Vasconia*.
14. Etxebeste, *Á Cloche-Pied*.

route of the Korrika crosses the territory with an endpoint and a goal, but in this case without a winner. The race involves participants completing a series of relays while carrying a wooden stick that represents the continuity and support of the community in developing the Basque language. The participants who accompany the leaders en masse join the race and leave it whenever they want; they cover the distance that suits them. When someone asks who has won, just as in the Caucus-Race in *Alice in Wonderland*, the Dodo declares "everybody has won." In other words, everyone wins if the Basque language wins. What is important in the Korrika is to run, to reach a certain point, not to arrive first. In her work on the Korrika, Teresa del Valle states that "discontinuous temporal reality is transcended through powerful, atemporal symbolic continuity. . . . This is the religious idea of overcoming time, overcoming the moment in which we live, in which we are immersed, with something transcendental imbued with distant animist and ancestral connotations."[15] This is a race without purpose, without a result, without a record.

For the anthropologist Joseba Zulaika, the absence and presence of a target is a key feature of two Basque behavioral models to define the notion of play—the *joko* and the *jolas*. The *joko* is competitive and bipolar, measured in time and space, clearly defined, and has an obvious winner. It is played seriously. Someone wins or loses. It can be summed up in the idea *bata ala bestea*, "one *or* the other." In contrast, the term *jolas* breaks the bipolarity of the *ala* or of the "or" to resituate itself in the idea of *bata eta bestea*, "one *and* the other." It is played for fun, to have a good laugh. There is no clear winner, one wins and loses at the same time. The action is full of ambiguities, and it is all "a big lie full of truth."[16] These behavioral models are closely tied to household values, in which household members relate to members of another household, with outsiders or *kanpokoak*, through *joko*, and to members of the same house, including those away from home or *etxekoak*, through *jolas*.[17]

When our parents were children, boys who played girls' games were often referred to disrespectfully as *mari-chica* or *mariquita* in Spanish, and *maritxu* in Basque (queer, girly); while girls who played boys' games were called *mari-chico*, *mari-muete*, or *mari-macho* in Spanish, and *mari-mutil* in Basque (butch, tomboy).[18] This separation in games played between members of the different sexes could indicate a gender difference in the emotional model that is linked to the activity of play. The

15. del Valle, *Korrika*, 173.
16. Zulaika, *Bertsolariaren jokoa eta jolasa*.
17. Etxebeste, *À Cloche-Pied*.
18. Etniker Euskalherria, *Juegos infantiles en Vasconia*, 58.

question that needs to be addressed could be formulated as follows: are there significant tendencies in the way subjectivity is constructed in the different genders in relation to the activity of play in the corpus of Basque children's games?

To begin to answer this question, I have divided the corpus of Basque games into three different classes: games that are exclusive to boys, games exclusive to girls, and those that are played by mixed groups. The results are conclusive: the majority of games are played by both sexes—61.9 percent of the games (533) or more than half of the total—while only 15.8 percent of the games (136) are played exclusively by boys and 22.3 percent exclusively by girls (192).

We can therefore conclude that the socialization learned through games affects the emotional character of Basque men and women in the same way. Games educate men and women following the same sentimental model that would imply a certain social parity in male and female roles, a preparation for running the household as the *etxeko-jaun* (the master of the household) or the *etxekoandre* (the mistress of the household). Nevertheless, there are two groups of games that are exclusive to each of the genders and that may imply a certain level of difference in the affective education of the sexes. I will focus here on resolving the differences shown in terms of the presence or absence of purpose in the play activity in order to deal with an important element in affective construction. To resolve this problem, from the general corpus of games I will exclude those that are exclusively played by boys or girls; games that are never played by members of the opposite sex at the risk of their being labeled as not masculine or feminine enough by their peers. From this I have generated a contingency table that analyzes the existing relation between both variables through a chi-square test (χ^2). Having ruled out independence theory,[19] a significant tendency can be observed whereby boys play more games with score memory than girls, who tend to participate more than boys in games without a purpose. This distinct form of socialization indicates that men's emotions will be more linked to results than women's, to a purpose that accounts for the emotional discharge, for the drama, and for the denouement, with a beginning and an end. In contrast, girls will tend to organize their emotions in a more pronounced way than boys into a set of affective anecdotes without chronological or causal order, based on a cloud of elements.

The study of the Basque social system in relation to the presence and absence of purpose reveals an intermediary point between what

---

19. The chi-square of 35.12 shows a relation of 0.01. The contingency table is not presented here to avoid overloading the text, and instead only the results are discussed.

Dorothy Lee describes as a linear culture (that of the United States) and a nonlinear one (that of the Trobrianders). In his comparative study of communicative contexts—linked to purpose and its absence—in relation to the justice system and commerce in the United States and Japan, Edward T. Hall, the founder of proxemics, concludes that "the French culture is a mixture, a mélange of high- and low-context institutions and situations,"[20] confirming the Basque balancing of purpose and non-purpose to be a European tendency.

The Experience of Those Involved in Basque Sentimental Education

Until now I have presented the structure and social system that organizes and underpins the way participants codify reality. Language, calendar, play time, purpose, intention, and result are all independent of the subjects involved. However, the subjects interpret events according to different circumstances in a way that allows individuals a margin of activity in specific social contexts, revealing individual differences among subjects faced with the same reality. My interest in the study of these differences has led me to develop a quasi-experimental research project between different universities, whose main objective is to analyze the existing relations between sports games that are organized on the basis of motor skills and emotions as designated by the participants, considering gender as well as the sporting background and cultural origin of the participants.

In my case, I selected cooperation-opposition sports games that I organized into four sessions of an hour and a half each. Two of the sessions were devoted to games with a score and the other two to those with no scores. After each game I handed out a post-test GES questionnaire (Games and Emotions Scale), to which an open question was attached in which the interviewees could explain their comments. The subjects were asked to score their emotions from 0 to 10 (joy, happiness, humor, anger, friendship, sadness, embarrassment, surprise, compassion, fear, rejection, and love). After this they selected the emotion with the highest score and explained in writing why they had given it this score (to a maximum of three emotions). The experiment was carried out with university students in their first and second year at the UPV-EHU, the University of the Basque Country, on 339 subjects during the 2010–2011 academic year. In this chapter I will focus on interpreting some of the explanations that the participants attributed to their decisions insofar as they related to the purpose of the game. We

---

20. Hall, *Beyond Culture*, 109.

must take care when attempting to interpret these results. The emotional state of each person is sensitive to a multitude of stimuli because it is a multidimensional essence; in other words, it is organic, psychological, and social. The sports games in which the subjects participated had to meet certain uniformity requirements and avoid parasitic variables. The motor situations presented in the experience are included in the same domain of motor action[21]—that is, they are analogous with regards to motor action criteria. There are two key precepts by which motor activities are organized, both of which are linked to the way the information is processed: on the one hand, the player's relation with space, and on the other, relations linked to other participants. Making decisions on the basis of processed information is without doubt a feature of intelligence; and in motor-skill decisions, the intelligence developed is, clearly, motor intelligence. The context in which surfers balance on their boards while riding the waves of Mundaka or Biarritz is precisely the space that surrounds them, the space in which they are literally submerged. All the surfers' actions are determined by the size of the waves, the direction they come from, the point at which they break, the irregular surface of the wave's gradient, and by the presence of "noodles" that make the water curl back into the sea from the shore. The uncertainty of space is a source of information and also, it must be said, of affectivity. In a diametrically opposite way, the actions of a *pelotari* (player of the Basque court game *pelota*) are carried out in an "empty" space, both in Jorge Oteiza's aesthetic sense and in terms of the information it generates. There is no spatial intelligence in the pelota game which means that it is highly unlikely that the space will be a significant source of emotions. What exists is a relational intelligence of interaction between the players. A *pelotari* hides his real intentions from his adversaries and must make them believe that he is going to cut the ball short in order to send it to the *txoko*, the "corner" where the walls meet, on the opponent's side. The ball always responds in the same way when it is hit against the wall; it follows the same laws of physics. This meta-communication that hides the real truth of the action has to be hidden from the adversary but visible to the partner with whom they share the court and alternate hits. This is a real challenge for social intelligence in action, an intelligence not used by a surfer in relation to other surfers, who only interact in relation to questions about the twists and turns needed to ride the waves. The presence and absence of uncertainty in the space, and in relation to partners or opponents, are the main principles according to which the different areas

---

21. Parlebas, *Juegos, Deporte y Sociedades*, 161–66.

of motor action are classified.[22] Uncertainty about the information is also a source of emotions, which means that its control as a variable is essential in order to interpret the information correctly. The distinguishing criteria that we have considered here is not intelligence, but the absence or presence of scoring, the uncertainty of the scoring. Other experiments in the same conditions are being carried out in other domains of motor action.

The hypothesis that I aim to verify is that the explanations given by the subjects concerning the emotions they feel during cooperation-opposition games tend to reproduce the absence or presence of purpose in the play structures presented.

As an initial step, I first identify sentences that include temporal references to the internal logic of the game, that is, to its rules. In the case of the game of *corta-hilos* (cut the cord),[23] for example, we read that "the surprise element was really strong because *at times* you didn't expect to be crossed and if you were the one catching, you also found yourself in situations with unexpected crosses." In the case of *balón real*[24] one subject writes, "It's good fun because *when* you're winning, you start to mess about with the players on the opposing team." The terms "at times" and "when" are italicized to make the reader aware of the idea of temporality that, as can be noted in the texts, refers to what has happened during the game.

The different possible cases are organized according to the reproduction of the purpose, which is central for the result, or in terms of its absence on the basis of a model of anecdotes that explains the process followed. We find two possible ways of explaining the emotions. First, they are explicit references to the results, to victory and defeat, and the act of scoring. Second, they are references to changes in the sociomotor roles. Then we study the relationship between the process and the structure of the play time.

In score memory games, emotion is generally explained according to the result of the game: victory, defeat, or the act of scoring. Some examples of explicit references to results are:

---

22. Ibid., 265–67.

23. The principle of the game of corta-hilos: the pursuer chooses any player as a target, but if any other player crosses an imaginary line that joins both players, he becomes the target. When the pursuer traps the target, they change roles.

24. The principle of the game of *balón real*: it is similar to dodge ball. A team wins if it reaches 100 points first by hitting its opponents with the ball as long as it does not exceed that number. There are therefore two ways of winning: if you reach a hundred points, or if the other team exceeds a hundred points. This can happen because the value of each player is unknown for the opposite team (e.g., the hidden king is worth 30 points, and a valet 10). This is a game with incomplete information, and with a symmetrical dual structure in teams.

- Good humor: I really enjoyed playing the game even though we didn't win. I really enjoyed playing the game so it didn't matter that I had lost.
- Happiness: Even though I lost, I had a really good time playing *balón quemado*. It was really good fun.
- Sadness: I feel great sadness for the loss of a game that I used to play as child.
- Hope: In the beginning we were about to lose, but we kept going and in the end we won.
- Happiness: I feel happy because we won.
- Joy: I had a really good time, and to top it off we won.
- Anger: I felt angry that I didn't manage to achieve the result I wanted.
- Joy: With achieving points and winning.
- Joy: When I caught one of the opponents and we won the game.
- Happiness: I felt happy when we'd gotten 10 *passes* (game targets).
- Joy: Most of all when we got the stone (the target).

It is also possible that in case of games with score memory, emotion is explained through a multitude of anecdotes linked to changes in the players' roles. For example:

- Hope: Being in jail and waiting to be freed.
- Sadness: Being one of the last to be the catcher and with the game finishing before I had my turn.
- Anxiety: I was out really fast, so I didn't get a chance to take part in the game and I wanted to play.
- Anger: Because I didn't get the chance to throw one single ball.
- Embarrassment: I spent most of the game in jail and I didn't make the most of the chances I had to get out.
- Joy: Because I managed to get out of jail quickly.
- Anxiety: When I had the ball and lots of my teammates came toward me I felt anxiety and hampered because I was surrounded by too many people.
- Anger: Anger when we lost the ball.

In games without memory, the subjectivity generated is tied to a string of anecdotes that are linked to a network of socio-motor roles. Here I present some examples of explicit references to role changes:

- Happiness: I had a really good time, and on top of that I wasn't even caught.
- Hope: I was the one who had to run behind my teammates and

when at one point I couldn't, I felt a little embarrassed and wanted it to be over.
- Happiness: I enjoyed the game, especially when I saved myself.
- Surprise: Sometimes I didn't know how to get to the corner, and it caught me unexpectedly.
- Hope: I was hoping I wouldn't be captured all the time because I didn't want to run so much.
- Anxiety: We had to be very attentive to be able to run out suddenly.
- Good humor: I was sitting out for most of the game because of an error.
- Compassion: When someone was running, I tried to pass the ball to get him free as soon as possible.
- Anger: I spent ages as "it" and couldn't catch anybody.
- Rejection: When I decided to switch places and the other person didn't do it, I felt rejected for having lost my place, rejected by the person who didn't make space for me.
- Sadness: Because they were busy catching people who were slower than me, they didn't come after me until many were already in jail. They caught the girls first and the boys after.
- Anxiety: Because they got me out at the beginning, and it was really difficult to get all the others.
- Joy: The game went well, I feel happy, even though some players held the ball for most of the game.

Of the 473 sentences analyzed in the games without a score system, only two refer to competition and winning, in both cases in the game of *cuba-libre*[25] (a version of the American *freeze-tag*). In the first case, the comment explains the absence of a role change, and in the second the person is referring to motor interaction. We can now turn to their arguments:

- Compassion: I felt sorry for the person who had to catch the others because their efforts were not rewarded with a victory.
- Good humor: In short, if we leave competition aside, and we take it as a game, it really is enjoyable. Everyone laughs their head off.

My hypothesis is confirmed by games without score memory. The

---

25. Principle of the game of cuba libre: the pursuer tries to catch the free players. When one of the free players feels at risk, he shouts "cu" and stops still wherever he is; then he is safe. Two players who are both in "cu" can grab hands and shout "ba," and if a free player goes under the bridge made by the arms of those who are in "cu-ba," this player shouts "libre" and the bridge breaks with all of them becoming free again. When the pursuer catches a free player, the two change places.

players' explanations express a multitude of anecdotes linked to the network of role changes, with no room for comments linked to results, to a purpose. In my study, linear explanations tied to results, victory, or competition, are present but very marginal, almost nonexistent.[26] In games with a score system, the model seems to be more divided. The great majority of the reasons given explain the emotion in relation to the result, and this goes for both winners and losers. But the perception of reality is not monolithic as in the case of games with a purpose. Participants are free from the dictatorship of the result to offer a freer interpretation that is more focused on play sequences that have been significant for the players. As in games without score memory some participants in games with score memory results justify their emotions through a series of anecdotes of temporal elements, irrespective of the purpose and the unfolding of victory or defeat.

The work on motivation in sports in the Basque Country in the light of Carole Ames's "Theory of Goals" and the concept of "Motivational Climate"[27] coincides with the results obtained in my experimental study. The aim of this research is to evaluate whether those new to the sport focus on "the task" or "the ego."

Subjects who are orientated toward the task play on the basis of a process whereby they compare their performance with their own abilities. In contrast, subjects orientated toward the ego show if they are competent or not by comparing themselves to others. Thus, people orientated toward the task direct their attention to the learning process, and believe that success is produced when people improve their own personal abilities; they use personal self-evaluation instead of social comparison.[28]

It is easy to see that the orientation of the task is linked to the absence of purpose and that the orientation toward the ego is linked to its presence, although we should nevertheless be prudent in making these comparisons.

According to the authors of the three studies of sporting activities in the Basque Country cited below, there is a greater tendency among young Basques toward task rather than ego. This is confirmed by the three separate studies. Jose Arruza discovers this tendency in the responses of thirteen- and fourteen-year-old soccer players in Gipuzkoa.[29] Silvia Arribas and Arruza also find it in their study of the reasons

---

26. It could be that this phenomenon is more developed in the United States than in Europe, insofar as this is a culture with a linear codification of reality.

27. Ames, "Achievement Goals, Motivational Climate and Motivational Processes," 161–76.

28. Arribas, Arruza, and Montes Etxaide, "Deporte escolar," 103–12.

29. Arruza, et al., *Estudio sobre la influencia del tiempo de practica de futbol reglado y libre*

fifteen- to eighteen-year-olds in Gipuzkoa gave for participating in as well as for abandoning physical-sport practice.[29] Arruza and his colleagues also found it in their study of the program for the initiation of globalized sport based on the teaching of values.[30] The discussion confirms that Basques who play sporting games with a score system (*joko*) interpret them in the dramatic terms of victory or in a more general anecdotal model. However, we can say little of games without purpose (*jolas*), which is a somewhat under-researched field.

Conclusion

The cultural construction of time is crucially dependent on the absence or presence of purpose, and each culture bases its reality on one alternative or another. In the case of Basque culture, a balance has been found between the linearity and nonlinearity of its reality. Young Basques who participate in sporting activities structure their explanations of the emotions they experience in terms of the result when competition is involved, and in terms of a model of affective anecdotes linked to role change when no such comparison is present. The importance of the competitive *joko* is unquestionable—the model of behavior performed against outsiders (*kanpokoak*)—in today's world. But the value of *jolas*— the model of behavior performed at home (*etxekoak*)—is also important as a space for friendship, love, and companionship, and as a set of unquantifiable rules comprising a multitude of affective anecdotes. The importance of sports games in the sentimental education of future citizens is crucial.

Physical education, which underpins the socialization of the new generations by offering different motor skills, games, and sports, must be aware of its own responsibility in terms of constructing the affectivity of students. Basques tend to decide between *joko* and *jolas*, and Americans between play, game, and sport, in order to construct affectivity in line with social principles. This debate is clearly ideological, a debate between the importance of performance and social competition driven by the pleasure of winning, and the preponderance of the pleasure found in sharing as equals. The sooner we reflect on time and its hidden influence in educational programs, the more time we have to direct it in the right channel. So *much to do, so little time!*

---

en jóvenes jugadores de 13 a 18 años.

30. Arruza, González, and Bizkarra, *Influencia en el deporte escolar de un programa de iniciación deportiva globalizada, basado en la enseñanza de valores.*

Bibliography

Ames, Carole. "Achievement Goals, Motivational Climate and Motivational Processes." In *Motivation in Sport and Exercise*, edited by Glyn C. Roberts. Champaign: Ill., Human Kinetics, 1992.

Arribas, Silvia, José A. Arruza, and Lorena Gil de Montes Etxaide. "Deporte escolar: factores psico-socio-estructurales que lo determinan." "Kirol Hezitzailea. Gogoetak eta Ekarpenak; Deporte Educativo. Reflexiones y Aportaciones." Special issue, *Ikastaria. Cuadernos de Educación* 15 (2006): 103–112.

Arribas, Silvia, and Jose A. Arruza. *Motivos de participación y causas de abandono de la práctica físico-deportiva en jóvenes guipuzcoanos de 15–18 años*. Donostia-San Sebastián: Gipuzkoako Foru Aldundia; Kirolarte, 2004.

Arruza, Jose A., et al. *Estudio sobre la influencia del tiempo de practica de futbol reglado y libre en jóvenes jugadores de 13 a 18 años*. Unpublished manuscript, 2003.

Arruza Jose A., Itziar González, and Teresa M. Bizkarra. *Influencia en el deporte escolar de un programa de iniciación deportiva globalizada, basado en la enseñanza de valores*. Donostia-San Sebastián: Gipuzkoako Foru Aldundia; Kirolarte, 2004.

del Valle, Teresa. *Korrika: Basque Ritual for Ethnic Identity*. Translated by Linda White. Reno: University of Nevada Press, 1994.

Benjamin, Walter. *Illuminations*. Edited with an introduction by Hannah Arendt. Translated by Harry Zohn. Frankfurt: Harcourt, Brace & World, (1955), 1968.

Carroll, Lewis. *Alice's Adventures in Wonderland*. New York: Heritage Reprints, 1941.

Elias, Norbert. *Time: An Essay*. Oxford: Blackwell, 1992.

Etniker Euskalherria, *Juegos Infantiles en Vasconia*. Bilbao: Eusko Jaurlaritza, 1993.

Etxebeste, Joseba. *Á cloche-pied: Les jeux sportifs traditionnels et la socialisation des enfants basques*. Sarrebruck: Editions Universitaires Européennes, 2012.

Hall, Edward T. *Beyond Culture*. New York: Anchor Press, 1976.

Lee, Dorothy. "Lineal and Nonlineal Codifications of Reality." In *Symbolic Anthropology: A Reader in the Study of Symbols and Meanings*, edited by Janet L. Dolgin, David S. Kemnitzer, and David M. Schneider. New York: Columbia University Press, 1977.

Parlebas, Pierre. *Juegos, Deporte y Sociedades: Léxico de Praxiología Motriz*. Translated by Fernando González del Campo Román. Barcelona: Editorial Paidotribo, 2001.

———. *Activités Physiques et Education Motrice*. Paris: Editions Revue

Education Physique et Sport, 1990.

Rosenblueth, Arturo, Norbert Wiener, and Julian Bigelow. "Behavior, Purpose and Teleology." *Philosophy of Science* 10, no. 1 (1943): 18–24.

Zulaika, Joseba. *Bertsolariaren jokoa eta jolasa.* San Sebastian: Ediciones Baroja, 1985.

———. *Basque Violence: Metaphor and Sacrament.* Reno: University of Nevada Press, 1988.

10

COOPERATIVE GAMES, EMOTIONS, AND GENDER FROM A SOCIAL PERSPECTIVE

Pere Lavega

In order to live in any society or culture one has to learn how to manage the system of meanings it uses.[1] Indeed, it is through this set of shared meanings[2] that human behavior can be interpreted, guided, and established in different relationship spheres. When it comes to learning how to signify meaning and to relate socially with others, motor games offer a privileged space that is akin to a laboratory of social relationships,[3] one that is shaped by the meanings and symbols of the society in question.

Motor praxeology—the science of motor action[4]—provides a theoretical basis that reveals the properties or internal logic of any motor game. According to the tenets of motor praxeology, a motor game constitutes a motor situation (of a praxic nature) that is coded (rule-governed), and which may or may not be regulated by social institutions (institutionalized). The rules of every motor game establish a system of rights and obligations that authorize or sanction the type of motor action that can be performed. Thus, when a group of people decide to play a game they bear witness to the democratic pact through which its

* This study has received funding from Spain's Ministry of Science and Innovation through R+D+i projects DEP2010-21626-C03-01, DEP2010-21626-C03-02, and DEP2010-21626-C03-03. Additional funding was given by the Institut Català de les Dones (Catalan Government's Institute for Women's Affairs), Ref. U-95/10. Financial support was also provided by the Catalan Government's Agency for the Management of University and Research Grants (AGAUR-INEFC), Ref. 2009SGR1404, VCP/3346/2009, as well as by INEFC (attached to the University of Lleida). The INEFC also provided funding through its 2011 call for research. Finally, the authors would like to thank Óscar Farrús (INEFC) for his help with the use of new technology to gather and process the data, Dr. Jaume March for the statistical analysis, and Dr. Francisco Lagardera (INEFC, University of Lleida) for reviewing the present text.

1. Geertz, *The Interpretation of Cultures.*
2. Kashima, Yamaguchi, Kim, Choi, Gelfand, and Yuki. "Culture, Gender, and Self," 935–37.
3. Parlebas, *Juegos, deporte y sociedad.*
4. Ibid.

rules are accepted.

Any motor game can be thought of as a praxeological system[5]—that is, a system with an internal logic that imposes a set of obligations and that guides the players to relate to one another in a way that is consistent with the rules of the game. From a social perspective, various studies have shown how the internal logic of a motor game contains distinctive traits of the society in which it is played, such that these games have an extraordinary capacity to act as socializing agents.[6] In relation to the type of motor interaction they involve, four kinds of motor games can be defined: psychomotor games (with no motor interaction), cooperative games, adversarial games, and cooperative/adversarial games.[7]

The contribution of cooperation to societal well-being has been widely recognized by various disciplines such as biology, anthropology, sociology, social psychology, and economics, although it continues to be overlooked or only superficially addressed in the field of physical education. In this regard, the present study seeks to illustrate the educational potential of cooperative games and to study the effects that the internal logic of such games may have on the emotions experienced by male and female participants. The theoretical framework applied is based on the theory of motor praxeology,[8] a psycho-pedagogical model of emotion,[9] and a sociological perspective on gender.[10]

The theory of motor praxeology considers that families of games should not be grouped hierarchically according to their value. Rather, it identifies domains of motor action that can be grouped according to the dominant features of the internal logic that is common to a given family of games. For players, these features will have praxic, cognitive, affective, and social consequences, which will vary considerably depending on the domain in question. In terms of affect, each family of games may trigger different emotional experiences among participants.[11]

Far from being theoretical processes, emotions are practical experiences associated with human action[12]—in other words, they repre-

---

5. Lagardera and Lavega, eds., *La ciencia de la acción motriz*.

6. See Etxebeste and Urdangarin, "La socialización tradicional vasca"; Parlebas, "Une rupture culturelle," 9–36.

7. Lagardera and Lavega, *Introducción a la praxiología motriz*.

8. Parlebas, *Juegos, deporte y sociedad*.

9. Bisquerra, *Educación emocional y bienestar*.

10. Puig, "La situación de la mujer en el deporte al iniciarse el siglo XXI," 67–80.

11. Lavega, Mateu, Lagardera, and Filella, "Educar emociones positivas a través de los juegos deportivos," 111–39; Lavega, Filella, Agulló, Soldevila, and March, "Understanding Emotions Through Games," 617–40.

12. Ben-Ze'ev, *The Subtlety of Emotions*.

sent trends within action.[13] As regards cooperative motor games, it will only be possible to predict possible emotional trends or consequences among players if we understand the different features of the internal logic of these games.[14] The concept of internal logic implies that players in any game must respond to the relationship with other players, to the relationship with both space and time, and to the relationship with the material used.[15] Hence there is a need to identify the features or characteristics of each one of these four relationships or areas of motor action.

Research that has studied the internal logic of several hundred cooperative motor games[16] has identified the following key variables.

Relationship with Other Players in Cooperative Motor Games

Cooperative motor games require players to interact positively with one another so as to achieve a certain motor goal. In order to consider the relationships that are established between players in greater depth, it will be useful to study the following two aspects further.

The System of Roles

The concept of role is related to the fact that the rules of the game may establish certain rights or prohibitions for one or more players. When all players take part under the same conditions, the game is said to have a single role—what Parlebas refers to as a fixed-role system.[17] By contrast, when a game includes more than one role, one or more players may direct the cooperative relationships of the others, or at least have a direct influence on their decision-making. Other terms used to refer to this aspect are the power-dependency relationship, multiplex roles, and the multiplicity or number of roles.[18] In this case, the role system can be said to be one of "local exchange,"[19] since the motor interaction among players is always based on cooperation.

Density

Density refers to the number and type of connections that are established by participants in a social network.[20] It is said to be high when a person's relationships have strong links with those of others in the net-

13. Frijda, "What Emotions Might Be?"
14. Lagardera, "La lógica deportiva y las emociones."
15. Parlebas, *Juegos, deporte y sociedad.*
16. Lavega, "La investigación en los juegos tradicionales y en los juegos cooperativos."
17. Parlebas, *Juegos, deporte y sociedad.*
18. Ibarra, "Personal Networks of Women and Minorities in Management."
19. Parlebas, *Juegos, deporte y sociedad.*
20. Weber and Messik, "Conflicting Interests in Social Life," 377.

work.[21] Density is also directly related to group size, and cooperation is usually greater in small groups.[22] Cooperative motor games may show two kinds of density: high and low. High density refers to the situation in which there is cooperation between all those involved—that is, motor interactions take place between all the players. By contrast, low density means that there is interaction between certain players only; in other words, each player interacts with specific others, generally those situated to one side, in front or behind.

Relationship with Time

The final result or score may or may not be taken into account in a cooperative motor game, and there are therefore two possibilities: a game involving winners and losers (a zero-sum game or exclusive competition,[23] in which one team defeats the other); and a game in which the objective does not involve overcoming an opponent.

Relationship with the Material

Cooperative motor games may or may not require the use of material. In the latter case, the motor interaction takes place through bodily contact, whereas in the former the participants communicate with one another through the exchange or shared handling of a given object or objects.

Relationship with Space

The presence or absence of information is another aspect to be taken into account. Cooperative motor games may be played in a stable space that does not generate any information (that is, there are no unforeseen circumstances), or alternatively in an unstable space, one that includes the presence of changes or information (uncertainty) that must be deciphered by the participants.

The Strategic Pact

When several people have to solve a shared problem, the internal logic of the situation requires them to reach an agreement so as to organize their response.[24] This means that there has to be a strategic pact negotiation and the exchange of information, and concessions may have to be

21. Kitayama, Markus, and Kurokawa, "Culture, Emotion, and Well-being."
22. See Kerr, "Illusions of Efficacy"; Messick and Brewer, "Solving Social Dilemmas"; Weber and Messik, "Conflicting Interests in Social Life."
23. Parlebas, "Health and Relational Well-being in Traditional Games.
24. Parlebas, *Juegos, deporte y sociedad.*

made.[25] In some cases, however, it can be the game itself that organizes the players' behavior, assigning them an order or position in the playing area. In these situations the players need to perform coordinated motor actions that enable a pact to be made without interrupting the game.

Activated Processes: Automatic Motor Behavior or Decision-Making

Depending on the type of motor problem to be solved, cooperative motor games may require the players to produce automatic, cyclical behaviors, or alternatively they may have to make decisions about situations that must be dealt with in different ways in each sequence of the game.

By considering all these variables, we can see that when a person decides to participate in a cooperative motor game he or she will have to adapt his or her motor actions to each of these different features of the game's internal logic. Note, however, that although a game may simply require the players to run, jump, or pass a ball, each participant will do so in a distinct, individual, and characteristic way. This means that in addition to activating their muscles, the players invest the game with their own personality, activating the cognitive dimension (through decision-making), the affective dimension (by expressing emotions) and the social dimension (by relating to others). All these dimensions form part of the broad concept of motor behavior.[26]

Emotion from a Social Perspective

Far from being absolute states, emotions are relationships that are shared socially, even though they are expressed and experienced in a particular way by each individual. As David Le Breton states,[27] emotions constitute forms of affiliation to a community; they are ways by which members of the community communicate and remain joined to one another. Le Breton uses the expression "affective culture" to refer to the repertoire of meanings and values associated with emotions, this being what renders a feeling intelligible.

Rafael Bisquerra[28] describes emotions as complex states within an organism that are characterized by a certain excitation or perturbation that predisposes the organism to make an organized response. Emotions are generally produced as a complex reaction to an internal or external event, such that the evocation of an emotion requires the con-

---

25. See Hyder, Prietula, and Weingart, "Getting to Best."
26. Parlebas, *Juegos, deporte y sociedad*, 85.
27. Le Breton, *Las pasiones ordinarias*.
28. Bisquerra, *Educación emocional y bienestar*.

currence of a situation (event or occurrence) or the presence of a potentially emotive stimulus. Furthermore, for the emotional process to develop there needs to be not only a perceived event but also an evaluation and appraisal that confers affective connotations to the stimulus.

Emotion is thus a multidimensional response that a person makes on the basis of his or her subjective appraisal of the meaning of an event (in this case, a motor game). Note, however, that the different dimensions of an emotion are not juxtaposed or isolated from one another, but instead are indivisible, superimposed, and compact parts of a single system. The key dimensions of emotions are biological/organic,[29] cognitive,[30] and social,[31] although one should not forget that emotions also have a motor facet (physical or behavioral).[32]

According to the classification of emotions developed by Bisquerra,[33] there are three broad types of emotions, the categories being distinguished by their relationship to the expected objectives of the persons involved. The three categories are: positive emotions (joy, humor, love, and happiness), negative emotions (fear, anxiety, anger, sadness, rejection, and shame) and ambiguous emotions (surprise, hope, and compassion).

A Gender Perspective on the Emotions Produced in Games

Within the broad field of physical activity, sport continues to be a predominantly male sphere. Indeed, sport has historically been akin to a laboratory of masculinity[34] that has served to reproduce the traditional model of maleness. However, advances in society have seen the gradual consolidation of equal rights, and the increased presence of women in sport has been accompanied by the creation of new organizations and greater diversity in terms of how the activity is understood.[35]

In the sense that men and women assign different meanings to the practice of sport, one can see that a specifically female culture of recreational motor activity has now emerged as something clearly distinct from that involving men. Traditionally, of course, women have been stereotyped as being emotionally unstable, gentler, more delicate, and as showing greater understanding, obedience, and cooperation,

29. See Averill, "A Constructivist View of Emotion."

30. See Lazarus, "How Emotions Influence Performance in Competitive Sports."

31. See Kitayama, Markus, and Kurokawa, "Culture, Emotion, and Well-being."

32. See Parlebas, *Juegos, deporte y sociedad*; Damasio, *Y el cerebro creó al hombre*.

33. Bisquerra, *Educación emocional y bienestar*; Soler, "Les relacions de gènere en l'educació física a l'escola primària."

34. Soler, "Les relacions de gènere en l'educació física a l'escola primària"; Puig, Lagardera, and Juncà, "Enseñando sociología de las emociones en deporte."

35. Puig, "La situación de la mujer en el deporte al iniciarse el siglo XXI."

whereas men were characterized as being in control of their emotions and of displaying dynamism, aggressiveness, competitiveness, and leadership.[36]

Interestingly, various studies of traditional games have noted how such games are often regarded as male, female, or mixed.[37] It has also been reported that women prefer cooperative games, whereas men tend to opt mainly for games involving a contest between individuals or teams.[38] Research into traditional children's games has similarly observed how a distinction is made between male, female, and mixed games, this being associated with the social roles that characterize the local context.[39]

Given that gender is above all a sociocultural category that influences the subjective appraisals made by individuals, one would expect to find differences between the emotional responses of men and women taking part in motor games, just as there are gendered differences in other spheres of life.

Gender, Cooperative Motor Games, and Emotions: Research in Progress

Sporting games, gender equality, and emotional education are all central issues as regards societal well-being in the twenty-first century. With this in mind, an interdisciplinary research project was begun in 2007, bringing together researchers from universities in Spain, the United Kingdom, Switzerland, Portugal, and Brazil. As this research is still in progress, the present chapter reports only the preliminary results obtained from the study of cooperative games in Catalonia (Spain).

The study in question took the form of a pedagogical experience for students in a degree course on physical activity and sport. Specifically, the students took part in a program designed to teach emotional physical education, the focus being on the first stage of teaching emotional competences,[40] which corresponds to developing awareness of one's own emotions.

---

36. Puig, Lagardera, and Juncà, "Enseñando sociología de las emociones en el deporte."

37. See Etxebeste, "Les jeux sportifs, éléments de la socialisation traditionnelle des enfants du Pays basque."

38. Benenson, Roy, Waite, Goldbaum, Linders, and Simpson, "Greater Discomfort as a Proximate Cause of Sex Differences in Competition."

39. Etxebeste, "Les jeux sportifs élements de la socialisation traditionnelle des enfants du Pays basque"; Lavega, "La investigación en los juegos tradicionales y en los juegos cooperativos," 77–116.

40. Bisquerra, *Educación emocional y bienestar*; Salovey and Mayer, "Emotional Intelligence."

Previous studies by our group[41] found that each family of sporting games or domains of motor action, grouped according to the common features of their internal logic,[42] triggered different amounts of positive, negative, and ambiguous emotions. As regards the intensity of emotions, the highest levels corresponded to cooperative games, while the weakest emotions were reported in the context of psychomotor games (those with no motor interaction between players). The emotions aroused by adversarial and adversarial/cooperative games were somewhere between these two extremes. The results also showed significant differences between men and women, with the latter reporting less intense emotions.

These preliminary results confirmed the direct correspondence between domains of motor action and the experience of distinct emotions. In other words, depending on the internal logic of the game, the players involved experienced a different range of emotions. This effect was also found to be independent of the players' geographical location, which means that the internal logic (the nature of the motor game) took precedence over the external cultural logic (the region or country in which it was played). As a result of these findings, it was decided that each research center, despite being located in a different region and country, could focus on one particular family of sporting games. In the case of the University of Lleida (Catalonia, Spain) the focus turned to cooperative games.

In line with the theoretical framework of reference two main research objectives were proposed:

1. To study the relationship between the relevant features of the internal logic of cooperative motor games and the experience of positive, negative, and ambiguous emotions as reported by players of these games; and
2. To take a gender perspective on this question--that is, to study the relationship between the relevant features of the internal logic of cooperative motor games and the experience of positive, negative, and ambiguous emotions according to whether the players were male or female.

Participants

Participants were 307 first- and second-year students (93 women, 214 men, M_{age} = 20.42 years, SD = 2.162) on two degree courses on physical

---

41. Lavega et al., "Educar emociones positivas a través de los juegos deportivos"; Lavega et al., "Understanding Emotions Through Games."
42. Parlebas, *Juegos, deporte y sociedad.*

activity and sport. The courses were offered by the Catalonian Institute of Physical Education (University of Lleida). All the students gave their informed consent to participate in this research, which was also approved by the Ethics Committee of the University of Lleida.

Measures

An exhaustive review of the specialist literature on sporting games and emotions revealed no instrument capable of relating positive, negative, and ambiguous emotions—which have been identified by authors such as Richard S. Lazarus and Rafael Bisquerra[43]—with the four domains of motor action and the presence or absence of competition.[44] Therefore, a specialist international research group for sporting games (GREJE) and a pedagogical research group (GROP) that specialized in teaching emotional skills spent two years developing an appropriate instrument.

This instrument consisted of the following parts for each cooperative game:

1. Winners and losers vs. noncompetitive: identification of the type of game played; and
2. Emotions generated by each game:
   (a) positive emotions: joy, humor, love, and happiness;
   (b) negative emotions: fear, anxiety, anger, sadness, rejection, and shame;
   and (c) ambiguous emotions: surprise, hope, and compassion.

Participants were asked to rate each emotion on a scale from 0 to 10 depending on the intensity felt while playing each game.

Psychometric Properties of the Questionnaire

The questionnaire was validated[45] by studying the following properties:

1. Acceptability. For each question, ceiling and floor effects, skewness and kurtosis were calculated;
2. Reliability. Internal consistency, as measured by Cronbach's alpha, was good for the questionnaire as a whole ($n = 357$; $\alpha = 0.92$), and similar results were obtained for each type of emotion: positive ($\alpha = 0.92$), negative ($\alpha = 0.88$), and ambiguous ($\alpha = 0.93$);
3. Construct validity. Confirmatory factor analysis was used to test the structure of the questionnaire and reproduced this structure adequately. The final model, which consisted of twelve factors,

---

43. Lazarus, "How Emotions Influence Performance"; Bisquerra, *Educación emocional y bienestar.*
44. Parlebas. *Juegos, deporte y sociedad.*
45. Lavega et al., "Understanding Emotions Through Games."

showed good fit indices ($\chi^2 = 7125.79$, df = 4174). The model did not include an overall higher-order factor.

Procedure

The research procedure involved the following stages:

Educating Students' Emotions

Participants received four hours and thirty minutes of theoretical and practical teaching on emotions, this being based on the models developed by Bisquerra, Lazarus, and Peter Salovey and John D. Mayer.[46] In these sessions, students learned how to identify their own emotions by means of exercises involving game situations.

The main practical component of the study was conducted once it had been confirmed that the students had no further doubts in terms of identifying their own emotions.

Selection and Application of Cooperative Motor Games

A total of twenty cooperative games were used, covering all the different features of internal logic explained above. The objective of the games involved players moving or exchanging objects and/or the coordinated movement of participants. Each of the games was first played competitively (games 1, 2, 3, 4, 5, 6, 7, 8, 9, and 10 in table 10.1), namely with winners and losers, and then noncompetitively. The next section describes the noncompetitive games (games 11, 12, 13, 14, 15, 16, 17, 18, 19, and 20 in table 10.1).

Introducing Oneself (Movement/Exchange of Objects)

Each team forms a circle, with each player having a ball. The first task is to pass a ball from player to player until it arrives back at the first player. This motor action is then repeated with two balls until all the balls are in play. In the competitive version, a team is awarded a point each time the other team makes a mistake.

Rope Jump (Movement of Players and Object). Each team has to come up with a creative way of jumping simultaneously over a rope. In the competitive version the two teams each have a rope and are situated in parallel to one another, with one team being awarded a point each time the other team makes a mistake.

Leapfrog (Movement of Players). The first player takes up the tradi-

---

46. Lazarus, "How Emotions Influence Performance in Competitive Sports"; Bisquerra, *Educación emocional y bienestar*; Salovey and Mayer, "Emotional Intelligence Imagination."

tional stooped position so that the second player can leap over him/her and take up the same position a few meters in front. The other players then take turns to leap along the line such that the group as a whole moves from one area to another. In the competitive version, the first team to reach the other end of the playing area is the winner.

Passing the Hoop (Movement/Exchange of Object). The players of each team hold hands, and must also hold two hoops. The hoops must be passed from player to player, without letting go of one another's hands, until they arrive back at the starting point.

Transporting a Floor Mat (Movement of Players and Object). Each team has to transport a floor mat to the other end of the playing area. They have to lift it off the floor and move without holding onto the mat, the objective being to leave it upright at the other end of the playing area.

Switching poles (Exchange of Object/Movement of Players). The players form a circle, and each one of them has his or her hand on top of a waist-high wooden pole, which is positioned vertically on the floor. When given the signal, they each take their hand away and move around the circle, the aim being to catch their neighbor's pole before it falls to the ground. In the competitive version of this game, a team is awarded a point every time the other team makes a mistake.

Cooperative Skates (Movement of Players). The players stand in a line with one foot each on one of two giant "cooperative" skates, to which their foot is attached by a strap. They have to lift one foot and then the other at the same time so as to move in unison. In the competitive version, two teams compete to get to the other end of the playing area first.

Raising a Hoop (Movement of Players and Object). Each group has a hoop that is initially placed on the floor but which they then have to raise above their heads as if it were a hat.

Knot (Movement of Players). Standing in a circle, each player grasps (at random) the hand of two other players, one with each of his or her own hands. The task is then to undo the knot and reform the circle but without releasing one's grip.

Body Segments (Movement of Players). Each team has to get to the other end of the playing area as quickly as possible, with each player always being in contact with a teammate's body according to the combination of body segments that is called out (for example, head, ear, back, head, ear, back), as if they were a rigid block in motion.

Each of these games was also played competitively, the winner being the first team to gain two points. Each team comprised of six to eight players. Table 10.1 describes the different features of the internal logic of the above-mentioned cooperative games.

Data Recording

Each student was given a questionnaire and a pen. The teacher began by explaining the game that they had to take part in. After playing each game, the students had to immediately fill in the questionnaire, rating the intensity of the different emotions experienced on a scale of 0 to 10, where 0 meant they had not felt that emotion and 10 that they had felt it with maximum intensity. The questionnaire was answered individually.

Table 10.1. Identifying the different features of the internal logic of the cooperative games used in this study

	Density		Conditions / roles		Use of material		Final score (winner)		Processes activated		Strategic pact	
	Low	High	1 Role	>1 Role	No	Yes	No	Yes	Decision making	Automatic behaviors	No	Yes
1. Introducing oneself (competitive)	1	0	1	0	0	1	0	1	0	1	0	1
2. Raising a hoop (competitive)	0	1	0	1	0	1	0	1	1	0	0	1
3. Knot (competitive)	0	1	1	0	1	0	0	1	1	0	0	1
4. Body segments (competitive)	0	1	1	0	1	0	0	1	1	0	0	1
5. Rope jump (competitive)	0	1	1	0	0	1	0	1	0	1	0	1
6. Leapfrog (competitive)	0	1	0	1	1	0	0	1	0	1	1	0
7. Passing the hoop (competitive)	1	0	1	0	0	1	0	1	0	1	1	0
8. Transporting a floor mat (competitive)	0	1	1	0	0	1	0	1	0	1	0	1
9. Switching poles (competitive)	1	0	1	0	0	1	0	1	0	1	1	0
10. Cooperative skates (competitive)	0	1	0	1	0	1	0	1	0	1	1	0
11. Introducing oneself (noncompetitive)	1	0	1	0	0	1	1	0	0	1	0	1
12. Raising a hoop (noncompetitive)	0	1	1	0	0	1	1	0	1	0	0	1
13. Knot (noncompetitive)	0	1	1	0	1	0	1	0	1	0	0	1
14. Body segments (noncompetitive)	0	1	1	0	1	0	1	0	1	0	0	1
15. Rope jump (noncompetitive)	0	1	1	0	0	1	1	0	0	1	0	1
16. Leapfrog (noncompetitive)	0	1	0	1	1	0	1	0	0	1	1	0
17. Passing the hoop (noncompetitive)	1	0	1	0	0	1	1	0	0	1	1	0
18. Transporting a floor mat (noncompetitive)	0	1	1	0	0	1	1	0	0	1	0	1
19. Switching poles (noncompetitive)	1	0	1	0	0	1	1	0	0	1	0	1
20. Cooperative skates (noncompetitive)	0	1	0	1	0	1	1	0	0	1	0	1

Note. 0 = Absent, 1 = Present. The games used had the following distribution as regards the features of internal logic: Density (low, 30%; high, 70%); Roles (1 role, 75%; >1 role, 25%); Material (no objects, 30%; with objects, 70%); Use of Final Score (winner/loser, 50%; noncompetitive, 50%); Activated Processes (automatic behaviors, 70%; decision making, 30%), Strategic Pact (pact involved, 70%; no pact, 30%). All the games (100%) were played in a stable space.

Statistical Analysis

The data were analyzed using a model based on generalized estimating equations (GEE), Gaussian family, identity link, and exchangeable correlation. The statistical software used was SPSS v.15.0 and STATA v.11.

The model considered six within-subjects factors and four between-subjects factors. The six within-subjects factors were: (1) roles (1 role, >1 role); (2) material (with objects, without objects); (3) score/no score (winner and loser, noncompetitive); (4) processes (automatic behaviors, decision-making); (5) strategic pact (pact involved, not involved); and (6) type of emotion generated (positive, negative, and ambiguous). The four between-subjects factors were: (1) gender (male, female); (2) age; (3) sporting experience: domain (no experience, psychomotor, sociomotor); and (4) sporting experience: competitive level (no experience, recreational, local competition, high-level competition).

Results

The 307 participants generated 63,021 observations under the different experimental conditions. For each student, the minimum and maximum numbers of observations were, respectively, 78 and 260 (average 205) (Wald chi^2 (12) = 49077.32, Prob. > chi^2 = .000).

Types of Emotions and Cooperative Motor Games

The statistical analysis revealed significant differences (p < .001) between the three types of emotions (see Table 2). Positive emotions activated significantly higher intensity ratings (M = 6.15, SD = .171, 95% CI 5.81, 6.48; p < .001), than ambiguous emotions (M = 3.11, SD = .184, 95% CI 2.75, 3.47). Positive emotions activated significantly higher intensity than negative emotions (M = 1.07, SD = .164, 95% CI 0.75, 1.39; p < .001).

Intensity of Emotions and the System of Roles (Internal Logic)

There were significant differences between cooperative games with a fixed-role system (single role) and those that allowed a local exchange of roles (those with more than one role) (see table 10.2). Games with more than one role elicited significantly higher intensity ratings (M = 3.55, SD = .170, 95% CI 3.22, 3.88) than games involving a single role (M = 3.33, SD = .169, 95% CI 3.00, 3.66; p = .043).

The highest intensity ratings corresponded to games with more than one role, those in which at least one person had the possibility of leading the cooperative behavior of other team members. For instance, in the leapfrog game the role of "leaper" alternated with that of "frog."

Note, however, that the "frogs" could take the initiative by varying the height of their body and/or the distance between them and the next "frog." Similarly, the "leapers" could choose how hard they pressed down with their hands on the back of the "frog" over which they were leaping. In the "cooperative skates" game, the first player could lead the group by determining the direction and orientation of the movement made by the other players who formed the cooperative skate.

Intensity ratings were lower for games involving a single role, those in which all the players took part under the same conditions. In the games "introducing oneself," "switching poles," "transporting a floor mat," "knot," "rope jump," "body segments," and "passing the hoop," all the players could perform the same types of motor action.

Intensity of Emotions and the Strategic Pact (Internal Logic)

There were significant differences between cooperative games that required players to make a strategic pact and those that did not (see table 10.2). Games involving a pact elicited significantly lower intensity rating (M = 3.38, SD = .164, 95% CI 3.06, 3.70) than games that did not required a strategic pact to be made (M = 3.50, SD = .168, 95% CI 3.17, 3.83; p = .007).

Table 10.2. Results obtained when applying the GEE population-averaged model to all the variables

Variables	B	Std. Error	Lower Limit	Upper Limit	Chi^2- df		p
			95% Confidence Interval		Hypothesis contrast		
Age	0.017	0.0251	-0.032	0.067	0.484	1	.487
Gender: Female	-0.768	0.2184	-1.196	-0.340	12.374	1	.000
Sporting experience: domain—Psychomotor	-1.061	0.7526	-2.536	0.414	1.987	1	.159
Sporting experience: domain—Socio-motor	-1.193	0.7432	-2.650	0.263	2.578	1	.108
Sporting experience: Recreational	1.418	0.7583	-0.068	2.904	3.496	1	.062
Sporting experience: Local Competition	1.367	0.7416	-0.086	2.821	3.399	1	.065
Sporting experience: High-level Competition	1.347	0.7475	-0.118	2.812	3.247	1	.072
Positive emotion	2.750	0.1113	2.532	2.969	610.182	1	.000
Negative emotion	-2.229	0.1194	-2.463	-1.995	348.410	1	.000
Density: Low	0.116	0.1053	-0.090	0.323	1.219	1	.270
Roles: 1 Role	-0.174	0.0864	-0.344	-0.005	4.076	1	.043
Material: Without Objects	0.181	0.0604	0.063	0.300	9.027	1	.003
Score: Noncompetitive	-0.340	0.0392	-0.416	-0.263	75.046	1	.000
Score: Winner	0.060	0.0415	-0.022	0.141	2.061	1	.049
Processes activated: Automatic behaviors	-0.187	0.1342	-0.450	0.076	1.935	1	.164
Pact: No Strategic Pact	0.142	0.0524	0.039	0.244	7.308	1	.007
Female Gender * Positive Emotion	0.573	0.2072	0.167	0.979	7.644	1	.006
Female Gender * Negative Emotion	0.387	0.1826	0.029	0.745	4.486	1	.034
Female Gender * Density: Low	-0.041	0.1501	-0.335	0.253	0.074	1	.785
Female Gender * Roles: 1 Role	-0.089	0.0913	-0.268	0.090	0.955	1	.328
Female Gender * Material: Without Objects	0.046	0.0702	-0.092	0.184	0.430	1	.512
Female Gender * Score: Noncompetitive	0.099	0.0713	-0.041	0.239	1.919	1	.166
Female Gender * Score: Winner	0.168	0.0846	0.002	0.334	3.932	1	.047
Female Gender * Processes: Automatic behaviors	0.029	0.0993	-0.165	0.224	0.086	1	.769
Female Gender * Without Strategic Pact	-0.041	0.0749	-0.188	0.106	0.302	1	.582

Note. Reference category for the independent categorical variables in the GEE population-averaged model: 1. *External logic*: Gender = male; Emotion = ambiguous; Sporting Experience Domain = Without experience; Sporting Experience Level Competition = Without experience; 2. *Internal logic*: Density = high; Roles = >1 role; Material = with objects; Score/No Score = defeat; Processes = decision making; Pact = strategic pact required. The variables highlighted in gray are those which produced statistically significant differences.

Games involving a pact were those in which the players had to agree on ways of cooperating prior to taking any action. For example, in the game "introducing oneself," the players had to decide how to combine the different paths that the ball could follow; in other words, they had to consider the teammate from whom they would receive the ball and the teammate to whom they would throw it. In the "raising a hoop" game, they had first to agree how they would begin to lift this object, and then share the effort required to support it during the different stages of its rise and fall. In the "knot" game, each player had to decide how to join hands with two other players, and also how to change position within the group without letting go during each sequence of the game as the knot changed its formation. Finally, in the game "transporting a floor mat," the players had to agree on the position that they would each take up, and on how they would actually transport the mat to the other end of the playing area.

Intensity ratings were higher for games that did not require a strategic pact to be made. In these games the players merely had to take up a position and wait their turn, so there was little need for organization or agreement. Examples of these games are "switching poles," "passing the hoop," and "leapfrog."

Intensity of Emotions and the Use of a Final Score (Internal Logic)

The presence or absence of a final score (winner/loser) produced significant differences in the intensity of emotions (see table 10.2). Winners had significantly higher intensity ratings (M = 3.63, SD = .166, 95% CI 3.31, 3.96) than losers (M = 3.49, SD = .166, 95% CI 3.17, 3.82; p < .049). Losers had higher intensity ratings than participants in noncompetitive games (M = 3.20, SD = .165, 95% CI 2.88, 3.52; p < .001).

Intensity of Emotions and the Use of Objects (Internal Logic)

The use of material (objects) in cooperative games was associated with significant differences in the intensity of emotions (see table 2). Games that did not involve an object elicited significantly higher rating intensity (M = 3.54, SD = .169, 95% CI 3.21, 3.88) than games involving objects (M = 3.34, SD = .164, 95% CI 3.02, 3.66; p = .003).

The highest ratings corresponded to games that did not involve an object, the greatest emotional intensity being reported for the "body segments" game. The "knot" game, "body segments," and "leapfrog" all required players to engage in direct motor interaction with the bodies of other participants. In the other games, however, the motor interaction was mediated either by the exchange of an object (pole or hoop), the movement of an object (floor mat, skates), or by having to jump without touching an object in the air (rope). These latter games (involving objects) were associated with lower ratings of emotional intensity.

Gender and the Intensity of Emotions (External Logic)

There were significant differences in the intensity of emotions according to the gender of participants (see table 10.2). The ratings by men (M = 3.64, SD = .174, 95% CI 3.29, 3.98) were significantly higher than those by women (M = 3.25, SD = .175, 95% CI 2.91, 3.59; p < .001).

Gender and Types of Emotions

The interaction between the variables "gender" and "type of emotion" (positive, negative, and ambiguous) also yielded significant differences (p = .006 and .034) (see table 10.2). Men had significantly higher intensity ratings in positive emotions than women (p =.006). Men also had significantly higher intensity ratings in negative emotions than women (p = .034) (see values in table 10.3).

Gender and Score (Winner/Loser) (Internal Logic)

No significant gender differences were observed in the context of noncompetitive games (p = .166). However, there were significant differences (p = .047) between men and women when the game involved winners and losers. Men winners had significantly higher intensity ratings than women winners (p = .047). Men losers had also significantly higher intensity ratings than women losers (p = .047) (see tables 10.2 and 10.4).

Non-significant Relationships Between Variables (Emotions/Density and Emotions/Processes Activated)

In these cooperative games there were no significant differences (see table 10.2) as regards the relationship between the intensity of emotions and the internal logic variables "density" (p = .270) and "processes activated" (p = .164).

Non-significant Relationships Between Variables: Gender (External Logic) and Other Variables of Internal Logic

No significant differences were found (see tble 2) when comparing the intensity ratings of men and women in relation to the following features of internal logic: density (p = .785), roles (p = .325), material (.512), noncompetitive format (p = .166), processes activated (p = .769), and strategic pact (p = .582).

Non-significant Relationships Between Variables: Sporting Experience of Participants (External Logic) and Emotions

The statistical analysis revealed no significant differences in intensity ratings in relation to the sporting experience of participants, whether for the domains of motor action (psychomotor , p = .159; sociomotor, p = .108) or as regards the level of competition (recreational sport, p = .062; local competition, p = .065; high-level competition, p = 0.72) (see table 10.2). However, it is worth noting that participants with no sporting background had higher ratings than did those with some sporting experience in the psychomotor and socio-motor domains (M = 4.10, SD = .613, 95% CI 2.90, 5.30). With respect to the level of competition, the highest ratings corresponded to participants with recreational experience of sport (M = 3.73, SD = .298, 95% CI 3.15, 4.32).

Table 10.3. Results obtained when applying the GEE population-averaged model to the variables "gender" and "type of emotion"

Gender	Type of Emotion	Mean	Standard Deviation	95% Confidence Interval	
				Lower Limit	Upper Limit
Female	Positive	6.08	.195	5.70	6.46
	Negative	0.91	.175	0.57	1.26
	Ambiguous	2.76	.217	2.33	3.18
Male	Positive	6.21	.182	5.86	6.57
	Negative	1.23	.172	0.90	1.57
	Ambiguous	3.46	.201	3.07	3.86

Discussion

The aim of this study was to examine the relationship between cooperative motor games and the emotional experiences of participants, specifically as regards gender and the different features of the games' internal logic. The results obtained can be discussed according to the following sections.

Table 10.4. Results obtained when applying the GEE population-averaged model to the variables "gender" and "score"

Gender	Score	Mean	Standard Deviation	95% Confidence Interval	
				Lower Limit	Upper Limit
Female	Noncompetitive	3.01	.176	2.67	3.36
	Winner	3.48	.180	3.13	3.83
	Loser	3.25	.182	2.90	3.61
Male	Noncompetitive	3.39	.174	3.05	3.73
	Winner	3.79	.174	3.45	4.13
	Loser	3.73	.177	3.38	4.07

Emotions and the Internal Logic of Cooperative Games

First, the results confirm the tenets of Parlebas's theory of motor action and Bisquerra's theory of emotions, which together provided the theoretical basis for the present study.[47] More specifically, differences were observed as regards the three types of emotions studied. The highest intensity ratings given by participants in the cooperative motor games corresponded to positive emotions, while the lowest ratings were those for negative emotions. The values for ambiguous emotions (surprise, hope, and compassion) were intermediate between these two. These results are consistent with the findings of previous studies that considered different domains of motor action in sporting games.[48] It should also be noted that the social nature of cooperative motor games not only encourages but actually requires players to relate positively to one another. This highlights the key role that these games can play in terms of providing a natural environment in which positive emotions can be fostered within a relational context.[49]

Detailed knowledge of the internal logic of cooperative motor games is a necessary step in revealing not only the praxic processes that take place within this family of games, but also the affective consequences they may have. Of the four features that define the internal logic of all cooperative games (the relationships with other participants, with time, with space, and with material), three were associated with significant differences in terms of the emotions experienced. The aspects that had a significant effect on the ratings of emotional intensity were: competitive vs. noncompetitive games (relationship with time); the use of objects (relationship with material); and the number of roles and the need to make a strategic pact (the relationship with others).

As regards the relationship with time in cooperative games, the results showed that the ratings of emotional intensity differed according to whether or not the game ended with a final score. The most intense emotions were produced in what Parlebas[50] refers to as exclusive competitive games (or zero-sum games), in which the outcome involves one team defeating the other. In these games, the emotional intensity ratings of both winners and losers were higher than those reported by participants in noncompetitive games. This finding is consistent with

---

47. Parlebas, *Juegos, deporte y sociedad*; Bisquerra, *Educación emocional y bienestar*.

48. Lavega et al., "Educar emociones positivas a través de los juegos deportivos"; Lavega et al., "Understanding Emotions Through Games."

49. Kaiser and Wehrle, "Situated Emotional Problem Solving in Interactive Computer Games"; Salen and Zimmerman, *Rules of Play*; Shahid, Krahmer, and Swerts, "Alone or Together."

50. Parlebas, *Juegos, deporte y sociedad*.

previous research that also found that the emotional experience of participants was more intense in competitive team games.[51] In the present study, the main difference was observed between winners of competitive games and players of noncompetitive games, although there was also a slightly less significant difference between losing participants in competitive games and players of noncompetitive games. The smallest difference in emotional intensity ratings was that between winners and losers in competitive games.

It should be noted, however, that these data contradict our group's previous findings regarding affect and different kinds of sporting games, in which the highest ratings of emotional intensity were obtained in noncompetitive cooperative games.[52] There are two possible reasons for this discrepancy. First, these previous studies used cooperative practices based on introjective motor skills, while varying a certain aspect of the internal logic between games. Specifically, cooperation was geared toward developing awareness of self and others (greater self-knowledge) through the use of strategies such as breathing exercises or cooperative massage, such that each participant's attention was focused inward. However, in the games studied here, the participants' attention was directed outward, toward the shared task that had to be successfully performed. The second possible explanation for the different results concerns the novelty of the task, an aspect that has been studied by various authors.[53] Here the students began by playing the competitive format of the games, and this may have led to them being less interested when it came to playing the subsequent noncompetitive version, which was no longer a completely novel task.

With respect to the use of material, the results show that emotional intensity ratings were higher when no objects were involved, that is, the players only made contact with each other's bodies. This body-to-body contact fosters positive and direct communication, which has repercussions in terms of the intensity of the emotional experience. If one compares the emotions produced in games involving the different domains of motor action, the use or not of material does not in itself determine the type of emotion that will be produced.[54] However, in the case of cooperative motor games, the absence of material does heighten the affective experience of participants.

---

51. See Burton-Chellew, Ross-Gillespie, and West, "Cooperation in Humans."

52. Lavega et al., "Educar emociones positivas a través de los juegos deportivos"; Lavega et al., "Understanding Emotions Through Games."

53. See for example Scherer and Brosch, "Culture-Specific Appraisal Biases Contribute to Emotion Dispositions."

54. Lavega et al., "Educar emociones positivas a través de los juegos deportivos"; Lavega et al., "Understanding Emotions Through Games."

As regards the relationship with others, the results concerning the system of roles show that the most intense emotions were experienced in games with more than one role. There are two possible interpretations for this finding. First, in games in which roles can be switched, one or more of the participants may act as a leader and direct the actions of the group, thereby emphasizing the commitment aspect of the motor interaction. This finding is consistent with previous studies that have argued that the emotions reported by participants reflect the relationships they have maintained with one another and the position they have each occupied in the group.[55] An alternative interpretation is that games that allow players to switch roles involve a greater repertoire of motor responses and relationships, thereby exploiting to the maximum the positive interactions that may occur between participants. This notion has been previously discussed by other authors.[56]

The other aspect associated with the relationship to others was the strategic pact. The results in this regard showed that the emotional experience was more intense when players did not need to interrupt what they were doing in order to plan the group's strategy and organize themselves. A possible explanation for this finding is that in a game that does not require a pact to be made, each player can immediately focus on solving the problem at hand, thereby avoiding a loss of momentum during the game. Young students who have been socialized in a context of audiovisual consumption, in a culture of immediacy, or in what some authors have referred to as a channel-hopping culture or a culture of the spectacle,[57] find in games without a strategic pact the opportunity to obtain immediate recompense for each of their motor actions.

Gender and Emotions in the Context of Cooperation

When men and women had to test their social competences through the motor interactions required by the specific cooperative tasks, significant differences were observed in the emotional experiences they reported. Specifically, the intensity ratings of men were higher than those of women for all three types of emotion (positive, negative, and ambiguous). These results are in line with previous research that also found that men reported greater emotional intensity than women in the context of psychomotor, cooperative, competitive, and coopera-

55. Buck, *Human Motivation and Emotion*; Matsumoto, Yoo, and LeRoux, "Emotion and Intercultural Communication."

56. Green and Rechis, "Children's Cooperative and Competitive Interactions in Limited Resource Situations."

57. Ferrés, *Educar en una cultura del espectáculo*.

tive/competitive games.[58]

When we analyzed from a gender perspective the relationship between the emotional intensity ratings and the different features of internal logic (density, roles, strategic pact, material, automatic behaviors/decision making), we observed significant differences between men and women in the context of competitive games. The difference between the ratings of men and women was greater when both were losers, as compared with when they were both winners. These results are consistent with previous findings regarding the processes of social dialogue among men and women in competitive contexts,[59] and the differences observed may be explained in terms of the social and cultural nature of the emotions. In this regard, various studies of children's motor behavior in specific cultural contexts have shown that cooperation is much more present among girls.[60] Similarly, research on the development of emotional literacy also confirms that women express a much weaker preference for competitive games than do men.[61]

To conclude, the present findings confirm that cooperative games can make an important contribution to the field of physical education. Further research is now required to elucidate in greater detail the ways in which such games can be used to foster emotional competences among both men and women.

Bibliography

Archer, John. "Childhood Gender Roles: Social Context and Organization." In *Childhood Social Development: Contemporary Perspectives*, edited by Harry McGurk. Hove: Lawrence Erlbaum Associates, 1992.

Averill, James R. "A Constructivist View of Emotion." In *Emotion: Theory, Research, and Experience*. Vol. 1. *Theories of Emotion*, edited by Robert Plutchik and Henry Kellerman. New York: Academic, 1980.

Benenson, Joyce F., Rosanne Roy, Angela Waite, Suzanne Goldbaum, Lisa Linders, and Anna Simpson. "Greater Discomfort as a Proximate Cause of Sex Differences in Competition." *Merrill-Palmer Quarterly* 48, no. 3 (2002): 225–47.

Ben- Ze'ev, Aaron. *The Subtlety of Emotions*. Cambridge: MIT Press, 2000.

Bisquerra, Rafael. *Educación emocional y bienestar*. Barcelona: Praxis,

---

58. Lavega et al., "Understanding Emotions Through Games."
59. Archer, "Childhood Gender Roles."
60. Etxebeste, "Les jeux sportifs"; Lavega, ed., *Traditional Games and Society in Europe*.
61. Benenson et al., "Greater Discomfort as a Proximate Cause of Sex Differences in Competition"; Hendridson Eagly, *Sex Differences in Social Behavior*; Roy and Benenson, "Sex and Contextual Effects on Children's Use of Interference Competition."

2000.

Buck, Ross. *Human Motivation and Emotion*. New York: Wiley, 1988.

Burton-Chellew, Maxwell N., Adin R. Ross-Gillespie, and Stuart A. West. "Cooperation in Humans: Competition Between Groups and Proximate Emotions." *Evolution and Human Behavior* 31, no. 2 (2010): 104–8.

Damasio, Antonio. *Y el cerebro creó al hombre. ¿Cómo pudo el cerebro generar emociones, sentimientos y el yo?* Barcelona: Destino, 2010.

Eagly, Alice Hendridson. *Sex Differences in Social Behavior: A Social-role Interpretation*. Hillsdale, N.J.: Erlbaum, 1987.

Etxebeste, Joseba. "Les jeux sportifs, éléments de la socialisation traditionnelle des enfants du Pays basque." Ph.D. diss., University of Paris V-Réné Descartes, U.F.R. de Sciences Humaines et Sociales, 2001.

Etxebeste, Joseba, and Clara Urdangarin. "La socialización tradicional vasca: una guía para la elaboración de un programa de Educación Física." In *Evaluación e intervención en el ámbito deportivo*, edited by Joseba Etxebestre and Clara Urdangarin. Vitoria-Gasteiz: Diputación Foral de Alava, 2006.

Ferrés, Joan. *Educar en una cultura del espectáculo*. Barcelona: Paidós, 2000.

Frijda, Nico H. "What Emotions Might Be? Comments on the Comments." *Social Science Information* 46 (2007): 433–43.

Geertz, Clifford. *The Interpretation of Cultures*. New York: Basic Books, 1973.

Green, Vanessa A., and Ruth Rechis. "Children's Cooperative and Competitive Interactions in Limited Resource Situations: A Literature Review." *Applied Developmental Psychology* 27, no. 1 (2006): 42–59.

Hyder, Elaine B., Michael B. Prietula, and Laurie R. Weingart. "Getting to Best: Efficiency versus Optimality in Negotiation." *Cognitive Science* 24, no.2 (2000): 169–204.

Ibarra, Herminia. "Personal Networks of Women and Minorities in Management: A Conceptual Framework." *Academy of Management Review* 18, no. 1 (1993): 56–87.

Kaiser, Susanne, and Thomas Wehrle. "Situated Emotional Problem Solving in Interactive Computer Games." In *Proceedings of the IXth Conference of the International Society for Research on Emotions*, edited by Nico H. Frijda. Toronto: ISRE Publications, 1996.

Kashima, Yoshihisa, Susumu Yamaguchi, Uichol Kim, Sang-Chin Choi, Michele J. Gelfand, and Masaki Yuki. "Culture, Gender and Self: A Perspective from Individualism–Collectivism Research." *Journal of Personality and Social Psychology* 69, no. 5 (1995): 935–37.

Kerr, Norbert L. "Illusions of Efficacy: The Effects of Group Size on Perceived Efficacy in Social Dilemmas." *Journal of Experimental Social Psychology* 25, no. 4 (1989): 287–313.

Kitayama, Shinobu, Hazel R. Markus, and Masaru Kurokawa. "Culture, Emotion, and Well-being: Good Feelings in Japan and the United States." *Cognition and Emotion* 14, no. 1 (2000): 93–124.

Lagardera, Francisco. "La lógica deportiva y las emociones. Implicaciones en la enseñanza del deporte." *Apunts de Educación Física* 56 (1999): 99–107.

Lagardera, Francisco, and Pere Lavega. *Introducción a la praxiología motriz.* Barcelona: Paidotribo, 2003.

———, eds. *La ciencia de la acción motriz.* Lleida: Ediciones de la Universitat de Lleida, 2004.

Lavega, Pere, ed. *Traditional Games and Society in Europe.* Barcelona: Asociación Europea de Juegos y Deportes Tradicionales, 2006.

———. "La investigación en los juegos tradicionales y en los juegos cooperativos." In *Investigación y juego motor en España*, edited by Vicente Navarro and Carmen Trigueros. Lleida: Universitat de Lleida, 2009.

Lavega, Pere, Mercé Mateu, Francisco Lagardera, and Gemma Filella. "Educar emociones positivas a través de los juegos deportivos." In *Docencia, innovación e investigación en educación física*, edited by Miguel A. Torralba, Miguel De Fuentes, Juan Calvo, and José F. Cardozo. Barcelona: INDE Publicaciones, 2010.

Lavega, Pere, Gemma Filella, Maria Jesús Agulló, Anna Soldevila, and Jaume March. "Understanding Emotions Through Games: Helping Trainee Teachers to Make Decisions." *Electronic Journal of Research in Educational Psychology* 9, no. 2 (2011): 617–40.

Lazarus, Richard S. "How Emotions Influence Performance in Competitive Sports." *The Sport Psychologist* 14, no. 3 (2000): 229–52.

Le Breton, David. *Las pasiones ordinarias: Antropología de las emociones.* Translated by Horacio Pons. Buenos Aires: Ediciones Nueva Visión, 1999.

Matsumoto, David, Seung H. Yoo, and Jeffrey A. LeRoux. "Emotion and Intercultural Communication." In *Handbook of Applied Linguistics.* Vol. 7. *Intercultural Communication*, edited by Helga Kotthoff and Helen Spencer-Oatley. Berlin: Mouton de Gruyter Publishers, 2005.

Messick, David M., and Marilynn B. Brewer. "Solving Social Dilemmas: A Review." Vol. 4 of *Review of Personality and Social Psychology*, edited by Ladd Wheeler and Phillip Shaver. Beverly Hills: Sage, 1983.

Parlebas, Pierre. *Juegos, deporte y sociedad: Léxico comentado en praxeología motriz.* Translated by Fernando González del Campo Román. Barcelona: Paidotribo, 2001.

———. "Une rupture culturelle: Des jeux traditionnels au sport." *Revue Internationale de Psychosociologie* 20, no. 9 (2003): 9–36.

———. "Health and Relational Well-being in Traditional Games." In *Traditional Games and Social Health*, edited by Guy Jaouen, Pere Lavega, and Carlos de La Villa. Ribera de Duero, Spain: Asociación Cultural La Tanguilla; Europeen Association of Traditional Games and Sports, 2010.

Puig, Nuria. "La situación de la mujer en el deporte al iniciarse el siglo XXI." In *Deporte y cambio social en el umbral del S. XXI*, edited by Margarota Latiesa, Pilar Martos, and José Luis Paniza. Madrid: AEISAD-Esteban Sanz, 2001.

Puig, Nuria, Francisco Lagardera, and Ferrer Juncà. "Enseñando sociología de las emociones en deporte." *Apunts EF y Deportes* 64 (2001): 69–77.

Roy, Rosanne, and Joyce F. Benenson. "Sex and Contextual Effects on Children's Use of Interference Competition." *Developmental Psychology* 38, no. 2 (2002): 306–12.

Salen, Katie, and Eric Zimmerman. *Rules of Play: Game Design Fundamentals*. Cambridge: MIT Press, 2003.

Salovey, Peter, and John D. Mayer. "Emotional Intelligence: Imagination." *Cognition and Personality* 9 (1990): 185–211.

Scherer, Klaus R., and Tobias Brosch. "Culture-Specific Appraisal Biases Contribute to Emotion Dispositions." *European Journal of Personality* 23, no. 3 (2009): 265–88.

Shahid, Suleman, Emiel Krahmer, and Marc Swerts. "Alone or Together: Exploring the Effect of Physical Co-presence on the Emotional Expressions of Game Playing Children Across Cultures." In *Fun and Games*, edited by Panos Markopoulos. Berlin: Springer Verlag, 2008.

Soler, Susanna. "Les relacions de gènere en l'educació física a l'escola primària: Anàlisi dels processos de reproducció, resistència i canvi a l'aula." Ph.D. diss., University of Barcelona, 2007.

Weber, Mark J., and David M. Messik. "Conflicting Interests in Social Life." In *The Handbook of Negotiation and Culture*, edited by Michele J. Gelfand and Jeanne M. Brett. Stanford: Stanford Business Books, 2004.

Part 3

PASSION

11

Bridging Practice and Desire: Football Rivalry in Mostar, Bosnia and Herzegovina

Gary Armstrong and Emily Vest

> *Violence—apart from endemic football hooliganism—*
> *is just a memory and unlikely to return.*
> —International Crisis Group, Bosnia: A *Test of Political Maturity in Mostar*

At the signing of the Dayton Peace Accords in December 1995, what the global media referred to as the "Bosnian conflict" came to an end.[1] Like many places in the former Yugoslavia, the medieval city of Mostar—a medium-sized city in the southwest of the nation of Bosnia and Herzegovina (BiH)—stood battered, in places reduced to rubble, and cleaved in half physically and demographically. Living on one side were the Bosnian Croats, whose political leaders looked to exclude all others of a different ethno-political background from every aspect of city life. On the other side were the Bosniaks,[2] who looked to create a multi-ethnic state, but one in which they were in the majority and held

* The authors are indebted to Adnan and Denis of the Velež Red Army fan group. Our thanks are also due to Dirim Ozkan for his generosity with contacts. The research was also facilitated by Adnan Karalić and Mirko Milošević. Sincere thanks are due to Joseba Zulaika, Joseba Extebeste, Clara Urdangarin, and Mariann Vaczi for their invitation to contribute to this collection and their assistance with editing. Full epigraph citation: International Crisis Group. Bosnia: A Test of Political Maturity in Mostar (ICG. Sarajevo/Brussels: Europe Briefing No. 54.2009),3.

1. The General Framework Agreement for Peace in Bosnia Herzegovina (more commonly known as the Dayton Peace Accords) brought to an end the conflict in Bosnia. The Accords established the Constitution of Bosnia and Herzegovina and the political framework of the country, achieved by creating two highly decentralised entities, the Serb Republika Srpska (RS) and the Bosniak/Croat Federation, each with its own government and law-making capacities. Key posts in the national governments are rotated between the different ethnicities. Since its implementation, the Dayton Accords has been much criticized for creating a political structure that has led to a separation of ethnicities and has in effect frozen Bosnia in a postconflict state unable to move past ethnic antagonisms. In 2011 the European Court of Human Rights ruled that the Accord was discriminatory against Jews, Roma, and others not of a constitutional ethnicity (Bosniak, Serb, or Croat) because these people are unable to hold these key rotating government posts.

2. *Bosniak* is a term for a Bosnian Muslim, but it does not have a particularly religious reference. The term *Bosniak* differs from *Bosnian* in that *Bosnian* is an all-inclusive word for any citizen of Bosnia, irrespective of ethnicity or religion.

political control. Divided physically, culturally, and religiously, the previously united city of Mostar was coming to accept the abnormality and instability of the postconflict milieu as routine. One sign of normality in this schism was the ability of the city's two professional football clubs to assume both their training and matches. The two clubs had always in various ways represented the people of Mostar, most notably in religion and politics, but the clubs were to become now more than ever a focal point of ethno-political identity—a visible sign of the differences between the city's two major ethnic factions. The story of the two professional Mostar clubs is, in a sense, the story of the city, reflecting the changing circumstances of the region. The clubs are vehicles for the bitterness that endures around ethno-political issues and for the way in which the communities choose to present themselves. Football-related antagonism is forever symbolic, frequently verbal, and less frequently but potentially violent; matches remain a key flash point in the uneasy relationships between Bosniaks and Croats some twenty years after the war.

The violence that accompanied a Cup match between the two clubs in September 2011 has meant that all subsequent matches, on the orders of the Football Federation[3] (known colloquially as Savez) have been played without the presence of visiting fans.[4] Furthermore, violence at the game between the Serb team Borac Banja Luka and the predominantly Bosniak team FK Sarajevo that same week led Savez to ban all visiting fans for the remainder of the season.

The Balkan Battlegrounds

Conflict has been a way of life for many people in this region for decades. The Yugoslav conflicts of the 1990s were the most violent on European soil since World War II. Placing a figure on the number of casualties remains a highly politicized act, but best estimates are that in the former Yugoslav region between 1991 and 2000 approximately 140,000 people were killed and almost 4 million people were displaced (International Center for Transitional Justice). The conflicts were characterized by violence between different ethnic groups (Serbs, Croats, Bosniaks, and to a lesser extent Slovenes, Montenegrins, and Macedonians) within the region and became notorious for the targeting of ci-

---

3. The Football Federation of Bosnia and Herzegovina, *Nogometni/Fudbalski Savez Bosnie I Hercegovine (N/FSBiH)*

4. Having drawn against each other in the Bosnian Cup, the two sides were scheduled to meet three times in under a month. The violence accompanying the first cup match on September 28, 2011, led to the matches between the two teams played on the following October 2 and 19 to be played without fans.

vilians, particularly in the pursuit of ethnic cleansing policies.[5]
Media reporting of concentration camps around Prijedor, Bosnia, in 1992 portrayed images eerily similar to those in Nazi Germany, but it was the daily Bosnian Serb gunshot sniping at Sarajevans during the three-year siege of the city under the noses of the world's media that kept the conflict in the global eye. Such global consciousness was not sufficient to prompt intervention, and the UN troops (UNPROFOR) present to protect civilians did not have a mandate to engage, only to protect. This mandate was not sufficient to protect the citizens of the Bosnian town of Srebrenica, which fell to the Bosnian Serb army in July 1995. Soon after, almost eight thousand Bosnian Muslim men and boys disappeared, an act later judged by the International Criminal Tribunal for the Former Yugoslavia (ICTY) to be genocide. Since the cessation of violence, the ICTY has been prosecuting serious crimes committed during the Yugoslav conflicts, including crimes against humanity that include acts of genocide, systemic rape, and massacres, as well as the destruction of sites of cultural heritage and religious buildings.[6]

---

5. A variety of conflicts based on a variety of causations were defined as the Yugoslav Conflict. The conflicts have to be considered as a series of separate conflicts, albeit inter-related. The chronology was as follows: Following Tito's death in 1981, increasingly nationalistic tendencies were visible in the economically stronger republics of Yugoslavia, most notably Slovenia and Croatia, particularly in reaction to the perceived Serb dominance and increasingly nationalistic Serb politics in Belgrade. Following a December 1990 referendum, Slovenia declared independence from Yugoslavia in late June 1991. The Serb-dominated Yugoslavian Army (JNA) sent tanks into Slovenia but met more resistance than expected and withdrew after ten days. Croatia held a referendum in May 1991 and declared its independence, also in late June 1991. Croatia's Serbs, who made up a sizable minority in Croatia, lived mainly in the east of Croatia and in the Krajina region bordering the west of Bosnia. They were particularly concerned about their marginalization and formed a quasi-statelet, the Republic of Serbian Krajina, which declared independence from Croatia in December 1991. Serbia supported the Croatian Serbs, and with international recognition of the country of Croatia violence became inevitable. In particular, the eastern city of Vukovar suffered massacres and a brutal three-month siege at the end of 1991, while the coastal city of Dubrovnik (a designated UN heritage site) was also bombarded. The war in Croatia ended in August 1995 with Operation Storm, which was a strong push by the Croatian Armed Forces against the Serbs to regain control of parts of Croatia claimed by separatist Serbs. This military action was described as the largest European land offensive since World War II. Lasting four days, this battle effectively ended the war in Croatia.

Macedonia declared its independence in September 1991, but it did not experience much resistance from Belgrade. But there was a large conflict between ethnic Albanians and Macedonians near the Macedonia/Kosovo border in Macedonia in 2001 that almost escalated into full-scale conflict. The Kosovo War (1996–99) started when the resident Albanians (who make up the majority of people in Kosovo) began seeking independence from Serbia. Kosovo holds an important role in Serbian history and Serb nationalism, so Serbia was naturally inclined to fight that break-up tooth and nail. The conflict came to an end with NATO fighter planes bombing Belgrade in March–June 1999.

6. Two national courts, based in Sarajevo and Belgrade, were also established to try

The region of the former Yugoslavia that is of particular concern to this paper is Bosnia, which held a referendum for independence from Yugoslavia in March 1992. The violence began shortly after as Serb paramilitaries who opposed Bosnia's independence began the notorious ethnic-cleansing policy in northeastern Bosnia. The Bosnian Croats and the Bosniaks began the conflict as allies against the Serbs, who wished to remain as part of Yugoslavia, but ultimately their contradictory views on the fate of an independent Bosnia led them to turn upon each other.[7] The fighting in Bosnia varied according to where one lived; in some areas the Croats and Bosniaks were allies, in others they were enemies. At times, matters were very confusing. Frequently what happened was atrocious.

Who Are You? Real and Imagined Identities

Historians generally agree that the Bosnian Croats, the Bosnian Serbs, and the Bosniaks descend from a single people.[8] The Bosniaks became distinct from the others during the Ottoman occupation (1463–1878), when they converted to Islam, which was a prerequisite for those working in the Ottoman administration. Such conversions led to a demographic pattern whereby the Bosniaks tended to be urban-based. The Bosnian Croats and Bosnian Serbs, far from being ethnically or historically "Croatian" or "Serbian," are understood to have been the rural-based populations who picked up the Croat Catholic or Serb Orthodox faith because of their proximity to the Croat and Serb borders. Although they were newcomers to this strand of faith, the peoples in the region were also learning at the time about the ideology of nationalism, which was coming to prominence throughout Europe. Already sharing a sense of religious community, many Serbs and Croats who were developing a sense of nationality felt that those in a neighboring state who shared a similar religion/language were surely an exiled people belonging originally to the Serbian/Croatian nation. In this milieu, they claimed the Christian populations in neighbouring Bosnia as their own.

In Mostar, as in the rest of Bosnia, the most noticeable of these

---

war crimes, but they faced serious problems, including lack of transparency and insufficient witness protection.

7. The Bosniaks wanted a separate Bosnian state, while the Croats wanted to partition the country, with some parts joining Croatia. Although the Bosnian Serbs (who wanted large parts of the country to remain with Serbia) and the Bosnian Croats had seemingly similar aims, the Croats required Bosnia to be independent from Yugoslavia in order to achieve their aims, hence the unlikely alliance with the Bosniaks against the Serbs.

8. Malcolm, *Bosnia*; Judah, *The Serbs*.

"ethnic" differences is religion, the other nationalist distinctions of language and culture being inapplicable. It is an irony that although defined by their religion, most Bosnians are not especially devout practitioners of their religious beliefs. Nonetheless, religious orientation makes up an important part of Bosnian identity. In Mostar, to be Croat is to be Catholic, and Christian symbolism is used both as a moniker of who the Croats are and as a definition of who they are not, in a dichotomy akin to the syntactic nature of footballing rivalries.

The Bridge of Sighs: Seeking the Reachable

In early November 1993 at the height of violence around the southern Bosnian city of Mostar, the Croatian Defence Council (*Hrvatsko Vijeće Obrane*, HVO, the de facto Bosnian Croat army) began to bombard Mostar's ancient soaring, single-span *Stari Most* (Old Bridge) crossing high above the emerald waters of the Neretva River. The bombardment targeted the bridge throughout the day until it could no longer withstand the onslaught and crumbled into the water. The destruction of the bridge was for many a most symbolic depiction of the collapsing Yugoslav regime.[9] As the bridge disappeared, so did the most visible reminder of a once unified city, a city formerly celebrated for its tolerance during the brutal years of World War II. An ethnically mixed city, the 1991 census of the city's then 126,000 inhabitants revealed the way they described themselves: 29 percent were Croat, 34 percent were Bosniak, 19 percent were Serb, and the remaining 18 percent considered themselves as Yugoslav or "other."[10] Many found it difficult to describe what they were, being products of the mixed marriages that were common at that time.[11] Although many Mostar neighborhoods were historically mixed, there was a tendency for Bosniaks to live on the east side of the Neretva under the shadow of Mt. Velež, and for Croats and Serbs to live on the flatter, more sprawling west side.

By the end of 1992, after months of bombardment by the besieging Serb-led Yugoslav army, almost all the Serbs had deserted the city. The remaining Bosniaks and Croats had jointly resisted the Serb attacks, but once the Serb forces withdrew they turned upon each other, the Croats expelling the Bosniaks from their traditional west-side base, and the Bosniaks removing Croats from the east.

The bridge was rebuilt in 2004, eleven years after its limestone arch

---

9. Coward, *Urbicide*.

10. The category "other" includes people describing themselves variously as Roma, Jewish, or Hungarian, and it includes those not wishing to describe and define themselves as any one ethnic group.

11. About a third of marriages in Mostar were thought to be mixed. See Bose, *Bosnia After Dayton*.

was shelled into submission. The young men of the city were quick to resume their traditional machismo pastime of leaping from the bridge into the river before an audience. But such a visible token of reunification could only achieve so much in this postwar milieu; the wounds of the conflict proved—and have proven—hard to heal. Mostar remains a ruptured city; its population of 72,000 is served by two bus stations, two fire departments (unified in 2005 but still operating separately), two postal services, two phone networks, two electricity companies, two utility services, and two universities. In 2010 Mostar endured a year without a mayor because neither side of the divided city was prepared to allow someone from the other side to hold the office. The football clubs are an integral part of these dualisms. Their weekly fixtures permit many of the residents of Mostar to celebrate their sense of difference from their fellow citizens. Football, a game of many contradictions, relies on such sentiments for its support.

As a pastime with enthusiasts across religious and ethnic divides, football is considered by many the world over as harnessing the potential for building upon a shared passion. Inevitably, those aspiring to build peace in areas of conflict may see in football qualities that could be utilized to their cause of bringing enemies together around a mutual enthusiasm. Those who promote the game—be it the apparatchiks of the games' global governing body, the FIFA, their European counterparts in UEFA, or for that matter the games' corporate sponsors—are never shy of publicizing what the game can facilitate for issues of human rights. The discussion that follows does not set out to deliberately challenge such viewpoints. The purpose of what follows is to offer a socio-historical analysis of football in one city in Bosnia Herzegovina where the actuality of how the game is conducted and supported carries with it an alternative narrative to that provided by those whom we might best term "football evangelists."

Football Rivalry: Noblemen and Citizens

Mostar's two professional football clubs have represented their supporters' s ideals and passions since their inceptions in the early years of the twentieth century. The Croats, traditionally looking toward Croatia and taking pride in their Croatian heritage, have tended to support HŠK[12] Zrinjski Mostar; while other residents of the city, with its long Communist heritage, have historically followed FK[13] Velež Mostar. Both clubs have a long history of resistance and defiance of the dominant political regime, but it is only recently, in the years since the latest

---

12. *Hrvatski Športski Klub* (Croatian Sports Club)
13. *Fudbalski Klub* (Football Club)

conflict, that their identities have turned and are shaped by their animosity toward one another.

The football rivalry between Zrinjski and Velež has a long history through a period of great change and upheaval throughout Bosnia. The clubs played their first game in 1922 in a period when the newly formed Kingdom of Yugoslavia[14] (of which Bosnia was a part) was vulnerable to both ongoing nationalist tensions between the different provinces and to the growth of support for Communism in the increasingly industrializing nation.

Zrinjski was, as it is now, part of a wider sports club created and named after the Zrinjski Croatian aristocratic family, which explains their nickname of *plemći* (noblemen). The club has played football since 1905, but was banned by the authorities following World War I (1914–18) for its perceived nationalist tendencies, which ran counter to the newly formed Kingdom of Yugoslavia of which Bosnia was now a part. Although they were encouraged to participate in a Yugoslav Sports Club, the Croats felt excluded and marginalized by the Serb population, so they left to establish their own exclusively Croat club in 1922, with ambitions to represent their Croatian identity both within the city and across the region. FK Velež was also founded in 1905, also in defiance of the dominant political regime. Its original incarnation, as the *Radnicki* (workers) sports club (hence the nickname of *Rođeni* or "citizens"), was also for a time disbanded. The players, who had effectively lost their club and who posterity tells us came from all over the city, met together to discuss the creation of a new sports club. Their Communist origins can be seen reflected in their Red Star choice of club emblem and in their philosophy of ensuring that the club was open to all regardless of ethnicity. The club enjoyed relative success and significant popularity in Mostar, with some 35,000 supporters regularly attending its games.[15]

The 1920s were turbulent times for the Kingdom of Yugoslavia. The Communist Party, divided over whether Yugoslavia was ready for a Workers' Revolution, split from its more revolutionary cadres and began a campaign of terrorism that included an attempt to kill the Prince Regent and led to a ban of the Communist Party altogether. During the same period, Croatia became increasingly resentful of perceived Serb dominance and questioned the centralization of power in Belgrade. Organizations such as the revolutionary and ultra-nationalist Ustaša

---

14. The official name of the Kingdom of Yugoslavia was the Kingdom of Serbs, Croats, and Slovenes. It was founded in 1918 and proclaimed by the Prince Regent Alexander I, who became king in 1921.

15. According to the club's official website www.fkvelez.ba.

Croatian Revolutionary Movement began to use terrorist tactics as they sought to create an independent Croatian state.

In such times, the authorities became less tolerant of the display of nationalist symbols and emblems. Because of this, the HŠK Zrinjski was banned from playing in a tournament in Dubrovnik because the colors and coat of arms on their team shirts were considered emblematic of Croatian nationalism.[16] FK Velež also ran into problems with the Yugoslav authorities. After a call by the Communist Party to start an armed revolt in 1929, Velež lost its president, who was jailed for his political sympathies, and many supporters, and it was unable to fulfill its matches until it could recruit younger members not known to the authorities.

Nationalist tensions, particularly among the Croats, continued to strengthen throughout the 1930s. It is during this period that the importance of football clubs in Bosnia as a vehicle for the expression of submerged identities became evident. The state knew that it was vulnerable to tensions between different ethnic groups, most notably Croat aspirations to regional expansion. At this time, overt displays of nationalist colors and emblems by fans of HŠK Zrinjski was a deliberate and very public statement of support within Bosnia for Croatia's regionalist claims as well as a most obvious re-assertion of Croat identity. The neighboring FK Velež meanwhile was resisting the dominant state identity by continuing to stress its Communist roots. By 1940, crowd demonstrations against the Yugoslav regime frequently followed football matches, with police arresting those considered ringleaders.[17]

---

16. The Croatian flag is based around the *Sahovnica*, the red and white checkerboard emblem of Croatia, most evident on the playing shirts of the HSK Zrinjski players.

17. The Velez club website tells the reader how, on September 1, 1940, Velez played a match against Crna Gora of Podgorica in Montenegro, after which demonstrations occurred against the regime. Many banners were displayed with messages such as "Down with Imperialism," "We Want Bread and Work," and "Down with Tyrants—We Want Freedom." That night, police took into custody anyone identified as part of the demonstration. The website continues:

September 2, 1940 the demonstrations continue in Mostar, main strike for the working people is a huge deal at this time in the city, the city is in shock. Some are asking for the people to attack the policemen and free their protestors from jail. In the club everyone agreed that it is best for the club to take all the trophies, all archives, money and jerseys be put in a safe place. On September 2, 1940 Velez was told that it was not functionable anymore and they needed to shut down. Practices were forbidden, but because of the generosity of club MOSK [MOSK Jedinstvo; the word means "Unity"] players still practiced and worked out, even though forbidden to play for players held their heads high and went to Tuzla and Split with their club. When the police chief of Mostar found out that Velez had competed in Dalmacija, he did everything in his power to find out how this happened. He had found out through the newspaper about what was going on even though the players gave out the information. After all of this a member of Velez Mesak Cu-

The Kingdom of Yugoslavia was split into six regions (known as banates) in 1929, the borders of which were specifically designed to avoid following ethnic or religious boundaries, in theory diluting the increasingly obvious nationalist fervor. The Croats resisted this idea, and by 1939 they had obtained an agreement for a degree of autonomy for a new, Croat-based banate.[18] The agreement was designed to include as many ethnic Croats as possible, and great swathes of Bosnia were annexed to the new banate, including much of Herzegovina and its de facto capital, Mostar, ostentatiously placing the region under Croat control. When the forces of Nazi Germany invaded in 1941, the Nazis were swift to recognize the Banate of Croatia as an independent country. Control of the Independent State of Croatia lay in the hands of the Ustaša (Croatian nationalists), although in reality it was known to be a puppet state of Nazi regime. The state's claims to sovereignty were also recognized by FIFA, which admitted it is a member in 1941. Croatia quickly moved to establish its footballing credentials by forming its own national Croatian league, a league immediately joined by HŠK Zrinjski Mostar's Croat team.[19]

Partisan Fanship

World War II in BiH was a particularly complex and brutal affair. The Axis-Allied conflict was only one aspect of the violence occurring throughout the country. The nationalist tensions evident in Yugoslavia prior to the war manifested themselves in a particularly vicious concomitant civil war. The civil conflicts between the Ustaša, Četniks, and Partisans were of notable violence, and atrocities were committed by all parties. The Croat nationalist movement, the Ustaša (Ustasha), which had allied itself with the Nazi movement in order to obtain quasi-independence as the Independent State of Croatia, had been, prior to the war, a right-wing terrorist movement.[20] Once in power, the

---

murija took all the trophies and everything else wrapped newspaper around it and put everything in barrels of petroleum and buried it somewhere. During the war he was arrested and taken away, he died in Sarajevo, Mesak Cumurija took his secret to the grave. After the war there was a search for the missing items but they were never found. War came to Mostar and Velez as a symbol of workers and freedom becomes forbidden by fascist government which have held in Mostar. Velez became a symbol for the freedom fighters because a chunk of its fans are in the partizan party [sic].

18. Cvetković-Maček Agreement, signed in August 1939.

19. As Croatia, they were admitted into FIFA in 1992.

20. The Ustaša were Croatian nationalists who envisaged a greater Croatia that included Bosnia. They were anti-Serb and anti-Slovene. In 1933 they presented a document they called "Principles," which sought to exclude non-Croats from political life. Those they considered undesirable were to be subjected to mass murder. The Ustaša saw themselves as descendents of the Goths, and they claimed stronger links to the

Ustaša were responsible for the construction of concentration camps in Yugoslavia, including the infamous Jasenovac camp in which some 100,000 Serbs, Jews, and Roma are estimated to have been killed.[21]

The Croats met resistance. Many Serbs took up arms in the war years and joined their own Serb nationalist movement known as the Četniks (*Chetniks*), a name synonymous with Serbian nationalism. Originally formed as a resistance force against the Ottomans, the later Četniks were particularly violent during World War II.[22] Many in Bosnia, particularly among the Muslim population, were uncomfortable with the overt nationalist sentiments of both the Serb and Croat movements, and in the face of brutal violence by both organized a multi-ethnic resistance group, which went under the name of the Partisans. Formed in resistance to the Axis occupation, the Partisans drew support from all ethnicities across Yugoslavia. Confusingly, they fought against the Četnicks (who also fought against the Nazis) and the Ustaša (who fought with them), and they received support from the Allies, who considered them the militia most likely to be successful in disrupting the Nazis. The Partisans—led by the General Secretary of the Communist Party Josef Tito—liberated Belgrade and then Sarajevo from the Nazis. While embracing the multi-ethnic nature of the Partisans, the Bosniaks were not always comfortable with their Communist links, particularly with what they perceived as the Partisans' suppression of religious expression. On top of this, the Bosniak choice of whom to fight *for* was complex and very localized; examples exist of Bosniaks fighting for all of the main warring factions. The choice was informed by diverse factors, such as who was in control locally, ethnicity, neighboring ethnicity, and a variety of historical antecedents.

Considering the FK Velež's strong Communist background, it is unsurprising that many of its players and members joined the Partisans. When Mostar was liberated in February 1945 and the Communist

---

Germans than to the Slavs. Their activities were based around resisting the Yugoslav authorities, but they then assassinated the Yugoslav King Alexander I. Croatia's army in 1941 was comprised mainly of non-Ustaša men, but the Ustaša organized a militia, said to consist of five seven-hundred-man battalions who had a reputation for mercilessness.

21. Nick Hawton and Marko Kovac, "Balkan 'Auschwitz' Haunts Croatia," BBC News, April 25, 2005. Estimates of numbers of casualties in any of the wars fought in Yugoslavia remain enormously political. Serbs put numbers killed at Jasenovac at between 700,000 to 1,000,000, while the Croats continue to insist that the figure is under 10,000. See Glenny, *The Fall of Yugoslavia*, 203.

22. Serbs who fought against Bosniaks/Croats in the most recent conflicts were referred to as Cetniks. The word has come to be an insult (in the same way that "Ustasha"/"Turk" is against the Croats/Bosniaks).

Party of Yugoslavia (*Komunistička partija Jugoslavije*: KPJ) took control, Velež was swiftly reformed, playing its first match barely a month later. HŠK Zrinjski, with its strong ties to the Croatian regime, did not fare so well in Communist Yugoslavia. On coming to power after the war, Marshal Tito was determined that in order to form his vision of Yugoslavia it was vital that the country put the brutal civil war and its long history of nationalist tensions behind it. He was well aware of the power of nationalist symbols in providing a focal point for the coalescence of animosities. Tito's promotion of the mantra "Brotherhood and Unity" relied upon all the ethnic groups in Yugoslavia to transcend nationalist frictions.[23] HŠK Zrinjski, with its Croatian *šahovnica*[24] colors and the Croatian coat of arms on its shirts, along with its history of playing in the Independent State of Croatia's league and its strong history of Croatian nationalism, was banned by Tito—a ban that remained in force for the next forty-seven years.[25]

By contrast, this postwar Communist period was a golden time for the Communist club, FK Velež. It qualified for the top Yugoslav league in 1951, and although struggling against teams such as Red Star Belgrade and Hajduk Split, it continued to play top-level football until the 1990s.[26] FK Velež attracted crowds of 25,000 and in time built a stadium to accommodate such numbers. The Bijeli Brieg (White Hill) Stadium, which to this day remains the second largest stadium in BiH, was

---

23. "Brotherhood and Unity" was a Communist Party slogan created in response to the divisionary policies of those trying to control Yugoslavia during World War II. The slogan reflects Tito's ambition to put the brutal and very violent and bitter civil war (and associated atrocities) behind in order to create his idea of a new, unified Yugoslavia.

24. The Croatian red and white checkerboard emblem even today is closely linked to Croatian nationalism.

25. Zrinjski was not the only club banned. The Serb club FK Slavija in Sarajevo and NK Hrvoje from Banja Luka, as well as the Belgrade clubs SK Jugoslavia and BSK Belgrade, suffered the same fate. Still other clubs failed to reform after the war. According to sources the authors spoke with among fans of Red Star Belgrade—which was founded after the war—these clubs were dissolved by the Communist authorities because they were deemed to have been collaborators by stint of their participation in football matches during the war. SK Jugoslavia's stadium, offices, and players went on to form Red Star Belgrade, whereas BSK Belgrade re-formed as OFK Belgrade. Red Star fans do not claim SK Jugoslavija to be the same club, whereas OFK Belgrade claims BSK Belgrade's history to be a part of their club. In the predominantly Bosniak city of Tuzla, three prewar clubs that had represented the three different ethnicities in the city were not re-formed after the war. Instead, football supporters coalesced behind the Communist-backed FK Sloboda club. This postwar period witnessed the inception of many new clubs, most notably Red Star and Partisan in Belgrade and FK Sarajevo in the city of that name.

26. Other notable achievements of the FK Velež club were appearing in the final of the Marshal Tito Cup in 1959 and progressing to the quarter finals of the UEFA Cup in 1974.

completed in the west side of the city in 1971. The stadium welcomed fans and players of all nationalities. With such success and within such an environment and without a local rival, FK Velež became *the* Mostar team, the team that represented the entire city and saw itself as a haven of tolerance, beyond ethnic identity. FK Velež was a club that celebrated the Tito vision. This was fine so long as Tito lived.

The Search for Heroes: Nationalisms and Football

Following Tito's death in 1981, long-suppressed nationalist antagonisms began to reappear across Yugoslavia. With the benefits of hindsight, we can see the omens of a return to armed conflict in the region echoing around the football stadiums. Football clubs throughout the 1980s became a focal point for those seeking to demonstrate and articulate nationalistic sympathies. Placards made by fans appeared on the terraces at games containing overt political messages alongside nationalist symbols, songs, and chants bearing political proclamations.[27] Red Star Belgrade in particular became the hub of Serb nationalism; to support Red Star was to support Serbia and Serbdom. Dinamo Zagreb, the strongest Croatian team, based in the Croatian capital Zagreb, also attracted increasingly nationalistic supporters. By the mid-1980s, both teams had supporter groups that maintained an organizational structure beyond the football stadium. Red Star had the Delije (Heroes), led by the soon-to-become infamous paramilitary leader Željko Ražnatović (more commonly known—in notoriety—as "Arkan"). Dinamo Zagreb had a fan group known as the Bad Blue Boys (BBB). Both groups were ultra-nationalists and, throughout the 1980s, willing to use violence against those perceived as footballing-political opponents. Their behavior was the most obvious indication of the rise of nationalist feelings within each republic of the federal state of Yugoslavia.

Throughout the 1980s, the economically stronger republics of Croatia and Slovenia were increasingly agitating for greater autonomy. This agitation was strongly resisted by the Serbs, who preferred to be the dominant province within a large federation rather than a separate country. Such tensions paved the way for increasingly nationalistic politics, amplified by the Serb politician Slobodan Milošević's use of Serb nationalism to consolidate his political power. Nationalist tensions reached a new height in 1990 with the surprise victory for the Nationalist Croatian Democratic Union (*Hrvatska Demokratska Zajednica*, HDZ) party in the Croatian elections.[28] A game between Red Star

---

27. Čolović, *The Politics of Symbol in Serbia*, 260.

28. Founded in 1989 as the Communist control of Yugoslavia was loosening, the Croatian Democratic Union party (HDZ) was led by Franjo Tudjman. Many assumed

and Dinamo in Zagreb in May of that year was to many onlookers an inevitable focus for fan violence, but few had anticipated the extent this violence could take. The notorious Arkan and three thousand of his Red Star *Delije* arrived ready to fight the Bad Blue Boys. There was strong evidence that both groups had planned for violence at the game; stockpiles of stones and weapons were evident on both sides. The deployment of acid to dissolve the metal barriers meant to keep the fans apart and off the field, allowed rioters to break through, overwhelming the police.[29] Hundreds of people were injured in the ensuing brawls in the stands and around the perimeters of the field. The fighting lasted for over an hour and only ended when part of the Makismir Stadium was set afire. This match proved to be "the last game before the collapse of the Yugoslav League and with it the state itself."[30] It is an overstatement to suggest, as some have, that this event was the beginning of the Balkan wars. However, the disorder reflected the mood of the time and was the most visible indication of the violence that was to come.

Following HDZ's victory at the polls, Croatia declared its independence. In neighbouring Bosnia, the Bosnian Croats swiftly followed the Croats' lead and proclaimed the Croatian Community of Herzeg-Bosnia to be a distinct entity, announcing also their intention to secede from Bosnia in order to unite with Croatia.[31] Mostar was to be the capital of this new entity.

A Siege Mentality: Taking Sides in Mostar

The towns and cities in BiH generally elected representatives with moderate political opinions. The rural areas were the more likely to support nationalist parties. In the run up to the Bosnian conflict, Mostar had not been a place associated with nationalistic sentiments—indeed, the people of Mostar took pride in their reputation for resisting the mutual

---

that its extreme nationalist tendencies would not be attractive to Croat voters in the 1990 elections, but in the face of the prominent Serb nationalism being preached by Slobodan Milosevic, many Croats saw the HDZ as the best method to leave the discredited Communist system and obtain independence from the state of Yugoslavia, which many Croats believed hindered Croatia's economic development.

29. Foer, *How Soccer Explains the World*, 16; Wilson, *Behind the Curtain*, 110.

30. Dave Fowler, "Football, Blood and War," *The Observer* (UK), 18 January 2004.

31. Herzeg-Bosnia is a term whose meaning depends on who is asked and when it is used. Croats in the early twentieth century used it as the name for the whole of Bosnia and Herzegovina. More recently it has come to mean the Croat-dominated parts of Bosnia. In 1991 Croats in BiH declared a distinct and separate political, cultural, economic, and territorial entity called the Croatian Republic of Herzeg-Bosnia—which the ICTY discovered was founded with the intention of seceding from BiH in order to unite with Croatia. In this new region the Croatian currency was used. Herzeg-Bosnia was never recognized internationally, and the region joined the Federation of Bosnia and Herzegovina in 1994 when the Croats and Bosniaks signed the Washington Agreement.

loathing and recriminations that had accompanied World War II—but the general opposition to the city's nationalist political parties had been fractured. Although Bosniaks outnumbered Croats in Mostar, the nationalist Croat HDZ party took control of the city when the Bosniak and moderate Croat vote was split between Communists and Reformists.[32] Following declarations of independence from Yugoslavia by Slovenia and Croatia, it became inevitable that Bosnia would have to follow suit. This was to cause the Yugoslav army (now a predominantly Serb force) to surround Mostar and subject it to siege and bombardment, as they were doing just fifty miles away to the Croatian city of Dubrovnik (also a UNESCO World Heritage site). The Serb residents left during this period,[33] leaving the Bosniaks and Croats to resist the Serbs by organizing a joint defense against the Serb forces (under overall command of HVO but with units of both Croat and Bosniak ethnicity). Serb forces withdrew from the city in the summer of 1992 but continued to shell it throughout the autumn. The Serbs were losing ground, with the HVO gaining territory throughout the summer. Unable to take the city, the Serbs resorted to smashing it and so destroyed the Franciscan monastery, the Catholic cathedral, the bishop's palace, and the Karadzoz-bey mosque, as well as an estimated thirteen additional mosques. Meanwhile, Bosniaks from villages surrounding Mostar flooded into the city, seeking refuge from the increasing Serb violence. Although the Bosniaks were now an absolute majority in the city, it was the Bosnian Croats who held political and military power.

No longer subject to Tito's ban, the HŠK Zrinjski—the Croats' football club—was reformed in 1992 at the important Catholic pilgrimage site of Međugorje.[34] The choice of such a site would not have been lost on the Bosnian Muslims. In this time of conflict, to be Croat was to be Catholic, and a club reconvened in Međugorje would be a club for Croats alone. Soon after its re-founding, HŠK Zrinjski played friendly matches with other Croat clubs, then helped to establish the First League of Herzeg-Bosnia, a football league for Croat clubs in the Croat-declared quasi-state within Bosnia.

Across the city, Velež, whose 1991–92 season had come to an abrupt halt with the Serb siege, fared less well. By March 1993 its equipment

---

32. Andjelic, *Bosnia-Herzegovina*.

33. According to the 1991 census, there were 23,909 Serbs in the city, which was almost 20 percent of the total population. There has been no census since 1991, but very few Serbs are thought to live in Mostar today.

34. Since 1981 six Catholics in Međugorje, some fifteen miles southwest of Mostar, have claimed to have seen and received regular messages from the Virgin Mary. Since then the site has become an important European Catholic pilgrimage site, attracting around a million visitors annually.

and belongings had been confiscated by the Croat armed force, the HVO, effectively shutting the club down. They managed to reform in 1994 and joined the Bosniak Football Association's league, run from Sarajevo. Their participation during the war years was sporadic, matches occurring when players could be found and when clubs could travel across the country through front lines, but they did manage to play at least three times (albeit with three defeats).

By May 1993, tensions between the Croats and the Bosniaks had reached a crisis point, and once the Serb siege of Mostar had been broken, the two previous allies turned on each other. The catalyst for the violence was the premature Croat attempt to implement the Vance-Owen peace plan,[35] which gave them control of Mostar, but Croat military actions across Herzegovina in April 1993, including the notorious cleansing of Bosniaks from the Laška Valley, had already led to a complete disintegration of relations between the two sides. In May 1993 the HVO launched an offensive against the Bosniaks, expelling them from their apartments and houses. Some 2,500 were arrested and taken to the FK Velež's Bijeli Brijeg Stadium, where they were detained at gunpoint. Eventually they and some 20,000 other Bosniaks were forced to leave the west side of the city and move to the eastern side. Bosnian Croats living on the east side of the city meanwhile were forcibly expelled under threat of violence by the influx of Bosniak refugees.[36] The city became effectively divided in two: the Bosniaks and the FK Velež club on the east of the river, the Croats with their newly re-formed HŠK Zrinjski now occupying Velež's Bijeli Brijeg Stadium on the west side.

---

35. The Vance-Owen Plan put together by the UN Special Envoy Cyrus Vance and the European Country Representative David Owen was negotiated in the first half of 1993. It split the country into ten semi-autonomous regions, but it was overtaken by events in Bosnia; ethnic cleansing and territorial gains rendered the plan obsolete. However, the idea of semi-autonomous regions was preserved and is reflected in the final Dayton Peace Accords, which created the Republika Srpska and divided the Bosniak Croat Federation into ten semi-autonomous cantons, reflecting the ethnic divisions.

36. During the 1992 conflict, people were forced to leave Mostar at gunpoint or left when it became obvious that the war was coming to them (they knew about the likelihood of ethnic cleansing). Bosniaks were briefly held in camps (including the football stadium). Accommodation for people displaced by the war saw people sheltering in places that others had left to move to a refugee camp or became refugees abroad. Prior to the conflict, a lot of property in the city was allotted to the occupiers as part of their working for an organization (a factory, for example). This left a huge headache for the city authorities when it came to working out ownership of property in the post-conflict milieu. The Dayton Accord stressed the importance of returning property to those who had been forced to leave it, and a Property Law Implementation Plan (PLIP) was put in place to work through the return of properties to their original owners. Such allocation remains a complex process, because many owners cannot return to their property until the people now living there have managed to reclaim theirs and so on. Controversies around the return of property remain to this day. There are still refugee camps in BiH.

This occupation/appropriation remains a source of massive tension/ celebration to this day.

In the years immediately after the conflict, FK Velež played in the eight-thousand-seat Vrapčići Stadium located in a suburb of eastern Mostar, while continuing to call Bijeli Brieg their "home" stadium. Shame over the loss of "their" stadium led some fans to refuse to attend games against HŠK Zrinjski when played at Bijeli Brieg. Others refused to attend any FK Velež game until the club could once again play in the "stolen stadium." The fans of HŠK Zrinjski have erased all traces of Velež from the stadium in favor of the red and white šahovnica emblems, and they love to taunt fans of their rivals with chants that remind them, in words that suggest both defeat and cowardice, that they "gave up" their stadium.

Fortunately, in the immediate postwar period the HŠK Zrinjski and Velež clubs did not meet on the football field in a competitive fixture. The former played within the Herzeg-Croat Football Association league, and the latter joined the Bosniak Football Association similarly formed in 1992. During the conflict, the two clubs managed to play a few games, but without the use of their stadiums or any equipment, they were handicapped from playing in the top leagues.[37] The postconflict years required a rebuild. Starting with what fans remember as just "a simple field to play on," FK Velež began to collect remittance monies from fans forced abroad during the conflict, and at the same time the team was adding players to replace those lost as war casualties on the front lines or to the wages offered by neighboring HŠK Zrinjski.[38] Because of these factors, the immediate postwar performances of FK Velež were poor. The team was soon relegated to the lower leagues. An inability to gain promotions into higher leagues characterized FK Velež over the next decade. HŠK Zrinjski, on the other hand, fared well in the league consisting of Bosnian-Croat clubs, competing most seasons with Široki Brijeg for the top spot. However, with the FIFA and the UEFA refusing to recognize the Herzeg-Croat Association, Bosnian Croat clubs could not qualify to play in European competitions. With the Bosniak and Bosnian Croats in an (uneasy) political alliance to create the single political entity of the Federation of Bosnia and Herzegovina, and with no possibility of European football for the Bosnian Croats, a unification of the

---

37. The three football federations in Bosnia formed in 1992 did their best to organize informal leagues, but travelling to and from games was difficult, so football was played largely at a regional level. There was a Bosniak football league in 1994–95, and a Croat league in 1993–94. The Bosniak and Croat leagues merged in the 2000–1 season, and the Serb league joined in the 2002–3 season.

38. For example, Slaven Musa moved to HSK Zrinjski in 1992 and played for other BiH clubs. He is now in his second season as manager at HSK Zrinjski.

Bosnian Croat and Bosniak leagues became inevitable, finally occurring in the 2000–2001 season, although playoffs between the winners of the two leagues had been taking place since 1998.

In the twenty years since the end of the BiH conflict, Mostar has witnessed huge steps forward in terms of conflict resolution. At times, however, such resolution is accompanied by enormous political stalemate. Looking on the bright side, the worst of the war damage has been repaired. Schools enroll pupils of both ethnicities, taught at the same time (albeit in separate classes). The tensions so evident in the city immediately after the conflict, with Croats trying to prevent Bosniaks from returning to the west side, have abated, with both ethnicities able to come and go freely and without incident across the bridges that once separated the populations.

But things below the surface remain uneasy. The bitterness evident around the football matches in the city are the most visible and aural indication of latent and unresolved resentments. Feeling that the Bosniaks are represented in Sarajevo and the Bosnian Serbs in Banja Luka, Croats feel keenly the lack of a recognized capital in Bosnia. They thus seek a city where they are indisputably in the majority and can retain cultural control. Consequently, the Croats see Mostar as their quasi-national capital and thus the home for Croat cultural, social, and business institutions. This state of affairs has political channels but is played out most obviously via football.

Mayoral Impulses: War without Bullets?

In 2009 a political stalemate led to an implosion in Mostar's political scene and made the city "ungovernable." The cause was the intervention of those tasked with peace-sustaining and nation-building, namely, "the international community." New laws imposed in 2004 by the NATO High Representative, designed to encourage a multi-ethnic political coalition, sought to replace the concept of one city mayor and a deputy of alternate ethnicity with one mayor who would—ideally—be seen as representing all residents.[39] Such an imposition came with an informal understanding that the political parties would alternate

---

39. The High Representative is the Peace Implementation Council (PIC) representative in BiH. The HR answers to the PIC, which first met in Bonn, Germany. The High Representative has wide powers to establish peace in BiH and has the authority to impose laws and sack politicians frustrating the peace process, but he generally tries to persuade the Bosnian governments to do the law-making using their "Bonn Powers" as an emergency measure. Because the HR is not elected by or answerable to Bosnians at all, his situation is criticized by native Bosnians as a neo-colonial imposition. One man who held the office between 2002 and 2006 was the former leader of the Liberal Party of the UK, Paddy Ashdown. He once sacked sixty Serb MPs in one go.

their support for different ethnic groups, so just as the Bosniak Party of Democratic Action (Stranka Demoktratske akcije, SDA) supported the Croat HDZ Mayoral candidate in 2004, so the HDZ would return the favor in 2008.[40]

By the time of the 2008 elections, there was a marked decline in support for the nationalist Croat HDZ party, both within Mostar and in the surrounding countrywide. Their traditional support splintered as some of the electorate moved to support more extreme Croat nationalist parties (including the splinter group HDZ 1990) and others became less nationalist, wooed by some Bosniak politicians who had begun to appeal to non-Bosniak voters. In several towns in the region, the HDZ lost the municipal mayoral office to the Bosniak SDA, and crucially the party lost the Croat seat of the national state presidency to the multi-ethnic SDP. Feeling threatened and determined to hold onto power in Mostar by any means, the HDZ refused to endorse a Bosniak mayoral candidate.[41] This led to an intense period of political maneuvring that left the city without a mayor and therefore without a budget; payments to employees of the City Council were not made for over a year. The implication of such an action—namely, that the Croats would never permit a Bosniak mayor in Mostar—worsened relations between the two groups. Politically, the HDZ was losing its hold as the dominant party among Croats, and the threat of losing political control of Mostar, the symbol of Croat culture in Bosnia, was keenly felt. It was precisely at this point that the violence between the football supporters, and specifically the actions of the right-wing, intensely nationalist HŠK Zrinjski supporters, significantly worsened.

The first match between the two Mostar clubs since 1938 took place in 2000. This was an exhibition match hosted in the Kosevo Stadium in the city of Sarajevo.[42] Since then, the two clubs have met regularly, in both league and cup competitions. Derbies between the two Mostar clubs have over the past fifteen years often been accompanied by fan violence. Strangely, violence between fans has become more noticeable as the threat of violence and intimidation in day-to-day life has receded for most of the citizenry of Mostar. Both Mostar clubs have active "fan groups"; the HŠK Zrinjski fans take their inspiration from the Southern European *Ultras* phenomenon. By contrast, the FK Velež fan group seeks inspiration from England—hence the nomenclature

---

40. International Crisis Group, "Bosnia."
41. Ibid.
42. The FK Sarajevo club stadium is the largest in BiH and is owned by the City of Sarajevo. Reconstructed in 1984 for the Winter Olympics, it is occasionally used for BiH national games, although the national team generally prefers to play in the city of Zenica.

"Red Army." The *Ultras* consist exclusively of Croatians reflecting the support base for HŠK Zrinjski as a whole. The Red Army is predominantly Bosniak, although other ethnicities are also present, reflecting the club's multi-ethnic heritage.

In 2008, with Croat politicians under pressure and the Croat project within Bosnia under threat, fights between fan groups outside the stadiums were common. The level of violence and ethnic animosity was such that one well-respected football official at the May 2008 derby match at FK Velež's Vrapčići Stadium commented to the researchers that this was one of the few times that football violence was not due to the more "normal" hooliganism but was about the fans' ethno-political history. In truth, the distinction was difficult to define. The *Ultras* of HŠK Zrinjski's were involved in several incidents against other Bosniak teams around this time, including an incident in 2009 in which they set fire to a coach belonging to Sloboda Tuzla's predominantly Bosniak *Fukare* supporters.[43] Later that same year, a chance meeting between the predominantly Bosniak supporters of FK Sarajevo and HŠK Zrinjski in the town of Konjic led to mass brawling and led to the arrest of over fifty participants.[44] It was inevitable that the club closest to them, namely FK Velež, would also face the wrath of the HŠK Zrinjski fans.

As is very evident, to support HŠK Zrinjski is to celebrate being a Croat and to support Croat nationalist tendencies. Despite only re-forming as recently as 1992, HŠK Zrinjski is the dominant team in Mostar; its wins have been better than those of FK Velež, its stadium is bigger, and its attendance records have been larger. Moreover, it has significant financial sponsorship from the largest business in the region, the Croat-owned and -run Aluminj Mostar.[45] Its supremacy reflects the dominant Croat presence in the city since the conflict ended, as well as the importance of the instillation of the team's "Croatness" upon the city. When combined with the sense of vulnerability felt by

---

43. Tuzla's Fukare and Zrinjski's Ultras have a history of clashes. Games between the sides in both cities are often accompanied by disorder. In this instance, the Tuzla supporters were returning from watching a match in the Croat city of Siroki Brijeg. As they passed through Mostar, they were recognized by the Zrinjski Ultras and their bus was attacked. The word *fukare* has no simple translation into English. Our inquiries produced explanations that varied from "bums" to "bastards" to "street cats." A more elaborate attempt to explain the term sought to correlate the word with an uneducated rural (male) demographic who was street-smart if nothing else.

44. This was a chance meeting. The Sarajevo supporters were on their way to Mostar to play Velež. The Zrinjski supporters were going to play a Sarajevo team. Their collision in Konjic took the police by surprise.

45. The name of a Croat-owned Bauxite mine. Utilizing electricity from Croatia, the mine produces high-quality bauxite crucial in the production of particularly pure aluminum used in the manufacture of cars.

Croat nationalists, this makes the HŠK Zrinjski club an important part of the creation of a Croat identity in a city that is the most important part of a Croat-dominated territory in Bosnia. Similar to the Croatian clubs in Australia and the Basque clubs in Spain, HŠK Zrinjski represents a "submerged nationhood,"[46] a Croat micro-state within Bosnia. The club attracts passionate support because, unlike the Bosnian Serbs, the Croats did not obtain a separate, Croat-dominated entity but instead are part of an uneasy federation with the Bosniaks. The city of Mostar, as the intended cultural and political capital of such a desired state, holds particular resonance. An ethno-religious identity is also important; the Croats' Catholicism is central to their culture and specifically excludes the Bosniak Muslims and the Orthodox Serbs.

By contrast, to support FK Velež implies a rejection of Croatian nationalist impulses. The team's fans present themselves as welcoming to all ethnicities while rejecting all that HŠK Zrinjski stands for. But in fact, FK Velež fans are predominantly Bosniak, as are the players and club officials. The Velež club has moved from a once-dominant identity, one that claimed to represent the entire city, to today's resistance identity where supporters demonstrate their rejection of the overarching Croat ideal of the city. But most of all, as one of the FK Velež core members told us, the club declares to the Croats, "We are still here. You can force us from our homes, you can take away our stadium, you can take away our equipment, you can take away our players, but you can't get rid of us. We're still here, and we always will be." The club thus represents the on-going presence of what might best be termed "old Mostar," where Bosniaks and Croats once lived as Mostarians, not defined by ethnicity. The Bosniaks' desire for a multi-ethnic community in which they have the majority, and therefore political power, is represented by FK Velež, which although predominantly Bosniak is not a Muslim club; religion plays no part in its structure, identity, or support.

Such attitudes have implications at the national level. Despite their multi-ethnic ethos, fans of FK Velež rarely pass up an opportunity to rile their Croatian neighbors. Such attitudes have implication for football played at the national level. Although in many areas of Bosnia fans support all former Yugoslav national teams in any international match, Bosniaks in Mostar generally support whomever is playing against Croatia. In 2006, Bosniak Mostarians loudly and enthusiastically took to the streets to celebrate Brazil's victory over Croatia in the World Cup, much to the fury of Mostar's Croatians. In the ensuing disorder, property was damaged and one Bosniak was shot and wounded. In the

---

46. Anderson, *Imagined Communities*.

2008 European Championships, the Bosniaks publically supported the Turkish team in its last-gasp, nail-biting win over Croatia. In the violence that followed between rival fans, some twenty people were hospitalized and riot damage was evident throughout the city center.

Football-related disorder in the city continues to this day. There was a spate of fan violence within the space of a week in September 2011. HŠK Zrinjski fans invaded the field after FK Velež scored in extra time to knock Zrinjski out of the Bosnia and Herzegovina Football Cup. The victorious players ran off the field, but some were beaten as they left the ground. Earlier that week, a game between FK Borac Banja Luka—a Serb team from Banja Luka—and FK Željezničar was stopped when Borac fans invaded the field and threw missiles at rival supporters. As a consequence of these and other fan disorders, a temporary ban on away fans was put in place until April 2012. The consternation that such disorder provokes is not limited to the domestic authorities. The UNHCR was sufficiently concerned about football hooliganism and the nationalist element to mention it in a 2012 report, which noted that the "Nationalist rhetoric inspired violent incidents at football stadiums between Serbs and Bosniaks in Banja Luka and between Croats and Bosniaks in Mostar. The renewed ethnic dimension to football hooliganism reminded citizens of similar incidents at sporting events before the wars related to the dissolution of Yugoslavia in the 1990s."[47]

The After-Taste of Disorder?

At its most functional, football might assist some processes in BiH that seek to bridge ethno-political divisions. At the same time, particularly at club level, the game reflects the rotten body politic of Bosnia and perpetrates the fracture lines of this society. The game exists at its most innocent to entertain and engage. In Bosnia, football is not always innocent. Throughout the country, politics and its more shady machinations are never far from football; politicians are closely connected to football clubs, and clubs are financed by the state. Presidents and key club positions are often politically connected and motivated. Ironically, the nationalist politicians of Bosnia, who while ostensibly loathing each other, need their opponents for their own personal political survival: an atmosphere of fear and recrimination brings votes for their policies of promoting ethnic exclusion and protection. Before elections, mutual desecration of churches and mosques occurs, as does an increase of hostilities between fans of rival clubs. Although no politician would be easily connected to such fan groups and such behavior, popular gossip

---

47. UNHCR, "Nations in Transit 2012—Bosnia and Herzegovina," available at www.unhcr.org/refworld/docid/4fd5dd32c.html (last accessed November 25, 2013).

claims that politicians are providing support for those looking to create trouble, which in turn encourages a sense of ethno-political instability and vulnerability. Through football-related encounters, the underlying visceral hatred and division of a once-united city remains brutally visible some twenty years after the end of the Yugoslav conflict.

And so it continues, albeit with a unique anti-hooligan response. In mid-June of 2012, the Croatian national side was knocked out of the European Championship tournament co-hosted by Poland and the Ukraine. Their 1-0 defeat by Spain saw some two hundred Croatian fans in Mostar enter the city's main square in anger, chanting Croatian nationalist songs. Their presumed destination was a Bosniak neighborhood where their presence would have provoked a violent response. Their progress was prevented by police, who fought a pitched battle with the mob. Seven of the rioters were arrested, and three police officers were injured, along with damage to four police vehicles. Days later, a handful of Mostar citizens declared the following Friday evening the occasion for a public sharing of chocolate in the main square, where all those opposed to football-related disorder—and its implicitly ethno-political antagonisms—could gather to share their sentiments and confectionary. Under the mantra "Trade Chocolates Not Punches," the organiser of the event spoke of his desire to show the world that Mostar was not city of hooligans.

Abbreviations

BiH—Bosnia and Herzegovina (*Bosna I Hercegovina*)
Federation –Bosniak/Croat Entity of Bosnia and Herzegovina
FK—Football Club (*Fudbalski Klub*)
HDZ—Croatian Democratic Union (*Hrvatska demokratska zajednica*), Croatian nationalist political party. There is one in Croatia and a separate, although connected Bosnian Croatian political party of the same name.
HŠK—*Hrvatski Športski Klub* (Croatian Sports Club)
HVO—Croatian Defense Council (*Hrvatsko Vijeće Obrane*), the de facto Bosnian Croat army
ICTY—International Criminal Tribunal for the Former Yugoslavia
KPJ—Communist Party of Yugoslavia (*Komunistička partija Jugoslavije*)
RS—Republika Srpska, the Serb Entity of Bosnia and Herzegovina

Bibliography

Anderson, Benedict. *Imagined Communities: Reflections on the Origin and Spread of Nationalism.* London: Verso, 1983.

Andjelic, Neven. *Bosnia-Herzegovina: The End of a Legacy.* London: Frank Cass, 2003.

Bose, Sumantra. *Bosnia After Dayton: Nationalist Partition and International Intervention.* London: Hurst & Co, 2002.

Čolović, Ivan. *The Politics of Symbol in Serbia: Essays on Political Anthropology.* Translated by Celia Hawkesworth. London: C. Hurst & Co, 2002.

Coward, Martin. *Urbicide: The Politics of Urban Destruction.* Abingdon: Routledge, 2009.

FK Velež. "Club History: Period 1922–1940." FK Velež: Oficijelni website. At www.fkVelež.ba/index.php?option=com_content&view=article&id=837%3Aperiod-19221940-period-do-rata&catid=54&Itemid=89&lang=en.

FK Velež. "Renewal of Club: 1945-1951." FK Velež: Oficijelni website. At www.fkVelež.ba/index.php?option=com_content&view=article&id=839%3Aperiod-1945-1951-obnova-rada-kluba&catid=54&Itemid=89&lang=en.

Foer, Franklin. *How Soccer Explains the World: An Unlikely Theory of Globalization.* London: Random House, 2005.

Fowler, Dave. "Football, Blood and War." *The Observer* (UK), 18 January 2004. At http://observer.guardian.co.uk/osm/story/0,6903,1123137,00.html.

Glenny, Misha. *The Fall of Yugoslavia: The Third Balkan War.* London: Penguin Books, 1996.

Hawton, Nick, and Marko Kovac. "Balkan 'Auschwitz' Haunts Croatia." BBC News, April 25, 2005. At http://news.bbc.co.uk/1/hi/world/europe/4479837.stm.

HŠK Zrinjski. "Povijest kluba." HŠK Zrinjski. At www.HŠKzrinjski.ba/index.php?option=com_content&view=article&id=100&Itemid=55.

International Criminal Tribunal for the Former Yugoslavia. "Case No IT-98-34-T: Judgement: Prosecutor Naletilic and Martinovic." ICTY.org. March 31, 2003. At www.icty.org/x/cases/naletilic_martinovic/tjug/en/nal-tj030331-e.pdf.

———. "Appeals Chamber Judgement in the Case The Prosecutor v. Dario Kordic and Mario Cerkez." ICTY.org, December 17, 2004. At www.icty.org/x/cases/kordic_cerkez/acjug/en/040117_Kordi_erkez_summary_en.pdf.

International Crisis Group. *Bosnia: A Test of Political Maturity in Mostar.* ICG. Sarajevo/Brussels. Europe Briefing No. 54, 2009.

International Crisis Group. "Building Bridges in Mostar." crisisgroup.

org, November 20, 2003. At www.crisisgroup.org/~/media/Files/europe/150_building_bridges_mostar.pdf.

———. "Bosnia: A Test of Political Maturity in Mostar." crisisgroup. org, July 27, 2009. At www.crisisgroup.org/~/media/Files/europe/b54_bosnia___a_test_of_political_maturity_in_mostar.pdf.

International Center for Transitional Justice. "The Former Yugoslavia, Background." ICTJ website. At www.ictj.org/our-work/regions-and-countries/former-yugoslavia.

Judah, Tim. *The Serbs: History, Myth and the Destruction of Yugoslavia.* London: Yale University Press, 2009.

Malcolm, Noel. *Bosnia: A Short History.* London: Macmillan, 1994.=

Wilson, Jonathan. *Behind the Curtain: Travels in Eastern European Football.* London: Orion Books, 2006.

12

TOGETHER AND APART AT THE BASQUE SOCCER DERBY: A PRISONER'S DILEMMA

Mariann Vaczi

"They are very nervous," says my friend J., looking at his colleagues, members of the fan group Herri Norte, pacing up and down the small square in downtown Donostia-San Sebastián, Basque Country. "They are in *foreign territory* here." I see dozens of men gather, most wearing black jackets. They are standing in small groups or nervously walking through the square. Among the *rojiblanco* (red-and-white) or *txuriurdin* (blue-and-white) crowd of fans who come and go and socialize amicably, the combat fan group is silent and vigilant. Its tension is palpable. A group of teenagers pass by, pull out a soccer ball, and start kicking it around. They lose control, and the ball flies all over the square, bouncing on the walls, the roofs, and the tables of a sidewalk café, threatening to break cups and windows. It is bouncing ominously: just as it could break a window or hit the wrong person on the head, so could a brawl break out at any moment.

Suddenly I lose sight of my two companions, J. from the Athletic fan group Herri Norte, and K. from the Real Sociedad fan group Mujika. I see the two groups concentrated in a narrow street, each comprising some seventy persons, facing each other. There are no ordinary fans mixed among them, and the tight street turns into a specter of impending violence. Between the two groups there is a narrow demarcation line, a neutral zone where four people are gesticulating wildly. I recognize J. and K. among them; they are negotiating. Bodies become a field that betrays intention, because the wrong gesture might escalate into a brawl involving one hundred fifty people in a narrow downtown street.

At the high point of tension, when I look for an escape route because a fight seems unavoidable, somebody starts yelling, "*Independentzia! Independentzia!*," and then a name, "Aitor, Aitor, Aitor Zabaleta!," and finally *"Español el que no bote hey, hey!"* (Those who are not jumping are Spaniards!). The two groups, which were seemingly on the verge of a vicious brawl only a minute ago, are now jumping, chanting, and singing in unison: *"Hain ederra, hain polita da ta"* (How beautiful, how pretty), *"Gora, gora Euskal Herria, a, a, a"* (Let's go, Basque Country, let's go), *"Gu euskaldunak gara, Euskal Herrikoak"* (We are Basques/From the Basque Country). And finally, as the two groups dispersed toward the stadium, the streets of Donostia-San Sebastián echoed with the tune of the Soviet national anthem.

This episode at the 2010 Basque derby between Athletic Club and Real Sociedad fans is illustrative of the complexity of fan identification and behavior in the Basque Country. Group rivalry violence was suspended by the evocation of common desires (Basque national independence); common heroes (Aitor Zabaleta, a Real Sociedad fan murdered by fans of the ideological foe Atlético de Madrid); a common enemy (the Spanish state); a common cultural and language community (*Euskaldun*, Basque), and common ideological beliefs (Marxist-Leninist, "red skin," or left-wing skinhead anti-fascism). The leaders of the two rival groups—my companions, J. from Bizkaia province and K. from Gipuzkoa—became friends while having a beer after a fight: "One day our groups were fighting. I looked at K. and said, 'Let's have a beer instead.' And we did." Since then, these two leaders of their respective combat groups spend every Basque derby together with all their obliging rituals: the pregame quest for entrance tickets, eating, drinking, and, if necessary, fighting.

Theoretical Approaches to Fan Rivalry

As a result of violence in the 1980s in British soccer stadia, fan rivalry became a staple of sociological research in sports. Figurational sociology attributed fan violence to segregation in terms of class, age, and gender.[1] Anthropological research later rejected the class-based definition, arguing that many fans come from respectably middle-class backgrounds, and that antagonism is often symbolic.[2] Interpretations of soccer fan violence include pleasurable arousal, a "quest for excitement";[3] the enjoyment of "flow";[4] a "euphoric hyped-up sensation";[5] an expression of proud, tough masculinities and status as "hard men";[6] the construction of *communitas*, a liminal, undifferentiated community

1. Dunning, *Sport Matters*, 139–61.
2. Armstrong, *Football Hooligans*.
3. Dunning, *Sport Matters*, 147.
4. Finn, "Football Violence," 108.
5. Hobbs and Robins, "The Boy Done Good."
6. Dunning, *Sport Matters*, 148.

of equal individuals;[7] an aesthetic marking of territory through symbolic violence;[8] a ritual that creates solidarity and a code of honor for the expression of dominant masculinity;[9] and a ritualized pattern of social hostility contained within a stylized framework.[10] According to Richard Giulianotti,[11] the construction of meaning around soccer identities happens in terms of semantic or syntactic forms by establishing in-group and out-group boundaries, the former defining who fans are, and the latter who they are not. He contends that opposition between fan communities emerges because soccer tends to privilege the syntactic logic of external opposition. From an anthropological-structuralist perspective, Gary Armstrong and Giulianotti[12] identify seven basic relations of football opposition: the construction of conflicting identities, contesting power inequalities, resistance by submerged nationhood, the construction of local and minority identity, symbolic violence of exclusion, aesthetic codes, and the negotiation of capitalism. In their many shapes, soccer rivalries are intimately linked to social, religious, class, ethnic, and national divisions.

Spanish soccer rivalry is known for what Phil Ball calls *morbo*.[13] The word escapes easy definition in English by variously meaning morbid pleasure, disease, perverse fascination, unhealthy curiosity, risk, hostility, and ill-will. All of these *sentimientos* (feelings) are played out large in Spanish soccer; they summarize the heat of regional, provincial, and town rivalries. From the global, politicized spectacle of the *el Clásico* between Real Madrid and Barcelona, the *morbo* of Spanish soccer trickles down to the most inconsequential intervillage games and is ritually reproduced at the many derbies crystallized through century-long competition. Derbies in Spain emerge along two basic lines: geographical proximity (intra- and intercity, provincial) and/or political-ideological position. Regional-territorial rivalry has defined Spanish soccer from its inception, while ideological and political antagonism intensified with the transition to democracy after the death of Franco in 1975.[14] The permutations of identification may result in culturally specific cases such as the Athletic-Real derby: provincial, intercity rivalry within a region (the Basque Country) that positions itself strongly against

7. Finn, "Football Violence," 108.

8. Dal Lago and De Biasi, "Italian Football Fans," 85–86.

9. King, "Violent Pasts," 582.

10. Marsh, *Aggro*, 30.

11. Giulianotti, *Football*, 9–14.

12. Armstrong and Giulianotti, "Constructing Social Identities," 269–78.

13. Ball, *Morbo*.

14. Llopis-Goig, "Identity, Nation State and Football in Spain"; Vaczi, "'The Spanish Fury.'"

the Spanish state. Historical-diachronic analysis has shown that the Basque derbies are variously characterized by unification and antagonism, the former revolving around a common Basque identity, and the latter around the provincial basis of local fandom.[15] With history in mind, this chapter takes an ethnographic, synchronic approach to the particular derby of 2010, and understands it as an "interaction ritual,"[16] a face-to-face cultural performance in which individuals enact the ways they belong to the moral community.

Belonging, however, is not necessarily a straightforward affair, for internal contradictions between identities may emerge. I propose that the historical-cultural specificities of Basque soccer in Spain make the derby the site of a dilemma: how to be together as Basques, but apart as rivals. The dilemma between cooperation as Basques and competition as Athletic vs. Real Sociedad fans is not unlike the prisoner's dilemma, whose basic structure I will adopt here as an analytical framework to study derby interaction.

In the classic prisoner's dilemma, two individuals—members of the same gang—are accused of a crime and presented with an option to confess or to remain silent. The harshness of their punishment depends on their own as well as their accomplice's choice to cooperate (stay silent) or to betray (defect) the other. I will address the specifics of the prisoner's dilemma later on in this chapter. For now, it will suffice to emphasize the relevance of the dilemma's basic structure for the Basque derby: an arena where each party, each club, will necessarily pursue its self-interest (winning), and even "betray" the other by poaching players and trespassing on its youth academy. However, the external meta-consideration that they belong to the same "gang"— the same moral community (Basques in Spain)—imposes a mandate of cooperation. The result is a history of derbies in which interaction switches back and forth between friendly and hostile, united and antagonistic—a dilemma condensed by the street episode between the Herri Norte and Mujika fan clubs that I described above.

The dilemma between cooperation and conflict, I argue, is evidenced by an oscillation between three Basque performative models: *joko*, *jolas*, and *burruka*.[17] *Joko* refers to binary competition between two parties, typically males in a public setting, whose outcome is winning or losing. This performance model characterizes some of the most popular public contests in the Basque Country: soccer, the squash-like in-

---

15. Walton, "Basque Football Rivalries in the Twentieth Century."
16. Goffman, *Interaction Ritual*.
17. Zulaika, *Basque Violence*, 169–187.

digenous game *pelota*, rural sports,[18] the poker-like game *mus*, and the improvisational poetry contests, *bertsolaritza*.[19] *Jolas* refers to noncompetitive children's games that take place in a domestic setting, in which there is no winner or loser, and which are performed in the intimacy of the home. *Jolas* may also refer to a festive, carnivalesque mode of social togetherness; it is the ludic genre of "what matters is not winning, but participation." And finally, *burruka* variously means wrestling, a brawl or street fight between male individuals. *Burruka, joko,* and *jolas* are socially, culturally, and politically sanctioned performative models of rivalry, competition, and cooperation. Because of their Basque idiosyncrasy, they are suitable analytical tools for my exploration of the derby oscillation between competition and cooperation.

By way of a roadmap, this chapter has three main parts. First, I will explore the levels of what I call the Basque rivalry complex: interpersonal, kin group and neighbor, town and village, province- and nation-level rivalry, with reference to how these levels of competition are manifested in Basque sports and everyday interactions. Second, I will identify the performative models of *burruka, joko,* and *jolas* in the Basque derby, and how they create spheres of competition and cooperation. Third, I will seek to explain the Basque derby's oscillations between competition and cooperation as resembling a prisoner's dilemma.

The Basque Rivalry Complex

Basques have a remarkable, if under-researched, fondness for rivalry and competition. These phenomena serve two important purposes: subjectivization, because rivalry demarcates the subject and his or her stance taken against the other; and interaction, because competition keeps the competing parties within the kernel of a relationship. Rivalry and competition take place at various levels, as I will now show: interpersonal, kin group, town/village, provincial, and national. While some rivalries have their paradigmatic genres and actors, others agglutinate several of these levels in one event.

Interpersonal Rivalry

"The janitors at the university," a young Real Sociedad fan and professor at the University of the Basque Country (Bilbao), tells me, "are rabid Athletic fans. They have a huge Athletic Club flag in their office, right

---

18. *Herri kirolak,* rural sports, are rooted in traditional lifestyles related with farming: wood chopping, stone lifting, bale lifting, cob gathering, churn carrying, and dragging games, to mention a few.

19. Armistead and Zulaika, eds., *Voicing the Moment.*

by the entrance. Last year, each morning as I entered the building I jok-ingly said something demeaning about the performance of their team. They ended up challenging me to a bet about whose team would close the season better." Betting is one of the most pervasive interpersonal dynamics in the Basque Country. Basques will bet on just about any-thing, and the language of betting is ubiquitous in everyday conversa-tions: mothers challenge their children into finishing their meals first; *cuadrilla* (age-grade peer groups) arguments often end with a bet to fi-nally decide who is right; people of all ages and gender bet to support their point of view.

This particular bet between the professor and the janitors would structure their relationship for the rest of the season: each morning they engaged in a discussion over the standing of their bet and their teams, playfully teasing one another until a final outcome. Moreover, a bet is likely to become a cycle of bets, because the loser is obliged to challenge or accept the challenge of the winner the following season in order to vindicate his honor. Once a bet is in motion, it is almost impossible to step out of the ritual obligation to bet again and again. As staying within the circuit of the bet becomes a question of integrity, no one "who is good at being a man"[20] steps out of it, especially when it is formulated as *que no hay cojones . . .* , or "I bet you don't have the balls to . . ." The following year, when the professor's team was doing badly and he wanted to avoid the bet, he started to use the emergency exit instead of the front door. What the bet achieved was keeping the janitors and the professor within the kernel of interaction by suspending their so-cial, economic, and age differences, and situating them on a level play-ing field where the result was equally beyond their control.

Athletic Club's century-old tradition of signing Basques only is at-tributed to a bet with the fans of Real Sociedad. No one knows exactly how the "Basque players only" philosophy of Athletic started, but where fact is lacking, a verisimilar genesis is created: "I dare you to play with locals only!" The bet is believed to have come from Real Sociedad, which makes it all the more inescapable. What is certainly well recorded is how Bilbao's soccer culture started with a bet. At the end of the nine-teenth century, *Bilbainos* (inhabitants of Bilbao) jealously watched En-glish dockworkers kick around a leather ball downtown by the Nervión River, on the *Campa de los Ingleses* (Field of the Englishmen), where the Guggenheim Museum stands today. "Perhaps annoyed with the supe-riority that the English manifested," Terrachet writes, "one fine day the *Bilbaino footballmen* publicly challenged them to a game."[21] On May

20. Gilmore, *Manhood in the Making*, 30, 43, 82.
21. Terrachet, *100 años de historia del Athletic de Bilba*, 23.

4, 1894, these *Bilbainos* played, and promptly lost 0-5, their first soccer game against the English.

Kin Group and Neighbor Rivalry

"*Ni hilen naiz,/nire arima galduko da,/nire askazia galduko da,/naina nire aitaren etxeak/iraunen du zutik.*" "I will die,/my soul will be lost,/my progeny will be lost,/but my father's house/will still be standing."[22] This 1963 poem by the Basque poet Gabriel Aresti reveals that the Basque concept of the household, the farmstead or *etxe*, is an important metaphor of continuity, stability, and unity. Historically, the *etxe-baserri* (house-farmstead) constituted an autonomous social, political, and economic unit: it provided subsistence for a kin group or family, and granted juridical and political status in terms of inheritance and voting rights. In the Basque cultural imaginary, the *etxe*, and the relationship between *etxeak* as neighbors, is one of the richest reservoirs of identification and the symbol of traditional Basque culture.[23] The neighborhood (*auzo*) relationship among houses consisted of ritualized cooperation and reciprocal obligations in the way of subsistence, funerary services, and road construction.[24] Such was the identification of a family lineage with the *etxe* that the former was named after the latter; in the rare occurrence of moving, the family took as its last name the name of the house they moved into. The integrity of the *etxe* was a major concern, because it stood metonymically for the integrity of the family lineage; single inheritance by the oldest child (male or female) ensured that the *etxe* would not be divided, and it could be sold only with difficulty.

Besides reciprocal neighborly obligations, what characterized the relationship between *etxeak* and their kin groups was competitive rivalry. In his 1992 movie *Vacas* (Cows), Julio Medem explores the eerie relationship and lingering animosity between two neighboring families that starts with the 1875 Carlist War and lasts over three generations. Kin group hostility is visually dramatized in an *aizkolaritza*, or wood-chopping contest, between the two strongest sons of the respective households. Basque traditional games were inspired by competition between farmsteads: wood chopping, hay mowing, stone lifting, and cattle herding were agricultural activities turned into competitions.[25] These traditional sports paradigmatically took place between two individuals, behind whom entire lineages rallied to bet at village

---

22. Aulestia, *The Basque Poetic Tradition*, 175.
23. Zulaika, *Basque Violence*, 131–36.
24. Ott, *The Circle of Mountains*; Douglass, *Death in Murélaga*.
25. Walton, "Sport and the Basques."

fiestas. Rural sports have never become commercialized. Because it was intimately linked to the *etxe*, competition in these sports was often fierce to the point that contestants were "willing to risk the animals' health and their own family fortunes"[26] in the quest for honor.

Olatz González Abrisketa finds a similar antagonistic disposition along kin group lines in the Basque indigenous game *pelota*.[27] Town and village allegiances structure player preferences in general; in the case of farmsteads, it often occurs that a family will root for one particular player only because the neighboring family is rooting for that player's main rival. Such an almost obligatory "display of autonomy through an antagonistic positioning against friend, neighbor, colleague and even brother"[28] often has no motivation other than subjectivization through setting boundaries. Family lineage rivalry prompted the emergence of *pelota* to begin with; González traces the game back to a perpetual series of blood feuds among antagonistic clans or factions as early as the Middle Ages.[29] *Pelota*, whose paradigmatic modality is the singles hand game, is particularly apt to transmit the binary of what Roger Caillois calls *agôn*,[30] competitive combat. In a documentary on Basque political violence, the director Julio Medem chose *pelota* as a master metaphor for the antagonistic struggle between Basque political entities.

"When you play a regular soccer game," a Real Sociedad fan tells me, "you are like the cow that only has to pay attention to the grass. When you play a derby, you are like the bull that has to pay attention to his surroundings." This metaphor conceptualizes the derby through the rural world of the *baserri* farmsteads, where cows and bulls are a basic asset of subsistence. It also implicitly distinguishes between what Clifford Geertz would call the difference between "deep play" and "shallow play"[31] in his analysis of Balinese cockfights: the more a match is between near-status individuals and/or high-status individuals, the deeper the match. The derby is "deep play": the bull represents a higher-status game, while it retains allusion to the farmstead and the rural, egalitarian world of kinship competition.

The best analogy for the Basque soccer derby, John Walton remarks, is that of "the family at war within itself."[32] In light of kin group rivalry based on neighboring *etxeak*, we may also see it as two allied kin groups at war. The relationship between the kin groups really depends

---

26. Ibid., 459.
27. González Abrisketa, *Basque Pelota: A Ritual, An Aesthetic.*
28. Ibid., 102.
29. Ibid., 39.
30. Caillois, *Man, Play, and Games.*
31. Geertz, *The Interpretation of Cultures*, 441.
32. Walton, "Basque Football Rivalries in the Twentieth Century," 119.

on the context of competition. Geertz observes that in the cockfights of Bali, members of the same kin group feel obliged to bet on their player no matter how poor his chances; if their kin group is not involved, however, they will support an allied kin group against an unallied one.[33] Similarly, soccer competition is a network of shifting alliances, and the kinship analogy becomes apparent when Athletic and Real are not involved in direct competition. In such a case, Basque clubs often behave as allied kin groups against unallied ones. In 1984, when Athletic's championship title depended on the outcome of the derby, the Real goalkeeper, "who normally cleared the ball with a powerful kick upfield, began to throw it out with unerring inaccuracy, regularly finding the Athletic forward Dani."[34] When the winning ball went in, "it seemed as if [the goalkeeper] had a sudden attack of lumbago."[35] A reverse scenario is also well documented. When Real needed the derby victory for its second championship title in the early 1980s, with 2-1 on the score sheet and ten minutes left, Athletic player Goikoetxea went up to striker Sarabia, "gave him a friendly shake by the neck, said something in his ear and after that they strolled around quietly in midfield. The contest was over."[36] On the soccer field, therefore, both competition and neighborly or allied kin group solidarity influence club relations.

Town and Village Rivalry

Identity in the Basque Country is intimately linked to place. When two people meet, one of the first questions they ask is where the other is from—that is, the other's birthplace. The answer will have a certain determination for the subject, as if a local essence was assigned by birthright: they are put in a category and their interlocutor now feels privy to their character. Localities have stereotyped identities that are playfully reproduced in the most diverse social interactions. Locals are quick to remind you that "Urretxu is Urretxu, and Zumarraga is Zumarraga" (Gipuzkoa), even if the two villages emerged together in the fourteenth century and there is no visible physical sign of demarcation between them. Two villages only a few miles apart may be conceptualized as different worlds. "I can recognize a person from Getaria [Gipuzkoa] the second he opens his mouth," a man from Zarautz tells me—the two seashore towns are separated by a two-mile walk. In order to demarcate identity in close geographical proximity and hundreds of years of coexistence (Basque localities are some of the most ancient

---

33. Geertz, *The Interpretation of Cultures*, 437.
34. Walton, "Basque Football Rivalries in the Twentieth Century," 132.
35. Ibid.
36. Leguineche et al., quoted in ibid.

and insular ones), Basque villages, towns, and cities elaborate on stereotyped character features that in turn have nourished long-standing rivalries between these towns and villages. These rivalries are acted out in sports that are increasingly organized and commercialized—in, for example, regattas, *pelota*, basketball, and soccer.

The rivalry between Bilbao (hometown of Athletic Club in Bizkaia) and Donostia-San Sebastián (hometown of Real Sociedad in Gipuzkoa) is very elaborate; it is an "all-out war," as the media likes to present it. In popular media representations, a *Bilbaino* needs serious life adjustment skills to survive the "culture shock" presented by life in Donostia-San Sebastián, only an hour's drive away. And vice versa: for a *Donostiarra* (a person from Donostia-San Sebastián), Bilbao is *otro mundo*, "another world."

The rivalry between Bilbao and Donostia-San Sebastián is based on their cultural and economic roles as capitals of their provinces. Donostia-San Sebastián is a beautiful resort town by the sea with a population of 180,000, and a strong Francophile and historic aristocratic touch; it is the closest big city to the French border (twelve miles away), and it has enjoyed considerable interchange in terms of sophisticated tastes and lifestyles with France. French architecture, haute couture, haute cuisine, and sophistication cultivated by visiting celebrities, royalties, and political notables established a markedly posh and sophisticated character for Donostia-San Sebastián. The city's glamour is epitomized by its category "A" cinema festival, Zinemaldia, or the San Sebastián International Film Festival; since 1953, the Basque city has welcomed the greatest stars of American and European cinema. Added to this the highest concentration of Michelin-starred restaurants in Europe, there remains little doubt why Donostia-San Sebastián has been chosen to be European Cultural Capital 2016. Its residents are characterized as classy, fashion conscious, and somewhat particular, guarding fancies like daily strolls along the Concha, one of the most spectacular beach promenades of Europe.

Bilbao, in turn, was a paradigmatic industrial center for most of its history. Until the 1990s, tourists only stopped, if at all, en route to Donostia-San Sebastián. Bilbao was a heavily industrialized, working-class city with a murky, yellow river, cranes and ship decks at the heart of its downtown district, ubiquitous smoke that coated the façades of buildings black, and a decadent night life in its Palanca district. Bilbao was an industrial city through and through, with iron production and shipbuilding at its core. As opposed to Donostia-San Sebastián's francophilia, Bilbao was anglophile: historically, its most important business links were with Britain. It was through these commercial encounters between Bilbao and Britain that soccer was first played in the Basque Country; and Athletic still cherishes its British roots as patrimony.

It is exactly where the first game was played, on the Campa de los Ingleses, where one of the most spectacular buildings of the twentieth century now stands—Frank Gehry's Guggenheim Museum. Why it is in Bilbao and not in Donostia-San Sebastián, the fashionable arts center of the Basque Country, is illustrative of the differences in entrepreneurial mentality and financial resources between the two cities. When the idea of a museum of contemporary art came up in Donostia-San Sebastián in the 1980s, the Cultural Ministry of the Provincial Council of Gipuzkoa found the approximately twenty million U.S. dollars necessary for the project too much to spend on art, even if the arts were a hallmark of Donostia-San Sebastián's identity. A few years later, Bilbao bought the Guggenheim project for about ten times more (approximately two hundred million U.S. dollars) without the blink of an eye. What would have been considered anathema elsewhere—a fancy international museum in a historically industrial city of marked working-class propensities—was taken by Bilbao without hesitation. Historically, Bilbao has thrived on its spirit of adventure and risk-taking—in other words, on "having the balls" to engage in the most fantastic reveries, and even to realize them. Both its deep-sea fishermen venturing to Newfoundland and its capitalists making Bilbao a center of the Industrial Revolution reflect a deeply entrepreneurial spirit, but nothing compares to "the balls" it took to throw it all away and invite the Guggenheim Foundation to build, of all things, a museum. The city went through a series of urban renewal projects that saved it from post-industrial demise, all with a natural quality as though success was its birthright. The nonchalant readiness, and the lack thereof, to risk exorbitant amounts of money on a project of unforeseeable consequences is symptomatic of the conceived differences between Bilbainos and Donostiarras and, as an extension, between Bizkaians and Gipuzkoans: the former are said to exude a "cocky," larger-than-life image, the latter are more sober and realistic.

Provincial Rivalry

There is a great variety of terrain, climate, minerals, flora, and fauna in the Basque Country, which has produced distinct lifestyles and subsistence methods. Localities delineate themselves through various lines: "each province has its own personality which is made up of a variety of 'micro-worlds' along rural/urban, nationalist/non-nationalist, Basque speaking/Spanish-speaking lines."[37] Stereotypes thrive around the provinces: the loud, boisterous "city slickers" of Bizkaia; the shrewd, introspective *aldeanos* "peasants" of Gipuzkoa; and the *patateros* "potato growers" of Araba. One must emphasize, as does Raento, that geographical differences do not translate into substantial discrepancies when it comes to general welfare and quality of living; instead, their main purpose is symbolic boundary-making.

Sports reflect and perpetuate a narcissism of small differences. In her ethnography on the *pelota*, González quotes Retegi II, one of the best-known players of this Basque sport, describing fan communities as "a reserve of the exclusive ethos" of their province: "I would say that [spectators from] from La Rioja are very passionate; Gipuzkoans are more serious and demanding; the Navarrese assimilate well, they are happy and not aggressive; the Bizkaians are very Bizkaian, they love everything."[38] Javier Clemente, an emblematic former coach of Athletic and the Spanish national team, spoke to me in similar terms in an interview: "A Bizkaian soccer player is cocky, and takes risks; Gipuzkoans are more sober and realistic; the Navarrese are tough brutes."[39] The difference between the Bizkaian and Gipuzkoan fan communities, a fan points out, shows in their interpretation of league ranking: "With only three points apart in the ranking, fans of Real Sociedad talk about how to avoid relegation to the second division, and fans of Athletic talk about winning the Champions League [a star-studded competition involving the best teams in Europe as a whole]." As long as it is mathematically possible, Bilbainos will maintain a can-do attitude: "Athletic is in the finals as long as it is not eliminated." The belief in success is manifested by Athletic fans' habit of reserving hotel rooms and making travel arrangements for finals, as they did for the 2012 UEFA Europa League (the second most prestigious European competition) final in Bucharest, when their team is still in the octo-final qualifying rounds.

Provincial consciousness and identity are greatly nourished by the different daily press that Basques consume in Bizkaia and Gipuzkoa, which is why Benedict Anderson's thesis on imagined communities is very significant in this context. Communities are "imagined," Anderson argues, "because the members of even the smallest nation will never know most of their fellow members, meet them, or even hear of them, yet in the minds of each lives the image of their communion."[40] Print

---

37. Raento, "Territory, Pluralism, and Nationalism in the Basque Country of Spain," 214.

38. González, *Basque Pelota*, 247.

39. Javier Clemente, personal interview with author, May 2011 Bilbao.

40. Anderson, *Imagined Communities*, 6.

capitalism and the daily ritual of consuming the same news, Anderson argues, creates an imagined linkage in the readers' mind. The Basque daily press creates this linkage through provincial publications: the two major dailies, the Bizkaian *El Correo* and the Gipuzkoan *El Diaro Vasco*, are run by the same news agency, but they feature province-based news that becomes extremely exclusive when it comes to sports. The former features only Athletic and the latter only Real Sociedad, while both do their fair share of creating *morbo*: controversy and competitive animosity before derbies. For Basque nationalists, these hegemonic pro-Spanish news anchors use the derby to divide the Basque community along provincial lines.

National Competition

Armstrong and Giulianotti argue that Basque soccer serves to construct what Benedict Anderson calls "submerged nationhood"—resistant national identities in centripetal political contexts.[41] While Athletic does indeed tend to be seen as the national team[42] because of its recruitment philosophy and past connections with the Basque nationalist elite, fans in the provinces of Gipuzkoa, Araba, and Navarre certainly disagree. Strictly speaking, the "national team" of the Basque "submerged nationhood" is the unofficial soccer selection—*Euskal Selekzioa*.

The Basque national team was one of the first in Spain, created years before the Spanish national team was founded (1920), and established with the aim of representing the Basque people. In 1911, the Basque Nationalist Party youth organization *Juventud Vasca* initiated a championship called *Copa de Euzkadi*, or "Cup of the Basque Country." The purpose of this cup was to create support among fans, clubs, and directors for a Basque national team. The newspaper *Euzkadi* observed the following on the necessity of a national team in 1915: "For a while now there is talk about the constitution of a Basque team selected from the best of Bizkaia and Gipuzkoa with the objective of competing far away from the fatherland, in France, in England. . . . Those who are knowledgeable in these matters argue that this team, formed with no other purpose than the glory of Basque land, would achieve this splendidly, for the talents of agility, dexterity and resistance of the race manifested in the Basque teams."[43]

The most noted attempt to lend Basques visibility through soccer was the 1936–39 national team assembled by the ex-player and later pres-

41. Giulianotti and Armstrong, "Afterword," 273–74.

42. Walton, "Basque Football Rivalries in the Twentieth Century"; MacClancy, *Expressing Identities in the Basque Arena*; MacClancy, "Nationalism at Play," 181–99.

43. Gómez, *La patria del gol*, 29.

ident of the first Basque government, José Antonio Aguirre, during the Spanish Civil War. The Basque national team went on a three-year tour around Europe and Latin America with the purpose of raising money for the Republican Basque forces, including money to buy aircraft, and aid for the hundreds of children evacuated from the war zone. Many members of that national team never returned to the Basque Country. During the repressive Franco regime (1936–75), the idea of a regional soccer team was unthinkable.

The Basque national soccer team has been a much-contested ideological terrain. The Spanish sports federations do not allow the formation of official Basque teams, but even the unofficial Basque soccer team is thwarted by controversy. Throughout its history, the team has been variously called Vasconia, the Northern Team, Euskadi, Euskal Herria, and Euskal Selekzioa—the name of the entity has been subject to spectacular debates and social divisions along political-ideological lines. Each name designates a different imaginary of what the Basque Country is, or should be, in terms of its geographical and ideological boundaries. A disagreement over whether it should be termed the team of Euskadi (the political entity forming the Basque Autonomous Community and comprised of the three Spanish provinces of Araba, Bizkaia, and Gipuzkoa) or Euskal Herria (the larger historical Basque Country made up of four Spanish and three French provinces) resulted in such a political storm that the annual Christmas game was cancelled in 2009. This game stands symbolically for the Basque nation, but any attempt to pin down the boundaries of that nation conjures up historical-ideological antagonisms. The Basque soccer team is symptomatic of the impasses and fractures within Basque society, conditions that make it impossible to arrive at self-definition on a collective level. This, in turn, hinders efforts in the struggle for officialdom, and for Basque representation at the level of a nation.

Burruka, Joko, Jolas: The Performance of Cooperation and Competition

The street episode with which I began this chapter demonstrates that fans shift from one performative model to another; one moment they might be preparing for *burruka* or a fight, the next they engage in carnivalesque *jolas*, and finally they enter into competitive *joko* projected onto the teams they support. In each phase, a particular identity gains prominence over the rest. Combat group loyalty and male honor, city and provincial belonging, nationalist ideologies, and ethno-cultural values are variously activated; they motivate action one moment and remain suspended in another. Because they highlight a particular social relation from among the many, *joko, jolas,* and *burruka* become ritu-al occurrences in Roy A. Rappaport's sense--that is, they "impose sharp, unambiguous, qualitative distinctions upon continuous, ambiguous quantitative differences."[44] The performative models of *joko, jolas,* and *burruka* of the derby oscillate between various Basque life worlds, orga-nizing them into competitive or cooperative relations.

Burruka: An "Echo of Lost Dignities"

The climactic moment I described in the introduction between the two combat fan groups Herri Norte and Mujika did not result in casualties just then. The situation, however, remained tense; a few hours later I see three red-and-white jerseys chasing down a blue-and-white one by the Café Barandiaran; customers flee into the bars and shades are low-ered in haste to prevent flying chairs from breaking shop windows. A few minutes later, a Real Sociedad fan emerges with his face bleeding. "What happened?" I ask a member of Herri Norte. "He insulted us! He said 'Fuck Bilbao, fuck Marijaia,'" Marijaia is a female cloth figure sym-bolizing the week-long fiestas of Bilbao, the *Aste Nagusia.*

In the Basque Country, a fight or wrestling match between males is called *burruka,* which Joseba Zulaika considers a "culturally sanctioned institution." The male nature of *burruka* was associated with male do-mains such as bars, taverns, and competition in plazas. The purpose of these fights is to harm the other not more than necessary in order to show dominance, force, and honor. "In traditional Basque society," Zulaika writes, "the notion of violence itself is largely translated into and controlled through the *burruka* cultural institution. Involvement in a *burruka* does not necessarily imply a violent character."[45] What it always implies is a spirit of struggle over honor, dignity, and integrity, which must be defended. This performative model has gained a polit-ical meaning; ETA's activities were called *burruka harmatuta,* "armed struggle," and the Basque nationalist youth was for years involved in *kale borroka* or a "street-fighting" guerilla war of various intensity over decades, including rioting at demonstrations, throwing Molotov cock-tails, burning trash containers, and attacking anti-Basque nationalist party offices.

For rival combat groups, every derby encounter potentially be-comes a *burruka* over honor and integrity. As Jennifer Low writes, "there can be no honor that is ever untested [and] no test is definitive."[46] A sociohistorically sanctioned, ritually more elaborate equivalent of the

---

44. Rappaport, *Ritual and Religion in the Making of Humanity,* 95.
45. Zulaika, *Basque Violence,* 172.
46. Low, *Manhood and the Duel,* 52.

burruka model is the duel of honor—Herri Norte fans told me about fights that had rules and were supervised by a referee of sorts. *Burruka* and duel share two features; both are "echoes of lost dignities"[47] because they aim to restore honor and integrity (note above the fight over insulting Marijaia, a female figure), and both enter into an economy of non-equivalences—the readiness to sacrifice physical well-being for an abstract idea. The *burruka* of the derby, like a duel, is predicated on a certain intimacy between the two parties, and the insult is all the more exacerbated because it comes from nearby.

Herri Norte and Mujika consider themselves *abertzale*, Marxist, Basque nationalist, red-skin, anti-fascist fan clubs. Their most dangerous adventures take place in Madrid against fan groups that they consider radical right-wing, Spanish nationalist, and fascist. "If it hadn't been for us," a fan tells me, "these fascists would run amok with their harmful ideologies." There is a sense in which the combat fan group conceives of itself as the last line of defense and its *burruka* as a necessary, if little understood, struggle.

Joko: Athletic vs. Real

Clifford Geertz argues that the individuals who compete in and bet on the illegal cockfights in Bali are in an "institutionalized hostility relationship" called *puik*.[48] The parties involved will not speak or have anything to do with each other; they compete fiercely, "even manically." The causes of *puik*, Geertz adds, may be inheritance arguments, political differences, or wife capture.

A similar "institutionalized hostility relationship" exists between Athletic and Real Sociedad over player capture. By the 1980s, Athletic's localist, province-based (Bizkaia) philosophy could no longer keep the club competitive in a globalizing league, which is why it expanded its recruitment over the entire Basque Country. Consequent player poaching, and the snapping-up of the winner of the under-twenty-one World Cup Golden Ball, Joseba Etxeberria, from Real Sociedad aggravated club relationships to the point of freezing them. Each time an Athletic talent scout is spotted at Gipuzkoan youth games, the papers voice indignation over the "dirty exploits" of the *merengue vasca*, the "Basque Real Madrid," which is an unflattering comparison with reference to Athletic's symbolic and financial hegemony. Gipuzkoan fans never fail to remark on what they see as predatory behavior, and a derby is always a good occasion: "Basque soccer is what it is. Some create soccer players. Others try, and if they don't manage it, they can always pass by

---

47. Ibid., 5.
48. Geertz, *The Interpretation of Cultures*, 438.

Zubieta [the youth academy of Real Sociedad] and resolve our econom-ic problems."[49] In order to fend off the neighbor, Real Sociedad players have a special transfer-fee clause attached to their contracts; for Athlet-ic, they cost more than for any other team.

The competitive relationship between Athletic and Real Sociedad, on and off the field, corresponds to the Basque concept of binary, com-petitive play—*joko*. *Joko* is a pervasive competitive framework in the Basque Country; betting, rural sports like wood chopping, stone lift-ing, and oxen challenge, ram fights, *pelota*, regattas, and soccer fall into this category. Even *bertsolaritza*, the paradigmatic Basque cultural per-formance of improvised poetry, is practiced in a competitive form as a winner is profusely celebrated. The interpersonal dynamics of chal-lenging the other into a bet is in fact challenging to *joko*, binary com-petition. *Joko* is strictly a man's affair: woman as a *jokolari*, "player," is a cultural "oddity" that makes her "conspicuously abnormal, an evidently mannish woman."[50] Elsewhere I argue that one reason women's soccer faces particular challenges in the Basque Country is because women are not conceptualized as competitive *jokolariak* ("players").[51] Tradi-tionally, theirs is the domestic *jolas*, noncompetitive play model. *Joko* is male public performance, whose paradigmatic cultural forms are men playing the *mus* card game in bars, performing *bertsolaritza* and playing pelota in the plaza, and playing soccer in stadiums.

Zulaika notes the potentially pernicious, dysfunctional effects of competitive, bipolar *joko*. It can disrupt family life if a husband fre-quents bars too much, or is too given to *joko*. Money wagers can threat-en the well-being of a family: "people would *jokatu* everything they had, houses included, and even their wife if you didn't keep watch."[52] *Joko* is also a political metaphor; as opposed to the street fight *burruka*, or-dinary political strategizing is considered *joko*, whose paradigmatic visualization is the informal game of *sokatira* or tug-of-war, a favorite staple of Basque intervillage competition between teams consisting of the strongest of local youth.

Joko has been the characteristic mode of the Athletic-Real derby ever since the first game in 1905, whose *morbo* was already so anticipat-ed that "it was necessary to send three special trains"[53] to bring people from Gipuzkoa to Lamiaco, Athletic's first playing field. In 1908 there was talk of a combined team, but the plan was never realized. Instead,

49. *Diario Vasco*, 6 December 2010.

50. Zulaika, *Basque Violence*, 180.

51. Vaczi, "A Matter of Balls."

52. Informant quoted in Joseba Zulaika, *Basque Violence*, 175.

53. Mateos quoted by Terrachet, *100 años de historia*, 44.

the derby was increasingly characterized by insults, rudeness, fights, and police intervention.[54] The "institutionalized hostility relation" was already thriving under an accumulating bunch of grievances. In 1909 Athletic officially complained that Real's Atocha Stadium was unfit for its "anti-regulation conditions"; in 1912, Real Sociedad reported on Athletic for playing British players, as a result of which Athletic was stripped of its title. In the 1920s, the rivalry was somewhat more sanitized.[55] During the repressive decades of the Franco regime, with its ban on non-Spanish ethnic symbols in soccer as elsewhere, the derby was conceptualized as just other derby between two "Spanish" provinces. With the end of the repressive Franco regime in the 1970s, which Llopis Goig calls the "post-national" era of soccer in Spain,[56] regional clubs were increasingly free to assume politicized-peripheral identities. The 1976 Basque derby was one of the first politically subversive events of the post-Franco era; prior to the start of the game, the players from both teams displayed the still-banned Basque national flag, the *ikurriña*. The derby became a site of not only competition but cooperation as well—an event in which Basques could finally insert themselves, as Basques, in Spain.

Jolas: the Great Basque Fiesta

Atotxa soccer stadium, Donostia-San Sebastián, December 5, 1976. Athletic Club of Bilbao and Real Sociedad of Donostia-San Sebastián are soon to emerge on the field. The stands are on the verge of explosion. You can hear the alternating yells of "Athletic!—Real!" Mixed with those words, you can also hear, loudly, *Presoak Kalera!* "Prisoners to the street!" *Askatasuna!* "Freedom!" and *Amnistia!* "Amnesty!" The fanfare band *Los Anastasios* is playing beautiful Basque songs; there is a great Basque fiesta going on. It is 4:30, and the players of both teams, lead by the captains Iribar and Kortabarria, enter the field while the fanfare is playing *Batasuna* "Unity." The applause and the chanting are deafening. Suddenly, a bearded young man emerges between the two lines of players. He walks over to Iribar and Kortabarria, pulls out a piece of cloth from under his shirt, and displays an *ikurriña* [Basque national flag]. Iribar and Kortabarria hold it and raise it, and the three of them walk to the center. Both teams align on the two sides of the flag. Madness overcomes the stands. The applauding and yelling are ten times louder, and tears flood from our eyes.[57]

---

54. Walton, "Basque Football Rivalries in the Twentieth Century."
55. Ibid.
56. Llopis-Goig, "Identity, Nation State and Football in Spain," 60–61.
57. *Kirolak*, 7 December 1976.

The 1976 derby, which the following day one Madrid newspaper called a "separatist orgy in Atocha,"[58] has over the years turned into a "Basque fiesta" of political and cultural vindication. The 1976 absolute unanimity of both Athletic and Real locker rooms in their decision to display the still-banned symbol became symbolic itself; it was an act of cooperation that transcended institutional competition and provincial rivalry. The mandate to cooperate still resonates with the derbies today. Thirty-four years later in 2010, as the Spanish *Liga* game scheduling would have it, the Basque derby fell on the same historic date— December 5. After the captains Gurpegi and Aranburu emerged on the field followed by the two teams, they lined up by the sideline. A small girl dressed in *rojiblanco* (red-and-white), the colors of Athletic, and a boy in *txuriurdin* (blue-and-white), the colors of Real Sociedad, appear, holding the historic cloth, amid deafening cheers and applause. They hand it to the captains who, like their colleagues thirty years ago, hold it aloft. The stands go wild with emotion as the present connects with the past through the weatherbeaten spectacle of the *ikurriña*.

The derbies are surrounded with an air of fraternal unity and a display of Basque identity. The streets of the old town in Donostia-San Sebastián become a sea of red, blue, and white. The streets are full of posters expressing regional political aspirations: *"Euskal Presoak Etxera"* (Bring Basque Prisoners Home)—reflecting a desire to bring ETA prisoners back to jails in the Basque Country so they can be visited more easily.[59] The organization ESAIT (*Euskal Selekzioaren Aldeko Iritzi*), an advocacy group fighting for the officialdom of Basque sports teams and their participation in international championships, plans a *kalejira*, a demonstration in favor of Basque national teams--*"Euskera eta Euskal Herriko Selekzioa Ofizialtasuna Lortu Behar Dugu eta Lortuko Dugu!"* (We Have to and We Will Achieve the Officialdom of the Basque Language and Basque Teams).

Basque unity and collective memory were the major themes of the 2010 derby. After the display of the *ikurriña*, the pregame program proceeded with the promotion of the Basque language; only two days before, on December 3, the Basque Country had celebrated the "International day of Euskera" [Basque]. First, homage was paid to the recently deceased poet Xabier Lete—one of the artists whose concerts flashed the first secret *ikurriñas* in the mid-1970s. After a one-minute silence

---

58. MacClancy, "Nationalism at Play," 193.

59. The Spanish government maintains a policy of prisoner dispersion. ETA prisoners are strategically placed in prisons all over Spain in order to isolate them. This is a controversial matter because it inhibits the prisoner's right to be visited, and the family's right to visit. An important aspiration of left wing Basque nationalists is to bring ETA prisoners back to Basque Country prisons.

in his honor, his signature song, "Izarren hautsa" (Stardust), echoed from the loudspeakers and in the stands, evoking the Tree of Gernika, the symbol of Basque freedom that is still nurtured in the town that the Nazis destroyed in 1937:

> *Gu sortu ginen enbor beretik*
> *Sortuko dira besteak,*
> *Burruka hortan iraungo duten*
> *Zuhaitz ardaska gazteak. (...)*
> *Gure ametsa arrazoi garbiz egiztatuko dutenak.* [60]

> From the same trunk that we were born
> Other young branches will be born,
> Who will keep fighting,
> Who will be born by becoming aware of their future,
> Who will make real what for us is dream and desire.

After the homage to Lete, the Basque singer Etxe took to the field to sing Urko's famous song that he wrote to revindicate the use of the Basque language. Finally, the entire Anoeta Stadium sang the song *"Txoria Txori"* (Bird) in unison, a song often sung by and for political prisoners,[61] and which metaphorically presents the nation as a bird whose wing is broken and thus cannot fly.

The fiesta of brotherhood takes place in the *jolas* performative mode: cooperative play in the intimacy of the family in which men, women, and children participate equally. *Jolas* neutralizes the competitive, violent, disruptive edge of *joko* and *burruka*, just as the festival element celebrating common Basqueness neutralizes the violent-competitive aspects of the derby. The pregame event was *jolas*, a fiesta of being Basque, in which the themes of independence, cultural and linguistic continuity, suffering, and sacrifice were celebrated through the most significant Basque symbolism. With kick-off, however, "the fiesta was over and the hostilities started."[62] We enter the sphere of *joko*.

Together and Apart? A Prisoner's Dilemma

Anthropologist Gregory Bateson based his play theory on a visit to the San Francisco zoo, where he saw two chimpanzees playing. The animals were engaged in combat-like behavior (biting, chasing, wrestling, and so on), although it was clear to both parties that they were not fighting but playing. This, Bateson argues, is only possible if there exists an

---

60. Lyrics in Basque available at http://eu.musikazblai.com/xabier-lete/izarren-hautsa/ (last accessed on 25 November 2013).
61. Zulaika, *Basque Violence.*
62. *Diario Vasco*, 6 December 2010.

act of meta-communication: "This is play." In other words, the players agreed that "these actions in which we now engage do not denote what those actions *for which they stand* would denote."[63] For the Basque derby to become play and not fight, a similar act of meta-communication has to take place.

Arriving at that meta-communicative agreement, however, is not easy because of conflicting interests, which turn derby interaction into a prisoner's dilemma. In the classic prisoner's dilemma, a Faustian bargain is presented to two members of the same gang: cooperate or defect. The authorities lack evidence for a crime and offer the two gang members the option of confessing or remaining silent. If one confesses and his accomplice remains silent, the authorities will drop charges against him and the accomplice will do serious prison time. If the accomplice confesses while the first prisoner remains silent, the accomplice goes free and the silent party goes to prison. If both confess, both get early parole. If both remain silent, there will be a settlement for a lighter sentence. In short, the prisoner's dilemma is this: in the consideration that both parties understand the structure of the game and both belong to the same gang, would the prisoners radically seek to optimize their own, if more precarious, best interest with no regard for the other, or would they cooperate and settle for a less ideal outcome for the individual but one more ideal for both parties? What is important for our purposes here is that the puzzle illustrates a conflict between individual and group rationality: a group whose individual members pursue rational self-interest may end up worse off than a group whose individual members act contrary to rational self-interest.

The Athletic-Real Sociedad relationship may be seen as an iterated prisoner's dilemma in which the actors play not just once but in succession; they remember their and their opponents' previous actions and decisions, favors and grievances, and strategize accordingly. The iterated prisoner's dilemma is also called a "peace-war game," which captures the history of the Athletic-Real Sociedad derby relationship. It has been a tug-of-war between cooperation and betrayal, shaped by the pursuit of self-interest and its relaxation in the light of the other's decision. We have seen examples of cooperation: when one club had nothing or only a minimum at stake, it was ready to cooperate and lose games so the other party could maximize its benefit and win the league championship. Player poaching, on the other hand, is conceptualized as betrayal precisely because it comes from the neighbor, which is why it provokes retorsions like exorbitant player-transfer fees. The prison-

---

63. Bateson, *Steps to an Ecology of Mind*, 152.

er's dilemma becomes an intimate affair, for there is no dilemma if it is just another competitive relationship; neither Athletic nor Real Sociedad expects another team, for example Sevilla FC, to lose games for them so they can win the league, nor are they particularly disturbed, much less inclined to cry traitor, when Sevilla FC approaches their players. If it is just another competitive relationship, self-interest is shamelessly maximized as the laws of competition dictate.

On the horns of the dilemma is therefore this: to cooperate or to betray? To play or to fight? The Basque derby is a dilemma between individual (club) rationality and group rationality (Basque community), between antagonistic fight (*joko*) and cooperative play (*jolas*). If both parties (Athletic and Real Sociedad) aggressively, if rationally, pursue their self-interest in terms of winning and player purchase, they might be worse off as a group: vicious competition in sports may adversely affect cooperation and unity in social and political matters. It is this concern that lies behind the complaints of those who see the artificial generation of inter-province competition as a harmful aggravation of rivalry (*burruka*), and the curbing of cooperation (*jolas*) among fans. The declaration of the Basque derby as "a game of high risk" by the Spanish *Liga's* Anti-Violence Commission is considered to exacerbate the situation by creating a self-fulfilling prophecy.

But because it is a *Basque* derby, there exists a meta-communicative act external to the competitive arena: we belong to the same "gang," the same moral community. The repeated display of the *ikurriña* is such an act of meta-communication; so is the chanting of anti-Madrid and pro-Basque songs by Herri Norte and Mujika. At the moment of possible fight, fans remind themselves of Bateson's notion: "This is play." Despite all apparent hostility, these meta-communicative acts render the Basque derby qualitatively different from those on other playing fields in which they are absent--at matches against Madrid teams, for example. Even if occasional betrayal produces zero-sum games, the iterated "peace-war game" has to maintain, in the long run, a balance of win-win situations in order for the community to survive the antagonistic, divisive tendencies of competition. Beyond individual self-interest, there must remain a collective meta-communicative agreement that "this is play," whereby "everybody wins . . . and the final result is merely a prize granted to one side of the street or the other."[64]

---

64. *Diario Vasco*, 6 December 2010.

Bibliography

Anderson, Benedict. *Imagined Communities: Reflections on the Origin and Spread of Nationalism*. London and New York: Verso, 2006.

Armistead, Samuel G. and Joseba Zulaika. *Voicing the Moment: Improvised Oral Poetry and Basque Tradition*. Reno: Center for Basque Studies, University of Nevada, Reno, 2005.

Armstrong, Gary. *Football Hooligans: Knowing the Score*. Oxford: Berg, 1998.

Armstrong, Gary, and Richard Giulianotti. "Constructing Social Identities: Exploring the Structured Relations of Football Rivalries." In *Fear and Loathing in World Football*, edited by Gary Armstrong and Richard Giulianotti. Oxford: Berg, 2001.

Aulestia, Gorka. *The Basque Poetic Tradition*. Reno, Nevada: University of Nevada Press, 2000.

Ball, Phil. *Morbo: The Story of Spanish Football*. London: WSC Books, 2003.

Bateson, Gregory. *Steps to an Ecology of Mind*. St. Albans: Granada Publishing Limited, 1973.

Caillois, Roger. *Man, Play, and Games*. New York: Free Press of Glencoe, 1961.

Dal Lago, Alessandro, and Rocco De Biasi. "Italian Football Fans: Culture and Organization." In *Football, Violence and Social Identity*, edited by Richard Giulianotti, Norman Bonney, and Mike Hepworth. London and New York: Routledge, 1994.

Douglass, William A. *Death in Murélaga: Funerary Ritual in a Spanish Basque Village*. Seattle: University of Washington Press, 1969.

Dunning, Eric. *Sport Matters: Sociological Studies of Sport, Violence and Civilization*. London and New York: Routledge, 1999.

Finn, Gerry P. T. "Football Violence: A Societal Psychological Perspective." In *Football, Violence and Social Identity*, edited by Richard Giulianotti, Norman Bonney, and Mike Hepworth. London and New York: Routledge, 1994.

Geertz, Clifford. *The Interpretation of Cultures*. New York, Basic Books: 1973.

Gilmore, David D. *Manhood in the Making: Cultural Concepts of Masculinity*. New Haven: Yale University Press, 1990.

Giulianotti, Richard. *Football: A Sociology of the Global Game*. Cambridge: Polity Press, 1999.

Goffman, Erving. *Interaction Ritual: Essays on Face-to-Face Behavior*. New Brunswick, N.J.: Transaction Publishers, 2005.

Gómez, Daniel. *La patria del gol: Fútbol y política en el Estado español*. San Sebastián: Almed, 2007.

González Abrisketa, Olatz. *Basque Pelota: A Ritual, An Aesthetic*. Reno:

Center for Basque Studies, University of Nevada, Reno, 2013.

Hobbs, Dick, and David Robins. "The Boy Done Good: Football Violence, Changes and Continuities." *Sociological Review* 39, no. 3 (1991): 551–79.

King, Anthony. "Violent Pasts: Collective Memory and Football Hooliganism." *Sociological Review* 49, no. 4 (2001): 568–85.

Llopis-Goig, Ramón. "Identity, Nation State and Football in Spain: The Evolution of Nationalist Feelings in Spanish Football." *Soccer and Society* 9, no. 1 (2008): 56–63.

Low, Jennifer. *Manhood and the Duel: Masculinity in Early Modern Drama and Culture.* New York and Houndmills, U.K.: Palgrave Macmillan, 2003.

MacClancy, Jeremy. "Nationalism at Play: The Basques of Vizcaya and Athletic Club de Bilbao." In *Sport, Identity, and Ethnicity,* edited by Jeremy MacClancy. Oxford: Berg, 1996.

———. *Expressing Identities in the Basque Arena.* Oxford: James Currey, 2007.

Marsh, Peter. *Aggro: The Illusion of Violence.* London, Melbourne, and Toronto: J. M. Dent & Sons, 1978.

Ott, Sandra. *The Circle of Mountains: A Basque Sheepherder Community.* Reno: University of Nevada Press, 1993.

Raento, Pauliina. 1996. Territory, Pluralism, and Nationalism in the Basque Country of Spain. Ph.D. diss., University of Nevada, Reno.

Rappaport, Roy A. *Ritual and Religion in the Making of Humanity.* Cambridge: Cambridge University Press, 1999.

Terrachet, Enrique. *100 años de historia del Athletic de Bilbao.* Bilbao: La Gran Enciclopedia Vasca, 1998.

Vaczi, Mariann. "'The Spanish Fury': A Political Geography of Soccer in Spain." *International Review for the Sociology of Sport,* Online Ahead of Print February 2013. DOI: 10.1177/1012690213478940. http://irs.sagepub.com/content/early/2013/02/22/1012690213478940.abstract.

———. "A Matter of Balls: Women and Soccer in the Basque Country, Spain." Forthcoming in *Soccer and Society* 15, no. 1 (January 2014).

Walton, John. "Basque Football Rivalries in the Twentieth Century." In *Fear and Loathing in World Football,* edited by Gary Armstrong and Richard Giulianotti. Oxford: Berg, 2001.

———. "Sport and the Basques: Constructed and Contested Identities." *Journal of Historical Sociology* 24, no. 4 (2011): 451–71.

Zulaika, Joseba. *Basque Violence: Metaphor and Sacrament.* Reno: University of Nevada Press, 2000.

13

PROTECTION, DISCIPLINE, AND HONOR: A BOXING CLUB IN AN AMERICAN GHETTO

Loïc J.D. Wacquant

In the same way that it would be impossible to understand an organized religion such as Catholicism without studying in detail the organization behind it (in other words, the Roman Catholic Church), it would not be possible to understand the meaning and the deep roots of boxing in contemporary American society (at least in the lower social strata, where its inevitable and imminent demise is not regularly pronounced) without looking into the network of social and symbolic relationships that exist within and around training gyms—the hub and hidden engine of the pugilistic universe.

That simple word *gym* denotes a complex institution with many meanings, loaded with roles and symbols that are not always immediately apparent. On the surface, what could be simpler than a gym? The characteristics of these organizations are so constant that we might well quote George Plimpton word for word in his portrait of the famous Stillman's Gym in New York during the 1950s to describe any gym in contemporary urban America:

> You go down a dark staircase which reminds you of an old galleon's hold. You can hear the noise even before your eyes get used to the half-light: skipping ropes slapping the floor, the sound of leather against punch bags which clink as they sway on their chains, the cracking of speed bags, the stifled crackle of boots moving on the ring (there were two rings), boxers sniffing as they breathe through their noses and, every three minutes, the bell's loud ring. The atmosphere's like nightfall in a damp jungle.[1]

* This chapter is dedicated to Robert K. Merton in thanks for his advice while we were neighbors in New York, all too briefly. I am also grateful to the Society of Fellows at Harvard University, the French Government's Lavoisier program, and the Russell Sage Foundation for the support they have given me throughout this research project.

1. Plimpton "Three With Moore," 158. This description is valid for most of the coun-

Gyms are the forges in which fighters are beaten into shape, the workshops where armor-plated bodies prepare to throw themselves into the ring, the crucibles in which the delicate combination of technical skills and strategic knowledge (which together make an accomplished fighter) is honed. They are the furnaces in which fighters' flames of desire burn alongside a collective belief in the intrinsic values without which nobody would spend long between the ropes.[2] But gyms are more than that. It could well be that their avowed technical purpose (passing on and instilling sporting abilities) is in fact subordinate to the social and moral functions that lie hidden behind the activities that created them in the first place.

The aim of this chapter is to examine three of the main extra-pugilistic functions that boxing gyms offer those who go there to join in this popular cult of virility known as the Noble Art. In the first place, gyms protect people from the street, shielding them against the violence of the ghettos and the pressures of daily life. Like a sanctuary, they offer a closed, private, protected space in which people can "drop their guard" and escape the dull misery of a tedious existence. Unlike anywhere else, gyms allow their denizens refuge from the misfortunes that the culture and the economy of the street offer such young people who are despised and abandoned, born and locked into this "other America."

Secondly, gyms are schools of morality in the sense defined by Durkheim.[3] In other words, they are machines for producing the spirit of discipline, the sense of belonging to a group, the ability to respect other people as much as oneself, and autonomous will. These qualities are indispensable in developing the pugilistic vocation, but their main advantages, to all appearances, are in fact to be found far from the ring, in the most varied family and social contexts. Gyms are the support behind a "master plan for life" (*regulae magistra vitae*, as the Benedictines used to say) and provide mutual forms of social activity and control that, by regulating behavior and emotions, open the way to knowing oneself and others better, finding a practical form of wisdom involving calmness and acceptance of self.

---

try; boxing gyms worldwide have almost identical characteristics, and they are so alike that one could be mistaken for another. There are further descriptions of the New Oakland Boxing Club in Oakland, California, and the famous Kronk Gym in Detroit in Wiley, *Serenity*, 28–29; of the Rosario Gym at East Harlem, New York, in Plummer, *Buttercups and Strong Boys*, 51; and of the Cabbagetown Boxing Club in the Toronto suburbs in Brunt, *Mean Business*, 43–69. Ronald K. Fried gives a charming portrait of Stillman's Gym in its heyday in *Corner Men*, 32–53. Larry Fink's remarkable photographic report (coauthored with Katherine Dunn), "In This Ring," 30–35; and Barrat's *Do or Die* offer faithful visual portraits of boxing gyms.

2. Wacquant, "The Pugilistic Point of View."
3. Durkheim, *Moral Education*.

Lastly, gyms are vehicles for making daily life less banal, making routine and physical training the means of access to an exciting, unpredictable sensorial and emotional universe in which adventure, masculine honor, and prestige are combined. Belonging to a gym is a tangible sign of being accepted by a virile brotherhood that allows people to escape from anonymity and to earn the acceptance and admiration of the local community. These factors explain the attachment that most boxers feel for their gyms, often describing them as a "second family" and even a "second mother," which graphically illustrates how much protection and nourishment they believe their gyms give them.

An Old-Fashioned Gym on Chicago's South Side

In order to understand the different facets of gyms and the protection and benefits that they offer to the people who submit to their regime, it is necessary and sufficient to follow the foot soldiers of the Noble Art in their daily workouts and to be by their side as they go through their rigorous routines, which is an inextricable combination of the bodily and the moral, and which defines their condition and seals their identity. This is what I did for three years (from the summer of 1988 until the fall of 1991) in a black ghetto in Chicago where I learned the rudiments of the trade and where, having become friends with the gym's coaches and boxers, I was able to see at first hand the social origin and the development of fighters' careers.

Stoneland Boys Club is one of the fifty-two boxing gyms officially registered in the State of Illinois and one of the four most important professional gyms of its type in Chicago.[4] It is an "old school" gym, run by the seventy-year-old head coach's iron hand (he is internationally renowned, trained in the legendary Joe Louis's group, has worked on three continents, and has taken two of his protégés to the very highest levels in the world). In spite of its modest resources, the club has had an excellent reputation since it opened in 1977. Under the colors of the charity that generously lends it its facilities, Stoneland Club takes in around one hundred adolescents each year and also has around thirty regular members, of whom ten or twelve are pros.[5]

---

4. A professional gym is one in which pro boxers train (boxers paid for their work in the ring), as well as the amateurs who go to clubs of all types. Stoneland is a pseudonym; certain place names and people's names have also been changed in order to maintain the anonymity of those who wished it. There is a more detailed description of Stoneland, its immediate surroundings, and social structure in Wacquant, "Corps et âme," and "The Social Logic of Boxing in Black Chicago."

5. At the end of his career, Muhammad Ali, who has a house a few miles from there in the upmarket Hyde Park-Kenwood district, a white island of richness lost in the middle of the ocean of black poverty of the South Side, used to go there to train (which

The gym is located in a deprived area that is in steady decline, typical of the South Side, on an avenue lined with abandoned buildings and stores that are now burnt carcasses or boarded up with plywood; most of them were burned down by their owners who conspired with one or another gang in order to claim the insurance. Stoneland is a sort of no-man's-land to which parts of the black working class, marginalized by the polarization of social classes in the city, are consigned, victims of the United States' inflexible racial segregation and urban withdrawal.[6] Its exclusively black population is young (40 percent of the inhabitants are under twenty), most of them have no economic or cultural capital (half of the adults have not completed high school and a third of the households live below the official poverty level), and most of them are outside the labor market (only 44 percent of men are in paid employment and the same proportion of families need social benefits in order to subsist). In other words, Stoneland Gym is ideal for exploring a boxing gym's role in a black ghetto in an American city.

Being the only white person in the gym could have been a serious obstacle to my integration and have stopped me from getting into the boxers' social world had it not been for three compensating factors. First, the egalitarian ethos and racial color blindness of pugilistic culture (in the gym, that is) mean that you are accepted as soon as you enter the common discipline and "pay your dues" in the ring. Also, being French gave me a sort of outsider status with regard to the relationships of exploitation, scorn, and mutual distrust that are so common between white and black Americans. Lastly, my total acceptance of everything expected there, particularly in taking part in fights on a regular basis, won my ring colleagues' esteem, as demonstrated by their nickname for me—"Brother Louie"—and the range of other nicknames they gave me over the months.[7]

The "opportunistic" nature of my integration[8] should be added to

---

always led to outbreaks of public joy in the street). Most of the successful boxers from Chicago during the 1980s at one time or another trained at Stoneland, which—until it was closed in 1992, when the building was demolished and replaced by a parking lot as part of the street's "renovation"—was one of the main suppliers of fighters for the region's boxing evenings.

6. Mollenkopf and Castells, eds. *Dual City*; Massey and Denton, *American Apartheid*; Wacquant, "De l'Amérique comme utopie à l'envers," and "Red Belt, Black Belt."

7. Kurt H. Wolf defines the concept of "abandoning oneself" in an ethnic group as "total commitment, the suppression of previously held notions, belonging completely, identification and the risk of being wounded." The fact that I took my apprenticeship as far at the Chicago Golden Gloves in 1990, the most prestigious amateur competition in the area, greatly helped to consolidate my status in the club, as did daily demonstrations of solidarity outside the club. Wolf, "Surrender and Community Study."

8. Riemer, "Varieties of Opportunistic Research."

these factors. In fact, I did not join the gym with the specific aim of studying the boxing world. My initial intention was to use the gym as a "window" onto the ghetto, which was my first object of study, and it was not until after I had established myself in the Boys Club itself that I decided, with the support of those involved, to take on the gym as my second object of study. The friendship and trust that the regulars at Stoneland generously gave me allowed me to become one of them inside the gym, and also to go with them as they went around the South Side. It was by taking part in both everyday and special moments, pitiful and glorious moments in their everyday lives (marriages, births, and funerals; looking for a job and looking for rented accommodation; entertainment and business negotiations; quarrels with their wives, the social benefits offices, and the police) that I was able to gain a firsthand insight into the impact that the gym had on their lives. Finally, these ethnographic observations were crosschecked and completed using the main club members' stories from real-life, in-depth conversations with the fifty professional fighters in the State of Illinois in the summer of 1991, as well as conversations with their coaches and managers and systematic reading of the "indigenous" written material (specialist magazines and writing, biographies and autobiographies) and scholarly texts based on the latter (literary and historical writing).

A Sanctuary: The Gym as a Shield against the Street

"They's so many young guys out there rippin' an' runnin' an' doin' nothin'. The gym gives them a choice to do somethin' positive. Everybody doesn't choose boxin'. Some of 'em choose basketball, some of 'em choose to hang out on corners, but the gym is there for the guys who wanna get off the street for a while. Tha's one of the reasons why I'm glad the gym is there, because the street calls you and the street can eat you up, so the gym can call you an' you can get lucky and branch off into better thin's, but the streets [grimace] —you usually win' up on a dead-en' alley somewhere." These comments by Butch, a thirty-two-year-old firefighter who has spent fourteen years training at the Stoneland Gym, sum up the important role that the gym plays in his life.

The main raison d'être of boxing gyms in ghettos has little to do with sport itself. It is rather to offer an antidote to the dangers and temptations of the street, a barrier against the insecurity that hangs over the neighborhood and poisons every area of its existence. The gym is a sanctuary where men can escape for a few hours a day until they find a better way to get away from the tensions of everyday survival on the margins of a society that is as affluent as it is indifferent to them. This whole function is an everyday factor that goes completely unnoticed[9] and that has recently become even more crucial because of the institutional desertification and increased violence in interpersonal relationships that are hitting the segregated enclaves in American cities, brought about by the shrinking labor market and decreased government intervention.[10]

When I asked the coach at Stoneland which members of the club came to find shelter and a break there, he snapped back at me: "It's all of them, Louie. They all tryin' to keep off d'streets and getting' in trouble—tha's everybody." Contemporary Afro-American ghettos are Hobbesian worlds in which violence is endemic, an example of which is the fact that all the professional boxers at the Stoneland Boys Club, with one exception, have personally witnessed one or more murders. Eight out of eleven have also been victims of armed robbery.[11] Furthermore, most of the members of the gym have had contacts—and two of them still have contacts—with the gangs that fight to control the abandoned territories that make up the South Side and West Side of Chicago.

In such an "area of high insecurity,"[12] the most diverse crimes are everyday occurrences and the homicide rate is similar to that of casualties among American soldiers at the worst times of the Vietnam War. Consequently, public space has toughened to such an extent that it has almost disappeared, and danger is not a mere "cultural perception,"[13] nor is it merely characteristic of urban life. Rather, constant danger is a pressing, inescapable physical reality.[14] As evidence of the extent

---

9. This also includes people who really should be aware of this, such as the people in charge of the charity that donates Stoneland its facilities. Several distant observers of the ghetto believe that boxing adds to the ghetto's violence and they only tolerate the gym in their local branch at Stoneland with the greatest reluctance (even though they do not contribute any direct finance themselves). However, providing protection from the street has been gyms' prime function since the Noble Art became a working-class activity during the early decades of the twentieth century. For instance, Stillman's Gym in New York "was opened by two millionaire philanthropists as a charity aimed to get young people in from the street" (Plimpton, "Three with Moore," 158). From this point of view, history has been inaccurate, as the coach at Palmer Park Gym (which is where Sugar Ray Leonard started off) in the Washington, D.C., slums, explains: "Right at the beginning, when we started off, our aim was not producing boxers for the Olympics. Our main aim was to get young people off the street and away from the problems there. *Young people hooked on boxing don't have time to steal cars*" (added emphasis), quoted in Goldstein, *A Fistful of Sugar*, 51.

10. Wacquant, "Décivilisation et démonisation," 103–25.

11. In the whole city, six pro boxers out of ten have witnessed murders, with this varying considerably depending on ethnic-racial origin. This goes up to 70 percent among black fighters, compared to a quarter of their colleagues from Hispanic and white communities.

12. Wacquant, "West Side Story à Chicago," 53–61.

13. Merry, "Urban Danger: Life in a Neighborhood of Strangers."

14. Sánchez-Jankowski, "From Violent City to the City of Violence."

to which violence has become part of everyday life, witness the aston-
ished reactions of members of Stoneland's Gym when I asked them if
they had ever seen a man killed. The question seemed a bit naïve to
them, superfluous in fact. As my sparring partner Shante put it: "Tssss!
I seen, I seen coupla guys git killed in d'penitentiary. I witness a guy git
kill on the street. That ain't nothin'. . . Yeah, I mean . . . [giggles] I been
shot at, uh-uh, I been shot at many a times. [How many times?] Oh,
man! I say ten times, fifteen times, shi'! [And stabbed?] No, [perplexed]
I'm lucky I ain' neve' been stabbed, ain' that somethin'!"

I got the same reaction from Curtis, the star of the gym, who grew
up in an area next to Stoneland. When he sees an attack on the street,
he says you just "turn your head, look elsewhere. What can you do? That
happens every day." His pal Tony, who works part-time in a local Mc-
Donald's, proves to be just as familiar with violence when he says, "I
seen people shot. I seen people killed. I seen a person shot, killed that
was standin' right next to me an' I felt that it coulda been me an', hum,
the bes' thin' that I need to do was change my acquaintances."

Changing his acquaintances, leaving voluntarily and without dis-
honor (and so not exposing himself to sarcasm or retribution) from his
network of friends who sooner or later are going to go wrong, avoiding
hanging out in the wrong places, getting outside the gang's sphere of
influence (those vehicles for delinquency), in fact, getting under shelter—joining the gym is, above all else, a way to get off the street in order not to be "sucked up" (as they put in the ghetto) by the package of
downward spirals and destruction that come with it. As a bonus, the
gym offers the possibility of learning a self-defense technique whose
usefulness is obvious. "Now if it wasn't for boxing, where would they
be, where would they go?" says an old man who has become a referee
and who spends his free time doing volunteer work in a gym that is the
center of a Mexican district infested with gangs. "Lotta 'em would go to
jail. This gym, boxing, it saves lives, boxing. [He shakes his head] Not
only does it save a life of the individual, it might save yours or my life
because that guy might be out killin' somebody or robbin' somebody.
Instead he's out boxing. He's out saving his life. He's out saving your
life and my life. He's not out there, he don't have a gun, he's not going
to shoot us. It's a cruel world out there."

In fact, any young man who turns up at the gym every afternoon
does not have the time, energy, or even desire to get involved in the
dangerous or illegal activities that many of the adolescents in the ghetto, unemployed and looking for action, spend much of their time do-

ing.[15] It is of little importance whether this recruitment leads him to be a feeble or mediocre athlete, to being the gym favorite, to failing to become a pro, or to being a real terror in the ring. The simple fact of sweating in the ring, taking his frustrations out on punching bags, or loyally hitting a gloved-up and helmeted adversary like himself in the ring is enough to justify the gym's existence. As a coach from the black ghetto in Oakland put it: "I couldn't care less if one of these young men becomes a pro or even becomes a good amateur. I try to get them into something they'll be able to work at. To get them off the street. If they get fed up after two or three years and hold up a bank, at least they won't have done any hold-ups while they've been here." And he adds for good measure, "This isn't a church here, but it'll do the trick."[16]

Like clams, gyms seal up and shut out the noise and fury of the outside world. A gym has its own time requirements, its rules for communal life, its etiquette, and its trademark atmosphere of enthusiasm, all of which oppose everything in the street and compete to create a feeling of security that is cruelly lacking on the outside. In this "portion of space," set apart, in which the worldly worries of the ghetto are systematically excluded,[17] people can let off steam and get rid of their anger at their bad living conditions by punching sacks rather than rivals from the neighborhood. And it becomes possible to enjoy a social life that is completely impossible in the outside world. This is because all vindictive and violent behavior is formally forbidden in the gym, and exchanges with sparring partners, including when they are in the ring, are strictly controlled and coded, even though they may appear to a novice observer to be uncontrolled.[18] Each person has to treat others with courtesy and deference and can expect to be treated in the same way. If need be, any excessively lively antagonism between two members of the club can be sorted out between the ropes, but never outside them.[19]

---

15. Vigil, *Barrio Gangs*; Taylor, *Dangerous Society*; Bourgois, "From Jibaro to Crack Dealer."

16. Quoted in Wiley, *Serenity*, 30. It is the same story at the famous Petronelli Brothers Gym in Brockton, Massachusetts: "Coaches join the profession because they love it … That isn't what I'd have thought about getting a world champion like Marvin Hagler. Noting like that. I've done it to get young people off the street." Quoted in Anderson, *In the Corner*, 37. This could not be further from John Sugden's interpretation that the motivation behind amateur gyms was to produce professional boxers to earn money for the coaches. In fact, the vast majority of amateurs do not become pros, and only a tiny fraction of professional fighters earn more than a poor worker's salary. See Sugden, "The Exploitation of Disadvantage."

17. Émile Durkheim defines sanctuaries in this way in *The Elementary Forms of Religious Life*, 121.

18. Wacquant, "The Social Logic of Boxing in Black Chicago."

19. In the three years I went to the gym almost daily, I only saw three incidents that almost became violent.

Curtis explains: "Just the idea, the respect for the gym, that people have for d'gym an' the way [the coach] make everybody respect the gym an' respect people aroun' in d'gym, y'know: no foul language, I mean, no talkin' loud an' no tryin' t'star' a fight' 'cause you get probably beat up in sparrin'. Everybody is frien'ly an' open with each other, everybody talk."

Another advantage appreciated by the young (and not so young) people who look for sanctuary in the gym: nobody asks you about your personal life. You do not have to open yourself up and so become vulnerable, nor do you have to dwell on the problems and disappointments of everyday life. The punching bags are there, silent, immobile, hard; you can wrap up your hands, shadowbox to your heart's content in front of the mirror, play with the speed ball, skip, and forget about yourself. For ten, twelve, or fifteen rounds, the exercise takes you and frees you from your worries, constraints, and external dangers. As Tony says:

> See, to me the gym is like meditatin'. I find peace an' relaxation an' a peace of min' that's jus' like when I'm home with ma wife, with our own privacy at d'gym . . . than I do out here, out here on d'street, because we gotta go through a lot of . . . I'm tryin' not to get caught up in the bind . . . I try to fin' peace. [He says very quickly] The gym show me that I coul' do somethin'. The gym show me that I can be my own man. The gym show me that I can do other thin's than the gang-bangin', use drugs, steal, rob people, stick people up, or jus' end in jail.[20]

For the most convincing testimony of the boxing gym's protective properties with regard to the street, it is enough to ask the club regulars what would have become of them if they had not taken to the ring. Shante grimaces and then murmurs with a dark look on his face: "I prob'y be dead now to be hones', I'm serious. Or on drugs, or sellin' drug or gang leader or dead. Yeah, 'cause tha's what I was doin', I wadden doin' nothin' constructive." A detailed analysis of the boxers' stories confirms that it was joining the gym that allowed them, at least for a time, to escape from the destinies that the social weight of the ghetto seemed to have ready for them, and they illustrate the terrible life stories these "running buddies" had and their involvement in crime in the neighborhood before they joined the gym. There is not a single member of the gym who does not mourn a friend who died from an overdose or as the victim of violent crime, who has not lost a cousin who pushed "Karachi" or "angel dust" (two drugs that were fashionable during those years), or does not have a school friend locked up in a state prison.

---

20. Personal communication. Here and below.

A School of Morality: Discipline, Respect, and Taking Care of Yourself

The virtues of the gym are not limited to trying to insulate people from the possibility of finding themselves in "the wrong place at the wrong time," as they say in the ghetto. If the club believes itself capable of inoculating long-term against the street's deadly influence, that is because it is the basis for a framework of disciplined activity, a specific morality and exchange of emotions that, likewise, are barriers against individual and collective disorder. In other words, it is as much the social and moral space that the gym offers as the physical place and the training area that create an exclusion zone from marginalization.[21] Eddie, a thirty-three-year-old coach at Stoneland who makes his living as a metal worker, told me: "Well, in a neighbo'hood like this, [kids] come in d'gym and they find *cleanance*. They keep their self clean in a clean atmosphere. An' they learn self-discipline, how to take care of themselves, mentally an' physically. Learn how to get along with people, how to socialize in this world without bein' angry. Knowin' how to, y'know, knowin' *how to carry their self as a person*."

Discipline, respect, and acceptance of authority, physical and mental hygiene, a sense of responsibility and humility, confidence and self-control, patience and politeness: these are the qualities that the gym inculcates in its members by simply closing them into a network made up of physical routines and collective rules that all members must follow without fail. In fact, joining the club involves a solemn commitment (*sacramentum*) to behave "as a gentleman, a clean-cut person," and also to honor the fighters' code of ethics as far as possible. This means taking on an austere lifestyle, completely changing bodily, mental, and social habits and behavior, in their daily life in the ghetto.[22]

Seen from the inside, the training room is above all a discipline device. It stipulates certain specific objectives (mastering technical movements, understanding new tactics, improving mobility, and polishing intelligence in action) and provides the means to be able to do this. It stimulates, directs, limits, and contains the activity. The training

---

21. Which means that the gym's influence depends directly on the integrity of the organization that backs it and the authority of the coach who manages it, as this West Side boxer underlines: "Anybody can put a building in a neighborhood, and if the facility is not ran properly, I mean, you can just as well have gangs runnin' the gym, sittin' here on the steps sellin' drugs and so forth. But there's gotta be some commitment by the community, by the people in charge in general, that are gonna run this place."

22. It would be interesting to reexamine many of the analyses developed by Odile Arnold about joining convent life in the nineteenth century in order to describe the wrench from the ordinary world involved in taking up boxing. See Arnold, *Le corps et l'âme*.

room demands and imposes punctuality, regularity, and obedience; the smallest movements, the most anodyne activities, and the slightest interactions are subject to painstaking surveillance and minute measurement.

Getting up at dawn to do their daily roadwork (running is the bedrock of fight endurance), boxers have to train five or six days a week and unswervingly follow the program their coach draws up for them. During the two hours that each session in the gym lasts, they unceasingly repeat the same exercises as laid down by a finely tuned program:[23] they work with mirrors and with punch bags, skip, stretch, do sit-ups, and spar.[24] Each one on his apparatus, all the fighters work together in three-minute sessions separated by one-minute breaks (thirty seconds at Stoneland) that simulate fight rhythm and synchronize their movements. Taking into account the rigor of the physical training, the almost repulsively repetitive nature of the exercises, the difficulty of the tasks, not to mention the continual wear and tear on strategic parts of the body (particularly on the skin on their hands and also on their faces and feet), it is no surprise that all boxers say that training at the gym gives them a sharp sense of discipline.

In fact, the need for discipline does not stop at the club door—quite the contrary. This is because as well as providing technical know-how, the coach teaches his disciples the "art of self-governance," which is designed to subordinate their whole existence to the accomplishment of their vocation. Michel Foucault terms this vocation "pugilistic self-care"—in other words, a way of life, looking after the body and the soul in ways that are appropriate for and in line with the specific needs of the boxer's trade, and which can be summed up with the intrinsic notion of "sacrifice." Just as with *curia sui* in ancient civilization, the pugilistic ethics of sacrifice are both "a duty and a technique, a fundamental obligation and a series of carefully prepared procedures"[25] whose objective is to maximize boxers' physical and moral capacity at the moment of combat. This obliges boxers to severely restrict their social and family life in order to manage their strength, follow a draconian diet that allows them to reach their optimum "fighting weight," and—the hardest deprivation—abstain from erotic pleasure during the weeks before matches in order not to squander the energy so patiently accumulated. Needless to say, not all boxers follow the pugilistic catechism

23. Wacquant, "Corps et âme," 48–51.
24. For a clear and concise technical explanation of the objectives and ways of training boxers, I recommend the excellent manual by Bouttier and Letessier, *Boxe*. For a more detailed analysis of fight training as body work, see Wacquant, "Pugs at Work," esp. 70–75.
25. Foucault, *Résumés des cours, 1970–1982*, 148–49.

to the letter—far from it, in fact. Nevertheless, the professional moral of sacrifice is the norm that regulates all their activities. It is the ideal toward which each boxer strives as far as he is able.[26]

Because the members of the boxing club all conform to the same standards, face the same tests, and suffer more or less the same privations, joys, and frustrations, they end up admiring each other.[27] By respecting others, and having this respect returned, self-respect is achieved and confidence in their own abilities is gained or recovered. Collective life in the gym is also an instrument for self-reconstruction, for achieving one's own potential and meeting one's obligations, and this all stems from one's own value. For Lorenzo, who recently joined Stoneland along with his coach, the gym gives him "Respect, uh, pride about yourself. That's one thing that I've always learned from the gym, since I was growin' up, y'know. Comin' up outa rough neighbo'hood, lotta guys come out with no respect or no care for anybody. The gym taught me respect, uh, how to 'preciate myself an' to fulfill, y'know, life goal, to go out, that you have to work for a livin', y'know. Nothin's gonna come handy to you."

The gym also helps to hold back certain "individual appetites," which Durkheim describes as being "naturally insatiable," by removing its members from the social isolation that is typical of their districts of origin. It helps them open up to people who come from varied social backgrounds. According to Eddie, this type of social mingling, even if limited, is particularly enriching for young people from Stoneland: "They learn to cope with people from all over d'city, y'know, diff'rent people. Tha's important 'cause the social life is important. Also you just can't live in one neighbo'hood all your life an' not be able to socialize outside the neighbo'hood." In Shante's case, he left prison full of bitterness and profoundly alienated, and the gym enabled him to "decompress." This allowed him to recover his confidence in others and also, little by little, to find pleasure in other people's company. In the protected setting of the gym, he has been able to relearn, in his own words, "How to relate to people an' jus' y'know workin' with diffren' personalities. You know how the diff'rent people we got in our gym. Learn to relate, understan' people, understan' why this guy's like this, y'know, you get lessons of life in that gym basic'ly, yeah. To me boxin' is

26. Wacquant, "Pugs at Work," 75–82.

27. According to Keith, a pro boxer and member of Stoneland for three years, "We all in the gym, we go through the same thing. I don' care how good a fighter you is, 'cause even your best fighter have a hard time, in the gym, trainin', ev'ryday, sparrin', doin' all the work you got to do. So he would then begin to respect others, an' outside the gym, I think if the kid was in a gym, they train, they'll find out that, uh, it's guys tougher than 'em."

d'small part. The larger part is bein' everyday, relatin', listenin', talkin', understandin' this guy."

Finally, the gym continually reinforces the belief that in the ring, as in other places in life, individual determination and effort are the only guarantees of success. And people should depend only on themselves if they want to improve their lot. Reese is just sixteen; he had been a member of Stoneland Boys Club for two years when he realized that fighting in the street had become too dangerous: "What I'm taught here to do is self-discipline and self-reliability, to rely on one's self an' not depen' on others to work for you. I also learn here that, uh, there's no such thin' as I can't." So it comes as no surprise that without prompting, many boxers compare indoctrination in the gym with the regimented life in another total institution—the army.

None of the boxers or coaches doubt for a single moment that the imperatives of discipline, self-denial, and respect that prevail in the training room leave their mark, and that their influence goes far beyond the area in which they are initially nurtured. Smithie, a mid-heavyweight with a lot of information about his job as a coach in a center for juvenile delinquents, explains that, "It give 'em a bit of pride, individuality, self-worth, a direction . . . Now it may not offer them the direction in life in which they need to go in, but it gives 'em a direction in which how to reach for that direction, d'you follow me? Okay, see it's a formula that's utilized in a gym settin' that [he emphasizes] if you will convert that formula in life, you can survive an' you can succeed."

Knowing oneself and having control of oneself leads to a fighter's asceticism, which then gives birth to a feeling of internal peace. A young pro who is starting his career in a West Side gym puts it like this: "The boxing, the discipline I learn in boxin' I take outsi' the ring too. Yeah, it carries over, it matures me. It helps me grow up, to relax. I feel as though I'm a peaceful warrior. I'm a warrior, but I'm peaceful, you know, 'cause it's a time to box in the ring, but outsi' the ring, I shake my opponent's han' an' we frien's again. Tha's how life shoul' be."

Altogether, the values inculcated during a boxing apprenticeship are very close to the values of the dominant ideology of individual meritocracy.[28] So it is not without justification that the old coach at Stoneland states, with a certain gravity, that throughout his life dedicated to teaching the Noble Art he has "produced a fair number of good citizens." He also says that the brotherhood of coaches gives itself a mission that

---

28. In this, the boxing gym's role conforms to the historical function of popular sport that, far from being an instrument of rupture with the established order, has in fact contributed to the integration of the working class into the heart of bourgeois culture, albeit in a turbulent and fragmentary manner. See Hargreaves, *Sport, Power, and Culture.*

is not dissimilar from that of the missionaries who left to civilize the far-off African colonies, less in terms of spreading a formal religious doctrine than in reconstituting a network of the most ordinary bodily signs and actions.[29]

Adventure and Honor

The monastic, almost prison-like lifestyle that boxers adopt is, paradoxically, the source of their great inner spiritual and emotional richness. The "systemization of austerities"[30] that is required in order to prepare for fighting is in fact the beginning of a deep relationship with their own bodies, a concentration of psycho-physical forces and an intensification of emotions that makes daily training an invigorating, even heady experience, which is its own reward. It is difficult to put into words the invigoration of the senses that comes from immersion in the gym, or the magnetism of the visual, auditory, and tactile kinesthetic landscape in which the boxers find themselves.[31] Suffice it to say that those who find themselves momentarily removed from it feel a loss comparable to that felt by drug addicts without their dose.[32]

The boxer's way of life has an "experiential tension" that gives it many features that are characteristic of the adventures described by Georg Simmel.[33] The hours spent in the gym form a small island of time with cleanly drawn contours, isolated from everyday life and on a big wave at the same time, with a distinctive tropism that combines the known with the unknown, the routine with the unpredictable, the immediate with the timeless, and the will to conquer with submission to the powers of the universe that one has become part of. Training is a continual joust with oneself that calls for continual attention to oneself without respite and concessions; it is a sharp hermeneutics of one's desires, limits, and most deeply buried possibilities. Boxers take part in a quest to "exist intensely,"[34] in which putting their body and willpower to the test continually, deliberately sought-out and accepted risk, feared and muzzled pain, and controlled fear are used to stretch their limits. Gyms detach boxers from their pasts and push them to obtain by themselves the resources they need to put together their future and

---

29. Comaroff and Comaroff, "Christianity and Colonialism in South Africa."
30. Arnold, *Le corps et l'âme*, 139.
31. Wacquant, "The Pugilistic Point of View."
32. Incredible though it may seem in hindsight, during the most intense phases of this research I seriously considered giving up my intellectual activities once and for all in order to box full-time, with the objective of becoming a pro.
33. Simmel, "The Adventurer," 197.
34. Le Breton, *Passions du risque*, 27.

to contribute decisively to their own destiny.[35] It makes the individual his own arena of challenge and invites him to find out how to create himself better.

It is a kind of voluntary ordeal that starts again and again. The boxer's trial is a structure that generates sensations and meanings that are in opposition to those of the ghetto and makes life less dull (*Ausseralltaglichung*, as Max Weber puts it), removing the colorlessness of daily life and producing shared determination. Becoming a member of the gym means refusing to disappear in the crowd and be an ordinary Joe, condemned to perpetual social invisibility. It is shouting loud and clear, with all your body and soul, your determination to rise above the average, the mediocre, by joining a brotherhood wrapped in a virile mystique and a considerable aura in the black community.

The Noble Art is, in fact, part of the long tradition of physical professions that embody humble ghetto people's resistance and courage in the face of racial and social adversity.[36] Charles Keil shows in his classic study, *Urban Blues*, that show business figures, in which he includes singers, musicians, priests, comedians, disc jockeys, and sports figures (he specifically mentions Sonny Liston and Muhammad Ali), make up "that special domain of Negro culture wherein black men have proved and preserved their humanity."[37] Fighters are this type of cultural hero; they are one type of "masters of sound, movement, timing and rhythm"[38] who embody the central axiological positions of the ghetto's oral and kinetic culture: physical courage and the pleasure of performance, shrewdness and indifference to problems, resourcefulness, and taking risks, without forgetting an extreme sense of individuality. Better still, the fighter's vocation is doubly esteemed because it combines, albeit in an imperfect, unstable way, the masculine qualities respected in the street with the conventional values of individual effort and regularity that are sanctified by the dominant society. And fighters are supposed to earn a lot of money, which is the perfect union between

---

35. The Canadian champion George Chuvalo puts it very well in this way: "Life sometimes becomes tedious. . . . At least when you fight there is some action, you have a reason to live, something that makes you feel good. Fighting is very exciting. You train, you always have the feeling that you have a fixed goal. Something's going on. *Each combat can change your life.* You can be on top of the world, you can fight some no-hoper and lose—hey! You're in the soup. You fight with a guy who's better rated than you and it's you who goes up a step. *It's like history-making time*" (my italics). Quoted in Brunt, *Mean Business*, 165.

36. From Papa Jack Johnson to Muhammad Ali, African-American boxing champions have held a prominent position in defiance of white domination. See Levine, *Black Culture and Black Consciousness*; Roberts, *Papa Jack*; and Ashe, *A Hard Road to Glory*.

37. Keil, *Urban Blues*, 16.

38. Ibid.

what is expected in bourgeois districts and in the ghetto.

Gyms are adversarial places in which everyone (that is, every man worth being called a man) can achieve the public dignity that he is denied in the outside world by submitting to rules and rituals that are involved in becoming part of this separate brotherhood, becoming a gladiator of the ring. In the spotlight, everyone demonstrates his skill and his "heart" and also creates his own style, establishes his "brand," and in this way, achieves distinction. Gyms are places in which you become similar and unique at the same time, known and recognized by fellow members and, at the same time, different from them.[39] According to a white trainer who had moved from a gym in Little Italy of Chicago, this is one of the main attractions of the gym for the young people who go there and prepare for combat: "They go to the gym because they feel they *could be someone*, they *are* someone, they're *treated right*, they, they feel like they're really *doin'* somethin', and may be in the environment they're in, *they're nothin'*, they're *pushed around* by their own people and at least they go to the gym, they get away from things like that, an that's what changes them, people's lives."

The aura around boxing lets those who pursue it enjoy the admiration of the ghetto microcosm.[40] This is true whether a man is a useless fighter (a "bum") or a confirmed champion, a brave veteran or a rising hope, a green amateur or an experienced professional, and true whatever his skills in the ring and his career prospects—which are often even less bright than those he has in the unskilled labor market that he is trying to escape. These men all receive their peers' undivided recognition and approval.[41] And the circle of relatives, friends, and neighbors hold them all to be models to follow because of their aesthetic moral and their determination to succeed, as can be seen in my notebook:

> Dwayne has a small barber's shop on 73rd Street, by the railroad line that marks the run-down district's boundary, teeming with drug pushers, with the black bourgeois area where Curtis lives, Pill Hill (so called because of the number of doctors and other liberal professionals who live there). He has known Curtis and his

---

39. Seen from this point of view, boxing gyms are a structural equivalent to the street corners where the ghetto working (under) classes, who do not belong in other (more respectable) places for social activity, take command. "Jelly's is a place where you can be somebody, the basis for negotiating your status and in which people matter to other people; they keep up-to-date with what happens to other people. Among their peers, the group members can behave as peers." Anderson, *A Place on the Corner*, 192.

40. Hare, "A Study of the Black Fighter," 2–9.

41. Approval that the old coach at Stoneland puts in these terms: "It takes a helluva man to be a fighter. See, I give anybody credit tha' go up in there whether it's a three-round amateur fighter, win or lose, if he stays in there an' do his best and prepared for it or a ten or twelve-round profess'nal fighter. If he's ready, I'll pat 'im on his back."

family for sixteen years. They went to high school together and he boasts about being his official hairdresser. Before each fight (when he has money), Curtis goes to get his neck shaved in his salon and they talk about boxing. The discussion includes passing friends and long-term acquaintances: "A lotta friends come in and they see him they all talk to him, ask him when is his next fight or how they go by comin' to see the fight or you know where is it being held, and, uh, they wanna know, they just wanna know an' they like—they like to see him, when he comes around, he brightens up the place."

Dwayne and his friends envy Curtis's "career," which they see as being something exciting that will enable him to rise in society. He is a sort of local hero for them: "He's done a lot for the neighbo'hood just by boxing. Everybody looks up to 'im, an' he's a good, good person . . . The neighborhood is so congested with you know a lotta things. It's really good, encouraging to see someone really come from the neighbo'hood an' make it, make it good, you know. So it's, it's a wonderful thing. 'Cause it's really hard makin' it you know in a small neighbo'hood like this."

In this sense, it is revealing that the drug dealers who are the spearhead of the new "pillage capitalism" that now dominates the ghetto's economy[42] see themselves as being *below* the boxers in the local scale of prestige and merit. Rodney, a meat salesman in his native South Side who has been fighting with the pros at Stoneland for almost three years, says: "They look up to me, hey! that I'm gonna make it again, hey! They give me all, all the benefit that hey, 'cause I got a chance. [They think you're doing better than them?] Yeah, yeah. [Even though they're making more money?] Yeah, they think I'm doin' the right way, goin' the right way."

However slight their chances may be of rising in the boxing hierarchy and reaping its potential benefits, the most modest club boxers, as well as having the advantages of the prestige that the brotherhood has built up over decades, are on "the right road" to "make something of themselves." The gym offers them a valid alternative to illegal and immoral street trades and they grab it. And, with it, their lives.

Bibliography

Anderson, Dave. *In the Corner: Great Boxing Trainers Talk About Their Art.* New York: Morrow, 1991.

---

42. Wacquant, "De l'Amérique comme utopie à l'envers."

Anderson, Elijah. *A Place on the Corner*. Chicago: University of Chicago Press, 1976.

Arnold, Odile. *Le corps et l'âme: La vie des religieuses au XIXe siècle*. Paris: Seuil, 1982.

Ashe, Arthur, Jr. *A Hard Road to Glory: A History of the African-American Athlete*. Vol. 3. *Since 1946*. New York: Warner Books, 1988.

Barrat, Martine. *Do or Die*. New York: Viking, 1993.

Bourgois, Philippe. "From Jibaro to Crack Dealer: Confronting Capitalism in Spanish Harlem." In *Articulating Hidden Histories: Exploring the Influence of Eric R. Wolf*, edited by Jane Schneider and Rayna Rapp. Berkeley: University of California Press, 1994.

Bouttier, Jean-Claude, and Jean Letessier. *Boxe: La technique, l'entraînement, la tactique*. Paris: Éditions Robert Laffont, 1978.

Brunt, Stephen. *Mean Business: The Rise and Fall of Shawn O'Sullivan*. Markham, Ont.: Penguin, 1987.

Comaroff, Jean, and John Comaroff. "Christianity and Colonialism in South Africa." *American Ethnologist* 13, no. 1 (1986): 1–19.

Dunn, Katherine, and Larry Fink. "In This Ring." *Mother Jones* 18, no. 5 (September–October 1993): 30–35.

Durkheim, Émile. *The Elementary Forms of Religious Life*. Translated by Joseph Ward Swain. New York: Dover Publications, 2008.

———. *Moral Education: A Study in the Theory and Application of the Sociology of Education*. New York: Free Press, 1961.

Foucault, Michel. *Résumés des cours, 1970–1982*. Paris: Éditions Juillard, 1989.

Fried, Ronald K. *Corner Men: Great Boxing Trainers*. New York: Four Walls Eight Windows, 1991.

Goldstein, Alan. *A Fistful of Sugar: The Sugar Ray Leonard Story*. New York: Coward, McCann and Geogehan, 1981.

Hare, Nathan. "A Study of the Black Fighter." *Black Scholar* 3, no. 3 (1971): 2–9.

Hargreaves, John. *Sport, Power, and Culture: A Social and Historical Analysis of Popular Sports in Britain*. Cambridge: Polity Press, 1986.

Keil, Charles. *Urban Blues*. Chicago: University of Chicago Press, 1966.

Le Breton, David. *Passions du risque*. Paris: Anne-Marie Métailié, 1991.

Levine, Lawrence W. *Black Culture and Black Consciousness: Afro-American Folk Thought from Slavery to Freedom*. Oxford: Oxford University Press, 1977.

Massey, Douglas S., and Nancy A. Denton. *American Apartheid: Segregation and the Making of the Underclass*. Cambridge: Harvard University Press, 1993.

Merry, Sally Engle. "Urban Danger: Life in a Neighborhood of Strangers." In *Urban Life: Readings in Urban Anthropology*, edited by George Gmelch and Walter P. Zenner. Prospect Heights, Ill.: Waveland Press, 1988.

Mollenkopf, John H., and Manuel Castells, eds. *Dual City: Restructuring New York*. New York: Russell Sage Foundation, 1991.

Plimpton, George. "Three with Moore." In *Reading the Fights*, edited by Joyce Carol Oates and David Halpern. New York: Prentice-Hall Press, 1988.

Plummer, William. *Buttercups and Strong Boys: A Sojourn at the Golden Gloves*. New York: Viking, 1989.

Riemer, Jeffrey M. "Varieties of Opportunistic Research." *Urban Life* 5, no. 4 (1977): 467–77.

Roberts, Randy. *Papa Jack: Jack Johnson and the Era of White Hopes*. New York: Free Press, 1983.

Sánchez-Jankowski, Martín. "From Violent City to the City of Violence." Paper presented at the Journées annuelles de l'Association française d'études américaines, La Rochelle, France, May 27–28, 1994.

Simmel, Georg. "The Adventurer." In *On Individuality and Social Forms*, edited and with an introduction by Donald N. Levine. Chicago: University of Chicago Press, 1971.

Sugden, John. "The Exploitation of Disadvantage: The Occupational Sub-Culture of the Boxer." In *Sport, Leisure, and Social Relations*, edited by John Horne, David Jary, and Alan Tomlinson. London: Routledge and Kegan Paul, 1987.

Taylor, Carl S. *Dangerous Society*. East Lansing: Michigan State University Press, 1989.

Vigil, James Diego. *Barrio Gangs: Street Life and Identity in Southern California*. Austin: University of Texas Press, 1988.

Wacquant, Loïc J. D. "Corps et âme: Notes ethnographiques d'un apprenti-boxeur." *Actes de la recherche en sciences sociales* 80 (1989): 33–67.

———. "The Social Logic of Boxing in Black Chicago: Toward a Sociology of Pugilism." *Sociology of Sport Journal* 9, no. 3 (1992): 221–54.

———. "Décivilisation et démonisation: La mutation du ghetto noir américain." In *L'Amérique des Français*, edited by Christine Fauré and Tom Bishop. Paris: Éditions François Bourin, 1992.

———. "De l'Amérique comme utopie à l'envers." In *La misère du monde*, edited by Pierre Bourdieu et al. Paris: Seuil, 1993.

———. "West Side Story à Chicago." *Projet* 238 (1994): 53–61.

———. "The Pugilistic Point of View: How Boxers Think and Feel About Their Trade." *Theory and Society* 24, no. 4 (1995): 489–535.

———. "Pugs at Work: Bodily Capital and Bodily Labor Among Professional Boxers." *The Body and Society* 1, no. 1 (1995): 65-93.

——. "Red Belt, Black Belt: Racial Exclusion, Class Inequality, and the State in the American Ghetto and the French Urban Periphery." In *The New Urban Poverty in Advanced Societies*, edited by Enzo Mingione. Oxford and New York: Basil Blackwell, 1995.

Wiley, Ralph. *Serenity: A Boxing Memoir.* New York: Henri Holt and Company, 1989.

Wolf, Kurt H. "Surrender and Community Study: The Study of Loma." In *Reflections on Community Studies*, edited by Arthur J. Vidich, Joseph Bensman, and Maurice R. Stein. New York: Wiley, 1964.

14

A "Fistic Festival" in Reno: Promoting Nevada's New Economy

Richard O. Davies

The local press called it a "fistic festival" when the enormously popular former heavyweight champion Jack Dempsey promoted a prizefight in Reno on July 4, 1931. Unlike earlier high-profile matches held in Nevada, this one had little impact upon the boxing world. It was significant, however, because it demonstrated to Nevada business leaders the enormous potential of attracting large numbers of visitors to the city to enjoy the ambience of its newly legalized casinos.[1] The prizefight featured two prominent heavyweight boxers who were considered prime candidates to challenge reigning champion Max Schmeling for the title, but lackluster performances by both men set back their title hopes. Max Baer was a handsome and charming young man from Livermore, California, who as a teenager had delivered meat for a California grocer, and so was dubbed the "Livermore Butcher." His opponent, Paulino Uzcudun, was nicknamed the "Basque Woodchopper." A native of the Basque Country in Spain, Uzcudun was the reigning European champion and had come to America to seek bigger paydays and a chance to qualify to fight for the world heavyweight title. By pairing Baer and Uzcudun, Dempsey demonstrated that he had learned a great deal about how to play the fight game from his friend, mentor, and the nation's first great fight promoter, George Lewis "Tex" Rickard.

The Promoters

By selecting Uzcudun from among a half-dozen or so possibilities, Dempsey demonstrated a keen understanding of what sells tickets. The *Reno Evening Gazette* estimated that some ten thousand Basques lived in Nevada and contiguous western states, and that the popular and per-

---

1. For two perspectives on this high-profile fight, see Clifton, *Dempsey in Nevada*, 67–74, and Earl, "Blood, Sweat and Leather."

sonable Uzcudun would attract many of them to Reno. A report in the *Humboldt Star* confirmed that perception: "Basques in Winnemucca were joyous over the prospects of their countryman staging a battle in Reno and indications are that should the fight details be completed, an almost 100 per cent exodus of his countrymen here to the fight in Reno will result."[2] The handsome Baer was a popular twenty-two-year-old up-and-coming fighter from the San Francisco Bay Area whose flamboyant lifestyle had created the image of a serious playboy. Dempsey correctly believed that thousands of Bay Area fans would make the trek over the Sierra Nevada to support their man.

This fight excited the residents of Reno, who saw it as a potentially large payday at a time when the Great Depression was beginning to take a serious toll on the economic vitality of the small city of seventeen thousand. By his own admission, Dempsey had lost over $3 million in the stock market collapse that had sent the Dow Jones down 85 percent by the summer of 1931. He could not touch a trust fund that Rickard had established for him after he defeated the French dandy, Georges Carpentier, in the first million-dollar prizefight. Dempsey was eager to find a profitable new line of work, and he had done some apprentice promotional work with Rickard before his friend died suddenly of peritonitis in January 1929, with a tearful Dempsey cradling him in his arms.[3]

It is likely that Dempsey was invited to promote the fight by two Reno businessmen widely reputed to have close connections with criminal elements. Dempsey had become acquainted with them in his formative years as an unknown and impoverished itinerant prizefighter in Tonopah, Nevada, in 1915. Jim McKay and Bill Graham were now firmly established in Reno, where they operated several enterprises, some legal and some, as was common knowledge, not so legitimate. At this time, the thirty-six-year-old Dempsey was also seriously considering a comeback to regain the heavyweight title that he had lost to Gene Tunney in 1926. McKay and Graham were quite likely angling to become his financial backers should he make the attempt, which did not seem that much of a long shot given the rather unimpressive number of serious contenders to champion Max Schmeling.

McKay and Graham undoubtedly viewed the Baer-Uzcudun fight as substantially benefiting their several Reno enterprises by bringing thousands of affluent tourists to town for a long weekend. They owned and operated the largest casino in town, the Bank Club, and had in-

---

2. *Reno Evening Gazette*, 26 May 1931, p. 2; *Humboldt Star*, 8 May 1931, p. 1.
3. Roberts, *Jack Dempsey*, 265; Kahn, *A Flame of Pure Fire*, 430–31; Piattelli Dempsey, *Dempsey*, 225–33.

terests in other gaming enterprises. Before gambling was legalized in March 1931, they had operated several clandestine gambling establishments in Reno, apparently without any interference from local law enforcement. As soon as the governor signed the bill legalizing gambling in the state, they merely opened their doors, hung out a sign, and ran an advertisement in local papers that stated: "Grand opening today of the Bank Club. The club has been greatly enlarged, however the management remains the same." They also owned The Willows, a popular, exclusive supper club and speakeasy on the west edge of town. The Willows featured big-name entertainment and served top-shelf drinks during the declining years of Prohibition, and for that reason the maître d' carefully screened customers before admitting them to the club. These enterprising men also operated the city's largest brothel, the Stockade, which featured fifty cribs that were rented to independent working ladies. McKay and Graham were widely reputed to control the bootlegging industry in northern Nevada, and both ended up serving six years in the federal prison at Leavenworth for conspiracy and mail fraud.[4]

At this time, Graham and McKay were partners with banker and businessman George Wingfield in launching the city's thoroughbred horse-racing meet, complete with pari-mutuel betting, at the fairgrounds in Reno. That the prizefight would take place at a newly constructed wooden arena located in the racetrack's infield was no coincidence. Born in 1876 in Oregon, Wingfield came to Winnemucca in 1896 and worked as a ranch hand, but soon he was earning his living playing poker. Skill at the card tables led to ownership of a saloon and card parlor. He moved to Tonopah in 1901 where a gold and silver mining boom was underway and big money was being wagered, and it was there that he became a business partner with banker George Nixon. Wingfield became a multimillionaire (with an estimated worth of $25 to $30 million) by the age of thirty through "an incredible combination

---

4. Although Graham and McKay played major roles in the development of Reno during the 1920s and 1930s and a broad outline of their careers is recognized, most details of their lives remain unclear. They left behind no documentary record, although various oral histories and newspaper accounts confirm their unsavory reputations. In 1934, they were the prime suspects in the murder of a local bank employee who was to be the prime witness against them in federal court, but the body of Roy Frisch was never found after his mysterious disappearance. In 1939 they were convicted of conspiracy and mail fraud, sentenced to nine years in federal prison and fined $11,000, serving six years before returning to Reno and reassuming management of the Bank Club. In 1950, President Harry S. Truman granted both men a pardon, apparently at the request of a powerful Nevada politician, U.S. Senator Patrick McCarran. See Kling, *The Rise of the Biggest Little City*, 4–6, 57–58, and 106; Raymond, *George Wingfield*, 163–68; and Barber, *Reno's Big Gamble*, 105–11.

of ability, luck, and gambling prowess" in the bonanza that occurred in Goldfield. He and Nixon acquired several profitable mining companies under a holding company named the Goldfield Consolidated Mines Company, which was initially capitalized at $50 million in 1906. Over the next decade, Wingfield diversified his holdings with investments in ranch land and businesses, but he concentrated on banking. He also acquired a stable of thoroughbred racehorses. In 1914, when United States Senator Nixon died, Wingfield controlled four of the largest banks in the state. Nominally a Republican, Wingfield naturally gravitated to state politics as a means of enhancing his economic power, and from his office in the renamed Reno National Bank he became the unquestioned political and economic boss of the small state. He was both respected and feared as he fused his own economic interests with those of the state. Until his financial empire, having expanded to include twelve banks, collapsed in bankruptcy in 1932, Wingfield was accurately known as the "owner and operator of Nevada." By mixing his financial ambitions with his control of state politics, Wingfield worked assiduously to promote projects that would help the thinly populated state grow.[5]

Thus it was natural that Wingfield became a major, if silent, financial backer of Dempsey's foray into the arcane world of prizefight promotions. Wingfield was, after all, a member of the Nevada Agricultural Commission, which owned the fairgrounds racetrack, and for good measure he was also a founding and longtime member of the Nevada State Racing Commission. By becoming the front man for McKay, Graham, and Wingfield, Dempsey had all the financial backing and political clout necessary to stage a major prizefight. By his own admission, Dempsey was in severe financial distress due to his investment setbacks in the stock market crash, and he had no money to invest in the promotion.

Dempsey was well known in Reno, having won his first professional fight there in 1915 at the Jockey Athletic Club, and soon thereafter he fought several times in Goldfield and Tonopah before moving onto the national scene in 1919 and becoming one of the most famous and popular Americans of the 1920s. His return to Reno in April 1931 sparked rumors on several levels. Because he had rented a house, it was widely rumored that he wanted to establish residency in Nevada in order to divorce his second wife, Estelle. Because he had lobbied legislators to legalize gambling as part of Wingfield's covert campaign to do so, rumors circulated that he was scouting about for an investment opportu-

---

5. Raymond, *George Wingfield*, 1–217.

nity in a Reno casino. He never denied the concurrent speculation that he was contemplating a ring comeback, and he told reporters on April 11 that he wanted to referee some prizefights for the money but that he was considering a return to the ring.[6]

To many Renoites, however, those rumors paled in comparison to the speculations that he was in serious discussions with such heavy-hitters as McKay, Graham, and Wingfield to bring a major fight to Reno for the Fourth of July weekend. At a press conference on May 1, along with his business manager Leonard Sacks, he confirmed that he was hard at work putting together a big-name fight and that prominent local architect Frederic DeLongchamps had been commissioned to design an arena to accommodate an anticipated crowd of twenty thousand. Not coincidentally, Wingfield was in the process of updating the racetrack after several years of neglect. An upscale clubhouse, also designed by DeLongchamps, was under construction in anticipation of the opening of the racing season on Wednesday July 1.

Nevada Embraces Prizefighting

This announcement was met with widespread approval in Reno. It rekindled memories of 1910 when George Tex Rickard had truly "put Reno on the map" on another Fourth of July. On that date, which still resonates as the single greatest day in the city's colorful history, Rickard shrewdly exploited crude racial issues in promoting a heavyweight title defense by the controversial black champion Jack Johnson against the "Old Grizzly," the retired and undefeated former champion, the much-proclaimed Great White Hope, Jim Jeffries. On that day, with millions of Americans anxiously awaiting news of the outcome via Western Union wires, an estimated twenty thousand fans paid a record $277,000 to witness the fight held under a blistering summer sun. Both fighters earned historic paydays that were more than doubled by residuals generated by the company that distributed a film of the fight to motion-picture theaters as a feature attraction. Dempsey's announcement lacked the racial overtones of 1910, but it did mean that after a twenty-one-year hiatus, big-time prizefighting was returning to the town that now proclaimed itself "the Biggest Little City in the World." Dempsey and his trio of backers clearly hoped for another bonanza such as Tex Rickard had generated in 1910.[7]

Nevada was well established as a home to large-scale championship fights in the United States. At a time when prizefighting was illegal

---

6. Clifton, *Dempsey in Nevada*, 68–74.

7. Greenwood, *The Prize Fight of the Century*; Hagar and Clifton, *Johnson-Jeffries*; Roberts, *Papa Jack*, 85–107.

across the country, Nevada had hosted five championship prizefights between 1897 and 1912, three of which generated enormous national attention and contributed significantly to Nevada's unsavory reputation as the "Sin State," where brothels were legal, gambling dens operated without interference, and thousands came each year from around the country for the well-known "Reno fix"—that is, a "quickie divorce." Nevada's unique mining frontier heritage had bestowed upon the state a libertarian approach to human behavior that was ironically paired with a staunchly conservative economic and political posture.

In 1897, with the state population dipping near the forty thousand mark during the severe economic downturn of that decade, and as residents departed for greater economic opportunities elsewhere, the state legislature passed with amazing speed a bill to permit "glove contest" exhibitions at a time when the blood sport was illegal elsewhere. The explicit purpose was to permit a heavyweight championship fight to take place in Carson City. Although exhibitions of the manly art were held in many cities across the land, they were conducted outside the law but with the tacit approval of local law enforcement agencies. That level of tolerance, however, did not extend to high-profile championship fights, as Dallas promoter Dan Stuart discovered in 1895 when he invested an estimated $40,000 of his own money to bring together in a Texas ring the handsome and charismatic champion, "Gentleman Jim" Corbett, against wiry challenger "Ruby Robert" Fitzsimmons. Facing threats of a felony indictment by the Texas governor, Stuart was forced to cancel the fight two weeks before its scheduled date, and he was subsequently run out of Hot Springs, El Paso, and the territories of Arizona and New Mexico. For good measure he sought to hold the fight in a bullring in Juarez, but he decided against that possibility when Mexico's "president for life," Porfirio Diaz, ordered his militia to open fire if anyone associated with the proposed prizefight attempted to cross the Rio Grande. In every instance, the opposition to the Corbett-Fitzsimmons fight was firmly based on religious and moral grounds, with energized men of the cloth mobilizing a fiery political storm of opposition.[8]

The moral climate in Nevada's capital, Carson City, however, did not produce the howls of righteous outrage that had nipped at Stuart's heels all across the Southwest. Nevada was mired in a serious economic depression that had created a steady out-migration of residents, which lowered the state's population to just forty thousand—a condition that was prompting serious discussions in the nation's capital about the

8. Miletich, *Dan Stuart's Fistic Carnival.*

possibility of revoking Nevada's statehood status. Approached by an emissary dispatched by Dan Stuart, the governor and key legislators were openly receptive to permitting the fight to occur on Nevada soil. A few ministers raised the usual objections and were joined by a vanguard of the Women's Christian Temperance Union from Reno, but the enabling legislation sailed through both houses of the legislature and was signed into law by Governor Reinhold Sadler.

After two years of delay, Stuart's prizefight was thus held outdoors on a cold and snowy St. Patrick's Day in Carson City. It attracted an estimated crowd of five thousand. A flickering black-and-white film of the contest won by Fitzsimmons with a knockout in the fourteenth round was distributed across the country as the first genuine feature-length film, becoming the first great financial success for the infant motion-picture industry.[9] In 1906, the thirty-four-year-old Tex Rickard, who operated a thriving saloon and casino in the boomtown of Goldfield, orchestrated the improbable lightweight championship fight between the veteran champion, Joe Gans, and Oscar "Battling" Nelson, and he did so brazenly by announcing that the primary objective of the Labor Day event was to attract wealthy "sportsmen" to the three-year-old boomtown located in the middle of vast stretches of sand and sagebrush. Once the sportsmen were in town and properly liquored up, it was accurately assumed, hundreds of local mining companies, most of which held worthless claims but published attractive, if outlandishly inaccurate, advertisements, could unload their highly speculative stock upon the gullible visitors. No one in the world of prizefighting had ever heard of Rickard, but he ended all speculation that he could not raise the stupendous $30,000 purse he had announced when he stacked 1,500 glittering Double Eagle gold pieces in the window of the town's largest bank. Several hundred reporters were at ringside to provide their readers with exhaustive coverage of a fight that lasted for forty-two rounds under a blazing Nevada sun before Nelson was disqualified for felling Gans with a vicious low blow. Nevada was once more vilified from pulpits and in editorials across the land for what was now defined as "Nevada's Disgrace."[10]

The growing level of hysteria that characterized the opposition to prizefighting tended to obscure the reality that opponents were losing ground to the growing popularity of the sport. The influential Muscular Christianity movement that had gained momentum since it first appeared in the 1850s had prompted YMCA clubs to feature instruction

9. Streible, *Fight Pictures*, 52–95.

10. Samuels, *The Magnificent Rube*, 86–126; Aycock and Scott, *Joe Gans*, 152–79; Kille, "United by Gold and Glory," 65–97.

in the "art of self-defense" and to offer "scientific exhibitions" of "the manly art" to the public. This resulted from widespread acceptance of the rules first announced in 1866 in London by the Marquis of Queensbury, which were intended to reduce the brutality of the bare-knuckle brawls that had existed since the early days of the nineteenth century. The new rules featured three-minute rounds, a set number of rounds to eliminate the so-called "finish fight," no hitting below the belt, the use of padded gloves, a ten-second knockout, and the presence of a referee to enforce the rules. The growing popularity of boxing was especially evident among upper-class men, often of a moralistic Victorian persuasion (such as amateur boxer Theodore Roosevelt), who took up the sport as a means of physical conditioning. By 1910 and the great racial confrontation between Jack Johnson and Jim Jeffries in Reno, boxing had grown in general popularity, as evidenced in Nevada by the fact that women spectators were admitted, after considerable controversy, to watch the mayhem.

Between 1897 and 1910, thinly populated Nevada was thus host to three prizefights that attracted national attention and ever-increasing revenues.[11] Each produced a substantial profit, but more important, they attracted thousands of visitors who spent freely at hotels, restaurants, saloons, and not-so-legal gambling dens. Following World War I, however, Nevada lost its hold on the boxing market because its financial successes were not lost on entrepreneurs in major cities and revenue-hungry politicians in state capitals. There was also the emotional factor of patriotism. During the Great War, the army used boxing as a means of training recruits. This produced a wave of positive news articles about the merits of boxing, and the moral arguments against pugilism faded into irrelevancy. In the years immediately after the war, laws were changed in several heavily populated states to create state commissions to regulate the sport, and prizefighting, which had always lurked beneath the veneer of social probity in major cities, now became a prominent new component of the popular culture of the Roaring Twenties.[12] Tex Rickard, who had successfully promoted the Gans-Nelson and Jeffries-Johnson fights, moved his act to the big cities on the East Coast and in the Midwest, promoting five fights during the 1920s that generated million-dollar gates. In 1927, the famous rematch between Jack Dempsey and Gene Tunney that featured the so-

---

11. A fourth fight promoted as a heavyweight championship bout failed to attract either national media attention or many out-of-state fans. The 1905 Marvin Hart-Jack Root heavyweight fight in Reno drew only four thousand spectators and was ignored by the rest of the country.

12. Sammons, *Beyond the Ring*, 48–72.

called "long count," attracted one hundred forty thousand spectators to Chicago's Soldiers Field, and Rickard reported $2.6 million in ticket sales. Executives of the NBC radio network estimated that fifty million Americans listened to the fight as described by pioneer sportscaster Graham McNamee.

Basque Community Excited

This tradition of fusing frontier masculine culture with economic promotion was revived in 1931 when Dempsey announced the Baer-Uzcudun match. In this particular instance, the fight did not stimulate much in the way of national media attention as had the three great championship fights, but it did attract large numbers of visitors from the Bay Area where the flamboyant Baer had become the long-sought-after replacement for the handsome and debonair San Francisco native Jim Corbett. It attracted an even larger number of visitors supporting Paulino Uzcudun. Basque residents from as far away as Southern California, Colorado, Arizona, and Idaho made plans to be on hand in Reno to cheer for the first Basque athlete to rise to national prominence in the United States.

Probably at the insistence of his financial backers, Dempsey required as a condition in the contract that the two fighters would do their final four weeks of training for the fight in Reno. Their presence became daily fodder for local newspapers and attracted thousands of serious fight fans who came to Reno to watch them smack punching bags and go a few rounds with sparring partners. After some strained negotiations, it was determined that Baer would train at Lawton's Hot Springs west of town along the Verdi road, and Uzcudun would encamp south of town at Steamboat Springs on the Carson City highway. On May 19, Dempsey established his headquarters and ticket office downtown on Virginia Street, and he announced that tickets would also be sold in San Francisco, Oakland, and Salt Lake City. Mayor E. E. Roberts made the local newspapers when he purchased the first ticket, a $20 ringside seat. Reports out of San Francisco that counterfeiters were dumping phony tickets on the market forced business manager Leonard Sacks to implement a tracking system to record all legitimate sales. Basking in a wave of local adulation, Dempsey was soon thinking in an expansive way, telling local reporters that he was anxious to prove that Reno had not lost its ability to host a major prizefight, and that if his first venture proved successful in luring fifteen thousand or more spectators, he would go after even "bigger" matches for Reno.[13]

13. *Nevada State Journal*, 7 May 1931, p. 1; Clifton, *Dempsey in Nevada*, 78–79.

Baer appeared first in Reno on May 28, a pleasant surprise for Dempsey and fight fans because he had a reputation as a playboy who had neglected his training before previous fights as he pursued an aggressive social life. Aware of that reputation and of Dempsey's concern, Baer pledged that he would stick to business and avoid the newly opened casinos and supper clubs. Evidence that Baer truly was in town to win a fight was revealed when his entourage included ten sparring partners and a full-time trainer. Upon his arrival, Baer told a gaggle of reporters and onlookers: "I'm serious. No more playing around for me from now until this fight is over. I'm going out and get that big spiggoty quick! This is my big chance to get somewhere. If I muff it, I might as well hang up the gloves. So I'm getting down to business. A four or five round kayo of Paulino ought to get me a chance at the championship. That's what I want." He reiterated his seriousness of purpose by saying that he had brought only three of forty-one fashionable suits from his Livermore home. Nonetheless, Dempsey had reason to be concerned because Baer arrived in a sixteen-cylinder sports car driven by his chauffeur decked out in proper uniform and accompanied by a full-time social secretary. Upon his arrival in town, the chatter at the divorce dude ranches was reportedly quite lively.[14]

Uzcudun did not make it to Reno as planned by June 1, remaining in New York City until his favorite sparring partner, Juanito Olaquibal, arrived from Spain. According to his manager, Lou Brix, the Woodchopper planned a day's stop in Ogden, Utah, where a large celebration in his honor was planned that anticipated a gathering of "several thousand Basques of that vicinity." Anxious to get to Reno and begin serious training, Uzcudun spent only a few hours with his well-wishers in Ogden and proceeded westward where he was formally welcomed to Nevada in Elko by Reno businessman Martin Goñi, who owned and operated Toscano's Basque hotel and restaurant in Reno. Uzcudun was greeted at every stop across northern Nevada by cheering Basques, including a crowd numbering in the several hundreds in Winnemucca. His train arrived in Reno at 11 P.M. on July 4. Despite the late hour, he was welcomed by an enthusiastic crowd of several thousand. A brass band decked out in traditional Basque clothing added to the festivities at the train station. After greeting the crowd, Uzcudun was driven by Dempsey to the upscale Riverside Hotel that was owned by George Wingfield.

The next day he moved into his quarters at Steamboat Springs, which became a destination site for thousands of Basque fans who

---

14. Clifton, *Dempsey in Nevada*, 79–81.

were thrilled to watch their favorite go through his training routine. Before most workouts, the outgoing Uzcudun visited with his supporters and signed autographs. Robert Laxalt was then eight years old, and he later recalled that he and his father spent nearly every day in June at the training site. His father, Dominique, was an avid boxing fan whose wife ran their Basque hotel and restaurant in Carson City while he spent most of his days tending to his large flock of sheep high in the Sierra. "We practically lived at Steamboat Springs," Nevada's most famous native author would later recall.[15]

On June 14, the Reno Moose Lodge sponsored a barbeque picnic at the resort, with Uzcudun slicing meat for a hungry crowd estimated at twelve hundred. The *Nevada State Journal* reported that the turnout was "so heavy" that a "whole steer and 12 sheep were roasted over open pits."[16] Uzcudun thereupon thrilled his guests with a lively sparring session. Dempsey had correctly calculated that having the European Heavyweight Champion on the ticket would be essential to fill the large stadium that was rapidly taking shape at the fairgrounds. Eleven days before the fight, Dempsey and Nevada Governor Fred Balzar traveled to Winnemucca to address a banquet audience at the American Legion post. Dempsey curiously predicted that Baer would win the fight, but he urged the many Basques in the audience to come to Reno to support their man.[17]

The crowds at Lawton's Hot Springs were equally large and enthusiastic, but the composition of Baer's audience was decidedly different, featuring a large contingent of what one newspaper called "the pretty, blonde members of the divorce colony." For at least a week after his arrival, Baer attempted to adhere to his promise of focusing on the upcoming fight, but several reports that Dempsey received were not reassuring. Baer had been seen horseback riding in the Sierra foothills with a covey of divorcees, and apparently he had activated his three fashionable suits for nocturnal visits to Reno's nightspots. Dempsey sent a terse letter ordering trainer Dolph Thomas to ride herd on the handsome boxer, with specific orders that he could not use or even ride in his own automobile, could not go horseback riding, and could not be seen in Reno night spots. Baer responded with an angry blast, telling reporters that Dempsey's warning was "hardly justified" because the reports he had received were "outright lies." Nonetheless, he promised to train with greater seriousness of purpose, adding for good measure

---

15. *Nevada State Journal*, 5 June 1931, p. 1; Laxalt, "The Laxalts: Boxers in Spite of Themselves"; Clifton, *Dempsey in Nevada*, 79–85.

16. *Reno Evening Gazette*, 15 June 15, 1931, p. 1.

17. *Humboldt Star*, 24 June 1931, p. 1.

that he planned to "plaster 'Upsidedown' all over that ring."[18]

The prefight news reports filed by a growing number of reporters from major West Coast newspapers were filled with inconsequential news and the usual rumors, except for the afternoon when Baer's manager, Ancil Hoffman, showed up at Steamboat Springs and attempted to blend into the crowd. He obviously was there "to get a line on the Basque" but was discovered and confronted by Uzcudun's manager, Lou Brix, and told to depart the premises. Words were exchanged, and soon the two managers were clumsily rolling on the grass attempting to throw a punch or two. Hoffman was summarily tossed out of camp.[19]

Although the upcoming fight matched two prominent heavyweights who eyed the bout as an important step toward a shot at the title, the major figure in the news was first and foremost the promoter. Jack Dempsey had lost none of the star power that he enjoyed during his seven-year reign as champion. News reports, which he attempted to ignore, repeated speculations that he was seeing a divorce attorney while dutifully reporting when he was seen at restaurants with attractive young women. Dempsey also donned ring togs at both camps and went a few brisk rounds with sparring partners, much to the delight of the assembled. That he looked in fighting trim sparked a resurgence of rumors that he might make a serious attempt at a comeback at age thirty-six to regain the title. On June 21, over three thousand fans paid 25 cents to see him mix it up with Uzcudun's sparring partner, Al Gomez. On June 30, he knocked out Ole Johnson at Lawton Hot Springs with a left hook that awed the crowd, further stimulating speculations about a comeback.

When the eighty-four-page "official program" was released for sale at 25 cents a copy, the cover picture was of Dempsey, with neither fighter depicted. That publication, however, gave an indication that Dempsey intended to move aggressively into the fight promotions business, because it included a moving testimonial to the recently departed Tex Rickard signed by Dempsey.[20] Dempsey made more headlines when he announced that he had decided that he would serve as referee, just as Rickard had done for the Jeffries-Johnson match in 1910. He did so after both fighters had objected to the names of several potential referees, but the unstated fact was that his presence in the ring would undoubtedly attract additional fans to the event. Ticket sales had been sluggish, but immediately after this announcement "a rush

18. *Nevada State Journal*, 14 June 1931, p. 6.

19. *Nevada State Journal*, 20 June 1931, p. 1; Clifton, *Dempsey in Nevada*, 84–85.

20. *Official Program*, 84 pp., rare copy located in the University of Nevada Basque Library Collection.

for tickets" occurred.[21]

By the last days of June, with ticket sales brisk and record crowds expected, Reno residents advertised rooms in their homes for rent, and some even erected tents in their yards to make a few bucks. Several temporary campgrounds were also ready for business, having complied with Department of Health regulations. Dempsey announced that the arena had been completed on June 25, and he held a press conference in which he outlined thirty special rules that he would enforce as referee, the most important being that should the fight go the twenty-round distance, he alone would decide the winner. Dempsey and Governor Balzar appeared at a joint press conference, the major purpose of which was to scotch persistent rumors that the fight was "fixed," although those rumors did not specify which fighter would be taking a dive. And, as a sign of the arrival of a new era in transportation, Gilpin Airlines announced the inauguration of direct service from and to Los Angeles, with the officials at Reno's new Boeing Field announcing that a ground crew had been hired and a new control tower would be in operation for the arrival of the first scheduled flight on July 1.[22]

Reno public safety officials were also busy making preparations. The fire department announced that it had installed special water lines and hydrants at the fairgrounds and that a temporary building had been erected at which a pumper and a chemical truck were stationed. Police Chief John Kirkley announced that fifty plainclothes officers were being brought in from the Bay Area to circulate among the crowd, and that he had recently purchased a Thompson submachine gun and two high-powered Browning rifles, just in case. For good measure, Governor Balzar announced that uniformed members of the National Guard would patrol the grounds as well, on the lookout for pickpockets and violators of Prohibition.[23]

Betting at local gaming parlors picked up in the days before the fight, with Uzcudun money making him a slight 10/9 favorite. Newspaper accounts reported that heavy betting from Basques skewed the odds slightly in his favor. On Wednesday, July 1, the summer racing meet commenced before large and enthusiastic crowds, with special victory cups awarded in honor of Uzcudun, Dempsey, and Baer. Patrons in the new grandstand downed soft drinks and lemonade under the large sign that urged everyone to "Please Observe the Prohibition Law." That same day, Gilpin Airlines began delivering many Hollywood luminaries, who included Edward G. Robinson, the Marx Brothers,

---

21. *Reno Evening Gazette*, 22 June 1931, p. 7; *Nevada State Journal*, 15 June 1931, p. 6.
22. *Nevada State Journal*, 1 July 1931, p. 4.
23. Earl, "Blood, Sweat, and Leather," 26.

Tom Mix, Buster Keaton, W. C. Fields, Jack Warner, and Darryl F. Zanuck. Dempsey's business manager reported that sixty out-of-town reporters had secured credentials and fourteen Western Union lines had been established so that up-to-the-minute reports would flow out of the arena to the awaiting world. On the negative side, reports surfaced that downtown hotels had jacked up their prices to as much as an outrageous $40 for a room, although around town some rooms were reported available for 35 cents. Homeowners were even renting out their porches for sleeping because all the motor hotels, campgrounds, and hotels were booked, as were the two hundred Pullman cars that had been located on the main sidings just east of town.[24]

Twenty Blistering Rounds

The weather forecast was for 95 degrees at noon, when the fight was scheduled to begin. When the gates opened at 8 A.M., several thousand fans rushed into the general admission sections to secure the best of the $3 and $5 seats located in the back rows of the elegant arena. Some fans attempted to poach a seat in the more expensive reserved sections, but they were quickly escorted to the cheap seats by members of the National Guard. The *Nevada State Journal* reported that a "notable feature" of the crowd was the "number of women present," which its reporter estimated to be nearly half the audience. This was in sharp contrast to the earlier prizefights, in which the issue of whether women would be permitted into the arena was a topic of considerable concern to promoters Dan Stuart and Tex Rickard. Pictures of the crowd suggest, however, that the reporter's estimate was substantially inflated.[25]

At 10 A.M. the Reno Municipal Band, dressed in their summer white uniforms, began to entertain, and at 10:30 the public address announcer began introducing the celebrities present, beginning with Governor Balzar, Mayor Roberts, and the three men who financed the event—Wingfield, McKay, and Graham. The biggest applause was for Dempsey, who appeared in a natty outfit comprised of a bright green shirt and white flannel pants to wave at the crowd before disappearing back to his dressing room to prepare for his task of refereeing.

Shortly before the appointed hour, spectators were thrilled by a noisy fly-over by ten United States Army Air Force biplanes that had flown out of Mather Field in Sacramento. The pilots did a few rollovers and dives before swooping down low over the arena in preparation for landing on the dirt runway at Boeing Field. At 11 A.M., the first of four preliminary bouts began. The sun was beating down hard, and restive

---

24. Clifton, *Dempsey in Nevada*, 85–87.
25. *Nevada State Journal*, 5 July 1931, p. 1.

fans began to squirm as the resin began to seep out of the green wooden bleachers. Sale of "near beer" was brisk as the four-round prelims proceeded to the cheers of the fans. At noon, Dempsey reappeared in the ring and was followed by the two fighters. The telegenic Baer looked stunning in his bright blue robe, which bore a large seal of the State of California embroidered on the back, while Uzcudun wore a dark blue robe.[26]

The near-capacity crowd settled in for the main event. Both fighters, understanding that their progression toward a possible title fight hinged on this bout, began to throw serious leather from the sound of the first bell.[27] Uzcudun took several sharp blows to the face, but he countered with punches of his own. In the second round, Uzcudun seemed to want to end the fight as he tore across the ring at the bell and began flailing away wildly at Baer, who deftly made him miss while scoring with his own sharp counterpunches. In Round Three, Uzcudun scored with a sharp blow to Baer's nose, and the first blood of the fight began to trickle down Baer's face, and shortly thereafter his lip began to bleed from another blow. As the early rounds went by, Uzcudun seemed to be controlling the fight as Baer was forced to tie up his opponent in clinches. Both men were repeatedly warned by Dempsey for head butts. By Round Eight, the wise men at ringside had decided that Uzcudun was the superior fighter, but in the following rounds the Livermore Butcher Boy began to take the initiative as the heat and bright sun seemed to be slowing the 202-pound European. As Round Nine ended, Baer landed a solid blow to the head that sent Uzcudun back to his corner seemingly dazed.[28]

Subsequent rounds passed with both fighters having their moments, but they both tired under the relentless sun, and in the later rounds the number of clinches and head butts increased. The force of their blows seemed to disappear as arm wrestling and clinching increased, prompting some in the crowd to shout out demanding more action. The Associated Press reported that both exhausted men "butted like goats" during the final rounds.[29] The irritated fans apparently had no idea about the amount of energy that the two men had expended, as both now seemed determined to follow a strategy of simply attempting to stay on their feet until the twentieth round was completed.

While the two men were being splashed with water as seconds

26. *Nevada State Journal*, 5 July 1931, p. 1.

27. A detailed round-by-round description by the Associated Press was published by both Reno newspapers on July 5, 1931. The film of the fight may be viewed in the University of Nevada Basque Library.

28. *Reno Evening Gazette*, 4 July 1931, p. 1.

29. *Associated Press report*, July 4, 1931.

waved towels in their faces to cool them off before the final round, Dempsey leaned over to the press row and said to no one in particular that the winner would be the fighter who won the round. Both men seemed to sense that reality, and they tore furiously into each other, landing punches that brought the crowd out of its lethargy. In the final minute, Uzcudun scored with several punches to the midsection as Baer seemed too exhausted to do anything but try to avoid the incoming blows. The crowd came to its feet cheering, and within a few seconds after the final bell, Dempsey raised Uzcudun's hand in triumph.[30] The crowd's cheers affirmed the correctness of his decision.

The "Bounding Basque" had seemingly ended Baer's quest for a title shot, or so the newspapers reported. In a press conference after the fight, Dempsey was confronted by comments from reporters that they thought the fight had been "a little slow," if not boring, but he smiled and suggested that those who held such an opinion should try to go twenty rounds against a formidable opponent under a hot Nevada sun. Uzcudun readily confirmed that observation, telling reporters that he was frustrated by Baer's repeated head butts, but his biggest opponent had been the heat: "It was very hot out there in the ring and whenever I drew a deep breath it was like sucking in hot flames. My feet felt like balls of fire. Twenty rounds under a hot sun is like forty rounds under a roof at night."[31]

The pace of the fight had prompted several catcalls from the crowd, and the next day the *Evening Gazette* joined in the complaining, concluding that "the fight was nothing more than a wrestling and head butting contest . . . and only two or three solid blows were delivered during the entire 20 rounds." Because of the "ham and egg" show that Uzcudun and Baer put on, the discontented editorial writer concluded with a sneer, "Jack Dempsey, who was referee and promoter of the Reno affair, was the only attraction in the ring. Baer will have to return to his butcher delivery boy job in Livermore," and "Uzcudun really should go back to chopping wood or else get a job herding sheep."[32]

This note of discord, however, was lost in the euphoria produced by the downtown bonanza of fully booked hotels, overcrowded restaurants, and jammed casino floors. An unknown reporter writing in the Sunday morning edition of the *Nevada State Journal* tended to confirm the correctness of the decision earlier in the year to permit wide-open casino operations. "It was not the usual fight crowd," the writer noted, emphasizing that "they came to see the fight, but any fight almost

30. *Reno Evening Gazette*, 4 July 1931, p. 10.
31. *Nevada State Journal*, 5 July 1931, p. 8.
32. Ibid., p. 4.

would have done as well. They wanted to see Reno and there is only one Reno." He noted that the large crowds in town on Saturday night comprised "a tidal wave of merrymakers" that contributed to "the most colorful, crowded and generally noisy night in Reno's history last night as its thousands of visitors sought pleasure . . . that it was the biggest night in the city's history went undisputed. There was never another crowd like it here."[33]

Aftermath

Most of the out-of-town visitors remained in Reno for a boisterous Saturday night on the town, and Police Chief Kirkley was pleased that for the most part they remained peaceful. Several arrests were made for public drunkenness, and one pickpocket ended up in the city jail. The fire department had a much busier time responding to sixteen calls, all of which resulted from careless use of fireworks. The *Reno Evening Gazette* editorialized that the weekend was a great success, that the fight had "placed Reno on the Fourth of July map of the United States in large red letters." But in an effort to balance out the editorial with a nod to those few who had protested the holding of a prizefight, the writer carefully added, "As a method of observing the holiday, it may not have pleased everyone, but for those who like that kind of entertainment, it was unquestionably a success."[34]

Once the final accounting had been done, however, Dempsey and his backers were less than ecstatic. They probably were gratified that the early morning rush for the general admissions tickets had pushed them out of the red and to a modest profit level. Because of primitive bookkeeping, they could not provide a precise accounting of the number of tickets sold, and Dempsey glumly lowered his initial estimate; he now pegged attendance at between twelve and fourteen thousand. Local newspapers reported sharply differing reports on attendance and total revenues. When the accountants finished their work, a total gate of $79,666 was reported, but after the two fighters were paid (Uzcudun received $18,000, Baer $12,000), the eight prelim fighters received their modest stipends, federal entertainment taxes were paid, and all other expenses met (primarily the cost of constructing the arena), Dempsey and his backers cleared less than $1,000. The two local newspapers, citing different sources, reported that substantial discrepancies had come to light. Because the unknown number of individuals who held tickets to the horse races were granted free admission to the fight, the total number of tickets sold was reduced to an estimated 9,260, far be-

---

33. Ibid., p. 4.
34. Quoted in Earl, "Blood, Sweat and Leather," 49.

low the optimistic early predictions of 18,000.

Dempsey had earlier said that he hoped to promote another major fight in the same arena on Labor Day weekend, but this was not to be. The final accounting apparently sobered him and his backers regarding future promotions. They announced that Dempsey himself would enter the ring against the so-called Aberdeen Assassin, Leo Lomski, in a four-round exhibition instead of the promised fight between Uzcudun and top-ranked heavyweight challenger Jack Sharkey. The day after the fight, Dempsey departed for Portland, where he began a barnstorming tour of exhibition matches, often taking on two to four challengers in one evening. On August 19, Dempsey met Jack Beasley at the fairgrounds and after sustaining a bloody lip in the first round, knocked Beasley to the canvas three times in Round Two. Beasley bravely agreed to fight a third round for an additional payment, but he declined to go for an even greater payday by agreeing to a Round Four. Lomski the Assassin pulled out of the bout two weeks before Labor Day, and in desperation, with hundreds of tickets sold, McKay and Graham announced that Dempsey would take on five little-known challengers. An estimated ten thousand fans were in attendance to watch Dempsey knock out two of the men while going two playful rounds each with the others. He thereupon departed town for another series of exhibitions. Between then and February 1932, Dempsey fought fifty exhibitions, and he enjoyed such easy triumphs that he convinced himself that he could make a real comeback. But in Chicago on February 8, he suffered a humiliating defeat to Kingfish Levinsky. After completing a scheduled seventeen more exhibitions, he decided to hang up the gloves.

Dempsey also discovered that as a promoter he did not have the same magic as Tex Rickard. He moved on to other enterprises, primarily operating his famous New York City watering hole and steak house. He promoted his last fight in Reno on July 4, 1932, when he matched Baer and Levinsky, attracting a sizeable crowd, but the sizzle was gone. Shortly thereafter, the arena was demolished.

Contrary to a wave of negative reports after his loss to Uzcudun, Baer's career was not ended, and he won the heavyweight title from Primo Carnera in June 1934. He lost his first defense to James Braddock a year later. He thereupon repaired to Hollywood for an acting career that spanned twenty motion pictures.

Uzcudun's career leveled out, but he was given a shot at the crown in Rome in 1933, losing a unanimous decision to Carnera. He made one last attempt at glory in early December 1935, but he was knocked out in the fourth round by the rising young phenom, Joe Louis. Max Schmeling, who was in the audience to observe Louis, said that Uzcudun went to the canvas "as though he was struck by a bullet." The Basque Wood-chopper returned to his native Spain, joined the forces of General Francisco Franco in 1936, and after recovering from serious battlefield wounds, served in Franco's government briefly before becoming a police chief in the town of Valencia.

In the aftermath of the big Labor Day fight of 1931, Dempsey remained a major figure in the Reno, making the front pages when on August 17 he sued his wife of six years, actress Estelle Taylor, for divorce. Six weeks later, he spent thirty minutes in the Washoe County Court House to obtain the divorce he previously denied seeking. Surprisingly nervous, he told Judge Thomas Moran and a packed courtroom that he was seeking the divorce due to "extreme mental cruelty" on the part of Estelle. After less than thirty minutes, William Harrison Dempsey left the courthouse a free man. Like thousands of temporary Nevada residents that same year, he had been "Renovated."

Bibliography

Aycock, Colleen, and Mark Scott. *Joe Gans: A Biography of the First African American World Boxing Champion*. Jefferson, N.C.: McFarland & Company Publishers, 2008.

Barber, Alicia. *Reno's Big Gamble: Image and Reputation in the Biggest Little City*. Lawrence: University Press of Kansas, 2008.

Clifton, Guy. *Dempsey in Nevada*. Reno: Baobab Books, 2007.

Dempsey, Barbara Piattelli. *Dempsey*. New York: Harper and Row, 1977.

Earl, Phillip. "Blood, Sweat and Leather: Jack Dempsey and the Baer-Uzcudun Fight, Reno, July 4, 1931." Unpublished essay, no date, Nevada Historical Society.

Greenwood, Robert. *The Prize Fight of the Century: Reno, Nevada, July 4, 1910*. Reno: Jack Bacon & Company, 2004.

Hagar, Ray, and Guy Clifton. *Johnson-Jeffries: Dateline Reno*. Battle Ground, Wash.: Pediment Publishing, 2010.

Kahn, Roger. *A Flame of Pure Fire: Jack Dempsey and the Roaring '20s*. New York: Harcourt, 1999.

Kille, J. Dee. *United by Gold and Glory: The Making of Mining Culture in Goldfield, Nevada, 1906–1908*. 2008. Ph.D. diss., University of Nevada, Reno.

Kling, Dwayne. *The Rise of the Biggest Little City: An Encyclopedic History of Reno*. Reno: University of Nevada Press, 2009.

Laxalt, Robert. "The Laxalts: Boxers in Spite of Themselves." In 1974 *Sierra Nevada Golden Gloves*, District Amateur Boxing Championships program, Feb. 22-23, 1974.

Miletich, Leo N. *Dan Stuart's Fistic Carnival.* College Station: Texas A & M University Press, 1994.

Raymond, C. Elizabeth. *George Wingfield: Owner and Operator of Nevada.* Reno: University of Nevada Press, 1993.

Roberts, Randy. *Jack Dempsey: The Manassa Mauler.* Baton Rouge: Louisiana State University Press, 1979.

———. *Papa Jack: Jack Johnson and the Era of White Hopes.* New York: Free Press, 1983.

Sammons, Jeffrey T. *Beyond the Ring: The Role of Boxing in American Society.* Urbana: University of Illinois Press, 1990.

Samuels, Charles. *The Magnificent Rube: The Life and Gaudy Times of Tex Rickard.* New York: McGraw Hill, 1957.

Streible, Dan. *Fight Pictures: A History of Boxing and Early Cinema.* Berkeley: University of California Press, 2008.

15

Playing Basque in the Far West: Udaleku

Clara Urdangarin Liebaert

Basque clubs, gathered under the banner of NABO (North American Basque Organizations), organize an annual youth meeting called Udaleku (Summer Camp). Udaleku has two objectives: first, to promote Basque culture or Basque heritage in the U.S.; and second, to reinforce relations among members of the Basque community. The event is very popular among young people from the Basque clubs scattered throughout the West, since it gives them the opportunity to spend two weeks together, sharing formative activities and the hospitality of host families. This chapter seeks to understand the process of socialization of young Basque-Americans through the dances and motor activities they practice in Udaleku. It is part of the ethnography I conducted in 2003 within the Zazpiak Bat Basque Club in Reno, Nevada.[1]

Udaleku's Sociocultural Context

According to Argitxu Camus, the first colonies for young Basque-Americans—termed "music camp"—were organized in 1973 in Boise, Idaho. The main goal of these gatherings was to encourage Basque musical culture, especially dance and music, which at the time was considered essential for maintaining the cultural roots of the Basque-American community. NABO took over control of this somewhat costly initiative in 1977. After being held at three different sites in the same year, in 1978 a rotation system for hosting Udaleku in four areas was established: Northern California, Southern California, Nevada, and a final one among the states of Idaho, Oregon, Utah, and Wyoming. From 1991 on, participants were accommodated by host families in the area, thereby

* This study has received funding from Spain's Ministry of Science and Innovation through R+D+i projects: DEP2010-21626-C03-01, DEP2010-21626-C03-02 and DEP2010-21626-C03-03.

1. Urdangarin, "Bailando *Jauzi* Bajo Barras y Estrellas."

replacing the occasional use of hostels, university residences, and hotels. In 2001, the name "music camp" was replaced by that of Udaleku, which means summer camp in Basque.[2] I attended the 2003 Udaleku held in San Francisco.

The Euskal Etxea of South San Francisco: A Space for Basque Culture

Udaleku takes place in two main spaces: the Euskal Etxea[3] or Basque Cultural Center (BCC), and the family homes in which young people accommodated. The BCC is the hub of the program. It is a two-story building located in the southern reaches of South San Francisco. Its facilities include a restaurant and a bar open to the public, a large banquet hall with its own amphitheater, a kitchen, several meeting rooms, and a left-wall fronton or Basque pelota court. Construction of the building was overseen by a group of Basque entrepreneurs in 1982. The initiative, which entailed a significant economic risk and therefore became a matter of intense debates within the Basque Club, is currently a facility that any Basque community would be proud to have. On its façade, its name written in Basque in large green letters clearly identifies it from the outside. A fence of the same color surrounds the building and its large parking lot. This barrier, which separates the Basque facility from the street and surrounding buildings, underlines its functional yet respectable image: this is a bastion of Basque culture and a symbol of the Basque presence on the Pacific coast.

The family homes that Udaleku offers for lodging are scattered all around the San Francisco Bay Area. In addition to South San Francisco itself, these homes, which are located in Burlingame, Millbrae, Redwood City, San Mateo, and other towns, form a large metropolitan area that combined alveolar suburbs, streets, and commercial centers. Located over a varied topography including a mix of hills and coastline, the neighborhoods are well connected by a network of highways and local roads. U.S. 101, I-280, and I-380 (among others) are the main routes used to take the young people involved from their host family homes to the BCC, where most of the Udaleku activities take place.

The Domestic Group: Getting Involved

The camp organization requires the involvement of a group of people working together to successfully accomplish their mission. In addi-

---

2. Camus, *The North American Basque Organizations (NABO) Incorporated*, 172–81.
3. Euskal Etxea, which literally means "Basque house" in Basque, refers to a Basque club.

tion to the campers, there are four distinct roles for the supervising adults involved: directors, instructors, stewards, and host guardians. These roles are carried out by men and women linked to the Basque community and identified by the responsibility they assume in the performance of their duties.

There are ninety-two campers, which is the largest number a Basque organization has ever managed to that date. The campers are boys and girls from the Basque communities of the western United States—California, Nevada, Utah, Oregon, Washington, Idaho, Wyoming, and even two members invited from Argentina. The most heavily represented state is California. The age of the young people varies from eight to eighteen. But while the conditions for registration stipulate that campers must already have reached the age of ten to attend, the organization is flexible and accepts younger children as long as a family member, parent, or older sibling acts as a helper. Overall, more females take part than males: 56.5 percent are girls (fifty-two in number), and 43.5 percent are boys (forty). Of these, eight participants belong to the Reno Zazpiak Bat Club—six girls and two boys, making up 8.7 percent of the total.

From the first day, the camp director stresses the disciplinary code that the campers had to follow so that there can be no doubt or misconception about what is considered bad behavior. Udaleku rules emphasize good behavior during class performance and while lodging with host families. They underline the need to respect teachers, classmates, and colleagues, the prohibition of any drugs (including tobacco and alcohol), the obligation to participate in any activity that Udaleku organizes, the proper use of facilities and materials, and compliance with the spatial limits—in other words, campers cannot leave the BCC premises on their own account. The director makes it very clear that these rules are all serious matters. She would not allow any problems to affect the progress of Udaleku, so if someone does not follow these instructions, he or she will be expelled from the camp.

Participants are divided into eight groups, and each of these groups takes the name of a Basque province Nafarroa, Lapurdi, Gipuzkoa, Xiberoa, Bizkaia, Baxe Nafarroa, and Araba. There is also an eighth "province," the Diaspora.[4] Together, group members attend each of the culture courses, and together they are responsible for collecting dirty dishes and cleaning the dining room after lunch or dinner, when appropriate. The number of people in each group varies, ranging from nine members of Bizkaia to fourteen in Xiberoa, with an average of

---

4. The spelling of the Basque province names here is that used in Udaleku.

eleven to twelve members per group. Age in each group tends to be homogeneous with two elementary school groups, five middle school groups, and one high school group (all, as noted, given the name of a particular Basque province, with Nafarroa hosting the youngest group of campers and Xiberoa the oldest). By age-group, most of the young people involved are fourteen or under, with a smaller number of campers aged fourteen to eighteen.

In the BCC, the participants' relational exchanges are mainly developed within each group (or province) and between the group and each instructor. The campers have the opportunity to learn and have fun, provided they do not make any wrong decisions. This prolonged intimacy increases the links among the young people, so if they attended other Udaleku gatherings, they would be able to solidify their friendships. This is clearly the case in Xiberoa, the group composed of older campers. Some members of this group also enjoy the confidence of the teachers, who choose them to help in some of the tasks as their assistants. After the daily Udaleku sessions, these young people share and enjoy their autonomy surrounded by their host family and only a few Udaleku-mates.

The camp is coordinated by two directors, Valerie and Caroline. Both in their thirties, they are the project's main leaders. Their tasks include, among other things, adapting the NABO activities program to their site; seeking accommodation for participants and instructors; coordinating and guiding campers, teachers, and volunteers in their roles; supervising attendance and discipline issues; managing financial matters (from raising funds to ultimately balancing the books); and in short, promoting the overall functioning of the event. For all this, they count on the experience and personal opinion of Aita (Father) Martxel Tillous, the community priest and soul of the Udaleku gathering. They combine these leadership roles with those of instructors of dance, *txistu*, and *mus*.[5]

Along with the directors, ten instructors work at Udaleku. Their function of leading the campers through their learning process is complemented by other tasks, such as facilitating a climate of good interpersonal relationships, detecting and reporting back on any problems and irregularities, helping with safety issues on trips outside the BCC, and contributing to the general social environment. The instructors are made up of an equal number of men and women whose ages span a wide range from two nineteen-year-old former campers to seventy-year-old Aita Tillous. With the exception of four instructors from

---

5. *Txistu* is a kind of Basque flute that Udaleku campers learn to play. *Mus* is a Basque card game that is also taught in Udaleku.

the Basque Country, all the others have previous experience in summer camps, both as former campers and as instructors. They are all trained to teach in more than one activity, and although the tendency is to keep to their specific field of competence, they support one another in the different disciplines. They communicate mainly in English and Euskara, the Basque language. Their often informal meetings serve to adjust the learning pace to the interests and concerns of the participants. They also extend their social relationship outside camp obligations, such as when meeting together in the bar and occasionally at a restaurant at the end of the day.

Stewards are responsible for food preparation and distribution during the day at Udaleku. They are usually women whose sons or daughters are in the camp. They serve meals every day to the guests, who are well organized in line, requesting their preferred choices as they pass by. Food is prepared on the spot and occasionally delivered (from pizzerias and the like). Occasionally, some of these volunteers also take on an instructor's job. Thus, the restaurant's chef teaches bread-making in culinary class, and Rosa Mari, a participant's mother, helps out in Euskara language sessions.

Finally, the host families are in charge of accommodation and travel to and from the center. In this context, they provide the campers with a warm atmosphere in which their needs and wishes are intertwined with the host family's daily routines. Because the main daily meals are provided at the BCC, the guardians are only obliged to prepare breakfast and any snack they see fit to include. Living together requires continuous adjustments, and there may be small conflicts among the new family group. The clash of different habits and above all the typical adolescent quest for fun (involving, for example, staying up late and making noise) do not always goes hand-in-hand with the responsible adults' daily obligations and schedules.

The Schedule: A Time to Learn, a Time for Recreation

Time regulates the Udaleku colony's life. There is a program length, a time for every class, a time for the play-offs of the pelota, and timing coordination between all those involved in Udaleku. Campers' days are divided into two separate time periods—instruction and rest time. The former starts at nine o'clock and ends after dinner, about six o'clock in the evening. During these nine hours, campers learn about Basque culture in the BCC's meticulously programmed environment. In short, this is time for work. Then, from six in the evening through to the next day's session, the young people relax in their small family groups. This is time to rest.

The activity in the BCC is governed according to a shared schedule. Built and adjusted by the two directors, it informs all participants day-to-day. Following a school structure, topics are sequenced in units of one hour: an hour for each activity, and an activity for each hour. The day appears, from beginning to end, as a fragmented, divided, decisive, and immovable grid, dominated by a careful watch that synchronizes the general activity. In this education model, time is *well used*. Each hour has a goal, a purpose. The class is taught and learned. At the end of the day, however, this rigid structure is relaxed and offers participants some large and diluted slots, combining recreation with rest. Now the young people set their time fractions and organize themselves according to their host home's rhythm; they may take a long hot bath, listen to music, and sleep until the next day, or perhaps they might plan an interesting activity with the family or spend much of the night talking with another camper. Unlike the causal time associated with the school day, family evenings reveal a static and cyclic time that is more fitting for meeting up, welcoming new members, and living together as a family. What counts is to feel good and to satisfy the individual needs of the campers.

Basque dance, pelota, Euskara, *txistu*, and *mus*. Each group starts every morning with a tour of Basque cultural subjects set forth by the schedule. After one class they move on to the next one in cyclical fashion. If, for example, one day the Bizkaia group begins with Euskara, the next day they may commence with pelota. There are eight "provinces," and the existence of more provinces than subjects requires groups to join together, thereby overcrowding some classes, which is sometimes detrimental to their performance. At eleven o'clock, a sixty-minute break for lunch provides the energy to continue with the subjects not yet dealt with. The learning journey ends with two hours of electives; from three to five o'clock in the afternoon, campers join two of the five main subjects worked on during the day. Being able to choose according to the campers' own interests relaxes the dynamics. After dinner, which is served at five, the young people wait for their families to pick them up, while playing, talking, and practicing. The Udaleku schedule runs from sunrise to sunset and takes up the whole day.

Udaleku lasts twelve days, divided into two five-day units broken by the weekend. These two formative weeks offer different kinds of orientation. The first week, which is regular in the schedule, is essential in learning the subjects themselves. During the second week, the work gathers momentum in order to reach the ultimate goal of the camp—the exhibition of the acquired knowledge. This second week, which is full of projects, culminates on the last Friday. That day, there are pelota and *mus* playoffs and presentations on the culture of a particular Basque province, and campers finish rehearsals for the final festival—a dance spectacle, a *txistu* performance, and singing in Euskara before the parents. Campers receive no certification attesting their attendance or the level attained in their Basqueness, but all of them are aware of the final gala's significance so they focus on it intensely. Time sense in Udaleku is summarized in the principle of cause and effect of the performed action. The learning experiences attained in class need to be performed, exhibited. The campers' final performance demonstrates, before an audience the Basqueness they have achieved. And the vibrancy of this performance marks the level attained at this particular Udaleku. Being Basque here means demonstrating one's Basqueness, acting as a Basque.

Material Goods for a Basque-American Construction

The objects used in Udaleku demonstrate its material culture. Udaleku evokes Basqueness and encourages the construction of a specific Basque identity. According to Jean P. Warnier, objects must be understood in their action (that is, when they are used), not as inert or isolated elements (namely, in just their form and composition): "The praxic value can only be seen when the subject and his objects are in motion."[6] In 2003, I have studied objects in relation to their physical characteristics, but mainly as regarded their use and meaning in the Udaleku experience. Some of the objects used in the colonies are given to the campers to keep for themselves, others are to be shared, others are made by the students themselves, and finally, there are objects that each participant brings from his or her own Basque club back home.

The Udaleku summer camp provides the campers with a T-shirt, a *poxpolin,*[7] and a memory book. The poxpolin is handed out at the very beginning of Udaleku so that campers can play it in the music classes, practice on their own during their breaks, and use it for the final performance. Mastering the *poxpolin* allows the campers to experience and participate in the Basque musical tradition. Once Udaleku is finished and the campers pack their *poxpolin* in their luggage, it becomes an object of symbolic Basque decoration. Yet participants might keep playing it at home and even venture to show their learning at their home club meetings, as I witnessed at a potluck of the Reno Basque Club, Zazpiak Bat.

The T-shirt, expressly designed to celebrate Udaleku 2003, is white with a serigraphic pattern on its front that combines the event letters,

---

6. Warnier, *The Pot-King, the Body and Technologies of Power,* 3.

7. The *poxpolin* is a cheap, metal version of the *txistu* that is used by beginners.

with the Golden Gate and Basque symbolic themes in the colors of both the Basque and the American flag. The shirt has several uses. It is a garment that identified the participants as Udaleku members. It is a practical and distinctive marker to locate them in their trips outside the BCC and to show the outside community who they are. It is also a sign of the campers' passage through the experience that is revived when worn in subsequent community festivities. Finally, the memory book includes information about the camp on two CDs. Given by the organization to each participant at the end of Udaleku, it includes a group photograph of participants and instructors standing in front of the BCC, wearing their T-shirts, and holding the *poxpolin*. The book also includes the *txistu* scores performed and lyrics to the songs learned in class, so participants will not forget them. There is also a list of all the participants' names, with attached photos and email addresses, so they can keep in touch. There is a funny twist in the thematic photo selection of popular students. They feature the finest dancers, pelota players, and *txistularis*[8]; the students with the best Basque accent and the chefs most likely to succeed; and also the nicest guys, the closest friends, and even the most sneaky and willful classmates. To conclude, several class scenes complete the collection. Taken together, these become memory snapshots, images designed to help the campers narrate their own Basqueness and construct their personal and collective Basque-American identity.

Udaleku also provides material to be shared. These objects are essential for the students both in regular class time and at home with their families. They are school materials, such as pens, paper, books, brochures, and even computers used by the students to learn Euskara and prepare their research projects. They also include the music and CD player for dancing, pelota tools, *txistu* scores, and *mus* cards. One role of the instructors is to enable the use and disuse of this material, which is kept at the BCC. Moreover, this idea of sharing is extended to the host homes, where families provide their personal items (a bed, TV, sofa, and so on) to be used by these young guests.

The organizers encourage a relaxed style of clothing for everyday practice. However, for the final performance they ask participants to wear the dance costume they have brought from home. As a result, the uniform clothing that tends to characterize each particular Basque club's exhibitions is relinquished in Udaleku in favor of an amalgam of colors and fabrics. For example, the red, white, and black outfits worn by the Reno girls mix with the dark colors of the Salt Lake City danc-

---

8. *Txistu* players.

ers. And the red and white male garments blend with the black vests and pants that distinguish those from Winnemucca. The final festival therefore highlights each club's particular identity through the different costumes worn, while at the same time the *pluribus unum* of NABO becomes the dancing itself.

Some of the activities in Udaleku consist of making a crafted product to be used occasionally in class—for example, balls made from rubber gloves, wool, and tape, and pelota or jai-alai baskets made from plastic bottles. In cooking class, students learn to make bread that is later consumed at dinner, with everyone getting an opportunity to taste their own and their partners' work. Finally, all students prepare a report, a well-documented poster, or a Power Point presentation about their Basque province to be presented before the other groups.

Udaleku's material culture shows an apparent jumble of objects. The roughness of leather balls or *palas*[9] transmits an abrasive dimension of Basque culture in play and competition, yet the more sophisticated elements handled in bowling, for example, transfer modern neatness and precision to this other game. If ordinary clothes bring to mind everyday routine, putting on dance costumes marks out a difference, enforcing a traditional embodiment of the dancing exhibition. Moreover, sheepherder-style bread-making makes participants feel like they are eating a piece of Basque culture; this is very different from the more standard commercial and quotidian experience of consuming pizzas, hot dogs, and sodas. As a result, Udaleku introduces the young people to their ancestors' material culture, and this coexists with a mainstream American counterpart that meets their daily needs.

Finally, the decoration of the BCC is also a significant factor in the construction of Basque identity during Udaleku. First of all, an *ikurriña* or Basque flag, surrounded by pelota tools, ball competition trophies, and photographs of the sitting president of the Basque government, Juan José Ibarretxe, and the Minister of Culture, Miren Azkarate, are displayed in a showcase at the entrance to the premises. All these objects remind campers of their land of origin, their Basque heritage, their roots, and their ties with the Basque Country. Furthermore, another important object is evident just a few feet away: a plaque commemorating the construction of the building in 1982, containing the names of all those who made the creation of the BCC possible. Finally, the presence of a restored wagon near the front door stamps the footprint of a pioneer past, a shared history of sheepherders, a life already transformed and adapted to new and changing times.

---

9. *Pala* is a wooden racket or paddle used to play some of the pelota games.

The Curriculum in Udaleku

The Udaleku program offers young people a Basque curriculum in order to instruct them about their Basque heritage. This educational program is made up of dancing, pelota, Euskara, *txistu, mus*, together with cooking, singing, and a final research project. These subjects are linked to leisure, and specifically to Basque festive events. They build up a corpus, agreed upon within NABO, to transmit the traits that identify them as a group, to perform their Basqueness, and to highlight how the Basque community wants to be perceived by its fellow citizens. These subjects are the same activities that NABO sponsors through its clubs with the aim of supporting this common culture, both within and beyond each institution. The idea is related to the politics of minority recognition in multicultural societies expressed by Charles Taylor.[10] Youngsters join the Udaleku program to acquire this Basqueness, a Basqueness they learn and develop in the academic environment offered by the colony. In this way, the BCC becomes a real school, the Basque school of San Francisco, where campers learn the valued traits of Basque culture .

The schedule clearly distinguishes two types of instruction. A basic program organized by core subjects constructs the ethnic tour that each group has to make every day: dancing, pelota, *txistu*, Euskara, and *mus* (see table 15.1). Each topic is also reinforced as an elective at the end of the circuit. The second type of instruction is a complementary one, with classes that are introduced in the middle of the Udaleku session on a given and specific day. This is the case of cooking, singing, and the research project. Finally, it is important to emphasize the role of the recreational trips. Without being subjects in themselves, these trips are part of the program and undoubtedly contribute to this general Basque cultural training.

Curriculum Nature and Motor Corpus Weight

One important characteristic of the curriculum is its character. Nearly all the subjects in Udaleku acquire the form of significant skills in the

Table 15.1. Subjects that made up the Udaleku program in San Francisco, 2003.

Type of Subjects	Subjects
Core Subjects	dance, pelota, Euskara, *txistu*, and *mus*
Electives	dance, pelota, Euskara, *txistu*, and *mus*
Additional Subjects	singing, *sukaldea* or cooking, research project
Recreational Trips	*Jokoak* or games in the park, bowling
Others	lunch/dinner, lodging in families

---

10. Taylor, *Multiculturalism and the Politics of Recognition*.

language they belong to: campers play the *txistu*, dance, or cook. At no point is theoretical rote knowledge emphasized in any of the areas involved. Even when students are learning Euskara and undertaking the research project, the emphasis is on the functionality of the activities concerned. In the former, the aim is to stick to short conversations; in the latter, the aim is to seek information, prepare a report, and present it before the other students. Thus Basque culture as presented here is mainly practical.

Furthermore, these subjects receive differing degrees of importance in the curriculum, as demonstrated by the hours devoted to each of them. I have observed and counted the hours devoted by the campers to each subject in this cultural circuit. Thereafter, to this amount I have added an estimated time of elective courses, dividing the number of optional hours by the number of available options.[11] This provides a theoretical number that allows me to compute an unset and irregular practice encouraged by the choice. Finally, I have added the additional hours of cooking, time devoted to the research project, singing, and time spent on recreational trips. In total, the young campers perform seventy and a half hours in classes over the two weeks.[12] A study of the distribution of these hours by subject shows that most time is devoted to Basque dance (making up 21.75 percent of the total time spent on activities), followed by *txistu* (17.2 percent), and pelota (15.88 percent). Dance is the principal activity in Udaleku, which matches NABO data on participation in the different activities organized by the individual Basque clubs.[13] Indeed, as Lisa M. Corcostegui states, "In the diaspora, dance serves as the primary means of acquiring Basque identity, demonstration of cultural competence, and maintaining ancestral roots."[14]

The ten subjects in the Basque curriculum are very different from one other, which might lead one to speculate that the curriculum offers a highly diversified educational program. However, there is a clear underlying order to this outward atomization.[15] Below, I outline five categories of activity according to the expressive language that each practice demands. In the musical category, the activity is focused on

---

11. The time for electives is equal to the total of elective hours divided by the number of electives.

12. The total number of hours carried out by each practitioner is equal to the number of hours of core subjects, plus the theoretical time in electives, the number of hours of additional subjects, and the number of hours of recreational trips.

13. North American Basque Organizations. "NABO Membership Data." At http://www.nabasque.org/Members/Members-Data.htm.

14. Corcostegui, "To the Beat of a Different Drum," 304.

15. Parlebas, *Elementos de Sociología del Deporte.*

producing musical forms—*txistu* and singing. The verbal category is represented by learning Euskara and the traits of a particular Basque province. Another category is related to the activities of skill and chance, customized in the game of *mus*. A fourth category is culinary language, represented by the cooking class. Finally, there is the motor group, which mainly involves dance and pelota, but also elective games in Euskara and the two recreational trips: *jokoak* or games in the park, and bowling. The motor culture transmitted by these cultural categories, bearing in mind the number of activities that each contains, is significant because it represents almost half of the Basque cultural curriculum in Udaleku: 47 percent versus 53 percent of the remaining subjects. Thus, the results show a clear preference in Udaleku for these motor activities.

Why does Udaleku choose a high-load motor corpus? Motricity is a language, and like all languages its role is to create signs and express messages about culture and society. The game of pelota or every dance is a closed system, each possessing its own motor code policy. Learning how to dance a *jauzi* (a particular Basque dance) requires mastering the rules of this specific dance and knowing how to act in it. It is a practice that makes the dancers express themselves in motor language and communicate in the same motor codes with co-actors involved in the same situation. It is the same case with pelota and the rest of the sporting games. Moreover, languages other than motor codes are subsequently constructed on these original motor languages. And those supplemental languages, which possess a different nature, give additional references and meanings to motor actions. However, here dancers do not need to get involved in the traditional Basque calendar of the dances, respect the original place where they are danced, know about their particular history, or know to whom each one is traditionally danced. To perform dances and sports games in Udaleku, it is strictly essential (but also enough) to recognize and follow only what each motor code establishes. No further knowledge is required.

This is more difficult to achieve when it comes to learning Euskara. Motor practices, because they can be easily emptied of this dense referential load and because they acquire meaning in the development of their own motor rules, become easy topics to teach and learn. Moreover, the polysemic and adaptable nature they acquire in these conditions allows them to build and adjust their message and meaning to an American social and cultural reality, far from their European roots.

Basque Dancing

Basque dancing is one of the main activities in Udaleku, and there is broad agreement that it is an activity that best identifies Basque-Americans in the United States. Most of the campers have an opportunity to practice it in their hometown club throughout the year. This, however, does not eliminate the level differences that emerge among them: clumsy and rough steps coexist with light and rhythmic leaps. In 2003, dance classes take place at the end of the BCC banquet room. Illuminated by a single window, it is a large and open space with a parquet floor. The instructor reigns over this space. Her straight body attitude and lively feet reveals the marks of many hours of practicing, both in the club and in the Basque Country. She never at any moment displays an improper posture or an overplayed gesture. Practice, practice, and practice is the motto she promotes in transmitting several dances: *Jauzis*, *Lantz Zortzikoa*, *Agurra*, fandangos, and quadrilles. These dances have no secrets. Each is well-defined, and there is no improvisation; spatial order, geometric accuracy, musical timing, and group unity reign.

Basque dances are immersed in a musical structure. Every step, formation, displacement, and relation—in short, every action—gives meaning to the melody and also becomes significant when fitting into the rhythmic measures played by the music. The rhythm is usually binary, but also ternary, quaternary, and even the irregular 5/8 tempo make an appearance, as in the Agurra. No action related to the space, time, the other dancers, and objects can be considered without the temporal unit established by the song. The dancers practice in a group, cooperatively, through regular formations, linking musical stanzas to their choreographic counterparts. Without any dance tool, the dancers perform following a melody played on a CD player. Thus, immersed in an unchanging physical environment, without any possible surprise, they focus on adapting forms and figures—sequences of motor stereotypes—to each dance-implementing model. The least accurate practitioners try to repeat the lost actions, while the most experienced perform elements they already know, all the while attempting not to get lost when encountering misplaced legs still crossing the room.

Pelota in the Left-Wall Fronton

The subject of pelota is practiced in the left-wall fronton of the BCC. It is a well-lit, approximately 115-foot-long facility, decorated with the two conjoined American and Basque flags presiding over its *frontis* or front wall. The lesson is divided into three parts: it begins with a traditional game of chase, similar to the game of tag. This is followed by short games or exercises in hitting and giving direction to the ball, and it ends with a *putxe*, a traditional children's game played in the European Basque courts, in which everyone has a place. The organized chaos of the *stop* game, a kind of tag game, begins a lively session. The group of practitioners decides who will be "it" or the first chaser. Then the chosen person starts a pursuit with the intention of catching any player who is free in the field. If the chaser is successful, he or she and the person caught change roles: the chaser becomes a free agent and the person caught turns into the pursuer. At any time, when the pursued players feel that they are going to be captured, they can stop right there—immobilized—and yell "Stop!" coming to a halt with both arms outstretched. Thus these players are protected from the action of the pursuer, but they must remain motionless. In this way they wait until a free player comes close and touches them. At this moment they become free again and keep on playing. Sprints and pursuits happen in succession. Roles change. Nobody wins and nobody loses. All this action takes place without any scoring. Boys and girls, big and small, young and old, friends and strangers, play and interact together. The game ends according to the mutual will or tiredness of the players or, alternatively, when the instructor decides to end this first phase of the class.

The second part of the session starts with a kind of Miami jai-alai game. The side wall has been divided with parallel lines into several areas of activity: one for each four-person practice group. They will play two-points games. First, two campers play together, one against the other, while the others wait outside the court. The game begins when one of the players in the court serves the ball to the other. They have to hit it over a tape that has been placed along the left wall and make it bounce inside a reduced space. The first to score 2 points stays on the court and meets the next player, who has been waiting outside. Multiple games take place at the same time on the fronton as a whole. Enthusiastic players, in rotation, face one another's different level of practice. The variety of the game is revealed in the different ways it can be played: hand modalities (striking the ball with one's hands alone) or using a *pala* (racquet or paddle) or a *cesta* (basket, made out of plastic bottles). In order to encourage the groups, instructors sometimes also take part, attempting to hinder easy victories by the most skilled players and facilitating the action of the weakest.

Ten minutes before the end of the class, and facing the *frontis* altogether, the players have fun playing *putxe*, which French Basques know as *la porte*. This game may involve between five and twenty *pelotaris* (pelota players) in an all-against-all situation. The players decide among themselves who starts putting the ball into play. Then, no matter the order, participants hit the ball against the wall with their hand one by one. They cannot hit the ball after it has bounced twice in a row; the trajectory of the ball must go directly onto the *frontis*, above the *tx-*

apa[16] and below the padding at the top, and the bounce cannot go out of the space to the right of the court. Players who fail to do so become "dead" and must stand against the *frontis*, that is, in the *putxe*, while the others keep on playing. The game gets more exciting. If a dead player standing against the wall catches a fly ball, he or she exchanges places with the one who has hit the ball. When all but one player have been removed from the court and sent to the wall, the remaining player wins a prize, a *life* or *bizitza*, the right to fail once during the following game and not travel to the cemetery. This player will also restart the next *putxe*.

Electives to Highlight Individual Desire

If Basque dance welcomes the most outstanding dancers, pelota enrolls the highest number of people. In the former, instruction is more individualized and attention more focused. In the latter, the material provided by the instructors organizes *putxes* and free games. Whether in the fronton or in the banquet room the instructors are responsible for providing the proper environment. In the case of Euskara, a significant change takes place: teachers take the students outside the classroom, and even outside the building, to congregate in the parking lot outside. There they propose traditional games that use the Basque language as support for a playful ritual. The game *pi*, (also known as *pi jolasa*) is the main game of the afternoon.

Pi is a hide-and-seek game. One player is chosen to be the chaser. The game begins. With arms outstretched and all the players gathered around physically in contact, the chaser, also called *pi*, closes his or her eyes and starts counting loudly, in descending order from fifteen to zero (in Euskara): "*Pi hamabost, pi hamalau, pi hamahiru . . . pi bat; pi zero pi-pi.*" Meanwhile, all the participants flee to seek a hiding place. Finishing the counting, *pi* opens his or her eyes and, from where he or she is standing, tries to identify someone who is confused or poorly hidden. The formula "Pi Jessie" or "Pi Chris" (depending on the capture) is enough to make the discovered player leave the refuge and temporarily the game. If after three allowed steps for a better viewing angle the hunter cannot see anyone else, he or she restarts the countdown from a lower number with his or her eyes closed. During this short interval, players quickly leave their shelters to touch *pi*'s body and hurry to take refuge again between the parked cars, behind the old wagon, or by the outside staircase. When all the players are discovered, a new sentinel is chosen. The experience becomes interesting, and every day a group

---

16. The *txapa* is a metallic sheet that runs along the wall, parallel to the ground, about three feet high.

of about twenty kids gets together to play. Besides the satisfaction that the game itself produces, the chance to feel the air and the sun never fails to offer a friendly and pleasant environment.

Leisure Trips

Trips outside the BCC provides a break in the intense Udaleku program. In the first excursion, which is termed *jokuak* in the park, students and teachers go to play in Orange Memorial Park, a few hundred feet from the center. Here they encounter a pleasant stretch of grass and a spot in the shade of some trees. Once installed, the instructors mark three major areas with cones, forming corners of an equilateral triangle: they are the *house* or territory of each of the three teams participating in the contest: *azeriak, oiloak, eta sugeak,* or "foxes, chickens, and snakes." The game consists of catching the members of one group while avoiding being caught by the members of another group. It represents better than any other game the balance of nature: the chickens peck the snakes and keep away from foxes, the foxes prey on chickens and avoid the poison of the snakes, and the snakes bite the foxes and hide from chickens. Players on each of the teams, balanced in both number and age, are identified by colored bandannas: red, blue, and green. They tie the bandanna around their arm, ankle, or head. The game begins and the bravest players leave their burrows to catch their prey while avoiding being caught by their predators. They run, feint, laugh, chase, scream, run away, and catch opposing team members. When a player grabs an opponent they go together to the capturer's refuge. In the burrow, prisoners form a chain and wait to be freed by a teammate. By the time most of the members of any team have been captured, one of its free members manage to confuse the guards and release the prisoners, leaving that team to start over. Anyone who is tired just sits down for a while. The game allows some players to leave while the rest continue. In the background, from the swings, the youngest campers watch the show. One of them wants to play, takes a bandanna, and joins the group. Instructors and students, men and women, young and not so young, share in the taste of the recesses of the Old Europe.

Then some soccer fans among the group take a ball and prolong the enjoyment. Two goals are marked out on the ground with bandannas to create a bounded field that is enough to start the game. An improvised team made up Ellande, Marcel, and Jean challenges Megan, Domingo, and Cirbie. There is nothing transcendent about the game; the goals come one after the other but are lost in a nonexistent score. In *jokuak* in the park, time flies by on idle entertainment—so much so that it encourages instructors, guided by two local *pelotaris,* to get together that night and discover the hidden places of San Francisco.

A trip to the bowling alley takes place on Wednesday after lunch. The night before, the organization has warned the campers that Udaleku would only pay for one game, so if they want to play more, it has to be on their account. Brentwood Bowl, a facility located one mile away, is the leisure spot chosen. The expedition on foot, which lasts a seemingly endless half hour, is carried out without water or provisions—"Why don't we drive?" But the suffering disappears straightaway in the air-conditioned bowling alley. Wearing the obligatory court shoes, youngsters gather in groups by ages and predilections. The game is a confrontation between two teams over ten frames. Each team adds up the points earned by the pins knocked down in the two shots each player has in the frame. A player receives more points for knocking down all ten pins on the first attempt (strike) than by doing it in two tries (spare). The games go fast, except the ones played by the instructors, who have all gathered together on the same lane. While waiting for their teachers' game to finish, the campers take the opportunity to go to the arcade to buy a soda and play video games. Finally, they return to the BCC in the instructors' cars; they are in a hurry because the classes that day are not over.

Motor Corpus in Udaleku: Internal Logic

The motor corpus of activities in the Udaleku Basque curriculum acquires a significant importance. But what is this corpus like? What are its characteristic traits? What do its situations have in common and what distinguishes them? How can these motor characteristics be related to Udaleku's goals? In short, what is the motor code like, and what does it transmit in Udaleku? Motricity is a language, and like any other language, it possesses two different yet directly related realities: activity grammar and the actor's speech. The grammar of practice, its motor code, is a set of rules and customs within the motor sphere. Its existence and meaning are defined by its action—for example, when turning around with one's partner in the quadrilles, when pursuing a colleague who has just been released from the *stop* position, when discovering who is hidden behind the pickup in the parking lot, when knocking down the pins with a recently launched bowling ball, and when catching a fly ball and thereby becoming free in the *putxe*. I will now explore the internal logic[17] characteristics of these practices, the reality constructed by the rules, the essential properties of the action in relation to the space, to the other players, time, and objects, in order to

---

17. Parlebas, *Juegos, Deporte y Sociedades*, 302.

inspire the responses.

Practically all Udaleku activities interact with a steady, certain, expected, and predictable environment. In dances, pelota, bowling, and the games played in the park, the invariability of the physical environment is its essential property. Participants do not interpret the information generated by the performance place because it is irrelevant to the practice. In this sense, they have moved away from their forebears' lifestyle when carrying out these activities. The ability to know where one is going in the snow, to ride through the canyons, or to navigate along rivers—previously all so significant in Basque sheepherders' lives in the U.S.—does not concern this community anymore because Basque-Americans now live within the shelter of their towns and buildings. The ability to read the physical environment has lost all importance. Only *pi jolasa*, introduced in the Euskara elective, focuses its activity on a de-codification of an uncertain space. In this case, the playing field is a parking lot and players use the spots between the cars, columns, plants, or stairs as hiding places to avoid being discovered. The power to disappear temporarily fits with the audacity of seeking and finding playmates. In any case, the optional nature of the game constrains this spatial relationship only to the campers involved in the activity. Therefore, one might say that the motor culture acquired in Udaleku favors clearly bounded, controlled, safe games, with the Basque Cultural Center in San Francisco becoming its main stronghold .

Identifying the target subspaces that motor situations use— that is, the way practitioners take hold of the space in embodying the motor task—is another interesting point to study. In the dances, what guides the action is the accomplishment of figures, formations, and choreographic elements, following an aesthetic code accepted by the community's canons. Joseba Etxebeste terms these types of subspaces "strongly rhythmic spaces."[18] The importance of these subspaces, characteristic of the dances, is somewhat balanced by the importance gained by fixed material targets. In pelota classes, the success of the activity is achieved when, after being hit, the ball touches the floor twice before being returned by the opponent. The same spatial relationship is seen when kicking the ball into the soccer goal and in knocking down the pins in bowling. Other material targets, this time related to a human and living nature, become a third place in the motor corpus. They identify themselves with the purpose of catching, touching, or hitting the opponent's body, with or without the ball. It appears in the *stop*

---

18. Etxebeste, *Á Cloche-Pied* , 64.

game and in the *pi jolasa*.

Relationships among participants are built through *sociomotor* situations. They are developed in motor interaction among participants, meaning that one player's actions determine the actions of the others.[19] These situations occur when someone is dancing with a partner or a group of partners, when running away from foxes or catching snakes, when surprising a hidden playmate, or when returning the other team's serve. In Udaleku, the motor cooperation typical of the dances is complemented by the presence of adversaries in pelota, and of adversaries-companions in the sporting games in the park.

Time in Udaleku practices slows down and swirls in a cycle that emphasizes the enjoyment more than determining a winner. As in dances, in the corpus of games there is no comparison and measure of success among the players. Even the soccer game embraces the same tendency. Improvised during *jokuak* in the park, and apparently played to win, the activity escapes the rigorous duality of the sport; constant entries and exits occur among participants and so continuous changes of team are allowed to balance the groups.

However, during the second week, as the end of the Udaleku session approaches, the nature of the pelota games changes. Playoff games are introduced to seek Udaleku winners in different categories. While there is still *putxe* for those who do not participate in these playoffs, the pelota schedule is adapted to allow more time for those who are now competing with one another. The sense of game time thus changes, as does the attitude of practitioners. Now they expect immediate outcomes, and emotions become polarized.

As regards material culture, I observe that Udaleku activities tend to be practiced with specific materials; most evident are the CD player necessary for the dances and the pelota instruments. Even the "American" outing to the bowling alley is an example of this, highlighting the use of a large infrastructure, sophisticated technology, and very specific features. As an exception to this general tendency, traditional games like *stop* and *pi jolasa* do not require any tools to play.

Motor culture in Udaleku is mainly dominated by sociomotor situations in certain spaces, without victory, and with tools to practice. However, against the prevailing trend of the program, bowling stands out through its more exceptional traits. The throws to knock the pins down are not executed in motor interaction, and the team's final score reflects the addition of each individual player's achieved points. Therefore bowling is a *psychomotor* practice. As this is collective action

---

19. Parlebas, *Juegos, Deporte y Sociedades*, 427.

through the simple aggregation of individual action, I would classify it as *comotricity*, following Pierre Parlebas.[20] Furthermore, the lack of a score—characteristic of Udaleku motor practices—underlines the temporary nature of this American activity, which stresses the importance of the victory.

Articulation of Internal Logic in Its Sociocultural Context

In my study of Udaleku I have focused on the question of Basqueness within American cultural dynamics. In this context of reference, the socialization of young people involves the internalization of a proper communication code that is perhaps different from European Basqueness. The summer camp's *ethnomotricity*[21] introduces us to Basque people who, on one side, are proud members of American society, perceiving themselves as such, while on the other hand they loudly claim their distinction from other Americans, deepening their ethnic heritage in Basque camps. As William A. Douglass notes, "There is almost a sense today in which an American who has no ethnic identity suffers from a certain impoverishment of the spirit. In this regard, WASP has become the saddest ethnic designation within the lexicon of American ethnic relations."[22]

Young Americans acquire in Udaleku an essentially motor instruction. Dances, games, and sports stand as fundamental constituents of the program instilled by NABO. This motricity requires learning self-referential tasks that are meaningful in themselves, independent of the referential context in which they were once conceived. If there is no change in the rules of the ball games, campers will be able to play them anywhere: Zarautz in the Basque Country, San Francisco, California, or Boise, Idaho.

The site chosen for developing the Basque curriculum is the Euskal Etxea, a well-supplied facility that offers the assured and risk-free environment characteristic of their motor corpus. Here, Basque-American volunteers from all over the West come to practice sociomotricity: they dance quadrilles and *jauzis*, and dispute *putxes* and pelota games. Through these practices they get in touch with both Basque and non-Basque objects in a blending of roughness and sophistication, tradition and modernity, heritage and mainstream. The schedule, organized over the two weeks of the colony, coordinates and dispenses a cyclic activity—that is, without victory. Motor action, through dances, games, and sports, leads to a Basqueness that articulates the activities them-

20. Ibid., 73.
21. Ibid., 227.
22. Douglass, "Basque-American Identity," 191.

selves and their context.

Udaleku teaches instrumental skills. It shows *how to do* things: how to dance, play pelota, sing, play the *txistu*, and play cards. The colony provides the young people with practical tools that will enable them to participate in the Basque-American community's events, whether the campers' final performance or in a social *mus* tournament at their own club back home. They learn to act like Basque-Americans, and in doing so, the grandchildren of old-time sheepherders are assimilated into their Basqueness. Indeed, as Clifford Geertz would say, in doing so, they deepen in it.[23] In Udaleku, one learns *to be* in the action, and learns these actions. Being Basque, then, means acting like a Basque.

This learning is done in relation to others, a sociability that is inherent to motor action and that unfolds in other areas. Playing pelota, young Basque-Americans meet other Basque-Americans and develop friendships. When dancing, they pair up with new comrades, and among them a newfound camaraderie may emerge. Sociomotor situations, without score, are the keys for these links: they do not measure who is better or worse, but rather they set up the circumstances in which all participants can share a good time. The relationships built in Udaleku will be nourished at the scattered festival meetings throughout the Far West during the summer months. Just as families and friends use NABO events to meet each other, young people feel drawn to share the calendar of events with their new friends. The networks that join the different clubs are built in Udaleku.

In this relationship process, veterans begin to take responsibility for novices. In the same way as in traditional culture, older siblings take care of the little ones, the most experienced dancers or the most talented *txistu* players take care of small groups of learners. Young people internalize teamwork: they take Euskara classes while offering help in the *mus* classes, or they take turns cleaning the dining room. This model of *anticipatory socialization*[24] is also a feature among the adults: parents welcome campers to their home, the grandmother helps serving the food, instructors from other clubs teach dance, and the community priest encourages *txistu* learning. All are part of a social network that is becoming more and more intertwined.

Being in the action means committing to the club, to the community, and Udaleku shows how one can acquire this commitment. The first necessary condition is to play pelota or to dance. Knowing how to do one of these two activities allows one to participate in exhibitions and therefore acquire an engagement with the group. As long as people

---

23. Geertz, "Art as a Cultural System," 1483.
24. Goffmann, *The Presentation of Self in Everyday Life.*

keep practicing, they gain expertise and their commitment to the community increases. As campers become adults, the commitment is no longer suggested by parents to gain autonomy.[25] Campers may assume new responsibilities and also diversify their performance expectations.

The Udaleku curriculum displays the icons that the Basque-American community needs to learn; those icons are the ones that they choose to identify and introduce themselves as a distinct ethnic group within the complex American multicultural community. The whole corpus of formative courses builds the Basque model chosen. It is a reinvented Basqueness, linked to leisure, with festive gatherings, and with ethnic demonstrations addressed to an American audience. These are Basques who dance, play pelota, and play *mus*; who sing and greet in Euskara; and who relate aspects of the history and culture of the land that their families left. This knowledge of Basqueness does not need to be too profound. It just has to meet community requirements to allow the Basques to differentiate themselves from other ethnic groups. A mixture of Old World and Far West references are employed in this "making of Basqueness"; pelota is combined with bowling in the Udaleku program in the same way as English is used with Euskara or the American and Basque flags are conjoined in the fronton.

Udaleku transmits a rigid and closed model of Basqueness. The icon-subjects, with their festive motivations that are ritually repetitive, encapsulate the instruction, highlighting the unchanging character of the Basque community tradition. On one hand, if Basque society in Europe projects itself through modernity, with Frank Gehry's Guggenheim Museum in Bilbao as an example, then conversely, Udaleku practices offer Basque-American society a past tradition in which they can reflect themselves. On the other hand, reproducing this model runs the risk of turning Basque-Americans, in the eyes of others, into a stagnant group, potentially subject to becoming amusement-theme parks, trapped in an outdated and uncreative cardboard representation. As Douglass anticipated a few years ago: "Today the Basque Country is a modern, urban-industrial society and open range sheep ranching is vanishing from the American scene. Consequently, to the extent that Basque-American identity remains predicated upon such symbols it runs the risk of becoming more show than substance. Its twenty-first-century representative may come to have more in common with the drugstore cowboy or the cigar-store Indian than with his forebears who tilled fields in Europe or herded sheep in the American West."[26]

---

25. Elias, *The Civilizing Process*.
26. Douglass, "Basque-American Identity," 196.

American Basqueness is commitment through action, an action that is conducted in a festive experience, and an action that young people perform mainly through dances, games, and sports that are carefully chosen as significant ethnic icons. In this sense, Udaleku acts as a *cantera* "quarry," as a resource and a school of Basqueness in the United States.

Bibliography

Camus, Argitxu. *The North American Basque Organizations (NABO) Incorporated: Ipar Amerikako Euskal Elkarteak: 1973-2007*. Vitoria-Gasteiz: Servicio Central de Publicaciones del Gobierno Vasco, 2007.

Corcostegui, Lisa M. 2005. To the Beat of a Different Drum: Basque Dance and Identity in the Homeland and the Diaspora. Ph.D. diss., University of Nevada, Reno, 2005.

Douglass, William A. "Basque-American Identity: Past Perspectives and Future Prospects." In *Change in the American West: Exploring the Human Dimension*, edited by Stephen Tchudi. Reno: University of Nevada Press, 1996.

Elias, Norbert. *The Civilizing Process*. New York: Urizen Books, 1978.

Etxebeste, Joseba. *À cloche-pied: Les jeux sportifs traditionnels et la socialisation des enfants basques*. Sarrebruck: Editions Universitaires Européennes, 2012.

Geertz, Clifford. "Art as a Cultural System." *MLN* 91, no. 6 (1976): 1473–99.

Goffman, Erving. *The Presentation of Self in Everyday Life*. Garden City, N.Y.: Doubleday, 1959.

North American Basque Organizations. "NABO Membership Data." At http://www.nabasque.org/Members/Members-Data.htm.

Parlebas, Pierre. *Juegos, Deporte y Sociedades: Léxico de Praxiología Motriz*. Translated by Fernando González del Campo Román. Barcelona: Editorial Paidotribo, 2001.

———. *Elementos de Sociología del Deporte*. Translated by Carmen García. Revised edition. Málaga: Instituto Andaluz del Deporte, 2003.

Taylor, Charles. *Multiculturalism and the Politics of Recognition: An Essay*. Princeton, N.J.: Princeton University Press, 1992.

Urdangarin, Clara. 2009. Bailando *Jauzi* Bajo Barras y Estrellas: Una Etnografia del Zazpiak Bat Group of Dancers de Reno, Nevada. Ph.D. diss., University of the Basque Country.

Warnier, Jean P. *The Pot-King, the Body and Technologies of Power*. Leiden: Brill, 2007.

16

Officiating and the Game: Professional Baseball and Perfection

T. David Brent

The officials, referees, or umpires of a team sports game are, in the minds of most observers, outside the game itself. They are necessary to determine the fairness of the outcome of each play down to the minutest aspect. But they are not usually considered players themselves.

I admit I shared this view until the sports historian and former college baseball umpire Dick Davies pointed out at the conference from whence this essay arose that the call of the umpires is determinative of the reality of the act that the players perform. In this sense, the umpires or referees are part of the game itself. They do not simply regulate it; they constitute it.

I have a friend with whom I used to talk with basically every second of every game of the Chicago Bulls basketball team. In recent years, post-Michael Jordan, Scottie Pippen, and Dennis Rodman, my friend says he is no longer interested in following the team with such fanatical consistency. Beside the fact that MJ, Scottie, and Rodman are no longer playing, he says that it is the "bad officiating" that has soured him on the game.

In my view, the beauty of the game has not diminished in the least, and the officiating, good or bad, has to be taken as part of the game itself. I'd like to illustrate this with a particularly poignant example taken from the history of the game of professional United States baseball.

The Perfect Game That Was Not

Twenty-seven up/twenty-seven down, no base runners, no errors, walks. Very rare—only twenty-four in over 120 years—something like twenty in approximately half a million games played in professional baseball history; distinction: automatic entry into the Baseball Hall of Fame. What happened: Armando Galarraga, a twenty-eight-year-old pitcher from Venezuela, pitched a perfect game for the Detroit Tigers on June 2, 2010. Or did he? On the final play of the game, the umpire called a batter safe at first despite the fact that everyone watching saw that he was out. The video replay confirmed that he was out. Yet the ruling was upheld, robbing Mr. Galarraga of his place in major-league history.

So what happened? Galarraga pitched eight and two-thirds perfect innings, but lost the perfect game on the twenty-seventh batter after what was ruled an infield hit. Rookie Jason Donald of the Cleveland Indians hit a ground ball to first baseman Miguel Cabrera, who tossed to Galarraga—who was covering first base—but first-base umpire Jim Joyce incorrectly called Donald safe on a close play, ending the perfect game and no-hitter. Completing the one-hitter, Galarraga threw 88 pitches, 67 of them for strikes. If he had completed the perfect game (83 pitches), it would have been the lowest number of pitches thrown since Addie Joss's 74 in 1908, and the shortest game since Sandy Koufax's perfect game in 1965. It would have been the second perfect game in the major leagues in just four days, Roy Halladay having thrown his on May 29, the fourth no-hitter of the season, as well as the third perfect game in twenty-four days.

Joyce issued a direct apology to Galarraga, acknowledging that the call was incorrect. Galarraga accepted the mistake gracefully, saying later, "Nobody's perfect."

Observers pointed to the handling of the situation as an example of good sportmanship on both sides. As a consolation prize, in what some called the most perfect PR event in history, Galarraga was presented two days later with a red Chevy Grand Sport Corvette convertible by General Motors, who sponsored the Tigers-Indians series, and he was presented with a "Medal of Reasonableness" for his response to Joyce's call at the Rally to Restore Sanity and/or Fear held in August 2010 in Washington, D.C. Galarraga and Joyce even wrote a book together, *Nobody's Perfect.*[1]

There are competing but not exclusive definitions of perfection, namely the legal and the individual, or, put in other terms, the individual's relationship with society and the individual's relationship with himself. In the legal context, there are rules but also there is judgment. The rules define fair play and foul play. However, the rules need to be interpreted in real time in every possible circumstance. In baseball, the umpire (and ultimately the Commissioner) is the final arbiter of any given play,

---

1. Galarraga and Joyce, *Nobody's Perfect.*

of whether or not a game is "perfect," and therefore how it is historically recorded. I doubt that there are any agents of chaos who would last long in the role of professional umpire who intentionally called every caught ball safe and every safe runner out. But like any legal system, there exists the potential for abuse and the opportunity for a fair man to be called guilty and a guilty man to go free.

In this light, it is interesting to note how everyone acknowledged that the lack of a perfect game for Galarraga was a mistake. Looking at the Wikipedia page, it appears that almost everyone said he should have been awarded the perfect game but also that Jim Joyce is one of the best umpires in the league; he always calls a fair game, but mistakes unfortunately can happen.

For the second view we have to do a bit more investigation. If the rules can be considered objective, then they must exist in some sense beyond observation. Galarraga can pitch a perfect game, and he just doesn't get acknowledgement. Or he could pitch a perfect game that is played without umpires, some sort of pickup game. In other words, the calls are subjective but they only govern what is recorded, not what "actually" happened. Isn't there the possibility of the pitcher throwing the game he needed to throw—as Galarraga says, the best game of his career—regardless of what is set down?

Moreover, calling a thing perfect does not have to mean that a thing is excellent. Sometimes it can mean that everything about it is "just so." Here I would like to acknowledge the element of chance that Michael Messner eloquently articulated at our discussion. Something might be called perfect because it has achieved in restraint or judicious craftsmanship something higher than a thing that is done to excess. A place for everything and everything in its place. If the term "perfect game" weren't an official one within baseball, I think there are a lot of situations where we might say this or that player had one.

The second meaning I think is very similar to excellence—that is, that perfection means the achievement of a state very like the Platonic ideal, sharing in all great baseball games equally. In that respect, from a moral view, perhaps what truly cements Galarraga's game as perfect is that he threw it within the rules, but it was not acknowledged, and yet he still displayed the composure and sportsmanship of a gentleman, going so far as to compliment the umpire and express concern about how he was dealing with the bad call.

I think it will be instructive here to look at some of the key differences between professional baseball and other team sports played with a ball. I then will focus on the notion of perfection as a limit of what can be achieved in both sports and in life generally. Finally I will try to define the complex of characteristics that determine what a perfect game really is.

How Baseball Is Different

There are many trivial differences between professional baseball and other team sports played with a ball, or for that matter any sport played with a ball. To begin with, the baseball season is longer than any other sport—162 games played over seven months. To the fans, this incredibly drawn-out season is magnificent. It is sometimes said that baseball is like an old flame—she is always there when you need her (or him). To paraphrase Kant, we will always return to baseball (that is, to metaphysics) as to a beloved one with whom we have had a quarrel.

There is no time limit within which the game must be played. Unlike soccer, football, basketball, or ice hockey, a baseball game can go on indefinitely until, perhaps, it is called by the umpires because of the danger it would cause, whether because of darkness or other factors. The role of the umpires is critical to this essay, but I shall reserve extensive comment upon it for later.

This temporal anomaly—remember, I am talking about team sports played with a ball, not bowling, billiards, tennis, or golf—is just the first of the distinctions that set baseball apart from other sports. I recognize that cricket and possibly rugby—for neither of which I have any knowledge or love—may be similar in this respect. In any case, the infinity within which baseball is played is a cause for wonder.

To go on with the more obvious aspects: the playing field is gigantic compared to all other sports. The distance between players is unprecedented in any other sport. It is even possible that some of the players will never be involved in a single play during the game. Separation by distance and individual isolation play a role in baseball as in no other sport.

The temporal and spatial anomalies of baseball are connected to the tremendous speed and the tremendous slowness of the game. Many people dislike watching or playing baseball because it seems so slow. I love it because action is always just about to happen. It's a game of "fast twitch" muscles, sudden isolated bursts, incredible speed, and long pauses, a game of inches, it is said, even though the field is sometimes nearly two times larger than a football stadium. It doesn't require the athleticism of other team sports for the most part, though athleticism can't hurt. The thing, though, for my purposes here is that the players are linked by common purposes over vast distances. Baseball is not a contact sport.

There is one key difference I would emphasize now that sets baseball apart from any other team sport played with a ball. With the possible exception of cricket, baseball is the only sport in which the offense does not possess the ball. How can this be? In every other team sport, with the partial exception of cricket, the *ball must score*. The ball may be carried by a person, but the person is ancillary to the ball. The ball must go into the basket, through the uprights, over the end-zone line, into the cup, the pocket, with or without the man who has carried it or kicked it or pushed it or putted it. In baseball, it is the *man who must score*; the farther away the ball, the better. In fact, the ball is your enemy. Being touched by it is one way of being put out. In a home run, the ball is hit so far away that in the case of a park with bounded walls it is ruled a "home run," but only if the batter touches all the bases including home base, the key base of all. It has been known to happen that a home run—a ball hit out of the park—is nullified if an infielder calls the ball back because the batter/runner has not touched a base. The runner is then called out. It is paramount that the runner touches all bases, including home, in order for the home run to count. (There is also the case of an "inside the park home run" where it is paramount only that the batter touches all the bases on the way home.) Thus, in baseball, *the person scores, not the ball*. I suspect this is one of the reasons baseball is so popular with children. It gives you an opportunity to do something important through your own body, not through something external, like a ball. You score. You become a hero by returning home.

Baseball is thus a fundamentally humanistic game the primary object of which, in terms of scoring, is to return home to the place you started out from. Like Ulysses in Greek mythology, or Ganesh in Indian, the hero is one who returns home after a long tour around the world. Baseball is inherently a humanistic and heroic sport. It has redemption built into it.

The idea that a "home run" could be nullified if the batter misses a base goes deep to the heart of what I am trying to say in this essay. There are many rules, codified over time, but always subject to change, that constitute any sport. That is not my immediate concern. Rather I wish to draw an implication from baseball's temporal, spatial, and person-centered anomalies.

From a purely spatial point of view, I hope it is not stretching the point to observe that there is another major anomaly. The center of the field—I'm tempted to say, of the game itself—is a widely regarded symbol of perfection: the diamond. And in the center of the diamond stands the key player of the game: the pitcher. I will now dwell briefly on the idea of perfection.

The Idea of Perfection

Analytic philosophers—analysts of concepts—must start out by describing or analyzing how terms are used in ordinary language. At least this is what I learned from my studies of the philosophy of J. L. Austin, whose notion of performative utterances is central to what I have to say about the concept of a perfect game in baseball.[2]

Every day, we use and hear the term *perfect*, or less commonly, *perfection*, quite a lot. Most usually it is used to mean simply, that will do. Let's meet at noon tomorrow. Perfect! How did you do on a test? Perfect. How is your blood pressure today? Perfect. I could of course add many more examples. In these usages it simply means: good enough, nothing to complain about, acceptable within the limits and constraints of a particular situation, game, or other means-ends pursuit.

In recent advertisements I've noticed two exemplars: Lexus, "the relentless pursuit of perfection," and Smirnoff, "the perfect mix for a great Bloody Mary." I know there are more, but I think these examples are enough to make my point. On the day-to-day level we have many examples of perfection, but perfection remains an unattainable goal, a Platonic ideal, to which we constantly aspire but never reach. As Galarraga said "Nobody is perfect."

I can't resist adding another example of the use of the term, this time from Freud: "We have, however, at the same time guarded ourselves against accepting the misconception that civilization is synonymous with becoming perfect, that it is the path by which man is ordained to reach perfection."[3]

Now what is unique about the American sport of professional baseball is that it gives the pitcher the faint possibility of throwing a perfect game. Within the humanistic framework of accepting errors, mistakes, and personal failings, there is still the possibility of triumph, of truly achieving perfection in the purest sense. I've reflected on this and can't come up with another example except from bowling or billiards, neither of which are true team sports with offenses and defenses. In bowling, you can get a strike every time for thirty frames and a perfect score of 300; in pool or billiards, you can "run the table" and not even let your opponent into the game.

Baseball, however, is played within an infinitely more complex situation. It is said that there are three kinds of umpires. The first says: I calls them the way they is. He is a staunch but naïve realist. The second says: I calls them the way I sees them. He is the subjective phe-

---

2. Austin, *How to Do Things with Words*.
3. Freud, *Civilization and Its Discontents*, 61.

nomenalist. The last says: they ain't nothing until I calls them. He is the post-modernist arbiter of reality. The call is a performative utterance that creates a reality rather than merely perceiving or recording one.

The Collaborative Process of Constructing Reality, and Armando Galarraga's Place in History

I hope I have said enough for us to draw some conclusions. In order for there to be a perfect game in the most ideal sense, a number of things must happen. No batter can reach base for any reason. This depends on the excellence of the pitcher, the excellence of the fielders, and the excellence of the umpires. In Galarraga's case, not all these factors were present—the umpire made a mistake. Therefore, it was not a perfect game. But we should and must take into account a number of other factors. The fans, the press, and sports fans everywhere were outraged by the triumph of the third kind of umpire: they ain't nothing till I calls 'em. Yet the generosity of the umpire, of the commentators in the media, of General Motors, and of Jon Stewart, the organizer of the Rally to Restore Sanity and/or Fear create a different picture. Ultimately, Galarraga did not achieve his automatic place in the Baseball Hall of Fame because of a technicality. But because of the collaboration of the players, the umpires, the fans, and the general public, Galarraga's achievement that day must be recognized as "perfect," not in the sense that "it will do," but because it shows us that the process of constructing what is real is a collaborative one, dependent on many complex factors coming together in the right combination over a period of time. To my mind, Galarraga's performance, while not technically perfect in itself, was a perfect example of how sports can be elevated to perfection.

The Future of Performance

Finally, I would like to say something that links the concept of a perfect game in baseball to the future of performance generally. Players are getting bigger, stronger, and faster. But if everyone is getting bigger, stronger, and faster, the playing field is still level. Individual talent will always be recognized. Or will it? As I've suggested, there is a moral and collaborative dimension to recognition that will never change because the collaborative and ultimately redemptive process is built into it. If the observers, the players, and the referees are all on the same page, you have a perfect game no matter what the technical outcome.

I have a good friend, the same one to whom I referred at the beginning of this essay, whose axiom is the truism that the team with more points always wins. I can't disagree with that on a purely logical basis. But the process of playing the game—playing a beautiful game, with all its drama and ups and downs—ultimately means more to me, and I think to history, than who gets credit or who gets into the Hall of Fame.

Bibliography

Austin, John L. *How to Do Things with Words*. Cambridge: Harvard University Press, 1975.

Freud, Sigmund. *Civilization and Its Discontents*. Mansfield Centre, CT: Martino Publishing, 2010.

Galarraga, Armando and Jim Joyce. *Nobody's Perfect: Two Men, One Call, and a Game for Baseball History*. New York: Atlantic Monthly Press, 2011.

17

A Life in Sport: Memory, Narrative, and Politics

Jennifer A. Hargreaves

My opening premise—that all authors and their texts are products of time, place, and personal experience—acknowledges the subjective element of research and writing. In this chapter, I examine my relationship to the past based on narratives about my early interest in sport and events that have influenced a very long career in education—teaching physical education in schools, training student teachers, and then moving to lecturing and research in sports history and sociology in universities. With age has come retrospection about the links between personal life, career experiences, national and world politics, and relations of power in sport, education, and culture. I refer also to intellectual and theoretical influences on my work and circumstances that impeded or enhanced outcomes. Put simply, I address relations between the personal (autobiography and private memory) and the political (wider society and collective memory). Inevitably, this process raises questions about the viability of memory.

In 2002, Pierre Nora claimed that "we are witnessing a worldwide upsurge in memory" and are in an 'age of ardent, embattled, almost fetishistic 'memorialism.'"[1] Certainly, there has been a burgeoning interest in memory and its uses in academia in recent years, attracting researchers from widely diverse disciplines and backgrounds. In the UK, there are university courses and doctoral theses and conferences with "memory" in their titles. In 2008 a UK journal entitled *Memory Studies* was published for the first time. A significant element of this upsurge has come from feminists,[2] but any claims for originality are misplaced. Although the terminology has changed, the use of memory in research is nothing new. It is an element of biography, oral history,

1. Nora, "Reasons in the Current Upsurge in Memory."
2. Radstone, "Memory, History and Events."

and life history—usually positioning the researcher as objective, as if separated from the story he or she is telling, and unreflective of personal involvement. It is also a significant element of autobiography, autoethnography, and narratives of self, which, in contrast, place the author at the center.

At the same time, the use of memory as a research resource has raised opposition and controversy, often because what is particular about its prominence is that it challenges the idea of one unified, official account of a period of history or a particular event (characterized as "dominant" or "official" memory). Using memory as a basis for research is a potentially provocative approach that can give voice to the experiences of disempowered, displaced, and neglected people, which has been the raison d'être of much of my work. The voices of the oppressed provide evidence, for example, of difference and identity, discrimination, and intrigue—foremost reasons for opposition from those who are in positions of power and wish to protect the status quo through "official" versions of history.

But I would argue that the denial of subjectivity distorts the truth anyway. Whether scientific or ethnographic in orientation, *all* researchers are personally implicated in the decisions about what research they do, what the purpose of the research is, how the research is carried out, what particular procedures and theoretical ideas underpin the research and analysis, whether or not it is supported by funding and who the funders are, what outcomes might be expected, and so on. All researchers have vested interests in, and preferences about, these issues and "the personality and biases of the researchers clearly enter into the [research] process[es] to affect the outcome."[3] However, good ethnographic researchers understand that memory on its own is insufficient. Memory is not insulated from social processes, and those social processes need meticulous investigation and sense made of their relationship to memory. This is a highly creative process, but also highly variable depending on the backgrounds and beliefs of the researchers.

Memory has been a constant feature of my research through the use of interviews and historical traces (such as archival resources, original documentary evidence, memorabilia, contemporary books, photographs, and film footage).[4] In the past, I have investigated the lives of other people and events, but here I focus on *my* life in sport. Autobiographical representation has been described as "an act of interpretation where the lived experience is shaped, constrained and

---

3. Anderson, Armitage, Jack, and Wittner, "Beginning Where We Are," 102.
4. Hargreaves, "Power, Privilege and Sportswomen on the Margins."

transformed."[5] My account is a selective construction of the past, positioned within particular discourses of identity and power and politics. In other words, there is an interaction between memory and history,[6] between my personal stories, the wider society, and collective or "official" memory. Cultural memory is a term that has been used specifically to indicate the relationship between the personal and the political, to show that they are interrelated, both part of culture, feeding off and influencing each other.[7] With this in mind, I refer to events that have influenced my opinions and interests, the type of research I have done, and the reasons I chose certain intellectual and theoretical approaches to make sense of the findings. Inevitably, this account raises questions about the vagaries and authenticity of memory, but nevertheless it is an attempt to throw some light on connections between the ways people think about and experience their personal bodies (notably in sport and physical education and exercise)—for example, the type of exercise and sports they do, the choices they make, the opportunities and difficulties involved and so on—and the relationship of those experiences to social, cultural, and political structures, relationships, and changes.

A Life in Sport

My life in sport developed from an early love of sport clearly influenced by my family background. My grandfather was a fishmonger and also an athlete. In the early years of the twentieth century he was the Billingsgate Fish Market hundred-yards champion, and he also held the record for running from the market to the top of the Monument and back.[8] The Monument is 202 feet high, accessed by way of a spiral staircase of 311 steps. Little is known about the role of sport in the lives of Billingsgate traders because the archival collection of memorabilia was lost during the 1980s when the market moved.

In the next generation, my father joined an athletics club and was a very promising middle- and long-distance athlete, but as the oldest son, he was forced into the family fish business and had little time to train. In 1948 he ran for the first time in the famous Windsor to Lon-

---

5. This was written in the publicity material of the International Conference "Landscapes of Self: Identity, Discourse, Representation," held at the University of Evora, Portugal, November 24–26, 2010.

6. Nora, "Between Memory and History."

7. See for example Erll, *Memory in Culture*.

8. Built in 1876, the old Billingsgate Fish Market was located on the north bank of the River Thames, in the City of London. It was the largest indoor fish market in the world. The original Billingsgate Market building still stands and can easily be recognized by the statue of Britannia on top. (The market itself moved in 1982 to Canary Wharf in East London.) The Monument to the City of London was built between 1671 and 1677 to commemorate the Great Fire of London and to celebrate the rebuilding of the City.

don marathon (known as the Polytechnic Marathon), which was always started by a member of the royal family.[9] My father trained mostly on Sundays, and I remember my (white-lower-middle-class-suburban) embarrassment watching him leave home with my infant brother on his shoulders and our family dog running behind. At that time it was exceptional to see runners or joggers on suburban streets, and my father was a focus for amusement and ridicule among local children.

My paternal aunt was also very sporty. She swam and played water polo for England in the 1930s and was a competitive diver, figure-floater (the precursor to synchronized swimming), and long-distance river swimmer. She also entertained enthusiastic local crowds in the big open-air municipal pools.[10] I learned to swim during the war at the age of four when the family was evacuated to Scotland, and I was the fastest swimmer of all the boys and girls at my primary school. At the age of nine I joined Beckenham Ladies' Swimming Club, on the borders of South London—the same club that my aunt had belonged to.

In 1948 my father took me to the London Olympics. I was a young impressionable girl, eleven years old. We went twice to watch the track-and-field athletics at Wembley Stadium, which had been converted at the last minute from a greyhound racing track to one for Olympic competitors. This truly was an austerity Olympics. One of my father's athletic colleagues put competitors up in his home, and his wife helped to make a uniform for her friend who was on the British team. The streets still reminded us of war. There were many damaged buildings and bomb sites (one at the end of our road), and we were on food and clothing rations. There was little excitement in our lives; with no spending money and no television, we made our own entertainment. I left home with huge enthusiasm, clutching my father's hand, and as we got off the bus we were swept along by the crowd going into the stadium. I wrote in an article in 1997[11] that during the men's 400-meter track event I fell in love for the first time—with Arthur Stanley Wint. My girlish emotions provide an example of what I call "embellished memory," but I shared also in the collective national memory about those Games—I saw Arthur Wint win the race. He was the first-ever Jamaican Olympic gold medalist.

My memory of Arthur Wint is still vivid, as are my memories of other black Afro-Caribbean athletes and black American athletes at those Games. It was, I believe, the first time I had ever seen a black person. I lived in an exclusively white suburb of southeast London,

9. Montemurro, *Any Danger of Getting a Cup of Tea?*, 193–202.
10. Hargreaves, *Sporting Females*, chap. 6.
11. Hargreaves, "Speaking Volumes."

and there were no black pupils at my grammar school[12] in Beckenham, another white middle-class suburb. Now I live in Dulwich, yet another suburb of southeast London, where much of the housing is hugely expensive (the late ex-Prime Minister Margaret Thatcher bought a house in Dulwich and so did the president of the Bank of England), and there are several very prestigious private schools there. But Dulwich is close to Brixton, where large numbers of black Afro-Caribbeans settled when they first immigrated to the UK from 1948 onward.[13] Today, the Afro-Caribbean population, joined by immigrants from Africa (and then from other countries across the globe), spills over into neighboring areas. In the upstairs flat next door to me lives a middle-aged black man, born in London, who took over his parents' flat when they went back to Jamaica to live. He plays golf and goes on golfing holidays and has a white partner. At thirteen years old, his son is crazy about football (soccer) and has a karate brown belt. Downstairs is an ethnically mixed group of young people, mostly from China and Southeast Asia. They have a table-tennis table in their back yard and play all the year round. My road is cosmopolitan, people from different ethnicities and classes, professionals and blue-collar workers living side by side, and there are private single-family homes, houses made into flats, housing association ownership, and sheltered accommodation for mentally ill people. From an all-white area, Dulwich has been transformed since the last war and is now representative of multicultural London. There are still mainly white areas, reflecting the residual class and ethnic divisions of the past with schools and sports clubs that remain exclusive and privileged coexisting with all-black sports clubs and ethically mixed facilities and users. The ways in which people in my area experience their bodies have changed with cultural, political, and demographic changes at national and local levels. Unlike when my father was the exception, men and women of all ages and ethnic backgrounds jog around the streets and in the local parks

Brixton triggers another particular memory from my past of a student who was studying for a joint degree in sociology and sport studies. She was doing an undergraduate thesis about the use of sport as social control, collecting data from a special scheme set up specifically to keep African-Caribbean kids off the streets. This was in 1982, following riots in Brixton (and other parts of the UK) the previous year. The

---

12. Grammar schools were the academically oriented tier of the tripartite system of state-funded public secondary education (grammar schools; technical schools; and secondary modern schools). They operated in England and Wales from the mid-1940s to the late 1960s.

13. On June 22, 1948, the *Empire Windrush* sailed into Tilbury docks from Jamaica carrying the first large group (493) of West Indian immigrants following World War II.

country was in recession, and Brixton had especially serious social and economic problems--high unemployment, poor housing, poor amenities, and a high crime rate. Lord Scarman, a high court judge appointed by the Home Secretary, described in a report that the rioting was the worst outbreak of disorder in the UK in that century. Lord Scarman's report urged that action was needed to prevent racial disadvantage—a fact of British life—from becoming an "endemic, ineradicable disease threatening the very survival of our society."[14] I was concerned for my student's safety at a time when there was palpable racial tension in the area, and so I insisted on driving her to Brixton and I used the opportunity to do some research myself. We were the only white people in the sports facility, but over many weeks we got to know and talk freely to the organizers and the black youths on the scheme. My memories of this specific sport initiative and the people we interviewed were mixed with memories of the ongoing social and political debates and racist and anti-racist discourses. The organizers acknowledged that the sports scheme was a form of social control that did nothing to address the underlying social issues that had caused the riots in the first place, but they nevertheless firmly believed that young people from Brixton, many of whom had been rioting the previous year, benefited from the scheme. They were safely "off the streets," most of them enjoyed the sports on offer, and many of them went on to join sports clubs in the area. It was a difficult but heady time, generating a lot of original, controversial, and enlightening data.

It is clear that personal memory can enhance and enliven narratives of events—in this case, can make the results of immigration legislation, demographic developments, policies of race and racism, and so on, seem more authentic and colorful. But a memory-based narrative is an act of interpretation and in the case of the sport-based Brixton initiative can be written in different ways—as we have seen, on the one hand, as a social benefit for deprived African-Caribbean youth, bringing better health and helping to reduce disaffection and crime, or alternatively, as piece-meal reform that does nothing to address deeper issues such as institutionalized racism, economic and social disadvantage, and police harassment.

However, I would not have come to these conclusions or taken a critical stance about my Brixton experience earlier in my life. I had passed the 11+ "scholarship" examination to gain entrance to a girls' grammar school (1948–1955). Known as the tripartite system, those who failed the 11+ went to (nonacademic) technical or secondary modern

---

14. Scarman, *The Scarman Report*.

schools. Although some girls at my school were working class, most of us came from middle-class backgrounds and were led to believe that we were "superior" and "privileged." At my grammar school we were inculcated with traditional and conservative ideas about education and about sport. In common with local secondary modern girls, who were mostly from working-class backgrounds, we played netball and rounders (a bat-and-ball game not dissimilar to softball) and had swimming and gymnastics lessons, but although ours was also a state-funded school, we played lacrosse, hockey, cricket, and tennis as well, in common with girls at schools in the private sector. There were distinct academic and sporting advantages along class lines for those of us at the grammar school. We had better facilities and opportunities to play a wider range of sports, and we had the benefit of some specialized coaching, as well as chances to compete in touring teams abroad—opportunities not available to secondary modern girls. I swam, played hockey, netball, lacrosse, and cricket for the school, and was the House Games Captain.[15] I also swam at club level and competed at the national swimming championships. Sports had become my passion, and in my free time I played rounders and tennis with a mixed group of girls and boys at the local recreation ground, spent summer days at open-air swimming pools, and went hiking and cycling and camping in the countryside.

By the mid-1950s, my love of sport had taken me to the famous Dartford College of Physical Education.[16] Having studied sciences at A-level (an academic qualification offered to students completing secondary education that served as a condition for entering college), I was in no doubt that science always reveals the truth, so in anatomy and exercise physiology lectures, I did not question the validity of science to explain cultural behavior. I was taught that "black" people have more mobility in their hip joints than "white" people and by their very nature were predisposed to be good at sport; and that men are innately more aggressive and competitive than women and hence better suited to sports requiring these qualities. Analysis of the physical body in sport was presented to us as if the body was intrinsically separate from social, economic, and political considerations.

---

15. Many traditional schools in the UK (private and public) had "houses" or different clubs within a particular school that competed with one another in a variety of sports and games.

16. Dartford College was a specialist college of physical education that ran a three-year teacher-training course when teacher training in other subjects was only for two years. There were no degree courses at the time (except at Birmingham University). We received an "elite" training. Anstey College, Bedford College, and Chelsea College were the other colleges offering three years of physical education teacher-training.

Later, during my time as a secondary school teacher and then as a college lecturer in the 1960s and 1970s, I started to reassess my previous beliefs. I was reading broadsheet newspapers, discussing national and world politics with colleagues, lecturing to student teachers in the history of sport and physical education, and becoming more and more interested in the social implications of the physical body. Students across the country (and in other countries in the West) had become highly radicalized, and during the 1970s they used sit-ins as political protests and to demand greater representation in the running of university affairs. (One of the first sit-ins took place at Southlands College in South West London where I was working). The politics of identity had become established by way of the American Civil Rights movement and the women's liberation and gay liberation movements. In South Africa Steve Biko declared that "the most potent weapon in the hands of the aggressor is the mind of the oppressed,"[17] and I joined the vigil outside South Africa House (the South African Embassy in London) in protest against the apartheid regime. In 1979, Margaret Thatcher became the first female prime minister of Britain, and the Ayatollah Khomeini declared Iran to be an Islamic Republic. Women demonstrators in Iran failed to stop the clampdown on their activities, including swimming in the sea, and wearing the black abaya in public places became obligatory.

The politics of sport was constantly in the news as well. Peter Hain became chairman of the Stop the (Seventies) Tour Campaign, successfully disrupting tours by the South African rugby union and cricket teams in 1969 and 1970, and in 1970 the IOC finally capitulated to pressure and banned South Africa from the 1972 Olympics.[18] In 1971 Evonne Goolagong became the first woman with aboriginal ancestry to enter and to win Wimbledon; in 1972 at the Munich Olympics the Black September Arab guerrillas massacred Israeli athletes; Olga Korbutt popularized female gymnastics with her unsurpassed skill on the beam; and I entertained Soviet gymnasts in my home, which was five minutes away from the National Recreation Centre in South London (arranged by my friend, Nik Stuart, who was the British National Gymnastic Champion, had come in fifth in the European Gymnast Championships, and was the National Gymnastics Coach). Later in the decade, I went on a sports study tour to the Soviet Union, led by Jim Riordan, who was a leading expert on sport in the Soviet Union[18]; Martina Navratilova defected to the United States; and the East German female athletes won gold med-

---

17. Stephen Biko was an anti-apartheid activist in South Africa during the 1960s and 1970s. He founded the Black Consciousness Movement and became famous for the slogan "black is beautiful." Biko was killed at the age of thirty-one while in police custody.

als in abundance with accusations of systematic drug abuse peaking at the 1976 Olympics. I invited Sam Ramsamy, Chairman of the South African Non-Racial Olympic Committee (SANROC)—exiled in London from 1976—to speak to my students about sport in apartheid South Africa. He came to the college every year until 1990, when he was able to return to his own country to be appointed president of the new National Olympic Committee of South Africa. Influenced by national and international events and politics and by a growing knowledge about the politics of sport specifically, I was becoming a critical thinker.

Philosophy of Physical Education

Also during the 1970s, progressivism was the dominant educational ideology enabling us to offer radical teaching programs. For example, we started to dent the resistantly gendered nature of physical education. At Southlands College, we introduced the first mixed-sex teacher-training course in the country. We had a radical philosophy: that all aspects of the physical education program should be for both sexes, preparing students to teach mixed classes in secondary schools as well as in primary schools. We interviewed all applicants, explaining that practical work was done in mixed groups. Most of the male students at that time had never danced, even at primary school; and none of them had danced at secondary school. I interviewed a male candidate who was a territorial rugby player from Yorkshire in the north of England, tall, very solidly built, all muscle, and with a strong neck. He sat facing me with his knees widely spaced and his hands clenched on his thighs. He was nervous but looked intimidating. I asked him the set question: "Have you ever done any dance?" He had a pronounced northern accent. "Aye," he answered. "Oh, good," I responded, "Will you tell me about it?" "I go oop [up] Lyceum every Saterdey night." The Lyceum was the local disco for crowds of young people and flowing beer. But the powerful rugby player I accepted for our course became a sensitive, skillful, beautifully coordinated, and expressive mover. He danced center-stage at a famous concert hall in London at an anniversary celebration of the Laban Art of Movement Guild.[18]

The story of this student is significant in the history of physical education in Britain. Several of the male students in his cohort and those in future years went into secondary schools and taught dance to boys. For the first time, boys from the age of eleven were being introduced to a wide range of movement, including artistic and aesthetic dance

---

18. The LAMG was founded in 1946, based on the work of Rudolph Laban, a pioneer in the evolution of modern dance whose theory of movement influenced the development of dance and gymnastics in British girls' education.

movement, as well as sports and gymnastics, collectively entitled movement education or physical education. We were broadening the movement vocabulary of boys and girls and deconstructing the distinctly
gendered character of the way in which they used their bodies. There
was notable opposition from male PE teachers and lecturers, and when
the government changed the training requirements for teachers and
made physical education a degree subject, the gendered separation of
physical activities was legitimized again.[19] Later on, at the government
level, the creative approach to movement was raised as one reason for
the low standard of British competitors in world sport. By the 1990s,
the emphasis on competitive sports and especially competitive team
games was symbolized by the prime minister, John Major, when in 1994
he declared, "I am determined to see that our great national sports—
cricket, hockey, swimming, athletics, football [soccer], netball, rugby,
tennis and the like—are put firmly centre stage."[20] In many schools,
the terminology changed from physical education to sport education,
and dance became a separate degree subject that attracted mainly female students. The focus on competitive sport in schools—including
primary schools—was reignited before and during the Olympic Games
in London in 2012, explicitly linked to the patriotic fervor about winning medals for Great Britain. The importance of developing in young
children of both sexes a wide and skillful movement vocabulary across
a range of physical activities (including aesthetic movement) before
specializing was devalued and overshadowed by the Olympic mantra
citius, altius, fortius ("faster, higher, stronger").

Critical Analysis of Sport

Throughout the 1970s, the intrinsic links between sport, physical education, culture, and politics—treated uncritically during my three years
at Dartford College—were integral to my work as an educator and were
part of national and world news. That was why I chose to study sociology at master's level in 1977.

My first sustained attempt to apply a sociological imagination to
the lives of women in sport was for my M.A. thesis when I went to the
archives of my old college and gathered data about its founder, Madame Bergman Österberg, and the incipient female physical education
profession in Britain. Madame Österberg came to London in 1882 and
became the leading exponent in Britain of the Swedish system of gymnastics, which she recommended initially for the education of large

---

19. Hargreaves, "Gender, Morality and the National Physical Education Curriculum."
20. From a transcript of John Major's speech on sport in schools at the Conservative
Party Conference, October 14, 1994. See Department of National Heritage, *Sport.*

numbers of working-class girls in elementary schools in London, and then to small groups of middle-class girls in elite private schools, and from 1885, to middle-class students in her college. She has been hailed by her biographers[21] as a woman ahead of her time, a liberator of girls' and women's bodies. But after interrogating the evidence and placing it within the social and political contexts of the time, I proposed a very different story: that during the late Victorian period, Swedish gymnastics were part of the structure of ruling-class hegemony through the direction and control, in an institutionalized setting, of the spontaneous activities of children; that Madame Österberg had ingratiated herself with members of the ruling classes and the political elite; and that her model of the legitimate use of the female body in exercise took an "ascetic" form, emphasizing moral rectitude and triumphing over proponents of more artistic and aesthetic forms of movement, notably Margaret Morris, dubbed the British Isadora Duncan, whose "more natural" method of movement had a far greater potential to change the social consciousness of women about their bodies.[22]

Moving into the 1980s and 1990s, I became increasingly interested in questions of agency, structure, and power in contemporary sport in Britain. I organized a national conference, sponsored by the English Sports Council, which resulted in the publication of an edited text titled *Sport, Culture and Ideology*, published by Routledge in 1982. The aim was to ask important questions about the character of modern sport, to examine topical events and polemical issues in sport, and to bring together sport academics and mainstream academics. For example, in the session about sport and international politics, the two speakers were Peter Hain and Jim Riordan, who presented papers about sport in apartheid South Africa and sport in the Soviet Union, respectively. Professor David Lane from Cambridge University, the renowned author of books about world politics and state socialism, was the chair.[23] The idea for the conference evolved from my growing interest in cultural studies and the application of Gramsci's concept of hegemony[24] to the analysis of sport. The conference attracted a lot of interest among journalists and sport administrators, as well as academics. It also attracted pejorative comments that became headline news in the *Sunday Express*, a right-wing tabloid newspaper—"Conference at Southlands College a Marxist Plot." The sports journalist David Miller was warning

---

21. May, *Madame Bergman-Österberg*; Webb, "Women's Place in Physical Education in Great Britain 1800–1966."

22. See Hargreaves, *Sporting Females*, chap. 4.

23. Lane, *The Rise and Fall of State Socialism*.

24. Gramsci, *Selections from the Prison Notebooks*.

the Sports Council to protect itself against the plotting of Marxist academics who wanted to destroy British sport! Miller telephoned the director of the Sports Council, Dicky Jeeps, an ex-England and British Lions rugby union player and a friend from the rugby "old-boy network," who responded by sending senior officials from the Sports Council—wearing the insignia of sport and maleness with their blazers, ties, and badges—hot foot to the conference to vet the proceedings. They could find nothing except high-level scholarly debate, but the intervention alerted me to the issue of male power and vested interests at the top levels of British sport. In academia, the conference book was hailed as a watershed publication and the scene was set for a more openly critical assessment of sport within the cultural studies tradition.

I was by now fully aware that most other academic publications were about established, mainstream, and elite sport and there was very little about issues of discrimination and exclusion in sports. Furthermore, there was a tendency for sport historians and sociologists to ignore sports and physical activities that were community-based and/or recreational in character.

Sporting Females in Britain

My next research project focused specifically on girls and women, in part to counter the male-gendered dominance of British sport history and sociology. I concentrated on issues of power, prejudice, and exclusion, seeking to provide an understanding of the particular difficulties that women from different backgrounds faced struggling for access to sport, or struggling against discrimination within it. Here is one example: I visited a netball club called Queens of the Castle, situated in an inner-urban area in Southeast London, the Elephant and Castle. All the members had working-class roots and were predominantly black (African-Caribbean). The club was run democratically; there was a truly caring, community ethos, based on an empathy with the problems and needs of young urban women. No form of discrimination (homophobia, racism, or bullying) was tolerated, and young, vulnerable club members—many of whom came from single-parent families or backgrounds of drugs and abuse—were protected as far as was possible. And it was a successful club, running four regular teams and winning games and tournaments. But the cultural values and behavior that these young women brought to the game were not favored by the netball establishment—a situation, the club's founder claimed, that "has a lot to do with race, and class, and money, and how you live and what language you use." The Queens' players based their opinions on memories of events and struggles that they had encountered. Theirs is an example of the value of memory-work in bringing to light, and understanding, examples of discrimination faced by minority groups.

Queens of the Castle was an organized initiative that reached beyond the insular context of netball, making a connection between sport participation and politics, and helping those who were marginalized, alienated, and powerless in mainstream sport. But it was a struggle that was doomed because of institutional discrimination. First, league competitions were held outside London where the teams' travel passes were invalid, so it was difficult and expensive for them to get to game venues (whereas white middle-class girls who lived closer to the competition locations were usually driven to them by their parents). Those who were selected to go for area trials claimed that they experienced discrimination on the court as well. They said they were not integrated into the game by the other players, many of whom were members of the same club team and so practiced set moves. But most damning to the club's survival was that the subsidy it had received from the local authority was terminated because the Conservative government of the time had passed legislation to cap local authority spending. Leisure pursuits were the first to suffer, because education and healthcare were prioritized. So the club folded.

Giving these netball players a voice to tell me their stories was a political act. It provided data that explained the link between "personal troubles and public issues."[25] It also brought into the open the particular struggles they had overcome to play netball and their ultimate failure to be able to do so.[26]

The case of the Queens of the Castle led me to prioritize questions of freedom and constraint. C. Wright Mills makes the point that "Freedom is not merely the opportunity to do as one pleases; neither is it merely the opportunity to choose between set alternatives. Freedom is, first of all, the chance to formulate the available choices, to argue over them—and then, the opportunity to choose."[27] The Queens of the Castle had no chance to formulate choices, and their case study illustrates the complexities of the relationship between freedom and constraint. I used the concept of hegemony in order to understand the unstable relationships between continuity and discontinuity and negotiation and accommodation that I discovered were ongoing features of the sporting lives of the women I was working with. Recognizing the sig-

25. Mills, *The Sociological Imagination.*
26. The club leaders approached different local businesses for sponsorship and I helped them with applications for funding from various bodies, but none were successful. See Hargreaves, *Sporting Females,* 250–55.
27. Mills, *The Sociological Imagination,* 121.

nificance of agency, Gramsci "sees history as actively produced by individuals and social groups as they struggle to make the best they can out of their lives under determinate conditions."[28]

I spent several years of research trying to throw light on the conditions under which, and the extent to which, girls and women from specific groups relating to class, "race," age, disability, and sexual orientation were able to control their own sporting activities. Their stories are included in *Sporting Females: Critical Issues in the History and Sociology of Women's Sports*, published in 1994.[29] But apart from one chapter about women in the Olympic Games, the research was exclusively about women from Britain, enhancing the Westernized and Eurocentric focus of most stories of women's sport. I was very aware that in the West we know remarkably little about the sports and physical activities of most of the women in the rest of the world. So the next major research project that I undertook had a definite international character, including participant groups from countries outside the West.

Sportswomen across the World

I worked for six years—between 1994 and 2000—carrying out research that culminated in the publication of *Heroines of Sport: The Politics of Difference and Identity*.[30] The title may be misleading because I deconstructed the commonsense images of heroines of sport that are associated with stardom, commodification, the winning of medals, and the narrow fabrication of nationhood. My participants were really the "unsung" heroines of sport—women from minority groups who had been excluded from, or marginalized in, mainstream sport, who had faced particularly harsh forms of discrimination, and whose achievements in the circumstances were remarkable. They included black women in South Africa, Muslim women in the Middle East, Aboriginal women in Australia and Canada, and lesbian women and disabled women across the world. The final chapter explores the question of representation--whether the leaders of the women's international sports movement adequately represented groups of women who were marginalized in mainstream sports. This is a question about colonialism and neo-colonialism. In the process, I revisited the politics of difference and identity, rejecting arguments for the failure of this interpretation as an explanatory tool for the present day, but also taking into account the complexities and multiplicities of late capitalist/postmodern/postcolonial societies.

All my research about women in sport has been positioned firmly

---

28. Grossberg, "The Formation of Cultural Studies," 29–30.
29. Hargreaves, *Sporting Females*.
30. Hargreaves, *Heroines of Sport*.

within the feminist tradition of scholarship that places women at the center of the research process and allows them, as far as possible, to have an authentic voice in the final product.[31] The project involved the meticulous collection of detailed personal narratives about the experiences—and the meanings placed on those experiences—of individual women and groups of women from minority groups and/or who live outside the West. The connections between culture, systems of meaning, and questions of power and politics[32] provided a rationale for the way in which *Heroines of Sport* was conceived and produced. Such a position recognizes the transformative interventionist potential of academic sport feminism--that if individuals and groups of women can tell their stories, bring to light problems and constraints, get their voices heard, then there is a chance (however small) for change. It is an example of academic politics that recognizes that struggles come from knowledge and ideas. I avoided the widespread engagement with postmodernism and the concomitant disengagement with social and material analyses of power.[33]

But there is an uneasy tension between academics who study sport from a critical stance and people who wield power as sport leaders or administrators or politicians. For example, on the occasion of the first-ever international conference on women in sport organized by the International Olympic Committee (IOC) in 1996, I was invited to give the opening address. I had agreed with the IOC that I would refer to women in sport in the recently liberated South Africa, a "new" country with "new" possibilities. I had just returned from a research trip to South Africa that included a group interview with black women in Guguletu, a township outside Cape Town. There were fourteen women sitting around a table, with a roving microphone. They explained to me that they still suffered from systematic discrimination—based on class and gender, as well as "race"—and they argued that the black men and women who had positions in the new sport organizations had forgotten their roots and were not helping women in the townships. They asked me to help: "*We* don't get invited to conferences, so please tell our story to the IOC in Lausanne--and wherever else you go. Tell them everything we have told you." I explained that I had no personal power to instigate a more democratic system of decision-making and resourcing, which was what they wanted, but I promised to tell their

---

31. Stanley and Wise, "'Back into the Personal'"; Stanley and Wise, *Breaking Out Again*; Stanley and Wise, "Method, Methodology and Epistemology in Feminist Research Processes."
32. Alasuutari, *Researching Culture*, 2.
33. Aitchison, "Poststructural Feminist Theories of Representing Others," 127.

story if I got the chance.[34]

Before the IOC conference began, I had received a request to send a copy of my paper to the conference organizers in which I had included some of the township women's stories of discrimination. As a result, the IOC asked me to change my paper and not to mention South Africa, just to talk about "women in society." Remembering my promise to the women from Guguletu and the IOC's original agreement about the title, I refused to do so, and as a result I faced distressing hostility. At the time, the IOC was putting money into the development of sports in South Africa, had built liaisons with the new black sports leaders and administrators in the country, and did not welcome dialogue. Following my experience at the conference, and taking account of the township women's stories, I presumed that the neo-elites in South Africa had created a sports system that incorporated divisions, privileges, and discrimination within the black community itself.

A major concern of postcolonial feminists is the risk of appropriation by white feminists like myself of the voices of the "Others."[35] Their concern relates to the argument that researchers should not study women from cultures and identities with whom they have no organic connection. However, in common with bell hooks,[36] I believe that those of us who are privileged have an obligation to support women from minority, oppressed groups. I also believe that there is huge potential for what has been characterized as "emancipatory research" to be carried out by members of the excluded, minority groups themselves, and further, that students from those groups should be encouraged to do such research. For example, one of my ex-Ph.D. students, Aarti Ratna, who is from a Gujerati Indian background, successfully completed her doctorate about British South Asian women in football (soccer) in 2008, and she now has a full-time, tenured university position. To my knowledge, she was the first British South Asian female researcher investigating the particular problems of racialization in football (soccer) faced by British South Asian women.[37]

Searching for Data

It is also important to encourage more historical research about women in sport. In the West, we know far less about the history of women's

---

34. Hargreaves, *Heroines of Sport*, chap. 2.

35. Hill Collins, *Black Feminist Thought*; hooks, *Feminist Theory*; hooks, "The Politics of Radical Black Subjectivity"; Mohanty, "Cartographies of Struggle; Mohanty, "Under Western Eyes; Spivak, *In Other Worlds*; Spivak, *Outside in the Teaching Machine*.

36. hooks, *Feminist Theory*.

37. Ratna, *British Asian Females*; Ratna, "Playing-up and Playing-down Intersections of Identity.

sport than about the history of men's sport, and the gender gap is much greater in countries in the developing world. Getting material can be quite hit-and-miss, and the chances of filling the historical gaps are diminishing as records go missing and old people die. For example, I had difficulties finding material about women's sport during the inter-war years (1919–1937). I was able to construct only a very partial picture by looking at archival materials, club records, newspapers of the time, pamphlets, magazines, programs, photographs, films, and memora-bilia of all sorts from many different sources. By chance, I found that my aunt had a trunk in her attic full of sporting trophies, photographs, and newspaper clippings. I knew that she was an elite swimmer but had no idea that she was also a figure-floater, a diver, an international water polo player, as well as competing in all the swimming strokes at short and long-distance events—including the five-mile race in the Medway River in Kent in the south of England. Most revealing was that she was a popular entertainer as well, doing tricks in the water with her husband-to-be with the special names of "monkey up a stick" and "the porpoise," and she performed double-person and triple-person dives with male and female club colleagues. Her memories, and the mate-rials she passed to me to support them, were invaluable. I interviewed lots of other old ladies as well, but I missed finding out about some important events because there were no records and no one alive who could be traced to tell the stories. Three key elderly women died shortly before the arranged dates of interviews with them. Because potential memories are lost, forgotten, and often biased, accounts are always in-complete.

When I was planning *Heroines of Sport*, I went to the archives of the British Workers' Sports Federation (BWSF) at the London School of Eco-nomics. I was keen to give an account about the participation in sport of women who were members of the BWSF, in an attempt to parallel the story about men told by Stephen Jones.[38] Although from membership fig-ures and lists of events it was clear that women were involved in a range of sports, female participation was sparsely reported in relation to the full accounts of men's events and the ideologies underpinning them. In South Africa, there was an even greater dearth of historical traces about black women (used here to denote all nonwhite women) in sport in apart-heid South Africa (1948–91). I went to the National Library of South Africa in Cape Town, but although I had the help of the deputy director with whom I spent six hours searching in every conceivable book, magazine, sports report, and newspaper, we found an unending amount of infor-

---

38. Jones, *Sport, Politics and the Working Class.*

mation about white men's sports, a fair amount about white women's sports, a smattering about black men's sports, but nothing about black women's sport. *Absolutely nothing.* Through this experience, the concept about women being "hidden from history"[39] was concretized in the specific context of apartheid South Africa, and the theoretical implications of the particular relationship between gender and "race" also came alive.

Eventually, when I visited the Women's Bureau of South Africa Resource Centre, I discovered past copies of *The Sowetan*, a newspaper that contained regular features about black women's sports. I photocopied as many articles as possible and then accepted the offer of help from one of the Centre staff, who copied all the remaining references and sent them to me in England. We had uncovered a significant part of the history of South African sport that had been forgotten. The Women's Bureau had never before had requests for material about sports.

On another occasion, I was interviewing two "colored" women who had been active members of the South African Council on Sport (SACOS, the non-racial anti-apartheid sports organization located inside South Africa) when they handed me a commemorative volume of the 1988 SACOSSPORT Festival, popularly called the "Black Olympics," which symbolized the past struggles of black people in sport during the apartheid regime. It was an invaluable record of the personal histories of the two women themselves, but they insisted that I should keep it because they wanted me to publish their story. The volume included written details and photographs of nonracial women's netball, softball, and track-and-field competitions. The photographs showed that the "sportswear" of many competitors was comprised of pieced-together items of clothing and that most of the women ran in bare feet. One of the feature articles recorded the anti-sexist, anti-racist, and feminist philosophies of the SACOS women who claimed that even in non-racial sport they were treated as "sex objects," their events were trivialized, and there was a lack of women's participation in decision-making.

Questions of Integrity

Questions arise all the time about the integrity of research findings such as those I have just described. Especially in the case of studying women in sport who come from minority groups and are not well known or celebrated, it is difficult to get information in the first place and the evidence is always only partial. When people's memories are a key source of data, the issue of reliability is crucial. When I interviewed Muslim women from the Middle East, they were nervous about giving information. Sports-

---

39. Rowbotham, *Hidden from History*.

women living in the Middle East have to accommodate to the political and patriarchal modes of power dominant within their own countries. Some of them are secularists at heart but tend to live two lives—the local life of Islam and the global one of the West. Muslim women throughout the Islamic diaspora are influenced by world politics, and their participation in sport has been further affected by the events of 9/11 and the London bombings of 7/7 and elsewhere. They have to cope with increased fundamentalism in the Middle East and with Islamophobia in the West.

Before the terrorist events, I interviewed a young Saudi woman who was a student in London and vacationed in Western Europe with her family. When I met her, she was wearing Western dress, working out in the local gym, and playing tennis and swimming with her university friends. On the beaches of Europe she wore shorts and a bikini and loved doing water sports. An arranged marriage was planned for her after she graduated, when she would assume a veiled life in Riyadh. She was very cautious about admitting that she enjoyed the Western European lifestyle that allowed her to indulge her love of sport because she was concerned about being "discovered." I have interviewed other Muslim women who were also in denial about taking part in sports and exercise without conventional Islamic covering and about their aspirations—as women—for a different, more active, way of life. They are constantly negotiating and renegotiating for sport and exercise opportunities. Similarly, their memories are constructed and reconstructed according to the context, and they assume varying identities relating to social, political, and religious pressures and changes at national, regional, and global levels.[40]

Another of my former Ph.D. students is from Kuwait. She was in her fifties when she arrived in London with a great deal of confidence and social sophistication. She was a devout Muslim but prided herself on having worn Western-style clothes throughout her professional career (except on special religious and ceremonial occasions). The only times I saw her with a head covering was, first, during tutorials in my study when she would take time to kneel and pray and, second, when she collected her Ph.D. qualification at the graduation ceremony at Brunel University in 2004. On both occasions she placed a lace scarf over her head; at other times, she allowed her beautiful black hair to swing freely. My student's Ph.D. was an investigation of the particular problems that girls and young women in Kuwait faced in their quest to take part in sports and other physical activities.[41] She already had

40. See Hargreaves, Heroines of Sport, chap. 3; Hargreaves, "Sport, Exercise and the Female Muslim Body."
41. Al-Haidar, Struggling for a Right.

many memories and experiences of the situation in her country that she developed through interviews with girls and young women, teachers, organizers, and policy-makers. Her thesis concluded with recommendations that she sent to relevant government officials from key Kuwaiti organizations and ministries (the Public Authority for Youth and Sport, the Ministries of Education and Higher Education, the Ministry of Health, the Ministry of Religious Endowments, the Physical Education Department in the Public Authority of Applied Education and Training, and the Ministry of Information and Communication). She returned to Kuwait to continue her quest to improve the opportunities there for girls and women to take part in sports and physical activity. But persuasion takes time, and after about three years, for some reason we lost contact. Then I received an unexpected email from her a few months after 9/11: "Dr Jennifer . . . I go to Mecca on pilgrimage and now I dress in Hijab—Islamic dress." She had reassessed her liberal interpretation of everyday Islamic dress requirements and had reassessed some of her Ph.D. recommendations for greater opportunities for girls and young women.

These particular examples of Muslim women from the Middle East throw up in a stark way the fraught problem of the integrity of a research process based on interviews and memories, but at the same time they demonstrate clearly the ways in which human, physical bodies are affected by wider social, cultural, political, and religious structures of power.

Although it is clear that I have theoretical preferences, I have tried to keep an open mind by allowing the analysis to evolve from the material realities of the women's lives, as in standpoint epistemologies.[42] An aim has been to situate each life history in its specific historical, cultural, and political (and so on) contexts and "to show how women's actions and consciousness contribute to the structuring of social institutions."[43] In other words, to relate private lives and personal problems to wider social structures and public issues. Further, I have taken account of the observation that "the social contexts within which different kinds of women live, work, struggle and make sense of their lives differ widely across the world and between different groupings of women."[44] A key focus of analysis has always been to take account of specific constructions of difference and identity, of the particular as opposed to the general, of relations of power; and of the dialectic between agency and constraint.

---

42. Stanley and Wise, "'Back into the Personal,'" "Method, Methodology and Epistemology," and *Breaking Out Again*.

43. Anderson et al., "Beginning Where We Are," 106.

44. Stanley and Wise, "Method, Methodology and Epistemology," 22.

Conclusion

I am writing this conclusion shortly after the 2012 London Olympic Games and Paralympic Games. I applied for tickets to attend them both, but unlike in 1948, I was unsuccessful. Although in 1948 there were no Paralympic Games, that was the year Sir Ludwig Guttman, a neurologist working with World War II veterans with spinal-cord injuries, established the Stoke Mandeville Games (named after Stoke Mandeville Hospital in Buckinghamshire) as part of a rehabilitation program.[45] They were the starting point for the modern-day Paralympic movement. The date was July 29, 1948, the very same day as the opening ceremony of the 1948 Olympic Games. I have absolutely no memories of the Stoke Mandeville Games and only learned about them as a student teacher. In contrast, the 2012 Paralympic Games, the second largest international sporting competition, smaller only to the mainstream Olympics, had huge media coverage and unprecedented public interest in their inspirational character. In 1948 we had no television at home, but in 2012, from the comfort of my sofa, I watched both the Olympic and Paralympic opening and closing ceremonies and many competitions. I was hugely excited by seemingly superhuman athleticism and epic sporting moments and more than once experienced a sense of national pride. So far, I retain warm memories of both the Games for their palpable and infectious "feel-good" factor. But I write this with caution! I am reminded also of the double meaning applied to the Austerity Games. First, it was a popular description for the postwar character of the 1948 Olympics, run on a shoestring in a country faced with economic bankruptcy, with volunteers and athletes who supplied their own uniforms, and when ordinary people put athletes up in their homes and gave them food from their own rations. But very few people know about the 2012 Austerity Games, a special event held one week before the opening of the Olympic Games for young people living in the shadows of the Olympic Park where there is widespread poverty. The 2012 Austerity Games was a fun day of sport organized by the Youth Fight for Jobs organization, backed by multiple labor unions, in protest at the estimated final staggering £24 billion (approximately $37.5 billion in August 2012) cost of the Games in a country facing a double-dip recession at a time when poor people were getting poorer. The demand of the Youth Fight for Jobs organization was that the housing facilities built for the Games not sold off as luxury apartments but instead be used to provide affordable housing to help the acute homelessness of people in the area, and also that local people be given low-cost access to the Olympic

---

45. For the history of the Paralympic Games see www.Buckssport.org/en/twentytwelve/Olympic_paralympic_history/.

sports facilities in order to ease widespread social and health problems.[46] Similar concerns have surrounded the Paralympics, which took place at a time when the government was planning radical benefit reforms that would make "tens of thousands of adults and children worse off."[47]

Now we have to wait and see whether or not the 2012 Olympic and Paralympic Games will result in the promised long-term benefits to disadvantaged people. My experiences of these two London mega-sports events confirm for me that memory is flexible and always "in the making, and that feel-good collective memories can become illusory and political fantasy."

Bibliography

Aitchison, Cara. "Poststructural Feminist Theories of Representing Others: A Response to the 'Crisis' in Leisure Studies' Discourse." *Leisure Studies* 19, no. 3 (2000): 127–44.

Alasuutari, Pertti. *Researching Culture: Qualitative Method and Cultural Studies*. London: Sage Publications, 1995.

Al-Haidar, Ghaneemah. *Struggling for a Right: Islam and Sport and Physical Recreation for Girls and Women in Kuwait*. London: Brunel University, 2004.

Anderson, Kathryn, Susan Armitage, Dana Jack, and Judith Wittner. "Beginning Where We Are: Feminist Methodology in Oral History." In *Feminist Research Method: Exemplar Readings in the Social Sciences*, edited by Joyce M. Nielsen. Boulder: Westview Press, 1990.

Department of National Heritage. *Sport: Raising the Game*. London: Department of National Heritage, 1995.

Erll, Astrid. *Memory in Culture*. Translated by Sara B. Young. Houndmills, U.K., and New York: Palgrave Macmillan, 2011.

Gentleman, Amelia. "Benefit Reform Will Penalise Thousands of Disabled People, Analysis Shows," *Guardian*, July 11, 2012.

Gramsci, Antonio. *Selections from the Prison Notebooks*, edited by Quintin Hoare and Geoffrey Nowell-Smith. London: Lawrence and Wishart, 1971.

Grossberg, Lawrence. "The Formation of Cultural Studies." In *Relocating Cultural Studies: Developments in Theory and Research*, edited by Valda Blundell, John Shepherd, and Ian Taylor. London: Routledge, 1993.

---

46. www.ukcancut.org.uk/actions/899; www.youthfightforjobs.com/wordpress/wordpress/?p=519.

47. Amelia Gentleman, "Benefit Reform Will Penalise Thousands of Disabled People, Analysis Shows," *Guardian*, July 11, 2012.

Hain, Peter. *Don't Play with Apartheid: Background to the Stop the Seventy Tour Campaign.* London: Allen & Unwin, 1971.

———. *Outside In.* London: Biteback Publishing, 2012.

Hargreaves, Jennifer A. "Gender, Morality and the National Physical Education Curriculum." In *Professional and Development Issues in Leisure, Sport and Education,* edited by Lesley Lawrence, Elizabeth Murdoch, and Stanley Parker. LSA Publication No. 56. Eastbourne, U.K.: LSA, 1996.

———. *Heroines of Sport: The Politics of Difference and Identity.* London: Routledge, 2000.

———. "Power, Privilege and Sportswomen on the Margins: A Research Story." In *The Sage Handbook of Fieldwork,* edited by Dick Hobbs and Richard Wright. London: Sage Publications, 2006.

———. "Speaking Volumes: On C. Wright Mills's *The Sociological Imagination.*" *Times Higher Educational Supplement,* March 21, 1997.

———. *Sport, Culture and Ideology.* London: Routledge and Kegan Paul, 1982.

———. "Sport, Exercise and the Female Muslim Body: Negotiating Islam, Politics and Male Power." In *Physical Culture, Power, and the Body,* edited by Jennifer A. Hargreaves and Patricia Vertinsky. London: Routledge, 2007.

———. *Sporting Females: Issues in the History and Sociology of Women's Sports.* London: Routledge, 1994.

Hill Collins, Patricia. *Black Feminist Thought: Knowledge, Consciousness and the Politics of Empowerment.* Boston: Unwin Hyman, 1990.

hooks, bell. *Feminist Theory: From Margin to Center.* Boston: South End, 1984.

———. "The Politics of Radical Black Subjectivity." In *Yearning: Race, Gender and Cultural Politics.* Boston: South End, 1990.

Jones, Stephen G. *Sport, Politics and the Working Class.* Manchester: Manchester University Press, 1988.

Lane, David. *The Rise and Fall of State Socialism: Industrial Society and the Socialist State.* Cambridge: Polity Press, 1996.

May, Jonathan. *Madame Bergman-Österberg: Pioneer of Physical Education and Games for Girls and Women.* London: University of London, 1963.

Memory Studies. See especially Volume 1, No.1 (2008).

Mills, Charles Wright. *The Sociological Imagination.* New York: Oxford University Press, 1959.

Mohanty, Chandra Talpade. "Cartographies of Struggle: Third World Women and the Politics of Feminism." In *Third World Women and the Politics of Feminism,* edited by Chandra Talpade Mohanty, Ann Russo, and Lourdes Torres. Bloomington: Indiana University

Press, 1991.

———. "Under Western Eyes: Feminist Scholarship and Colonial Discourses." In *The Post-Colonial Studies Reader*, edited by Bill Ashcroft, Gareth Griffiths, and Helen Tiffin. London: Routledge, 1995.

Montemurro, Annette. *Any Danger of Getting a Cup of Tea?* Coquitlam, Can.: Stony Creak Publishing, 2002.

Nora, Pierre. "Between Memory and History: Les Lieux de Mémoire." *Representations* 26 (1989): 7–24.

———. "Reasons in the Current Upsurge in Memory." *Transit: Europäishe Review* (2002). At http://www.eurozine.com/articles/2002-04-19-nora-en.html.

Radstone, Susannah. "Memory, History and Events." Notes and Bibliography of Radstone's talk given at the Arts and Humanities Research Council "After the Wall" Workshop. Bristol University, April 17, 2009.

Ratna, Aarti. 2008. British Asian Females: Racialised and Gendered Experiences of Identity and Women's Football. Ph.D. dissertation, University of Brighton.

———. "Playing-up and Playing-down Intersections of Identity: British Asian Female Footballers and Women's Football." In *Routledge Handbook of Sport, Gender and Sexuality*, edited by Jennifer Hargreaves and Eric Anderson. London: Routledge, forthcoming, 2013.

Riordan, James. *Sport in Soviet Society: Development of Sport and Physical Education in Russia and the USSR*. Cambridge: Cambridge University Press, 1977.

Rowbotham, Sheila. *Hidden From History: 300 Years of Women's Oppression and the Fight Against It*. London: Pluto Press, 1973.

SACOS. *SACOSSPORT Festival '88*. Cape Town: Bachu Books, 1988.

Scarman, Lord. *The Scarman Report: The Brixton Disorders 10–12 April 1981*. Harmondsworth: Penguin, 1982.

Spivak, Gayatri Chakravorty. *In Other Worlds: Essays in Cultural Politics*, London: Routledge, 1987.

———. *Outside in the Teaching Machine*. London: Routledge, 1993.

Stanley, Liz, and Sue Wise. "'Back into the Personal': Or Our Attempt to Construct 'Feminist Research.'" In *Theories of Women's Studies*, edited by Gloria Bowles and Renate Klein. London: Routledge and Kegan Paul, 1983.

———. *Breaking Out Again: Feminist Ontology and Epistemology*. New York: Routledge, 1993.

———. "Method, Methodology and Epistemology in Feminist Research Processes." In *Feminist Praxis, Research, Theory and Epistemology in*

Feminist Sociology, edited by Liz Stanley and Sue Wise. London: Routledge, 1990.

Webb, Ida. 1967. Women's Place in Physical Education in Great Britain 1800–1966, with Special Reference to Teacher Training. M.A. thesis, University of Leicester.

List of Contributors

Gary Armstrong is reader in the School of sport and Education, Brunel University, West London. He has widely published on football and supporter cultures and the role of sport in arenas of conflict. He is part of a research team currently undertaking an ethnographic inquiry into policing the 2012 Olympics. Among his publications are *Football Hooligans: Knowing the Score* (1998) and *Fear and Loathing in the World of Football* (2001, eds. with Richard Giulianotti).

T. David Brent was educated at the University of Chicago where he received his Ph.D. in philosophy in 1977. His doctoral thesis, *Jung's Debt to Kant: The Transcendental Method and the Structure of Jung's Psychology*, was directed by Paul Ricoeur. Dr. Brent has worked at the University of Chicago Press since 1974. He is currently the Executive Editor responsible for Anthropology, Philosophy, and related areas of the Human Sciences. Brent was also the inaugural editor for the Chicago Studies in Ethnomusicology Series, The John D. and Catherine T. MacArthur Foundation Series on Mental Health and Development, and Chicago Studies in Practices of Meaning Series.

Luc Collard is Professor of Sociology (2007), and director of the research group TEC "Techniques et Enjeux du Corps" at the University of Paris Descartes. He wrote his dissertation on risk and risk-taking behavior in sports in 1997, in which he combined education, sports and game theory. He published about forty articles and book chapters, and three books: *Sports, enjeux et accidents* (1998), *Sport & agressivité* (2004), *La cinquième nage. Natation & Théorie de l'évolution* (2009).

Richard O. Davies is Distinguished Professor of History Emeritus and is the author of a leading textbook on American sports history, *Sports in*

American Life: A History (Wiley-Blackwell, 2012, 2nd ed.). Other publications include *America's Obsession: Sports and Society Since 1945* (Harcourt Brace, 1993), *Betting the Line: Sports Wagering in American Life* (Ohio State Press, 2001), *Main Street Blues: The Decline of Small Town America* (Ohio State, 1998). He is co-editor of *500 Years; America in the World* (Pearson, 2007).

Bertrand During is dean of the Faculty of Sports Sciences at the Descartes Paris University, and director of the research group GEPECS at the Faculty of Human and Social Sciences at the Sorbonne V. His publications include *Une Fédération française du Sport pour Tous: Rêve ou Réalité?* (2010, with Amélie Coulbaut), *Education Physique, Sciences et Culture* (2001), Histoire *Culturelle des Activités Physiques* (2000). His research interests include the history and sociology of physical activities, the epistemology of motor practices, and the articulation of knowledge and values through action.

Joseba Etxebeste Otegi is professor in the Department of Physical Education and Sports at the University of the Basque Country (UPV-EHU). His research area includes the study of the sport games, their internal logic, their implications for education, and their social and cultural meanings. "La socialización tradicional, una guía para un programa de Educación Física" and "Juegos deportivos y socialización: el caso de la cultura tradicional vasca" are some of the articles he has written on the subject. He co-authored a book titled *Euskal Jokoa eta Jolasa, Transmitting Basque Heritage through Games and Play*. He has been Dean of the College of Physical Education and Sports (1989-93) at the University of the Basque Country.

Richard Giulianotti is a Professor of Sociology at Loughborough University, UK. His main research interests are in the fields of sport, globalization, mega-events, crime and deviance, and socio-cultural identities. He is the author or co-author of four books: *Football: A Sociology of the Global Game* (Polity, 1999); *Sport: A Critical Sociology* (Polity, 2005); *Ethics, Money and Sport* (with Adrian Walsh; Routledge, 2006); and *Globalization and Football* (with Roland Robertson; Sage/Theory, Culture & Society, 2009). He has published articles in leading journals including *British Journal of Sociology, Global Networks, International Sociology, Social Anthropology, Sociology*, and *Urban Studies*.

Olatz González Abrisketa received her B.A in Anthropology from the University of Deusto in 1997 and her PhD from the University of the Basque Country in 2004. She went on to become a lecturer in Social and Cultural Anthropology at that university. Her ethnographic research was published in 2012 by the Center for Basque Studies with the title *Basque Pelota: A Ritual, an Aesthetic.* She is interested in visual anthropology, and produced her first documentary in 2007, "Jørgen Leth on Haiti," featured in NAFA2009, amongst other festivals.

Jennifer Hargreaves played a pioneering role in the development of sport sociology, particularly (but by no means exclusively) with reference to the politics of gender, the social construction of the body, and issues of exclusion and discrimination. Her publications include: (1982) *Sport, Culture and Ideology*(ed); (1994) *Sporting Females: The History and Sociology of Women's Sports*; (2000) *Heroines of Sport: the Politics of Difference and Identity*;(2007) *Physical Culture, Power, and the Body* (co-ed. with Patricia Vertinsky). Jennifer co-edits the book series, *Routledge Critical Studies in Sport* and has co-edited *Routledge Handbook of Sport, Gender, and Sexuality.* Jennifer was awarded the North American Society for the Sociology of Sport (NASSS) best book of the year award in 1994 and the NASSS Distinguished Service Award in 2008.

Pere Lavega has been a lecturer (1991-1995), Senior Lecturer (1996-2006), and Professor (2007-present) in the area of Theory and Practice of Skill Play and Games at National Institute of Physical Education of Catalonia (INEFC) at the University of Lleida. He is co-author of *Introducción a la praxiología motriz* (2003), editor of *Games and Society in Europe. The European Culture to the ligth of traditional games and sports*, co-editor of *La ciencia de la acción motriz* (2004), co-editor (with G. Jaouen and C. De la Villa) *Traditional games and social health. Aranda de Duero (España)* (2010). He has also published "Traditional games in Spain. A Social School of values and learning" (*International Journal of Eastern Sports & Physical Education* 2007).

Jeremy MacClancy is Professor of Anthropology, Oxford Brookes University, and has done major fieldwork in the Basque Country and Vanuatu, as well as briefer spells in Nigeria, southeast Spain, the West of Ireland, and the London auction rooms. His publications include *The Decline of Carlism* (2000), and *Expressing identities in the Basque arena* (2007).

Michael Messner is professor of sociology and gender studies at the University of Southern California, where he has worked for 25 years. His teaching and research focuses on gender and sports, men and masculinities, and gender-based violence. In 2010, the USC Center for Feminist Research released the most recent update of his longitudinal study, *Gender in televised sports.* He is the author of several books, including most recently *It's all for the kids: Gender, families and youth sports* (California, 2009), and *King of the wild suburb: A memoir of fathers, sons and guns* (Plain View Press, 2011). In 2011, the California Women's Law Center honored him with its Pursuit of Justice Award, for his work in support of girls and women in sport.

Pierre Parlebas is Professor Emeritus of Sociology and Social Sciences at the Sorbonne-Paris V, a specialist in physical education and motrocity. He co-founded the journal *Science et Motricité* and the Association des Chercheurs en Activités Physiques et Sportives. His numerous publications include *Eléments de sociologie du sport* (1986); *Sociométrie, réseaux et communication* (1992); *Jeux, sports et sociétés* – Lexique de praxéologie motrice (1999); *Statistique appliquée aux activités physiques et sportives* (1992); *El joc, emblema d'una cultura* – Introduction in *Les jeux et les sports traditionnels* (2005); "Sociologie du sport en France, aujourd'hui" (*L'année sociologique* 2002); "Mathématiques, jeux sportifs, sociologie" (*Mathématiques et Sciences Humaines* 2005).

Clara Urdangarin Liebaert is professor in the Department of Physical Education and Sports at the University of the Basque Country (UPV-EHU). She is interested in the study of motor games and dances as cultural practices and significant elements of socialization. Some of her article publications include "Jokoa eta Jolasa Mundu Berrian;" "Reflexiones sobre la educación física de hoy a la luz de las características de la cultura tradicional vasca;" "Las danzas vascas en la diáspora. Análisis y significación en la cultura Americana." She has co-authored a book titled *Euskal Jokoa eta Jolasa, transmitting the Basque heritage through games and play.*

Mariann Vaczi (University of Nevada, Reno) is an anthropologist and sociologist specializing in sport. Her geographical focus is the Basque Country and Spain, where she has done extensive fieldwork. Her interests include the interfaces of soccer culture with identity, ethnicity, discourse, gender, ritual, politics, and nationalism. Her article publications have appeared in *The International Review for the Sociology of Sport, Sport in Society, The Journal of the Royal Anthropological Institute,* and the *South African Review of Sociology.* Her ethnographic monograph on Basque and Spanish soccer culture is forthcoming in the *Routledge Critical Studies in Sport* (October 2014).

Patricia Vertinsky is a Distinguished University Scholar and Professor of Kinesiology at the University of British Columbia in Vancouver,

Canada. She is a social and cultural historian working across the fields of women's and gender history, sport history and sociology, popular culture, modern dance and the history of health and medicine. Her numerous publications include *The Eternally Wounded Woman: Doctors, Women and Exercise in the Late Nineteenth Century* (1990), *Disciplining Bodies in the Gymnasium: Memory, Monument and Modernism* (with Sherry McKay, 2004), *Physical Culture, power and the Body* (with Jennifer Hargreaves, 2007).

Emily Vest has been living and working in Bosnia over the past 10 years. She has recently returned to the UK to complete her PhD examining the role of football in reconciliation processes in the country, with a particular focus upon small rural village teams in the Bosnian Serb Entity, the Republika Srpska. She holds a BA from Cambridge and an MSc in Development, Humanitarianism and Human Rights from Oxford Brookes University's Centre for Development Practice.

Stephanie van Veen completed her undergraduate degree in Kinesiology at the University of Western Ontario and her Masters of Arts degree in Kinesiology at the University of British Columbia. A former national level ice dancer, her Master's thesis research focused on the effect of judging practices on ice dancers' movement practices and choreographic styles. Stephanie was the recipient of the Fred Hume Graduate Scholarship in Sport History in 2012.

Loïc Wacquant was a student and close collaborator of Pierre Bourdieu. He is currently a Professor of Sociology and Research Associate at the University of California, Berkeley. He is specializing in urban sociology, urban poverty, racial inequality, the body, social theory and ethnography. His numerous publications include *Body and Soul: Ethnographic Notebooks of An Apprentice-Boxer* (2004); *Pierre Bourdieu and Democratic Politics* (2005); *Urban Outcasts: A Comparative Sociology of Advanced Marginality* (2008); *Punishing the Poor: The Neoliberal Government of Social Insecurity* (2009).

Cassandra Wells is a PhD student in the School of Kinesiology at the University of British Columbia. She previously published on collegiate sport scholarship policies and class- and race-linked meaning making among student-athletes. Her current work explores how sex-linked eligibility policies in elite sport rework relations between notions of fairness and biological bodies.

INDEX